MOVING ROMANS

Moving Romans

Migration to Rome in the Principate

LAURENS E. TACOMA

OXFORD
UNIVERSITY PRESS

OXFORD

UNIVERSITY PRESS

Great Clarendon Street, Oxford, OX2 6DP,
United Kingdom

Oxford University Press is a department of the University of Oxford.
It furthers the University's objective of excellence in research, scholarship,
and education by publishing worldwide. Oxford is a registered trade mark of
Oxford University Press in the UK and in certain other countries

© Laurens E. Tacoma 2016

First Edition published in 2016
Impression: 2

Published in the United States of America by Oxford University Press
198 Madison Avenue, New York, NY 10016, United States of America

British Library Cataloguing in Publication Data
Data available

Library of Congress Control Number: 2015950353

ISBN 978-0-19 876805-0

Printed and bound by CPI Group (UK) Ltd, Croydon, CR0 4YY

To the memory of Joost Mioulet (1963–2009), best of friends

Preface

This book is the result of a joint venture in more than one way.

Intellectually, it has been part of a wider project conceived by Luuk de Ligt and myself at Leiden University, the Netherlands. My thanks to the Netherlands Organization for Scientific Research (NWO) for funding 'Moving Romans: Urbanization, Labour, and Migration in Roman Italy'. I owe much to my collaborators in this project: first and foremost to Luuk de Ligt, whose support was extremely important for the project both at the beginning and in its final stages; to Rolf Tybout for epigraphical assistance; and to Miriam Groen-Vallinga for the many discussions that have widely extended the confines of Roman labour. I owe more to them than they probably realize.

I would also like to thank the two anonymous readers of OUP who read the draft manuscript very thoroughly. Their comments have helped me immensely in improving the text. That I have not in all cases heeded their advice is due to a combination of stubbornness and time constraints, in which the latter legitimated the former. Any errors or oversights are my own. In addition, I would like to thank the persons who have helped me turning the typescript into a monograph: at Leiden Marilyn Hedges, and at Oxford the staff at OUP, in particular Charlotte Loveridge, and Jeff New. I have been greatly impressed by their professionalism.

The book would not have been finished if I had not had the privilege of staying for a year in 2013/14 as a fellow at the KNIR, the Royal Dutch Institute at Rome. Such periods of uninterrupted work are exceedingly rare in academia, and I thank all those who have made it possible, both in Leiden and in Rome. Keeping track of the rapidly expanding literature has been a bit of an uphill battle, but—as far as battles go—not an unpleasant one in the wonderful library of the KNIR.

The largest debt I owe to my family, for their willingness to participate in the final stage of the project and move with me to Rome. I owe more to my wife Lily Knibbeler than I will ever be able to tell her; at a practical level she also read the manuscript and offered many suggestions to increase its readability. She even improved the previous sentence. I would also like to thank our daughters Laura and Charlotte for overcoming twice their reluctance: first to move to Rome, then to move back home. I also thank my foster-parents George and Els Keet-van Dril for the enthusiasm with which they joined our Roman project.

This book is dedicated to the memory of the one person who sadly could not share in the venture, my good friend Joost Mioulet. He died after a prolonged illness in 2009, before I seriously started working on this book. I have missed deeply not only his company, but also the many irreverent comments and silly jokes he no doubt would have made about my project.

Contents

List of Tables

1

Introduction: Migration Before Modernity

The contention that migration is part of becoming modern—for economies, cultures, or individuals—distorts and obscures geographical mobility rather than illuminates it.[1]

1. DE-MODERNIZING MIGRATION

This book begins with what seems a false start, outside the Roman world.

In 1971 the geographer Zelinsky formulated what he called the hypothesis of a mobility transition.[2] According to this hypothesis, a dramatic increase in mobility rates had occurred in the Western world as a response to modernization and industrialization, and similar transitions were discernible in developing countries. Zelinsky connected this change in mobility patterns to the demographic transition, the process by which modernizing societies changed from a demographic regime of high mortality and high fertility to one of low mortality and low fertility. The mobility transition that, according to Zelinsky, coincided with the demographic transition was an irreversible, patterned process consisting of several stages, in which mobility changed both in volume and in character. Once a predominantly sedentary and rural society with low levels of circulation became caught up in the process of modernization, due to a decrease in mortality rates population growth would occur. Soon the society would be incapable of hosting its growing population, and a logical response would be emigration. This emigration could take various forms: people could move to cities in their own country or move abroad to rural settlement frontiers or other pioneer zones. Just as the demographic regime would eventually adjust itself to the new situation by a drop in fertility rates, so mobility patterns would eventually also stabilize, but now at much higher levels

[1] Moch (1996) 8.
[2] Zelinsky (1971); what follows is a short summary of what is in fact a much more sophisticated stage-model.

than before the transition. This increased level of geographical mobility, so Zelinsky argued, was indicative of a much more profound social and mental transition: the world opened up.

In many ways Zelinsky's model was new, but the underlying assumption had a long pedigree. Like Zelinsky, many scholars before him had assumed that high levels of mobility were a property of modernized, industrial societies, and that, by implication, pre-industrial societies were essentially immobile. Zelinsky himself was explicit on the lack of mobility in pre-industrial times:

> Some circulation might occur, but normally within a well-trodden social space—for example, the daily journey to field, pasture, fishery, or quarry, trips to fairs, shrines, and courts, or the rather more extended sojourns of apprentices and students. The only persons freely to cross major social boundaries would be aristocrats, religious pilgrims and scholars, merchants, warriors, criminals, sailors, and so on, some of whom might elect to become full-fledged migrants or expatriates. Essentially, then, the universe of premodern, traditional communities was one of an array of cells firmly fixed in space with rather strong, if invisible, membranes surrounding each unit.[3]

A forceful image, but it was precisely this underlying assumption rather than Zelinsky's stage-model of the mobility transition itself that was subsequently criticized.[4] Pre-modern societies, so the critics objected, were far from immobile.

Historians of early modern Europe led the way in voicing criticism. They showed numerous instances in which levels of mobility were high. Although Zelinsky had discussed some data from pre-transition societies (both historical and underdeveloped ones) that corroborated his view,[5] other scholars subsequently pointed to many cases of the reverse, of the occurrence of high levels of mobility and migration in pre-industrial contexts.[6] To quote some of the major participants in the debate, 'our image of a sedentary Europe... is seriously flawed';[7] 'at least in western Europe, the early-modern period was bustling with movement, both temporary and definitive'.[8] The intuitive equation of migration with the well-known great waves of cross-continental emigration across the Atlantic that are so characteristic of the modern period had led to ignoring other types of migration. Some of these types were quite important in early modern Europe.[9] One can think of the seasonal mobility

---

[3] Zelinsky (1971) 234; other very similar statements at 222, 224.

[4] For summaries see Pooley and Turnbull (1998) 8–10 and Lucassen and Lucassen (2009) 348–9.

[5] Zelinsky (1971) 235.

[6] Relatively early examples of more generalizing criticisms are Tilly (1978) 63–5; Hochstadt (1983) esp. 196–7. For some figures pointing to high mobility in early modern Europe, see De Vries (1984) 213.

[7] Moch (2003[2]) 1.   [8] Lucassen and Lucassen (2009) 349.

[9] Steidl (2009) 7; Lucassen and Lucassen (2009).

of villagers,[10] but also of that of sailors, who moved in large numbers over substantial distances.[11]

The attested cases of high mobility in pre-industrial times inevitably led to a more fundamental point of criticism. Scholars pointed out that the link between the supposed mobility transition and modernization was tenuous.[12] Well before the Industrial Revolution, societies emerged with high levels of urbanization and open labour markets, elements that could be conducive to high levels of mobility.[13] Moreover, relatively high levels of mobility could emerge entirely independent of modernization, as happened in the peasant society of tsarist Russia.[14] There were even cases that flew fully in the face of the predictions of Zelinsky's model: cases where mobility rates decreased rather than increased after industrialization, such as in Germany.[15]

These criticisms and findings do not necessarily imply that a mobility transition of the type postulated by Zelinsky did not occur at all. In many societies substantial increases in the volume of migration have occurred after industrialiszation, and it is difficult to avoid thinking that in our present-day globalized world levels of migration are at an unprecedented level.[16] However, the crucial point is that the process did not commence from a stagnant situation. Furthermore, the transition seems to have constituted a quantitative rather than a qualitative change: 'it was not the underlying structural causes of migration that changed but rather its scale.'[17] Thus, the transition between the two stages was not as large and profound as Zelinsky thought.[18] To rephrase the implications of the debate somewhat: the hypothesis of the mobility transition might perhaps be a useful concept to analyse the exceptional nature of Western society (though it clearly is not always equally well applicable), but is not very helpful to understand pre-industrial societies. It only tells what they were not, and it is in some cases plainly wrong.

Zelinksy's hypothesis of a mobility transition may thus have formed a false start, but its importance lies in the fact that its rejection opened up new fields of research in the pre-modern period. Although there has been an understandable tendency to locate other transition points in migration

---

[10] Jackson and Moch (1989; 1996) 54.

[11] Lucassen and Lucassen (2009) for their importance; though it should be noted that they were already mentioned by Zelinsky as an exceptional category.

[12] Hochstadt (1983) 197–8.

[13] Lucassen and Lucassen (2009) 349; esp. 370–1 for the Dutch Republic.

[14] Lucassen and Lucassen (2009) 373, showing that Russian migration rates from 1500 to 1850 hovered around the European average.

[15] Tilly (1978) 63–5; Hochstadt (1983) 223–4, esp. 209: 'In all probability, German urban communities in the centuries before industrialization housed a more mobile population than they do now.'

[16] Sanjek (2003) 315.   [17] Lucassen and Lucassen (2009) 374.

[18] Lucassen and Lucassen (2009); (2010) in particular fig. 9.1.

history,[19] it is unwarranted to lump all societies before that supposed point of transition together into one immobile past. In fact, it has become increasingly clear that migration is a phenomenon of all times, not something that belongs to the modernized world, or something that is confined to Western Europe. Mobility occurs in many guises, but it appears in all human societies: it is 'a normal and structural element of human societies throughout history'.[20]

If mobility is a structural feature of all societies, but its modes vary from society to society, the implication is extremely important: a large part of earlier migration history still needs to be written. Over the past decades historians have done much work to fill the gaps. An immense number of studies have appeared analysing pre-modern migration.[21] At the same time, the venture has not been free from problems.

Firstly, the sources are usually rather fragmentary. Migration is by its very nature difficult to measure, even in the modern period. Unlike other demographic events, migration is not a finite property.[22] 'The evidence for migration before industrialization is still so scattered and unsystematic that generalizations about its frequency, form, distance, and particularly their relation to social structure, are tentative at best.'[23] The lack of solid data for almost all pre-industrial societies is not only an accident of survival, or due to the lack of a coherent research tradition. In a sense, migration as a quantifiable property is itself an invention of the modern nation-state, with its bureaucracy and the creation of relatively fixed borders that were thought to need protection against intruders.[24]

Secondly, delineating the boundaries of the subject has not been easy. With the rejection of Zelinsky's modernization paradigm, historians quickly realized that the focus of the research had been very much on the history of the Western world.[25] In consequence, migration historians have branched out

---

[19] So Lucassen and Lucassen (2009) 352: 'As for periodization, 1500 seems to be a sensible starting point. There had, of course, been movements out of Europe as early as the high middle ages, for example with crusading settlement in the Middle East or the peopling of Portugal's Atlantic islands. However, the "discoveries" were the catalyst for the real take-off, with colonists leaving for white settler colonies, both overseas and in Siberia, and migrants moving to trade posts and strongholds in Africa and Asia. Moreover, emigration, often forced, from eastern Europe to the Middle East started around this time.'

[20] Lucassen and Lucassen (1997) 9.

[21] Manning (2013[2]) 204: 'The study of migration has advanced dramatically in recent decades in its breadth and depth.'

[22] Pooley and Turnbull (1998) 7; likewise De Vries (1984) 200. Cf. for the Roman world in a similar vein Erdkamp (2008) 419.

[23] Hochstadt (1983) 3.

[24] Tilly (1978), though somewhat overstated, as prior notions of citizenship also created the need to fence off a privileged population and could generate a bureaucratic apparatus. For lack of general data on urban migration in the pre-industrial period, see Moch (2003) 44.

[25] In addition, Steidl (2009) 9 emphasizes that within European migration history the focus has been very much on the western parts of the continent.

their research both geographically and chronologically. Migration history has very much become world history.[26] But in the absence of a well-demarcated chronological and spatial framework, it is difficult to see where to stop. Even the boundary between human migration and the migration of animals has become permeable: though it is clear that, in the former, individual choice and socially-induced behaviour, and in the latter, collective biological constraints form major determinants, the distinction is not clear-cut.[27] And what governs the choices in studying migration patterns of particular populations? Is the aim simply to identify and analyse hitherto unknown migration patterns and systems in the infinite universe of world history?

Whereas these problems are to some extent practical ones, the third one is fundamental. The rejection of the modernization paradigm has deprived historians of a clear and easily usable interpretative framework. The lack of intellectual coherence has led to a search for new organizing concepts for the pre-modern period. Some of the new approaches focus on culture-contact and implicitly take migration as an engine for progress, an evolutionary (if not modernizing) assumption that may not be particularly helpful.[28] Another approach takes over contemporary concepts of transnationalism and diaspora and applies them to the pre-industrial world: the formulation of migrant identity is regarded as a complex and context-dependent attempt to come to terms with living in a new place without negating the ties with the homeland. However, while its contribution to acculturation theory is clear, the approach seems of less help in analysing particular modes and patterns of migration.[29]

Perhaps Zelinsky's ideas formed not such a false start after all. It seems that one of the most interesting options is to go along part of the route that Zelinsky travelled, without, however, adopting his stage-model of a mobility transition. It is clear that some societies have characteristics that seem conducive to high levels of mobility, such as high levels of urbanization and relatively open labour markets. But what is the exact relation of such characteristics with migration if modernization is left out of the equation?

It is here that ancient Rome can help.

---

[26] Hoerder, Lucassen, and Lucassen (2007) 28–9.

[27] See the interesting attempts to include the 'deep past' of Lucassen, Lucassen, and Manning (eds.) (2010).

[28] This applies in particular to the focus on cross-community migration in Manning (2013²). Cf. Lucassen and Lucassen (2010) 9, who, while using Manning's conceptual framework, note that 'this assumption should be discussed much more seriously'.

[29] Manning (2013²) 200–1 for discussion. Though note that some diaspora models predict substantial return migration; see Sanjek (2003) 323.

2. ROME THE COSMOPOLIS

In many ways the Roman Empire of the first two centuries AD forms a good case to study pre-modern migration without the interference of the modernization debate. It presents, to be sure, just one case out of many possible others. The migration patterns of each society have modes and characteristics that make them unique. But there are several characteristics that make the Roman case in general, and the city of Rome in particular, an interesting one.

The most important reason to study migration in the Roman Empire is its urbanized character. Judging by pre-industrial standards, the Roman urban network was unique.[30] Cities played a central role in society. The urban network was strongly hierarchical, levels of urbanization were relatively high, and some cities were astonishingly large. The empire contained one city of about 800,000 to 1,000,000 inhabitants, several cities with populations well over 100,000 inhabitants, but also a dense network of medium-sized and smaller towns. It has been argued that they formed an integrated whole. Rather than individual entities which interacted exclusively or primarily with their own territories, they formed an urban network with relatively easy communication.[31]

In pre-modern societies high urbanization is often an indicator of high levels of mobility. More generally, it is widely accepted that the quantitative properties of the urban network and the social composition of the urban population were major determinants of migration flows.[32] Such connections seem also apparent in the case of the Roman Empire, but there can be no doubt that the relationship between urbanization and migration was complex. During the first two centuries AD the cities of the empire blossomed and had flourishing populations. It is often argued that the Roman cities could only maintain their populations thanks to an influx of outsiders.[33] However, who these migrants were and how they were absorbed by the cities are questions that are only beginning to be studied.

The Roman Empire is also of interest because the mobility occurred in a vast space in peaceful conditions. Civil wars and crises apart, wars were normally fought at faraway borders. Although not all subjects might have swallowed the ideological construct of the *pax romana* whole, the number of internal wars and revolts was small. The Mediterranean Sea and a network of Roman roads connected the regions of the empire to each other. This interconnectedness did

---

[30] See e.g. Jongman (1990), and contrast the highly influential study of De Vries (1984) on urbanization in early modern Europe.

[31] Laurence (1999); Morley (1996) on Rome's position with respect to its hinterland. For the former notion see the classic article by Finley (1977).

[32] Jackson and Moch (1989; 1996); Lucassen and Lucassen (2009).

[33] e.g. Jongman (2003).

not necessarily lead to high levels of mobility for all the inhabitants,[34] but it certainly created conditions conducive to voluntary migration.

At the same time, levels of enforced mobility were high. The Roman world was a slave society. The existence of urban slaves in large numbers is often thought to have impeded the emergence of a labour market, which was dependent on a freedom of movement denied to slaves.[35] However, although slave and free labour can (and should) be analytically separated into two distinct groups, there was much more interaction than might have been expected. The distinction between slavery and freedom is primarily of a legal, not an economic, kind.[36] Moreover, given the high frequency of manumission of urban slaves and the subsequent integration of freedmen in the population, slavery was for many a transient state. Slave and free labourers seem to have been in many respects structurally equivalent. The similarities raise important questions about the differentiation between enforced transport of slaves and voluntary movement of free migrants.

The Roman state also played a significant role in inducing migration. Colonizations under Caesar and Augustus involved great numbers of people, transported over large distances.[37] During the whole of the imperial period, the army recruited masses of people from all over the empire who could be transported from one end of the empire to the other. After discharge, some veterans stayed in their new place, married, and acquired land; others returned home or went elsewhere. The Roman Empire was thus characterized by the simultaneous occurrence of significant levels of free mobility, enforced mobility, and state-organized movements.

The complex nature of Roman migration is best visible in the city of Rome itself. The composition of the city was extremely diverse: it contained the whole known world. '[I]t could be said with justice that the *urbs Roma* itself was one of the most vital images of the Imperium Romanum.'[38] It was the 'queen and mistress of the world'.[39] The presence of foreigners in the city was a *topos* in Roman literature: Rome was the epitome of the world, in which whole cities, and even peoples, had settled.[40] It functioned both as a symbol of

---

[34] As Wierschowski (1995) 17 rightly warns.

[35] Temin (2003/4) 513–14 for some historiography.

[36] Bradley (1994) 65; Temin (2003/4), forcefully arguing that 'most Roman slaves, particularly urban slaves, participated in a unified Roman labor market' (529).

[37] Scheidel (2004).

[38] Griffin (1991) 19. For general introduction to the way Rome functioned as symbol, see Hope (2000).

[39] Front., *De aquis* 88: *regina et domina orbis*.

[40] Athen. 1.20b, for Rome as ἐπιτομὴν τῆς οἰκουμένης and at 1.20c, 'one day would not be sufficient to enumerate the number of cities within heavenly Rome', ἐπιλείποι δ' ἄν με οὐχ ἡμέρα μία ἐξαριθμούμενον τὰς ἐν τῇ Ῥωμαίων οὐρανοπόλει Ῥώμῃ ἀριθμουμένας πόλεις, etc.; Ael. Arist., *Or.* 26.13, stating that everything comes together in Rome, and 26.61 for Rome as the centre of the whole world: ὅπερ δὲ πόλις τοῖς αὑτῆς ὁρίοις καὶ χώραις ἐστί, ἥδε ἡ πόλις τῆς

the might and power of Rome, and gave rise to a dystopian image of a city in which all the vices of the world came together.[41] Moreover, the way the Romans constructed their identity was grounded in the paradox that from its earliest beginning they had incorporated outsiders; in fact, they kept emphasizing the myth of their own foreign, Trojan, origin.[42]

The city of Rome formed the apex of the Roman migration system. It was a final destination for many persons coming from all parts of the empire, the point of departure for Romans going to the provinces, and a major hub of transportation for people on the move. It contained soldiers, slaves, and voluntary immigrants in high numbers.

All these elements mark out the city of Rome as a rewarding subject for the study of migration. Many of the characteristics of pre-modern societies that display high levels of mobility can be found there, in a combination that seems unique. They allow the relation between migration, urbanization, and labour to be studied without interference from modernization theory.

ἁπάσης οἰκουμένης, ὥσπερ αὖ τῆς χώρας ἄστυ κοινὸν ἀποδεδειγμένη; Sen., *ad Helv.* 6.2–3 (quoted Chapter 6, Section 1), stating that people come from everywhere to Rome; *ad Helv.* 6.4, where Rome 'may in a sense be said to belong to all', *quae veluti communis potest dici*; Mart., *De spect.* 3, 'what people is so remote or barbarous that it cannot be found in your city, Caesar?', *Quae tam seposita est, quae gens tam barbara, Caesar, ex qua spectator non sit in urbe tua?* Further Mart., *Epig.* 8.61, mentioning in passing all the peoples that Rome comprises, *omnes Roma quas tenet gentes*; Plin., *N.H.* 3.5.39, in which Italy is 'both nursling and parent of all lands', *terra omnium terrarum alumna eadem et parens*, and destined to become 'a single fatherland of all peoples in the world', *una cunctarum gentium in toto orbe patria*. For these and other, later, passages see Noy (2000) 31–3, Tozzi (2014); cf. also Sherwin-White (1973²) 425–44. For a more general exploration of Rome's representation in Latin literature, see, above all, Edwards (1996).

[41] For the latter, see e.g. [Q.Cic.], *Comm.* 54 for Rome as conglomerate of nations, *civitas ex nationum conventu constituta*, in which there are many intrigues; Sall., *Catil.* 37, stating that every evil flowing into Rome *sicut in sentinam confluxerant*; Luc., *Phars.* 7.405, for Rome containing the dregs of the world, the *faex mundi*; the famous (and over-cited) images in Juv., *Sat.* 3. 58–80 of the Orontes flowing into the Tiber; Tac., *Ann.* 14.20, where in a senatorial debate on the introduction of Greek spectacles in AD 60 it is stated that everything foreign that leads to corruption is on view in the capital, 14.44 on the dangers of having whole slave *nationes in familiis*; 15.64, Christianity coming to the capital *quo cuncta undique atrocia aut pudenda confluunt celebranturque*; Mart., *Epig.* 7.30 for a sexualized simile in which a *Romana puella* receives indiscriminately various foreigners; the imagery is used repeatedly by Lucian, e.g. in the *Nigr.* and in *De merc.* See again Noy (2000) 34–6, also citing other passages, and Laurence (1997); Holleran (2011) 160.

[42] e.g. Sen., *ad Helv.* 7.7, stating that 'the Roman Empire itself looks back on an exile as founder', *Romanum imperium nempe auctorem exulem respicit*. The paradox plays a large role in Claudius' speech about the admission of Gauls into the senate, see *C.I.L.* 13.1668 (the Lyon *tabulae*) and Tac., *Ann.* 11.23–25. Tschiedel (2003), Farney (2007), Gruen (2012) 4, with Cornell (1995) 156–9 for discussion of the historicity of the claim in the regal period. For the contribution of outsiders in later imperial times, see Aur. Vict., *De caes.* 11.13. Cf. Sanjek (2003) 317 for the importance of ideologies of migration in the modern world.

3. INTERPRETING ROMAN MIGRATION: SOME HISTORIOGRAPHY

In general, migration historians have not studied Roman migration patterns. Usually migration history is traced back to the early modern period of European history, but no further. The explanation is probably primarily a practical one, and has to do with disciplinary boundaries: migration history forms a sub-branch of social history, and social historians usually do not study periods before AD 1500.[43] So Moch, in her survey of European migration, started her research from AD 1650.[44] Hoerder, in another major survey of migration in history, pushed the starting-date back further, to well before AD 1500, but still did not reach Roman times.[45] Manning, in his brief but extremely wide-ranging discussion of migration in world history, started much earlier, with the beginning of human history, but his focus on cross-community migration led him to ignore migration within the Roman Empire.[46]

The migration historians can hardly be blamed for ignoring Roman migration, for they have not been well served by ancient historians (though archaeology has followed a different intellectual trajectory). To be sure, the presence of 'foreigners' in the Roman world has hardly been a secret. It forms a standard element in handbooks,[47] and from time to time more detailed studies of the phenomenon have appeared. Be that as it may, though, it is fair to say that there is no continuous research tradition of Roman migration as a subject in its own right. Although that situation is now rapidly changing, for a long time migration has not been placed high on the agenda of ancient historians.[48] Given the fact that ancient historians have normally been quick to pick up developing research interests elsewhere, the delay calls for explanation. At least three major reasons for the absence of interest may be given.

The first derives from a definitional issue. It seems likely that migration has implicitly been equated with voluntary movement.[49] In line with the assumption of a relatively immobile world sketched above in Section 1, such voluntary movement was believed to be limited, especially when compared to the

---

[43] Lucassen and Lucassen (1997) may serve as an illustration. Despite the statement that migration should be regarded as a 'structural element of human societies throughout history', the period before 1500 is left without discussion.

[44] Moch (2003[2]); likewise Hoerder, Lucassen, and Lucassen (2007).

[45] Hoerder (2002), starting AD 1000.

[46] Manning (2013[2]), though the Romans make some fleeting appearances in his book, see index s.v. 'Roman Empire'.

[47] e.g. Carcopino (1939) 75–6; Stambaugh (1988) 94–5; Kolb (1995) 457–65.

[48] Likewise Erdkamp (2008) 417, observing that there are many publications in which 'movement of people' occurs, but few that address 'mobility per se'. See also De Ligt and Tacoma (forthcoming).

[49] This assumption can be found e.g. in Frank (1916), discussed later in this chapter.

enforced movements of soldiers, slaves, and colonists. The latter movements
were not studied under the heading of migration, however. As the study of
these latter groups formed well-established research topics in their own right,
the need for a different organizational concept was not felt.

A second reason may have been that migration was seen as collective cross-
community migration rather than individual trans-local movement within
the empire. Quite naturally, the focus of such research was on the invasions
of tribes in late antiquity that marked (or were thought to have caused) the
collapse of the Roman Empire.[50] The period of the Principate was, from that
point of view, of less interest.[51]

The third, and possibly most important, explanation may be sought in the
all-pervasive influence of the concept of romanization in Roman history. The
interpretation of what exactly romanization entailed has been subject to many
changes, and each interpretation has given rise to new criticisms: the unilateral
nature of the process, the supposed superiority of Roman culture, the lack of
agency of the host population—all have been questioned, especially under
the influence of post-colonial theory.[52] Yet throughout all its permutations
romanization has remained a geographically static concept. The very essence
of the concept of romanization has been that people changed their customs by
remaining where they were: Roman culture was brought to them or taken over
by them, and thus locals could become Roman independent of movement
(apart from that of the Romans themselves). That in reality mobility occurred
was not denied, but it was not regarded as fundamental. In consequence,
processes of cultural interaction could be studied without taking migration
into account.

What the absence of a continuous research tradition on Roman migration
implied can best be demonstrated on the basis of the studies that have been
devoted to the foreigners living in the city of Rome in the Principate. Given the
disparate nature of the literature, it seems pointless to offer a complete
overview, but discussion of a number of works may show the diversity of
contexts in which migration was placed.

Migration is hardly ever regarded neutrally. One perspective which has
been very influential was to regard immigrants negatively, as a *de-romanizing*
force, as the enemy within. Immigration was studied in the context of slavery.
The best-known, and rather notorious, example of such an approach is a study
of Frank, who started from the observation that, among the thousands of
inscriptions of the city of Rome, many of the names that were recorded had a

---

[50] It is in this way that Roman migration appears in the world history of Manning (2013²)
86–8. See Todd (2001) 11–14 for historiography.
[51] Todd (2001) esp. 50–1.
[52] For overviews of the (rather large) historiography, see Hingley (1996); Freeman (1997);
Mattingly (1997); Woolf (1998) 1–23; Webster (2001); Le Roux (2004).

foreign sound.[53] He argued that the inscriptions showed that through manumission the servile element rather than free immigrants had come to dominate the population. Famously, he estimated that under the Principate 90 per cent of the population of Rome must have been of servile descent and originated from the east.[54] According to Frank, the preponderance of slaves and freedmen had moral repercussions: the 'race mixture' or 'foreign intrusion' it entailed led to a debasement of the Roman character, to decadence, and to the corruption of morals. There was an inbuilt tragic irony in Frank's argument: while the Romans were civilizing others in the provinces, they became slaves of their slaves. They brought about their own demise by importing internal enemies, with the result that, in the end, 'the people who built Rome had given way to a different race'.[55]

Very similar ideas could be found in analyses of the other end of the social scale. In discussions of the changing composition of the Roman senate, the gradual admittance of members of provincial background was painted in similar terms of intrusion. The term 'race suicide' was sometimes employed to describe the supposed unwillingness of Rome's senators to reproduce themselves, and the gradual acceptance of senators from the provinces was interpreted in negative terms.[56] Likewise, the changing composition of the Roman army in general and the praetorian guard stationed in Rome in particular was analysed in terms of barbarization: provincials whose loyalty to Rome and Italy was questionable brought about the demise of the empire.[57]

The interpretative framework of Frank was discarded after the Second World War.[58] In some ways it formed no more than a direct continuation

---

[53] Frank (1916) 689 'the cognomina all seem awry'; see also Frank (1927²) 202–18, where the arguments are repeated in a wider historical reconstruction; Frank (1934) for application to Ostia. McKeown (2007) 12–29 for the context and reception of Frank's ideas, and Mouritsen (2011) 2–3, 80–92 for the wider historiography on freedmen; both citing many views similar to those of Frank.

[54] Frank (1916) 690: 'By far the larger part—perhaps ninety per cent—had Oriental blood in their veins.' He also extended his conclusions outside Rome: 'it is evident that the whole empire was a melting-pot and that the Oriental was always and everywhere a very large part of the ore' (702–3).

[55] Frank (1916) 705. La Piana (1927) 247 for similar terms.

[56] e.g. Frank (1927²) 206. Hammond (1957) 75 with n. 3 for further refs., and 81 n. 23 for parallels between the senatorial and slave models.

[57] See the highly influential work of von Domaszewski (1967²) on the officers of the Roman army, speaking in his *geschichtlichen Überblick* of 'dieser unvermeidliche Sieg der Provinzen über das wehrlose Italien und den römischen Westen' in the early third century AD. 'Die Bauern aus den Wäldern Illyricums, die Bewohner des Atlas und die Wüstenreiter des Euphrattales, die das Kaiserheer in Italien bilden, hersschen im Reiche.' Note that the very substantial revisions of the *Überblick* by Dobson at pp. v, lix–lxi do not concern the underlying assumptions about 'barbarisation'.

[58] As McKeown (2007) 23 aptly observes, Frank's racist paradigm was never fully rebutted (though many scholars openly disapproved of it), but it 'simply disappeared'. Frank's thesis about the dominance of Greek slaves was in fact already rejected by Gordon (1924) 101, but it is interesting to see that even in her much more detached analysis, parts of Frank's framework survived: 'precisely that portion of the Roman world from which its government, its culture and its ideas proceeded, was derived to a great extent from a servile class, of no nationality and of a

of ancient dystopian discourse in which Rome was supposed to have attracted all the vices of the world. More importantly, its blatant racism had become extremely embarrassing,[59] and the connection between moral decline and social developments was no longer considered tenable. In other respects its influence lasted longer. His work epitomizes a long tradition of research into the presence of slaves and freedmen in the city's population. When Frank's work is discussed, it is in the context of debates about the 'intrusion' of slaves and freedmen in urban society,[60] and the more technical question of what may be inferred from the presence of Greek cognomina. Migration plays no great role in such discussions.

The influence of Frank's ideas can also be seen in the first full monograph on foreigners in Rome, by George La Piana. For all its length, La Piana emphasized that his aim was not to provide a complete overview of migration but something altogether different: he wanted to understand the rise of Christianity in Rome. La Piana started from the assumption that the earliest Christians in Rome were immigrants, and wanted to place their presence in the context of the oriental religions that the immigrants were supposed to have brought with them.[61] In many respects La Piana's work is now rather dated and heavily dependent on Frank. But it epitomizes a wider approach in which migration is studied for its contribution to religious history; immigrants are primarily regarded as carriers of foreign cults.

Another type of research has been provided by epigraphers. Especially after the Second World War, and no doubt under the influence of decolonization and changing views about cultural interaction, scholars started to study the presence of particular groups of foreigners in Rome on the basis of a more detailed exploration of the great mass of Roman inscriptions. For obvious reasons, the Jewish diaspora community had a much longer research tradition, though for the early empire the Jewish epigraphy from Rome is in fact rather meagre.[62] Many other ethnic groups living in Rome received treatment as

civilisation not their own. The conventionality, the waning literary and artistic inspiration, and the general creeping paralysis of ancient culture may find part of its explanation here' (110).

[59] For the resonance of such ideas among the Nazis, see briefly Isaac (2004) 238. It is telling, though most unfortunate and undeserved, that Frank's ideas have been appropriated by recent US white-supremacy organizations, who have reprinted his work.

[60] Gordon (1924); Ross Taylor (1961); Maier (1953–4); Huttunen (1974) 10–15, discussing also other responses to Frank's work. Mouritsen (2011) 1–9 for the difficulties inherent in the approach, cf. also 123 for more recent claims for very high numbers of freedmen in Rome.

[61] La Piana (1927), a monograph in the guise of an article, tellingly published in a theological journal. Parts had been published slightly earlier in Italian. The underlying ideas can also be found in Frank (1916) 706, who responded to other explanations of the presence of (so-called) Oriental cults: 'may it not be that Occidentals who are actually of Oriental extraction, men of more emotional nature, are simply finding in these cults the satisfaction that, after long deprivation, their temperaments naturally required?' And 708: 'These religions came with their peoples.'

[62] See the valuable overview by Solin (1983), with copious bibliography. Subsequent work includes many studies by Rutgers, e.g. (1998) and Cappelletti (2006).

well.[63] Similar epigraphic studies have appeared for the rest of Italy[64] and the western Roman provinces;[65] studies of the very rich epigraphy of the eastern half of the empire have been lagging behind, but are starting to appear as well.[66] Even apart from the fact that they are extremely useful because they bring highly disparate data together, many of these studies contain pertinent observations on the nature of Roman migration. At the same time, much of the discussion has focused on technical issues of identifying foreigners in inscriptions, rather than on migration itself. As these studies lacked a wider interpretative framework or a proper research context, they have for a long time played no central role in debates about the structure of Roman society.

In recent years the situation has been changing, and the epigraphic studies have found a new audience. In the wake of renewed interest in acculturation theory, an increasing awareness has arisen that it is worth exploring the subject of migration further.[67] In response to dissatisfaction with the concept of romanization, alternative concepts have been proposed to understand cultural interaction in the Roman Empire. Hybridization, creolization, and globalization—all have been employed to greater or lesser effect.[68] More generally, a growing resistance has arisen against the general notion that the ancient world was a static society.[69] The movement of goods, transfers of land,

[63] In particular in a series of studies by Cecilia Ricci, see e.g. Ricci (1993) on Egyptians. For synoptic treatment, see Ricci (2005). For Syrians, Solin (1983). For foreigners in late antique Rome, see, apart from Noy (2000), also Avraméa (1995) and Nieddu (2003), both with further references.

[64] See e.g. Simelon (1992) on Lucania and Buchi (2005) on the Veneto.

[65] For Gaul, see, briefly, Frézouls (1989), and in much more detail Wierschowski (1995) (with 23 n. 30 for further bibliography) and (2001); for Britannia, see Noy (2010a) 18–24 with further bibliography, and for Britons outside Britannia, Ivleva (2012); for a study of four specific centres in the West (mod. Chester, Mainz, Cologne, and Lyon), see Carroll (2006) 209–32; for Germania, see Kakoschke (2002) (with 28–30 for previous literature); for Raetia, see Dietz and Weber (1982); for Lusitania, see Stanley (1990); for the whole of the Iberian peninsula, Haley (1991) (with 11 n. 4 for further bibliography) with Holleran (forthcoming b); for North Africa, see Lassère (1977) 597–644; also Rebuffat (2004) (incl. Egypt) and Hamdoune (2006) (on the basis of funerary epigrams).

[66] For a study of female mobility in the Hellenistic period, including a discussion of inscriptions, see Loman (2004). Several of the papers in a forthcoming volume edited by De Ligt and myself will concern the Greek East: Hin (forthcoming) on Athens, Zerbini (forthcoming a) on Syria, Tacoma and Tybout (forthcoming a) on Greek epigrams. In addition, A. J. Yoo and A. Zerbini are editing a diachronic overview of mobility in Syria which will include epigraphic studies. For an early and very full papyrological study of Hellenistic and Roman Egypt, see Braunert (1964); cf. Adams (forthcoming) and Foubert (forthcoming).

[67] The fact that a number of conference proceedings have appeared on ancient migration and related subjects is telling. See Sordi (ed.) (1994); Sordi (ed.) (1995); Moatti (ed.) (2004); Bertinelli and Donati (eds.) (2005); Bertinelli and Donati (eds.) (2006); Moatti and Kaiser (eds.) (2007); Eckardt (ed.) (2010).

[68] Among others, Mattingly (1997); Laurence (2001); Webster (2001); Hingley (2005); Naerebout (2013).

[69] See in particular Osborne (1991), whose paper on mobility in classical Athens was in many respects a pioneering study. For deme mobility in classical Athens, see now also Taylor (2011).

levels of social mobility—all turn out to be higher than has been previously assumed. Cities are 'conceived of not as whole societies in themselves, but rather as prominent social exchanges in a dynamic human landscape, or as nodes in a set of highly agitated social networks'.[70] Increasing stress has been put on the connectedness of the empire in general and the Mediterranean world in particular. Connectivity is regarded as a structural characteristic of the history of the Mediterranean world, impervious to the political constellation of any particular period or state. Such interconnectedness assumes the existence of patterned mobility.[71] This idea finds a more formal expression in the application of network theory.[72]

The main virtue of the new theories of cultural interaction is that they assign wider meaning to migration. However, just as with the model of romanization which they intend to replace, the new theoretical frameworks might once again risk ignoring migration and mobility as a subject for independent analysis. Both the concept of connectivity and network theory call for greater precision.[73] For example, a statement like: 'We believe neither that most country folk were the grandchildren of country folk in the same region, nor that most inhabitants of nucleated settlements could claim to be third-generation inhabitants', is in itself thought-provoking, but is no more than a belief which calls for further scrutiny.[74] Comparative studies might show that levels of mobility could be extremely high in pre-industrial contexts, but this does not automatically imply the same for the Roman period.[75] Unlike

---

[70] Woolf (2013) 351; see also Woolf (forthcoming *a*) for the radical change in perceptions (and some criticism).

[71] Horden and Purcell (2000); connectivity is explained at 123 as 'the various ways in which microregions cohere, both internally and also one with another', the Mediterranean Sea at 133 as 'the principal agent of connectivity'. As Shaw (2001) 424 observes with regard to their work, 'they insist that the essential unity of the Mediterranean is far less a reified thing thing than a process—the impetus to connect the disparate parts'. Cf. also Laurence (1999) on road networks and the brief overview of ancient migration by Isayev (2013). Such ideas are not completely new; see Sen., *ad Helv.* 6–8 for somewhat similar Stoic thinking about the continuous movements of peoples in ancient times.

[72] Malkin, Constantakopoulou, and Panagopoulou (eds.) (2009).

[73] See the response to Horden and Purcell (2000) by Harris (2005), stressing on 9–10 the need for measurability, with further discussion by Horden and Purcell (2005); cf. also Horden and Purcell (2000) 130 ('Now in theory this [i.e. types of connectivity] can be measured'). For general exegesis of the arguments relating to mobility in *The Corrupting Sea*, see Woolf (forthcoming *a*). Gambash (forthcoming) rightly stresses that maritime connectivity and mobility need to be carefully distinguished.

[74] Horden and Purcell (2000) 380 (supposedly applying to the whole of the two millennia under scrutiny), see also 400. Cf. somewhat similarly Osborne (1991) 419, or Price (2012) 8–9 on the speed of Roman communication ('There was surely no-one in the Roman Empire like the Japanese soldier who fought in the Philippines during the Second World War, and refused to believe in the Japanese defeat, surrounding only in 1974'. Surely? No one?).

[75] Likewise Erdkamp (2008) 444: '[t]he fact that the population of early-modern England was incredibly itinerant does not necessarily lead to the conclusion that the inhabitants of republican Italy were equally mobile.'

with concepts such as urbanization or mortality, there are no natural con-straints to migration: its volume and nature differ from society to society. If in the ancient world movement across the Mediterranean is regarded as a structural property, numerous questions are raised about its limitations, about the structure and nature of the patterns, and about changes over time in the Roman period.[76] As a migration theorist already remarked in 1958: 'like all such universals, these cannot explain differential behavior: if all men are sedentary (or migratory) "by nature," why do some migrate and some not?'[77]

This situation has in part been remedied by two empirical studies on immigrants in Rome. In 2000 David Noy published a study of foreigners in Rome.[78] The book might be regarded as the culmination of the epigraphical tradition of the study of foreigners in the city. Noy's focus was on foreigners, not on immigration as a phenomenon per se, and he defined these foreigners as free civilians from outside Italy below the elite. Noy studied them on the basis of a wide range of written sources, but relied in particular on a set of over 1,000 inscriptions in which people mentioned their foreign origin.[79] Noy's questions, observations, and use of comparative material are extremely useful and have in many ways paved the way for a further exploration of the subject.

The second study is a dissertation by Kristina Killgrove from 2010.[80] It might symbolize the change in approach of the last decade. Like Noy's study, her work is also strongly empirical, but her evidence is of a new type: she bases her discussion on isotopic analysis of skeletal evidence from two graveyards in the vicinity of Rome: Casal Bertone on the eastern side, and somewhat further out, Castellaccio Europarco to the south of Rome. She used a sample of 183 skeletons, of which she subjected a sub-sample of 105 to strontium isotope analysis, and within these, fifty-five skeletons to combined strontium and oxygen isotopic analysis. Her work forms part of an increasing number of bio-archaeological studies that concern many parts of the Roman Empire. For obvious reasons, a relatively large part of her work is devoted to technical issues concerning isotopic analysis, but she placed her findings explicitly in the

---

[76] For example, the claim that late antiquity was 'an astonishingly mobile society' calls for comparison with previous and later periods. See Leyerle (2009) 113, who takes his inspiration from Horden and Purcell (2000); cf. Kakoschke (2002) 6 who assumes decreasing mobility due to the tying of people to their profession, and Handley (2011) for a full discussion of the epigraphic evidence.

[77] Petersen (1958) 258. Cf. also Harris (2005).

[78] Noy (2000). Somewhat similar to La Piana, Noy started his study in an attempt to contextualize the history of the Jewish diaspora in Rome. For briefer studies, see Dresken-Weiland (2003); Ricci (2005).

[79] Noy (2000) xi–xii for delineation of the subject; though Noy offers many valuable discus-sions of soldiers and slaves. I use '1,000 inscriptions' as a convenient round figure; Noy (2000) 59–60, table 1, gives 1,089 immigrants (excl. the 195 Jewish/Christian ones), but some inscrip-tions contain more than one person.

[80] Killgrove (2010a); the dissertation has remained unpublished, but a partial publication can be found in Killgrove (2010c).

context of migration models, in particular that of transnationalism, and also showed how isotopic research might contribute to answering new questions, for example on diet and health standards of Roman migrants. She argued on the basis of her samples for relatively high levels of immigration, and for the occurrence of many women among the immigrants, and pointed to the likelihood that many immigrants originated from within the Italian peninsula.[81]

Outside the city, many other studies are appearing that are directly or indirectly of importance for the study of Roman migration. Even apart from the virtual deluge of studies on cultural and ethnic identity, studies have appeared on seasonal mobility;[82] on female mobility,[83] on institutional restrictions on mobility,[84] on the relation between forced and free mobility,[85] on urban graveyard theory,[86] on living conditions, diseases, and levels of mortality in Rome,[87] and on the functioning of the Roman labour market.[88] There have also been attempts to integrate the large number of isotopic analyses of sites in the Roman provinces with the other evidence.[89]

Despite the discontinuities in the research tradition, the epigraphic studies on foreign groups, the two relatively recent monographs on mobility in Rome, and the studies on mobility-related topics have created good prospects for a further study of Roman migration as a subject in its own right. They form, each in their own way, good starting-points for further exploration of the question how Rome functioned in the migration system of the Roman Empire. There is a basis for further modelling.

4. STONES AND BONES

Studying migration before the advent of modern society is never easy. In the case of the Roman world, the source problems may appear large indeed—there are, for example, no autobiographical migration narratives, and especially the absence of statistically useable material is deplorable (though not particularly surprising). Arguably, this is more a matter of degree than a fundamental

---

[81] Killgrove (2010a) 28–30, 305 and *passim*.
[82] Erdkamp (2008), on the Roman Republic, with a follow up in Erdkamp (forthcoming).
[83] Foubert (2013); Woolf (2013).
[84] Discussed in a series of studies by Claudia Moatti, including Moatti (2000), (2006), (2007), and (forthcoming).
[85] Scheidel (2004); (2005), cf. also Scheidel (1997).
[86] Among others, Lo Cascio (2000); Jongman (2003); Hin (2013) 210–57.
[87] Scobie (1986); Scheidel (1994); Shaw (1996); Sallares (2002); Scheidel (2003); Morley (2005); Shaw (2006); Scheidel (2013); Oerlemans and Tacoma (2014); cf. also Aldrete (2007).
[88] Temin (2003/4); Holleran (2011), explicitly addressing the question to what extent migrants could be accomodated in Rome's labour market; Laes and Verboven (eds.) (forthcoming).
[89] Eckardt (ed.) (2010).

difference from the situation in other societies, but the problems remain nevertheless.

At the same time, both the epigraphic studies and the new isotopic evidence from physical anthropology show that Roman sources for the study of migration are not lacking. In fact, there is such an abundance of sources that this in itself forms an additional, practical reason for limiting a study of migration to the city of Rome under the Principate. The sources clearly have great potential, yet their fragmentary and incomplete nature should be acknowledged as well. It is therefore useful to discuss possibilities and pitfalls in some detail.

First of all there are the literary works in Greek and Latin that present stories of movements of individuals or particular groups, or discuss attitudes or report debates, in fiction, in historical narrative, and in geographical descriptions. However, despite their wide variety in form, substance, and relevance, all written works suffer from the classic problem of all Roman literature: its elite bias. Moreover, there is a more profound (and more interesting) problem with the literary sources: it is hardly a secret that they are literary constructs rather than reportage. The classic case is Juvenal's *Third Satire*, containing Umbricius' rant against foreigners.[90] It is quite dangerous to regard such texts simply as series of vignettes, from which one can freely choose (which is not to say they should not be used). For example, the extensive Roman literature on exile forms part of a discourse that is much more concerned with questions of Roman (and Greek) identity formation than with emigration.[91] Yet without the corpus of Greek and Latin literary works we would know next to nothing about the collective expulsions that occurred from time to time, about perceptions of travel, or about notions of foreignness and Otherness.

Then there is evidence in the legal sources, especially in the writings of the *Digest*. As with all the Roman legal sources, the legal works present both small case studies that are discussed by the jurists, and legal rulings that have a bearing on migration itself. The cases that are described are useful, but raise questions of typicality: their choice is determined by legal interest, not by the fact that they are representative of regular social life. The content of the law raises classic problems of the sociology of law: for whom was the law created, and to what extent was it followed? Moreover, it should be emphasized that the legal evidence does not contain a series of migration laws, nor does it present a coherent framework of attitudes about migration. It rather contains rulings on citizenship, on obligations towards the place of origin, and on the census, all of which may, but need not, have repercussions for the movement

---

[90] For which see Laurence (1997) with refs; for reading Juvenal in general, see e.g. Garrido-Hory (1998), who employs its *systèmes de références* (to ethnicity, slavery, etc.) for *decodage des pratiques sociales*.

[91] See in particular Whitmarsh (2001).

of people. For the analysis of institutional responses to mobility, such evidence is surely helpful.

Inscriptions form the main written source for the study of migration, and therefore require more discussion. The epigraphic habit culminated under the high empire, and tens of thousands of inscriptions survive from Rome, mostly in Latin, some in Greek. The epigraphical material forms, for more than one reason, an excellent source for research. One reason is the simple fact that there are so many inscriptions, another that they circumvent a large part of the disadvantages of the literary sources, and yet another that they offer more direct testimony of individuals. Mostly they are epitaphs, many of them consisting of hardly more than a name, others being more elaborate affairs. Some inscriptions directly testify to migration, by explicitly specifying the origin of the person named. (These will be called DOC inscriptions: *Denominazione di Origine Controllata*).[92] Others give indirect clues, such as the use of foreign names or of calendars that are in use elsewhere.[93]

The epigraphical evidence is abundant, but there are also reasons for caution.[94] Epitaphs form the main type of epigraphical source. Patterns of commemoration are hardly free from biases. It is well known that type of burial, the putting up of a written record, and what was recorded on it were all heavily dependent on cultural preferences. Roman funerary culture was very much directed at communication to third parties; self-representation was extremely important. One problem for the study of Roman migration through epigraphy is that identity was not expressed primarily in ethnic terms: in many cases, legal and social status were considered more important, and people omitted their origin. Another is that the dead were sometimes transported back to their place of origin to be buried there.[95] Both phenomena are of real social significance, but obviously hinder the identification of migrants. The case of senators is sobering: although prosopographical studies have ascertained the non-Roman origins of a great number of senatorial families, there are hardly any inscriptions from Rome in which senators mentioned where they came from. At the other end of the spectrum stand the soldiers stationed in Rome, whose naming patterns were highly standardized and included almost invariably their origin.[96] The general population seems to lie somewhere between these extremes. In

---

[92] Although it cannot always be established with absolute certainty, I take it that normally in DOC inscriptions we are dealing with first-generation migrants rather than their descendants. Likewise Solin (1983) 647, who argues that in the case of slaves this is virtually certain. The same applies to soldiers. Holleran (forthcoming *b*) cites some exceptions.

[93] For a full discussion of various types of inscriptions testifying to migration in a provincial context, see Haley (1991) 11–27. Noy (2010*a*) 13–18 for discussion of criteria; Bruun (forthcoming) for a useful overview.

[94] Explored further in Tacoma and Tybout (forthcoming *b*) and Tacoma (forthcoming *c*).

[95] Tybout (forthcoming).

[96] Tacoma and Tybout (forthcoming *b*) for soldiers from the Near East stationed in Rome.

their case, it seems that there were no hard and fast rules about in which contexts people decided to mention their origin and in which they did not.[97] In many inscriptions that lack a DOC designation there are hints that people came from elsewhere, yet it is also clear that these hints should not be confused with facts. The case of Greek cognomina serves as a sufficient warning: as has been pointed out in response to the research of Frank mentioned above, they were not only used by people originating from the Greek East, nor always by slaves, despite the fact that many Greek names had a servile connotation.[98] The understandable response among epigraphers has been to employ hard criteria to establish who is a migrant and to eliminate all uncertain cases.[99] But by limiting oneself to the certain cases a great deal of the other material is not taken into account. So, Noy's list of foreigners contains over 1,000 DOC inscriptions, but the number of inscriptions from Rome that is potentially relevant for the topic is easily larger by a factor of 10.[100] Put somewhat differently, the mention of origin that seems such a sound criterion in DOC inscriptions is just as subject to construction as any other identifier of migrant status.

Another difficulty is formed by the lapidary (literally!) character of the texts: they normally testify to individual movement only, by mentioning that someone originates from elsewhere, without providing any further information. Usually the motivation for the change of place can only be guessed at.[101] As individual attestations in themselves have little value, the natural response has been to analyse inscriptions in series. This is certainly justified, but the problem is that epigraphy is just as much about self-representation as about objective historical recording. In analysing inscriptions in bulk, scholars make themselves vulnerable to the hazards of patterns of epigraphical recording and survival. Given the biases in the epigraphic material, creating statistics is at best not fruitful, and consists of pseudo-science at worst. We know that the sources are biased, but the simple fact remains that it is impossible to establish with any

---

[97] A comparison with the naming patterns in the epigraphy of Hellenistic and Roman Athens is instructive: there, people used standardly either a *demotikon* (in the case of locals) or an *ethnikon* (in the case of immigrants), resulting in thousands of attestations of immigrants. See Gray (2011) and Hin (forthcoming).

[98] Numerous studies by Heiki Solin have established the poin; e.g. Solin (1983) 633–51, discussing the onomastics of Jews and Syrians; making in addition a similar argument about the employment of Semitic names, and about geographic names ('Die Bedeutung der sog. Her-kunftsnamen als Indiz für ethnische Herkunft hat man oft stark überschatzt', 643). For the latter argument, *C.I.L.* 6.13820, an epitaph for Caecilia Graecula, *natione Hispana* and *Graff.Palatino* 1.332, a graffito of *Nikaensis Af(er) Hadrimetinus v(erna?) d(omini) n(ostri)* are cases in point; see also in general the catalogue of Solin (2003²). Mouritsen (2011) 123–9 for the prevalence of Greek names among the servile population.

[99] e.g. Wierschowski (1995) 24–9, Solin (2007). See Noy (2010a) for a thoughtful discussion of criteria. For a different method of making use of onomastics, see Salomies (2002).

[100] A somewhat similar observation is made by Salomies (2002) 150–3, who in the *nomina* from Ostia finds many further hints of immigrants beyond those explicitly attested as such.

[101] As observed by Stanley (1990) 251.

exactitude in what ways the biases run. In creating statistics there is also the additional problem of small sample size: despite appearances, the number of attestations relative to the total number of inscriptions (let alone to the underlying population) is extremely small.[102] Breaking the epigraphic material down into smaller subsets almost invariably leads to small-number statistics that are, even within the data-set itself, meaningless. Statistics thus only have meaning *within* a sample, of which we know that it is skewed in ways that are beyond reconstruction. They might perhaps help to understand the nature of the sample, but certainly not that of the underlying population. The inscriptions should be used to direct our thoughts rather than to provide definite answers.

There is, of course, also non-written evidence for migration.[103] The topography of the city of Rome is exceptionally well known.[104] Despite the difficulties inherent in studying a city with a continuous history spanning almost three millennia, the immense and prolonged effort to reconstruct the city of the Principate has turned the study of its topography into a scholarly discipline in its own right. Although it certainly helps to have a physical context in which to locate the migrants, at the same time the topographical studies are pervaded by an awareness that much of the daily life of the mass of the population is beyond recovery.[105] For example, it is sobering to realize how few *insulae* have been brought to light.[106] But it is of some significance to know that there is no physical evidence for the existence of migrant quarters.[107]

Grave goods also have the potential to shed some light on migration, as some might have an ethnic connotation. For Rome, the prime example is formed by the grave culture of the Jewish catacombs. But these catacombs stem from a somewhat later period, and in the first two centuries AD the Jews have left remarkably few traces in the burial record.[108] It is, in fact, noteworthy

---

[102] See in general Maier (1953–4); cf. Huttunen (1974) 10–15. For example, in the case of Gaul, Wierschowski (1995) works with 640 inscriptions containing 659 persons and documenting 680 *Mobilitätsfallen*. This may seem a high number, especially in view of the general paucity of ancient sources. But the estimated total number of epigraphically documented names from the same area is *c.*13,000, the population is estimated at 5 million, and the inscriptions might cover some ten generations. See also the figures of Holleran (forthcoming *b*) for Iberia: only 473 inscriptions record *origo* on a total of 24,000 inscriptions included in the Hispania Epigraphica online database. For more figures from the western provinces with some further discussion, see Kakoschke (2002) 26–7.

[103] For some other forms of material evidence for migration in the Roman provinces (pictorial evidence, objects found outside funerary contexts), see Bender (1978) 21, Ivleva (2012) 41–2. Survey archaeology is also potentially relevant, though normally shifts over longer time-spans between different types of settlement are studied for which migration is a possible but not a necessary explanation. See the balanced discussion of Patterson (2006) 33–48.

[104] See the topographical dictionaries of Richardson (1992) and Steinby (ed.) (1993–2000), and, for shorter accounts, Coarelli (2007) and Claridge (2010²).

[105] e.g. Patterson (2010).   [106] Patterson (2000*b*).   [107] Tacoma (2013).

[108] See Noy (1998) and Rutgers (1998) 70–1 on the invisibility of the Jews of Rome in the Principate. Solin (1983) 731 on the situation in Ostia. For the catacombs see Leon (1995²); Cappelletti (2006) 143–91; Noy (2010*b*), all with further literature.

that in general in the city of Rome under the Principate most burial sites were distinctly Roman.[109] If we assume that families grouped their burials together, a modest form of ethnic clustering is to be expected. However, proper immigrant graveyards have not been identified in this period.[110] Burial was often arranged for by associations, so it is their membership that is mainly responsible for patterns of clustering.[111] The large elite *columbaria* contained slave households that were ethnically mixed (and also included *vernae*, locally born slaves).[112] The use of Egyptian and Egyptianizing objects and symbols in graves in Rome has very little to do with the presence of Egyptian immigrants.[113] The *equites singulares* seem to have had a separate graveyard, but in their case their military identity was surely more important than their immigrant status, and other units stationed in Rome show clustered burials but do

[109] Killgrove (2010*a*) 203: 'the vast number of graves uncovered in the last decade do not indicate that people individualized their identities in death in a material way that would identify them as nonlocals.' This applies also (with one possible exception) to the populations of Casal Bertone and Castellaccio Europarco studied by her, see (2010*a*) 300–1.

[110] A possible (but by no means certain) case of a late Republican graveyard of Campanian immigrants is presented by the so-called *Olle di San Cesareo* from the Via Appia, for which see *Terme* 4.31 with further refs, to which Adams (2003) 101–3; Shaw (2006) 93–101 and Graham (2011) should be added, the latter giving other possible interpretations of its social context. It is possible, but not certain, that in late antique Rome the degree of ethnic clustering increased. There has been some discussion of clustering of burials of Egyptian immigrants in the area around S. Paolo fuori le mura, but the evidence seems rather poor and there is certainly no separate Egyptian graveyard; see Nieddu (2003) 119. Similarly, the case made by Bertolino (1997) for a late antique *cimiterio nazionale pannonica* near S. Sebastiano at the third mile of the Via Appia concerns a couple of inscriptions only, not all of them equally securely assigned to the graveyard, though some clustering of Pannonians around the transferred remains of the Pannonian martyr S. Quirino seems to have occurred. In both the Egyptian and the Pannonian case, there are also certain cases of people buried elsewhere in the city.

[111] The absence of clustering of immigrant burials suggests that the claim of Verboven (2011) that ethnically based trade associations engaged in burial activities did not apply to the city of Rome. For a migrant burial in a *columbarium* at the Via Latina, see *C.I.L.* 6.6974; presumably amidst people from other walks of life. For probable clustering of a people sharing the same occupation, see *C.I.L.* 6.4417 mentioning an *ustrina saccariorum,* with Martelli (2013) 102.

[112] Cf. however Borbonus (2014), who argues that the *columbaria* function akin to immigrant graveyards as they contained socially marginalized persons; but that can only be true in a metaphorical sense, and Borbonus himself admits that 'the analogy should probably not be pushed too far' (12).

[113] See, on the multiplicity of meanings of Egyptianizing material culture in Augustan Rome, van Aerde (2015). For Cestius' pyramid in particular see Vout (2003); Borbonus (2014) 3 n. 4 for further literature; van Aerde (2015) 164–72. For a few rather exceptional finds of Egyptian-style mummies, one at the Via Cassia (the Grottarossa girl), the other at the Via Appia, see Toynbee (1971) 41–2. Such burial customs may perhaps belong to Egyptian immigrants, but given the widespread interest in Aegyptiaca that is by no means self-evident, and in the case of the Grottarossa girl it is now virtually certain that mummification was used locally, by people originating from Rome or its vicinity: see Ciuffarella (1998) with further refs. The point is also nicely demonstrated by the fact that an Egyptianizing small pyramid-shaped tomb was used in the Isola Sacra graveyard at Ostia/Portus by an immigrant from Aquitania in Gaul, see *I.S.I.S.* 21 (tomb no. 1) with Tacoma (forthcoming *c*).

not seem to have had collective burial grounds.[114] It is, in fact, noteworthy that immigrants who came from eastern areas where inhumation was the norm adopted cremation when they arrived in Rome.[115] Moreover, the very fact that the dominant form of burial in the city of Rome in this period seems to have been cremation adversely affects the presence (and preservation) of grave goods. At any rate, such material culture is more important for the study of acculturation and the expression (or the lack of it) of ethnic identity than for migration per se.[116]

What archaeology contributes to migration studies is, to a much larger degree, evidence from human skeletons. Some of this has been analysed by relatively conventional methods such as craniometrical analysis.[117] But quite exciting and revolutionary new methods have been employed, and in the past decade a parallel scholarly universe has come into existence with many studies that are relevant for the theme of Roman migration. Studies of modern DNA help to establish genetic lineages between the current population of Italy and their ancient predecessors, and help to understand at which periods of time immigrants entered the population.[118] Ancient DNA also has the potential to elucidate migration patterns in more direct fashion, though its retrieval is surrounded by formidable technical problems.[119] However, the best results thus far have been achieved by a different method: the analysis of stable isotopes from teeth and bones. There is a growing range of isotopic studies addressing Roman migration.[120]

---

[114] The graveyard of the *equites singulares* was located at the via Labicana, at the third milestone; it seems to have been deliberately destroyed by Constantine after the battle of Pons Milvius in AD 312. In consequence its exact layout remains unknown; what was to become the Mausoleum of Helena was built over the area. Speidel (1994a) 43 and *passim*. The graves of their predecessors, the *Germani corporis custodes* (less formally known as *Batavi*), have been found along the via Portuensis and the via Aureliana. See Speidel (1994a) 25-6. Soldiers of the praetorian and urban cohorts seem to have been buried in somewhat dispersed clusters along the via Flaminia (near Pons Milvius, Tor di Quinto, and, close by, via Vitorchiano), between other grave monuments. See Gregori (2012b) 170. Epitaphs of both have also been found at the via Salaria and the via Nomentana.

[115] Nock (1932) 329.

[116] Cf. Modéran (2004) 344–6 and esp. Cool (2010) and Pearce (2010) for discussion of the— often difficult—interpretation of ethnic grave goods in the provinces. Note also that elite burials with rich grave goods often consist of an assemblage of objects with very different provenances (e.g. the Grottarossa girl, see Toynbee (1971) 41–2, or the so-called Lady from York, see Leach et al. (2010)); the diversity probably served to convey a sense of wealth rather than point to the ethnic identity of the deceased.

[117] See Leach et al. (2009); Eckardt et al. (2010) 111–12; Leach et al. (2010).

[118] Woolf (2013) 361 for some brief remarks.

[119] See Prowse et al. (2010) for an interesting example of DNA analysis (in combination with isotopic analysis) of a graveyard belong to an imperial estate at Vagnari, Puglia. However, the finding that one person originated from Japan (or descended from people originating from that region) is remarkable, to say the least.

[120] For isotopic studies of migration in the Roman provinces, see e.g. Dupras and Schwarcz (2001) on the Dakleh Oasis in Egypt; Perry et al. (2009) on the mining area of Phaeno,

Analysis of isotopes is quite likely to become a main source of new information in the near future. It is based on the principle that during the growth of teeth and bones the food and water that is consumed produces a chemical profile that is geographically specific. By comparing ratios of stable oxygen or strontium isotopes in teeth and bones within a sample, it is possible to establish the extent of homogeneity. Individuals with a markedly different profile are assumed to have grown up elsewhere, and hence to be immigrants.[121] With the help of a reference population (either ancient or modern) or a hydrological profile of specific regions, it is in some cases possible to determine the origin of the immigrants.

Isotopic analysis is important, and bound to become ever more prominent in studies of Roman migration. One of the major advantages is that it may help to identify migrants that remain otherwise invisible.[122] But it would be naive to expect too much of it, and it would be a mistake to take it as hard factual evidence that speaks for itself. It does *not* present the reference population against which we can judge in what directions the written sources are biased. Apart from technical problems in the analyses (some, incidentally, quite formidable), major interpretative issues are raised.[123] In fact, some of the problems are remarkably similar to those of epigraphic sources.

At present there are relatively few isotopic studies available, and only two that are directly relevant for the study of migration to the city of Rome: one from Casal Bertone at the eastern suburbium, the other from Castellaccio Europarco south of Rome.[124] In addition, there is a study of the data of the

---

mod. Jordan; for Britain see, among others, Budd et al. (2004); Leach et al. (2009); Leach et al. (2010); Prowse (forthcoming).

[121] Killgrove (2010*a*) 48.

[122] So in the case of Killgrove (2010*a*) 183: 'there are no distinguishing characteristics, either biological or cultural, that would suggest that any of the individuals from Casal Bertone or Castellaccio Europarco originated somewhere other than Rome.' Likewise in the cemetry of Vagnari in Puglia, studied by Prowse et al. (2010), see 176: 'Evidence from the burials themselves (burial type, grave goods) does not provide a clear indication of differential burial treatment for foreigners *versus* locals.'

[123] Bruun (2010), a re-evaluation of Prowse et al. (2007), with response by Killgrove (2010*b*) 50: 'neither isotope nor osteological analysis can judge whether an individual came to Rome voluntarily or by force, or whether that individual was manumitted during life or at what age manumission occurred. Isotope analysis is not a panacea to the limitations in the archaeological and epigraphical evidence, but its utility for answering questions about migration to Rome has never been investigated.' See further Prowse (forthcoming) and Tacoma (forthcoming *c*). For further brief discussion see also Pollard (2012) 181–2: 'the enthusiasm for such studies (or, more accurately, our confidence in the validity of the interpretations) might need to be tempered a little, until we have developed a better understanding of the underlying biogeochemical mechanisms controlling the behaviour of such isotope systems, which is currently somewhat empirical.' Note that some of the problems noted by Bruun have been acknowledged by the researchers themselves, see e.g. Budd et al. (2004).

[124] Killgrove (2010*a*); for a description of the site of Casal Bertone, see also Musco et al. (2008) and some brief remarks in Catalano et al. (2013).

second- to third-century AD necropolis of Isola Sacra, that is located between Portus and Ostia.[125] But the number of publications is increasing at such a speed that this problem is likely to be overcome in the near future.[126] What nevertheless cannot be remedied is the scattered nature of the data: all concern very specific samples based on a couple of tens of specimens coming from sites with a very specific profile.[127] It therefore remains difficult to generalize from the samples. In addition, the outcome of the technical analysis is not as straightforward as one would think: foreignness turns out to be a matter of degree rather than something absolute. A sample produces a spectrum of isotopic values whose outliers are considered to be immigrants, but this leaves room for ambiguous cases.[128] Furthermore, the supposed local part of the sample may in fact have been born in a region producing the same isotopic profile.[129] In addition, the method is much better at identifying outsiders in a population than at establishing where they came from. In the absence of full information, the choice of a reference population (ancient or modern) remains a hazardous affair. And again, as with all studies based on burial sites, cemetery populations show biases (few infants and young children, fewer women than men) of which it is impossible to determine to what extent they were the product of culturally determined preferences in burial. One last obstacle is that, in the city of Rome under the early empire, many (probably most) people were

---

[125] Prowse et al. (2007), analysing oxygen isotopes from first and third molars. Further discussion by Bruun (2010), who pointed out that Isola Sacra contained the populations of both Ostia and Portus, not just Portus alone and the response of Killgrove (2010*b*); Killgrove (2010*a*) 245–50 for re-analysis; Hin (2013) 234–7 for further interpretation; Prowse (forthcoming); Tacoma (forthcoming *c*).

[126] Cf. the isotopic studies of ancient diet that have used a much wider range of skeletal samples. For samples from within Italy, see e.g. Sperduti, Bondioli, and Garnsey (2012) on Velia and Wallace-Hadrill (2011) 125–30 summarizing research on the *c.*300 skeletons found at the beach in Herculaneum.

[127] Sometimes the small sample size is caused by the limited number of burials, but sometimes it is also small relative to the graveyard population. See Prowse et al. (2007) 512 and Bruun (2010) 111–12 on the Isola Sacra data: 61 skeletons were analysed, on an estimated total number of 2,000 skeletons (of which *c.*1,000 are well catalogued). Likewise, isotopic analysis at a graveyard of the late antique mine of Phaeno in mod. Jordan concerned 31 skeletons of an estimated 1,700 buried individuals; see Perry et al. (2009); Dupras and Schwarcz (2001) studied 109 out of 383 excavated skeletons coming from a cemetry in the Dakleh Oasis which may have contained 2,000 burials; Leach et al. (2009) studied 50 individuals from Roman York, of which 29 came from a site that produced *c.*350 excavated skeletons. Obviously the realities of funding and specific requirements for the research play a large role. For the specific character of sites, Casal Bertone is a good example. It does in fact consist of two burial sites (a mausoleum and a necropolis), whose connection is unclear. Even if the connection with the nearby-located fullery remains tenuous, a comparison with other graveyards around Rome described by Catalano et al. (2013) makes it clear that in terms of age profile and sex ratio there are large differences between sites.

[128] See e.g. Leach et al. (2010) fig. 5, where a female is discussed whose isotopic strontium values fall with the local range, while the oxygen values are on the boundary between local and non-local, and the individual is still taken to be a migrant.

[129] As Bruun (2010) 112 has pointed out, this is a major problem in the case of the Isola Sacra data.

cremated rather than inhumated.[130] Most skeletal material from Rome is therefore of a relatively late date, late second or third century or later.[131] Although this certainly does not mean that skeletons from the earlier period are not available at all for analysis,[132] and ashes may contain unburnt skeletal material, the representative nature of the findings for establishing patterns of the general population is severely limited, especially as the choice between cremation and inhumation may have been class- and gender-specific.[133] Not only is it probable that the unclaimed bodies of the urban poor were cremated in mass pyres,[134] what is more important is that the slaves and freedmen that are so well known from the inscriptions from the *columbaria* cannot be subjected to isotopic analysis because they practised cremation.[135]

---

[130] The shifts between inhumation and cremation were traced on the basis of literary sources by Nock (1932) and Toynbee (1971) 39–42; for briefer comments see Noy (1998) 75–8, Fassbender (2005), and Hope (2009) 81–2. Cic., *Leg.* 2.22.56 and Plin., *N.H.* 7.54.187 suggest inhumation was the older custom, but the earliest excavated graves in Rome were cremations. The Twelve Tables allowed for both inhumation and cremation. Inhumation seems to have been the norm in the middle Republic, but already from the third century BC onwards cremation increasingly became popular, though aristocratic families adhered to inhumation for a long time. Cremation became dominant in Rome by the first century BC and remained so in the early Principate. Whereas Lucr. 3.890 may suggest that inhumation and cremation were both practised in the late Republic, Tac., *Ann.* 16.6.2 implies that by the time of Nero cremation was the norm (see also Petr., *Sat.* 111). The monumental *columbaria* with large numbers of urns, for which see Patterson (2000a and b), Hasegawa (2005), and the full study of Borbonus (2014), date from the Augustan period onwards. As Borbonus argues, underground or partially underground *columbaria* were confined to the first half of the first century AD. The above-ground *columbaria* that were made subsequently ceased to be built after Hadrian, though existing ones continued to be used. From the early second century AD inhumation came to be practised more frequently, and there is some evidence for second-century AD tombs with mixed burials (Nock (1932) 323–4). The shift is fully visible in the second- and early third-century burials at Isola Sacra, Ostia. Inhumation became nearly universal in the third century and was standard practice in the Jewish and Christian catacombs (though note that the chronology of their appearance is disputed, see the research of Rutgers, aong others (1998) 45–71). Macrobius, *Sat.* 7.7.5 at the end of the fourth century describes cremation as a thing of the past. This standard account might be in need of revision once the research on the ten sites around Rome described by Catalano et al. (2013) 23 is fully published: each of them has only a small proportion of cremation burials (mostly below 10% of all burials), but the dating of the graveyards (normally described simply as 'Imperial') remains crucial for the argument.

[131] See also Eckardt et al. (2010) 109 on Roman Britain: 'the necessity of using inhumation burials led to a bias towards the later Roman period . . .'

[132] See Gowland and Garnsey (2010) 137; Killgrove (2010a) 88–90; Catalano et al. (2013) for sites in the vicinity of Rome. The analysis can also be conducted on basis of already excavated material in museum collections.

[133] See in a somewhat similar vein Harris (2011) 48–50, who emphasizes that the prospect of a decent burial might have been absent for the lowest classes. For predominance of adult women among cremated individuals in a series of Roman graveyards, see Catalano et al. (2013) 23. Note that cremation is standard practice for the members of the association of the *cultores Dianae et Antinoi* at Lanuvium, see *C.I.L.* 14.2112 of AD 136, and that the association is composed of the poorer parts of the local population, including slaves.

[134] Bodel (2000) 133–4.

[135] Cf. Webster (2010) 53, who incorrectly blames the lack of possibilities for bioarchaeology of Roman slavery on the absence of slave graveyards.

One final problem applies to most sources in one way or another: they are very dependent on Roman burial practices and patterns of commemoration. Most of our attestations of migration (say 80 per cent of the epigraphic material and 100 per cent of the isotopic evidence) come from burial sites. In consequence, the Roman sources help to identify non-locals because they give information about their origin rather than trace migration as a process: we see them at destination, but not on the road.[136] Anyone working on the subject has to face the fact that, due to the particular way the sources are created, there is a distinct possibility that some forms of mobility have escaped documentation. Seasonal migration was hardly prone to epigraphical recording or to leave isotopic traces. In addition, the custom of bringing some of the dead who died elsewhere back home is likely to have erased much movement.[137]

There is, in sum, no shortage of sources, but all of these sources also have limitations. Even apart from the obvious fact that particular sources help to answer particular sets of questions, there is little reason to privilege one source type over another on *a priori* grounds.[138] The fundamental problem is that there is no way to determine on the basis of the ancient sources alone in what direction the sources are biased. These problems do not imply that the sources should be discarded—rather the reverse. But we should not depend solely on them for our analysis: they need a framework.

5. AIMS AND METHODS

The aim of this book is to create such a conceptual framework for understanding urban migration in the Roman world on the basis of a study of the city of Rome under the Principate, as a supplement to the more empirical studies that already exist. Empirical study and modelling are not binary opposites, and to some extent the relative proportion that is allotted to each of them is more a question of intellectual preference than of anything else. The present book is an attempt to model from the available knowledge the significant forms of migration to the city, permanent and temporary, better-documented and less well-attested. How did Rome function in the migration system?

This framework will be created by drawing on a number of insights which have emerged from studies of migration in other historical periods. These are

---

[136] Cf. Moch (2003[2]) 19 for a somewhat similar situation in early modern Europe: '[p]arish lists, occupational lists, and census data are limiting. They force the scholar to infer movement from static data; thus, they yield little information about the actual volume of movement, return migration, or repeated moves. As a consequence, these sources give the impression that historical actors moved infrequently and that they stayed at their destination.'

[137] Tybout (forthcoming).

[138] Cf. the debate between Bruun (2010) and Killgrove (2010*b*).

taken especially from the literature of early modern Europe. At the same time, there can be no question of mechanically applying models derived from the studies of later periods to the world of early imperial Rome. One needs only to think of the prevalence of slavery in the Roman world to realize that this would be a dangerous route indeed. In practical terms, this means that the comparative material will provide guidance in interpreting the scattered and fragmentary data, but that their applicability to the Roman world should not be taken for granted. At the same time, it implies a certain eclecticism in borrowing theories and concepts.

Scholars of early modern migration have advocated a systems approach.[139] Such an approach consists of two elements: firstly, it studies how various types of migration relate to each other; and secondly, it places migration in its societal context. In the Roman case, such an approach is not only advisable but almost mandatory. Much of what can be said about Roman migration can only be inferred through indirect means.

In Chapter 2 definitional issues and typologies are explored on the basis of ideas formulated for early modern migration. What is migration? How can it be classified? What was its volume? Where did migrants came from? In Chapter 3 institutional responses to migration will be studied: what was the legal status of immigrants? To what extent did the pre-modern state attempt to control migration? In Chapter 4 the implications of Roman family structure for migration patterns are discussed. In Chapter 5 urban migration theory will be subjected to further scrutiny. Chapter 6 discusses the capacity of the city to absorb migrants by studying the openness of the labour market. Chapter 7 discusses integration and the formulation of migrant identity. Chapter 8 places the findings for Rome in the context of the Roman world.

Chronologically this book focuses on the Principate, a period that comprises two-and-a-half centuries, from Octavian's emergence as sole ruler of the Roman world in 31 BC (or, to be more precise, his assumption of the title of Augustus in 27 BC) to the end of the dynasty of the Severi in AD 235. For the purpose of this study these exact dates have not much meaning, and in consequence sources from the first century BC onwards until the later part of the third century are taken into account where relevant. The roughly two-and-a-half centuries that the Principate comprise are taken as a unified period, and in consequence the focus is on structure rather than on change. Some scholars have pleaded for a more nuanced treatment, in which distinct periods are distinguished within the period of the Principate.[140] In itself their pleas are justified, as it is *a priori* unlikely that no changes occurred during a period of two-and-a-half centuries, and migration might assume a wave-like

---

[139] Jackson and Moch (1989; 1996) 61–2.   [140] Wierschowski (1995) 36–7.

character.[141] But these changes can only be analysed in a small number of cases, most notably in the changing composition of the soldiers who were stationed in Rome. For the rest, they are by and large obscured from view, if only because both inscriptions and skeletal material are usually not dated with exactitude. The issue is to find an acceptable level of generalization, and a structural analysis therefore seems more appropriate than a chronological one.

The focus is on the city of Rome because it constitutes the best place to study migration and test hypotheses. It formed the apex of the urban hierarchy, and there can be no doubt that it functioned in many senses also as the apex of the Roman migration system. The fact that the sources to study migration are much better than anywhere else in the Roman Empire is certainly no coincidence. At the same time, it is obvious that Rome cannot be studied in isolation—if only for the fact that migrants came from other places. Occasionally these other places are brought into the discussion.

After some consideration, it was decided to leave the material from Ostia/ Portus out of the discussion. It is clear that Rome's main sea harbour was connected in multiple ways with Rome, but it is also clear that it formed a world on its own. For obvious reasons, Ostia is of great interest for the theme of this book: both its exceptionally rapid growth in imperial times and its function as harbour city guaranteed a very high presence of immigrants.[142] Some of these people would continue to Rome, and there is also evidence for people who were active both in Rome and in the harbour.[143] But even apart from the fact that a significant distance separated the two cities physically, Ostia had its own peculiar character and was much more than the suburb of Rome for which it is sometimes taken.[144]

It should also be made explicit what the study is and what it is not. In the first place, this is not primarily a book about the city of Rome, but one about Roman migration. Within this field, this is a book about *urban* migration, not about migration *tout court*. The focus on migration to Rome implies that some other forms of migration will receive short shrift. It is internal migration that is

---

[141] See Hochstadt (1983) 207 for discussion of early modern German migration waves, in particular caused by wars and epidemics. As Manning (2013²) 193 observes more in general, 'it seems that flows of migrants along a single trajectory rarely last more than half a century without undergoing some change'.

[142] See among others Salomies (2002); Prowse et al. (2007).

[143] e.g. a grain merchant who made a dedication at Tivoli but was in all likelihood based in Ostia and thus presumably travelled up and down the Tiber, see *C.I.L.* 14.4234 with *Terme* 8.12 (*M(arcus) Caerellius Iazemis q(uin)q(uennalis) pistorum III et perpet(uus) codicarius item mercator frumentarius Invicto Herculi ex v(oto) d(onum) d(edit)*)—presumably a freedman; the *cognomen* suggests a Cappadocian origin. For Gaionas, who was active both in Ostia and at the Syrian sanctuary at the Janiculum, see the refs. in Steinby (ed.) (1993–2000) s.v. 'Iuppiter Heliopolitanus (Reg. XIV)' (J. Calzini Gysens) with Noy (2010*b*) 204 (who points out Gaionas may not have been himself a Syrian immigrant). For moving on from Ostia/Portus to Rome, see *B.G.U.* 1.27 and *P.Mich.* 8.490 and 491.

[144] As Bruun (2010) 110 points out.

at issue, not the settling of foreign tribes on Roman soil, nor the settling of Roman traders and soldiers on conquered territories. Colonization will only be discussed briefly, as it was primarily a phenomenon of the late Republic and the Augustan period, and was only to a limited extent connected to the population of the city of Rome. And by looking at the upper end of the urban system, movement within the rest of the spectrum of settlements or within settlements will not be discussed in any detail.

These exclusions entail a certain risk. This study might easily reinforce the idea that migration to the city was the dominant mode of mobility in the Roman Empire. There is indeed a possibility that this assumption is correct, but it should not be taken for granted, and it is certainly more relevant for voluntary migration than for forced and state-organized migration. Scholars of early modern Europe have increasingly warned against the idea.[145] By focusing on Rome, there is in fact a danger that the idea of a distinction between a mobile urban and an immobile rural world is reinforced.[146] It is quite possible that village mobility was large, but its study requires a different analysis, with different types of sources and different models.[147]

We need to start somewhere, and where better than in the heart of the empire?

---

[145] So Hochstadt (1983) 213 on early modern Germany: 'On the basis of the evidence presented so far, there is little reason to believe that cities were more mobile than villages. Migration affected all types of German communities, although the forms of mobility may have differed widely. Probably only a minority of German migrants fit the pattern of permanent rural-to-urban migration which is frequently taken for the norm.'

[146] Cf. Wierschowski (1995) 16: 'Für einen grossen Teil, nämlich die ländliche Bevölkerung, die nach vorsichtigen Schätzungen 80% ausmachte, nach anderen sogar 90%, bestand keine Veranlassung und auch kein Interesse, den angestammten Wohnsitz zu verlassen, da die bäuerliche Existenz durch das Verbleiben am väterlichen Hof geschichert war. Nur der relativ kurze Weg zum nächsten Wochenmarkt als Unterbrechung des täglichen Arbeitsrhythmus erforderte temporär befristete Mobilität, darüber hinaus eventuell auch einmal im Jahr, bei politisch Interessierten, der Gang in die Stadt zur Wahl der Magistrate.' In similar vein Kakoschke (2002) 3.

[147] As epigraphy is an urban phenomenon, the inscriptions are not particularly useful to analyse rural mobility (apart from the peasant's sons that joined the army, see Ivleva (forthcoming) and Veg. 1.3; cf. Noy (2010a) for some soldier's inscriptions from Rome mentioning village origins). Cf. Braunert (1964) on Egypt's *Binnenwanderung*; the papyri document rural mobility much better. Something similar appears when the epigraphical and papyrological sources from Syria are compared; see Zerbini (forthcoming a).

2

Conceptualizing Migration

> Migration may occur in stages with stops along the route for lengthy periods of time. It may be circular, bringing migrants back to their homes. Absence may be limited seasonally to a few months each year, to a few years, or extend for working life. Emigration constitutes an intentionally permanent move that, however, may be followed by secondary or return migrations when conditions at the destination become unsatisfactory.... Migration may be unintentionally permanent when migrants who plan to return 'next year' finally die in the receiving society; or it may be involuntarily permanent when exiles may not return because of hostile, even life-threatening regimes 'at home'. Migration involves a continuum from travel to lifetime emigration.[1]

1. DEFINING MIGRATION

Early modern historians of migration such as Hoerder (just quoted) have emphasized that an exclusive focus on permanent, 'don't look back' emigration as the dominant form of migration is unwarranted. Migration is a broader phenomenon: much migration has a temporary character and seemingly unrelated types of mobility may tie into a single migration system.[2]

Such complex forms of migration raise questions of definition and demarcation. Geographical mobility is the term that covers an extremely wide spectrum of movement in space, including short trips, random visits, travel, and tourism.[3] Migration concerns the more permanent parts of that spectrum, forms that consist of patterned movement and/or prolonged stays. Here, migration is defined as the movement of persons who change their residence

---

[1] Hoerder (2002) 14–15, in response to the question: 'What distance has to be covered, what cultural boundaries have to be crossed, and what decisions have to be made to define a "move" as a "migration"?'

[2] e.g. Lee (1966) 49. Cf. Sanjek (2003), though from a somewhat different perspective.

[3] For definitions of travel, see Foubert (2013) 391 n. 3.

from one place to another on a permanent or semi-permanent basis. For the purposes of this book, migration thus constitutes movement by humans into and out of the city of Rome, in which the change of residence is of some duration. The movement is trans-local and in principle spatially discontinuous: it is from one settlement to another.

A central concept in the current definitions of migration is the notion of permanency. A move should be permanent to be regarded as migration: '[w]hatever else migration is about, it is about moves that are relatively long and relatively definitive.'[4] But as this quote by Tilly also shows, permanency turns out to be relative. The problem is demonstrated by the use in the current definition of the slightly awkward term 'semi-permanent'. The term is used to include two somewhat different phenomena: seasonal migration (the regular patterned movement between two places with stays of some duration), and temporary migration (the movement into a place for a longer period of time, and subsequent return). What the exact duration of a stay should be in order to be considered permanent or semi-permanent remains unstated. Although it seems futile to formulate a too precise time-limit, one may consider several months as a reasonable minimum.

Issues of permanency apart, the definition that is used here is relatively straightforward and closely adheres to those that are currently in use in studies of early modern migration.[5] Very similar definitions are also used in the isotopic studies of Roman migration, no doubt for practical reasons as well, as they cover the type of migration that can be analysed through isotopes.[6] But migration has also been differently demarcated, both more and less exclusively.[7] Frank, who was interested in the 'intrusion' of foreigners in Rome, used an extremely inclusive concept of 'foreign descent', which remained further undefined and allowed him to regard an infinite number of generations of descendants of immigrants as foreigners. By contrast, Noy focused on free civilians from outside Italy below the elite. He thus excluded (at least in principle) the imperial aristocracy, soldiers, Italians, and slaves.[8] It should be clear that, thus defined, Noy's foreigners will have formed only a part of all migrants in the definition used in this book.

The definition that is used here falls somewhere in between these two extremes. In several respects it is inclusive. By including 'semi-permanent' migration and taking 'permanency' as a relative rather than an absolute concept, one problem that has haunted epigraphers dissolves: very often in

---

[4] Tilly (1978) 50. [5] Moch (2003²) 18; Hoerder, Lucassen, and Lucassen (2007) 36.
[6] Killgrove (2010a) 12. Note that aDNA works differently, establishing origin within maternal or paternal lineages; Prowse et al. (2010).
[7] Cf. Erdkamp (2008) 418, who adds a 'shift of subsistence strategy, either between jobs or between farms'.
[8] Noy (2000) xi–xii; though note that Noy offers many valuable discussions of slaves and soldiers, and includes them in his appendix of inscriptions.

the inscriptions it remains unknown to what degree a stay was intended to be permanent, especially in the case of voluntary migration.[9] The only sure indication is given when an immigrant built a grave monument in his new home *inter vivos*, and thereby signalled his intention to stay to the end of his days in the city, but cases where this is explicitly mentioned are scarce.[10] The focus is not only on immigration, but outbound movement is also taken into account (though the focus remains on Rome). Movement is not confined to persons of a particular social status. The definition also deliberately avoids statements about the degree of rupture, the question whether ties with the place of origin should be broken or be maintained in order to be regarded as migration proper. It is ironic that both the former and the latter option have been regarded as crucial to migration. Breaking the ties with the place of origin was essential to modernizing interpretations such as those of Zelinsky, but can also be found in the attempts at typology of Charles Tilly.[11] Conversely, the

---

[9] Epigraphers have in general eschewed definitional discussions but rather concentrated on the criteria to identify migrants. But cf. Solin (1983) 624–6, who in his study of Syrians and Jews in the western Roman Empire tried to limit himself to cases of permanent resettlement, but immediately had to concede that in the epigraphy this often remains uncertain. See also Solin (2003[2]) xxix, who in the context of his study of *griechischen Personennamen* remarked: 'Alles in allem ist festzustellen, dass es hoffnungslos ist, in Rom, dem Schmelztiegel der antiken Welt, zwischen "Stadtrömischem" und "Fremdem" mit letzter Sicherheit zu unterscheiden.'

[10] In our study of 146 epigrams testifying to mobility in the Greek East, we found only three cases of *inter vivos* monuments, see Tacoma and Tybout (forthcoming *a*). Roman examples include: *C.I.L.* 6.9677, in which a *q(uin)q(uennalis) corporis negotiantium Malacitanorum* builds *inter vivos* a grave monument for himself, his wife, his children, and their freedmen and descendants; *A.E.* (1979) 78, in which two hostages from Parthia build a tomb for themselves and their daughter; *C.I.L.* 6.9707, a grave monument for a Thracian moneychanger and his family. *C.I.L.* 6.15011 is a monument for a deceased son which is also intended for the eventual burial of the dedicating father, a Pannonian. *C.I.L.* 6.34466 is a monument for a Phrygian family. *C.I.L.* 6.29718 for a man from Nemausus (mod. Nîmes), who interestingly enough also held a local office. For movement out of Rome by people setting up memorials *inter vivos*, see *C.I.L.* 3.4869 from Virunum, Noricum (mod. St Veit an der Glan, Austria), for a couple with children, he from Rome, she from Aquileia. *C.I.L.* 10.6492 is a grave built in Ulubrae, some 50 km south of Rome, by a freedman who describes himself as *margaritarius de sacra via* for himself, his wife, and his brother. It is likely that the freedman resided and worked in Rome; perhaps he had property in Ulubrae. *I.L.Sard.* 57 is an epitaph set up in Cagliari in Sardinia for someone *domo Roma*, with a vacat after *vix(it) ann(os)* implying the information was to be supplied later; Bruun (1992) argues he was a trader following the army. Note, however, that in many cases the graves are built for a deceased relative, and the mentioning that the monument is also *sibi* seems formulaic and somewhat accidental (see Huttunen (1974) 30–2: in the inscriptions from Rome as many as 30% had a *sibi*-formula, but 61% of these concerned tombs for spouses and children). Such was the case with Monica, Augustine's mother. She had a monument built in Thagaste for her deceased husband and herself, but was buried nevertheless elsewhere, in Ostia. See Aug., *Conf.* 9.11.28 with Tacoma (forthcoming *c*), though Tybout (forthcoming) shows how exceptional this was. See for an ambiguous case *A.E.* (1953) 56, with Wierschowski (2001) 16.

[11] Zelinsky (1971) 225–6 (migration 'is a spatial transfer from one social unit or neighborhood to another, which strains or ruptures previous social bonds'); Tilly (1978) 50 ('Below some minimum amount of rupture, no move (however distant) constitutes migration'); somewhat similarly Manning (2013[2]) 192.

maintenance of ties is a crucial element in diaspora models. Although it does perhaps not function as a formal criterion to define what constitutes migration, the focus in such an approach has shifted to migrant identity and the subjective experience of living abroad. Migrants, in that perspective, are persons who personally bridge the gap between two cultures and remain either physically or mentally in contact with their homelands.[12] Interesting though such an approach is, it should be kept analytically separate from an analysis of migration patterns proper and not interfere with definitional issues.

The definition does not make pronouncements about the question whether the migrant moves of his own volition, or is forced to move by others. Where necessary, a threefold distinction by agency will be employed in this book, distinguishing between voluntary, state-organized, and forced migration, but the omission of agency in the definition is deliberate.

There can be little doubt that a significant part of Roman mobility flows consisted of forced movement, most notably, but not solely, that of slaves. There is among migration historians of later periods an increasing tendency to study forced and voluntary migration together.[13] It is based on the assumption that labour is an extremely important motive for migration, but that such labour migration should be understood not purely in economic terms. If regarded from a social perspective, the difference between forced and voluntary movement is less clear than it may seem. In many cases migrants that appear to move voluntarily are in fact enmeshed in a web of social and economic obligations. The freedom of free movers only concerns the decision to move itself, but they can still be forced to move by the conditions they live in.[14] More generally, in studies of labour relations it is increasingly emphasized that a spectrum exists from complete dependency to complete independency. Many people will not find themselves at the extremes of the spectrum but somewhere in between, and will have created within relatively constrained conditions some room for manoeuvre.[15] Such an approach is helpful, because Roman historians have started to emphasize that the distinction between slavery and freedom is primarily of a legal, and only to a lesser

---

[12] For applications of diaspora models to Roman migration, see Eckardt (ed.) (2010), Killgrove (2010a) 41–2 (including the related concept of transnationalism), and Ivleva (2012) 14–24. Cf. also Joshel (2010) for application to Roman slavery. Outside the Roman world, the concept of diaspora has sometimes been used rather inclusively to cover all kinds of migration— as Sanjek remarked: 'so, who is not a diasporee now?'—but also in a more narrow sense. Sanjek (2003) 317; Sanjek himself advocated a more restricted application, limited to specific forms of migration.

[13] Eltis (ed.) (2002). Cf Sanjek (2003) 317, emphasizing dissimilarities.

[14] Hoerder, Lucassen, and Lucassen (2007) 31: 'Allerdings verweist der Begriff der "freien", im Gegensatz zur "unfreien", bzw. "erzwungenen" Migration auf nur einen Aspekt, nämlich die Entscheidungsfindung von wandernden Familien und Individuen.' See also Hin (2013) 212–15.

[15] Lucassen and Lucassen (1997) 11–12; Eltis (ed.) (2002).

extent of an economic or social, kind.[16] As the free and the slave population
show in some respects structural equivalencies, it is useful to analyse them
together. Such an approach admittedly works better at the aggregate level
than for particular types of migration and mobility. Seasonal labour migration,
for example, clearly remained confined to voluntary migrants, but the fact
remains that it operated in a labour market where slaves were also working.[17]

The definition also includes the state-organized movement of soldiers. The
term 'state-organized' itself is admittedly somewhat awkward, but aptly con-
veys that the agency of the movement is external but that the movement is
not forced. Soldiers were recruited, normally of their own volition, but upon
enlistment could be transported wherever the state saw fit. In the case of the
troops stationed in Rome the situation was even more complicated, because
admission to these troops occurred often after service elsewhere and proven
suitability, and was regarded as a privilege.[18] State-organized migration is
included for similar reasons as forced migration: the motives and constraints
in which people decide to join the army are similar to those of voluntary
migrants.

But there are also some exclusions. One consequence of the definition is
the fact that the focus is on movement *between* places, not on movement
within the city. Post-mortem mobility is also excluded, though the return of
people who died abroad to their place of origin is certainly important for
understanding how migration was perceived.[19] Perhaps the most important
consequence of the definition is that the focus is firmly on first-generation
migration, on people who came newly to the city.[20] In demarcating migration
as a social phenomenon, there is always the question when a migrant stops
being a migrant. In the definition used here, people are considered as immigrants if they were born outside Rome, no matter how attached they became
to Rome. Conversely, people whose parents came to Rome but were themselves born in the city are not considered migrants, no matter how much they
affiliated themselves with their parental homeland. The focus is thus on
formal, objective criteria, rather than on subjective experience. The choice is
deliberate: the extent to which migrants and their descendants considered
themselves to be migrants and chose to express their identity in such terms
constitutes a separate, secondary issue, which will be addressed in Chapter 7.

[16] Bradley (1994) 65; Temin (2003/4), arguing that 'most Roman slaves, particularly urban
slaves, participated in a unified Roman labor market' (529).
[17] Erdkamp (2008) 418 and (forthcoming); De Ligt and Tacoma (forthcoming); De Ligt and
Garnsey (forthcoming).
[18] Less is known about recruitment than one might think. For a vignette showing the
complexities, see *Sent. Hadr.* case no. 1 (31.24–44; 387.11–21) with Lewis (1991) 274: someone
petitions Hadrian to enter the praetorian guard, to which the emperor replies that he should start
at the urban cohorts and after one year of service may be allowed to transfer to the praetorians.
[19] Tybout (forthcoming).   [20] Cf. Sanjek (2003) 315.

The point is of particular relevance for the Jewish diaspora community living in Rome: it consisted only in small part of first-generation immigrants in the definition used here,[21] and therefore plays only a limited role in the discussion.

2. TEN TYPES OF MIGRATION

Migration is by its very nature not only an unruly, but also a highly varied phenomenon. It is therefore not surprising that migration historians have identified many different groups of migrants. So an inventory covering European migration history from the seventeenth century to the present lists some 200 different migrant groups, running from Cossacks in Russia in the seventeenth century to Peruvian domestic servants in Italy in the twentieth century.[22]

The response to the presence of so many migrant groups has been predictable: to classify them in categories of shared characteristics. Although its actual usage varies, migration historians have often employed the typology of Charley Tilly. Based on what he called the social organization of the move, Tilly distinguished between four forms of migration.[23] Firstly, local migration, consisting of moves within a geographically contiguous area with a unified market of labour, land, or marriage. Secondly, circular migration, consisting of return movement, either occurring once or being repeated. Thirdly, chain migration, in which networks of people connect distant places, and in which those already at the destination provide aid, information, and encouragement to newcomers. Fourthly, career migration, in which people move because of the opportunity to change (improve) their social position. The major benefit of Tilly's typology is its wide use, which enhances possibilities of comparison.[24] At the same time, it should be noted that his categorization is based on the

---

[21] The point has been often made; see e.g. Solin (1983) 616, who also points out that by the time the Jewish inscriptions appear, most Jews would have lived in Rome for generations (706). A key passage is the description of Philo, *Leg.* 155–8, where Philo claims that many Jews had Roman citizenship and received grain in the dole. Expressions of Jewish identity in Rome are in fact even more complex, as ethnicity and religion merged in them. Note also that it is very likely that Jews did not originate solely from Palestine, but showed mixed origins, see Leon (1995²) 238–40 and the observations of Noy (2010*b*).

[22] Bade et al. (eds.) (2007).

[23] Tilly (1978) 51–5. As the typology did not cover all the major distinctions (as Tilly (1978) 56 himself already remarked), some migration historians have subsequently added two further types: colonization and coerced migration; see Moch (2003²) 17.

[24] Perhaps unsurprisingly, other typologies have been devised as well. For precursors, see Ravenstein (1885) 181–4, who classified migrants on the basis of distance and motive, and Petersen (1958), also discussing previous attempts. For successors, see Lesger, Lucassen, and Schrover (2002); Hoerder, Lucassen, and Lucassen (2007) 37 categorize migration by motive, creating four broad types: forced, flight/expulsion, economic, and cultural. Sanjek (2003) advocates a sevenfold typology covering wider forms of movement than first-generation migration alone.

application of multiple criteria: it is partly the type of move, partly the geographical space within which someone moves, and partly the motives for movement that determine its type. It is therefore not surprising that overlap occurs between the various categories, that some forms of migration can be categorized into more than one type, and that types of migration can mutate from one form to another. In the Roman case, examples of all four types of migration occur.[25] Nevertheless, many of the attested cases of migration can only with difficulty be classified into one of these types, for the simple reason that too little is known about them: mostly we see people at the point of destination, rather than on the move. Some forms can be surmised on theoretical grounds, but are not well attested. In particular chain migration is very difficult to identify. The use of the typology is so limited that it does not seem fruitful to employ it in the analysis of migration to Rome.

The pluriformity of European migration makes it rather unlikely that Roman migration was a monolithic phenomenon—an impression that is easily obtained when one relies on a single type of source.[26] One of the major advantages of studying migration in the city of Rome is that some of the variety can be demonstrated. At least ten major types of migration can be distinguished and will be briefly presented here. Some of the types have received an immense amount of scholarly attention (though not always under the heading of migration). In these cases, it is hardly possible to do justice to the scholarly discussion in this brief compass, and it seems neither necessary nor warranted to provide full annotation. Others require some more attention. Some, in fact, will receive more detailed treatment later in this book.

The first type consists of elite migration. Although it is normally not analysed under that heading,[27] one of the best-known types of immigration to Rome is provided by the imperial elite. Over time, more and more members of the senatorial and equestrian orders originated from outside Rome. Many of them transferred their domicile to the city.[28] No doubt entry into the imperial elite signified real advancement,[29] but as the new members of the elite originated from families of local worthies in the provinces that had a very similar outlook to those of Rome, theirs was geographical rather than social mobility. The widening geographical recruitment of the elite is best visible in the changing composition of the Roman senate.[30] In modern times its explanation

---

[25] Cf. Noy (2000) 53–6, for reference to the typology, with Zerbini (forthcoming *a*) for further discussion.

[26] For the need to differentiate between varieties of ancient mobility, see Woolf (forthcoming *a*).

[27] La Piana (1927) 196–7 was an exception. See now Eck (forthcoming).

[28] Plut., *Mor.* 470C for Greek members of the provincial elite coming to Rome.

[29] Hammond (1957) 75.

[30] The classic analysis is that of Hammond (1957), covering the period from the reign of Vespasian to the third century AD; for recent bibliography see Eck (forthcoming).

has generated a substantial amount of scholarly discussion: the failure of Rome's own elite to reproduce itself, the withdrawal from politics, proscriptions and executions by the emperor, the personal preferences of emperors and their need to have loyal supporters, have all been adduced.[31] At any rate, new senators set up a household in the city, and they were expected to own at least a part of their property in Italy.[32] Other aspiring members of the imperial aristocracy settled in Rome of their free will, though no doubt social expectations about proper elite behaviour played a large role. Rome functioned as a stage for elite life, and much of the daily transactions were conducted in the city.[33] Despite the centrality of Rome, members of the imperial aristocracy also led highly mobile lives. Many owned lands and residences in all parts of the empire. Senators originating from the provinces often kept a substantial concentration of their property-holdings around their city of origin. Such holdings determined their movements: they travelled between villas, made the occasional inspection visits that were, even for absentee landowners, unavoidable, and acted as local patrons.[34] Later in life they might in fact return to their home-ground.[35] Furthermore, members of the elite moved on a seasonal basis out of Rome, because it was too hot and too unhealthy to live there later in the summer.[36] Invariably they were accompanied by trains of attendants and baggage, so moving around will have involved massive efforts.[37]

---

[31] Hammond (1957) 74–5 with some of the older discussion; Hopkins and Burton (1983) 184–9.

[32] Plin., *Ep.* 6.19.4, stating that Trajan orders those who want to hold office to own at least one-third of their property in Italy, so that they do not use Italy as a mere *hospitium* or *stabulum*; SHA, *Marc. Ant.* 11.8, where Marcus Aurelius orders that *senatores peregrini* should own a fourth part of their property in Italy. See Eck (forthcoming). Cf. Aul. Gell. 1.12.8 on the choice of Vestal Virgins: they should not be the daughter of a man without residence in Italy, *neque eius legendam filiam qui domicilium in Italia non haberet*; not necessarily pertaining to the senatorial aristocracy, but certainly elitist in character.

[33] e.g. Mart., *Epig.* 10.30 (business at Rome keeps one from visiting the lovely villas in the countryside).

[34] Laurence (1999) 93–4, with reference to Pliny's letters. Cf. Eck (forthcoming), who stresses the ties to Rome. Cf. Taylor (2011) 124 for the consequences of dispersed holdings for mobility patterns and 'bi-locality' in classical Athens.

[35] Solin (1983) 667 states that many senators from the east had only a 'Behelfswohnung' in Rome. See further Ameling (1983) for one of the best-documented cases: Herodes Atticus, one of the great sophists of the second century AD, who remained an active member of the local Athenian elite and participated intensively in local politics. He had a decidedly local base: much of his life was spent at his estate at Marathon, whereas his stays in Rome (and elsewhere) were limited to relatively brief periods of time, mainly connected to office-holding.

[36] The extremely luxurious villas both in Latium and in Campania, for which see Adams (2008) and D'Arms (1970) 116–64, point indirectly to the importance and structural pattern of such seasonal moves. For literary references, see e.g. Plin., *Ep.* 5.6.1–2, where the health of Tuscany in summer is discussed.

[37] Laurence (1999) 140–1. SHA, *Elag.* 31.5 states that the future emperor as a private person never travelled with fewer than 60 wagons—a sign of his extreme decadence, to be sure, but also implying that large trains were normal.

We might imagine a rather complex choreography of aristocratic movement circling around Rome.

Closely connected to aristocratic migration was the second type: administrative migration.[38] Many new members of the elite, though certainly not all, entered the imperial aristocracy through holding office in Rome. In the reverse direction, from Rome, every year a great number of individuals set off to administrative positions in the provinces. Thanks to the survival of hundreds of *cursus* inscriptions and the prosopographical studies that have been based upon them, the phenomenon is exceptionally well documented.[39] Such postings were on a temporary basis, and could run from several months to several years. Once in their province, many of these administrators travelled around in their provinces on inspection tours and in order to judge court cases.[40] Somewhat less well documented but part of the same phenomenon is the administrative mobility of imperial slaves and freedmen who were sent to the provinces to occupy lower-ranking positions in the Roman administration or to administer imperial property. Again, such postings could take up several years. A counterpart is the inbound mobility into Rome of official representatives and ambassadors from provinces and cities, though their stays were normally of much shorter duration.[41] In the patterns and structures of its mobility it was certainly institutionalized, but the Roman administration remained relatively small, and professionaliszation hardly occurred. Arguably, it was precisely this non-professional aspect which generated so much movement into and out of Rome.

The third type consists of educational migration.[42] Many young men travelled to one of the large cities of the empire for educational purposes,[43] and stayed there for prolonged periods of time. Although there is some evidence (not from Rome itself) for educational migration by younger people,[44] most of

[38] For an introduction, see Garnsey and Saller (1987) 20–6. Bowersock (1965) for Greeks in imperial service in the time of Augustus.

[39] It seems futile to give a bibiography; for the nature of *cursus* inscriptions Eck (2009*b*) is important.

[40] Marshall (1966) for an analysis of itineraries of governors in the late Republic. See, apart from Pliny's correspondence with Trajan in Plin., *Ep.* 10, also Arrian's *Periplus maris Euxini*, though see Rood (2011) for the underlying identity politics.

[41] Noy (2000) 100–6, showing the large number of such visitors, and pointing to a number of cases where a temporary visit turned into a permanent stay. See also Habicht (2001) with further literature. Eck (forthcoming) for the effects of senatorial patronage on local communities.

[42] Noy (2000) 91–7, Ricci (2005) 33, Moatti (2006) 122–3, also for discussion of some of the sources that are cited here. The educational system remained virtually unchanged until late antiquity, for which see Kaster (1988) and Cribiore (2007).

[43] Sen., *ad Helv.* 6.2 adduces *liberalium studiorum cupiditas* as one of the motives for coming to Rome. See Kaster (1988) 21, who speaks of 'an archipelago of cities where schools of liberal letters were to be found. This distribution encouraged a good deal of island hopping.'

[44] Plin., *Ep.* 4.13 for schools in neighbouring cities frequented by *praetextati*, something similar in Tac., *Agr.* 4, stating that Agricola was born at Forum Julii but educated from early youth onwards at Massilia, and in Aug., *Conf.* 2.3.5, where Augustine visits a school in nearby

it will have occurred at the later and final stages of the curriculum.[45] Educated by house teachers or at local schools for the first parts of their training, young elite males often spent some time elsewhere—often far away from home—to finish their education.[46] Such stays ranged from a number of months to a number of years.[47] Also in view of the fact that such stays outside the home-town will have been expensive,[48] it is not surprising that educational migration is mainly visible in the case of the elite.[49] Rome was quite naturally one of the educational centres involved. Already by the end of the Republic the city had become a centre of education for legal studies,[50] literature, and philosophy. The presence of many great scholars helped to attract students from all over the empire. Schooling revolved around personalities; there is very little evidence for institutionalized, purpose-built schools.[51] After a number of months or years students returned home, or moved elsewhere. Such educational patterns nat-urally paved the way for more prolonged stays or returns later in life. In addition, there was also outbound movement by young members of the elite

Madauros; cf. *C.I.L.* 12.118 for regional educational mobility of a 16-year-old, and for similar mobility of teachers see *C.I.L.* 8.26672 with Hamdoune (2006) 1014.

[45] *C.I.L.* 13.2040 might be an exception. In this epitaph from Lyon someone *annorum X in studiis Romae de(cessit)*. But Noy (2000) 92 may be followed in his suggestion that the ten years refer to the length of study rather than the age of the deceased. A late law, *C.Th.* 14.9.1 (AD 360), states that students can remain in the city up to the age of 20, but the phrasing suggests that in reality many remained longer. Cf. *C.J.* 10.50.1 (Diocletian and Maximianus) which gives age 25 in the case of students in Berytus.

[46] In *Dig.* 5.1.18.1 the difficulties of a *filius familias* staying abroad are discussed. In cases of theft and injury, but also in such cases that follow from contractual obligations, such as the recovery of a loan, such *filii familias* are allowed to start court proceedings themselves, without having to wait for their *pater familias*.

[47] The data assembled by Cribiore (2007) 323–7 on Libanius' pupils suggest that normally a stay would take about three years, but there was significant variation. In *C.J.* 10.40.2pr. Alexander Severus reiterates a Hadrianic law that states that only after stays of 10 years were students regarded as having changed their *domicilium*, suggesting that normally such stays were much shorter. Cf. *C.Th.* 14.9.1 (AD 360) (stays up to the age of 20) and *C.J.* 10.50.1 (Diocletian and Maximianus) (stays in Berytus until the age of 25), both already mentioned above.

[48] *Dig.* 5.1.18.1 and 12.1.17 make the connection between educational stays in Rome and *viaticum*, travel money, though it seems that sons used their money also actively for different purposes, such as loans. See Aug., *Conf.* 2.3.5 for high costs that necessitate a gap-year which allows Augustine's father to save money for Augustine's subsequent education in Carthage. Cf. Mart., *Epig.* 3.10 for high monthly allowances by fathers to wasteful sons.

[49] In *Dig.* 50.1.36pr. a student is approached by his home village to deliver a letter to the emperor; relatively high status is implied. In Lucian's *Somnium* such education is presented as a costly elite pursuit. In Philostr., *Ap.T.* 7.42, a student owns several slaves in his home town. The ruling that during their study in Rome students *debent excusari*, presumably referring to immunity from municipal obligations, also suggests membership of local elites, see *Frag.Vat.* 204. For the three sons of Herod the Great being educated in Rome, see Jos., *B.J.* 1.435 (the youngest son dies in Rome while there for his education), cf. 1.445, 452, 455.

[50] *Frag.Vat.* 204 for students of law. Philostr., *Ap.T.* 7.42 has a young man who was sent by his father from Messene in Arcadia to study law in Rome.

[51] For legal schools, see Liebs (1976) 236–9 on Juv., *Sat.* 1.128 with scholia and discussing the *stationes* mentioned by Aul. Gell. 13.13.1.

in Rome, most notably to Athens.[52] A somewhat different type of educational migration may also have occurred below the elite, in the context of apprenticeship arrangements (which will be discussed in a different context in Chapter 6, Section 3). Lucian, in a small (semi-)autobiographical *Somnium*, nicely demonstrates that for some people there actually was a choice between pursuing an education or becoming an apprentice (in his case, that of a sculptor).[53] The apprenticing out of sons (and slaves) was widespread among skilled workers. Apprenticeship systems in later periods could induce large-scale migration streams.[54] However, it seems that in the Roman world apprenticeships normally involved little travel, and that they took place within the community, or covered only small distances—in fact, the apprentices may have stayed at home during their apprenticeship.[55] Perhaps longer distances could be covered for apprenticeships in the more specialized jobs at the higher end of the occupational ladder.[56] Somewhat similarly, people trained as doctors or architects might also be thought to be in between the skilled apprentices and the elite sons that prepared themselves for leading positions in the empire, and they might have travelled significant distances to receive their training.[57]

Closely intertwined with educational migration was a fourth type of migration, consisting of the movements of intellectuals.[58] Grammarians, rhetoricians, orators, writers, and philosophers could and did serve as educators, but also performed in public and could act as moral advisers to the leading men in the state.[59] Somewhat similar mechanisms applied to people working in relatively high-ranking jobs, such the medical or legal professions, or sculptors and architects.[60] As this was the world of literati, it is extremely well documented.[61] The great majority of such intellectuals who were active in Rome

---

[52] Bonner (1977) 90; Gray (2011) 59 on Romans entering the Athenian ephebate.

[53] Likewise Mart., *Epig.* 5.56 discusses training for occupations of different standing.

[54] See Moch (2003[2]) 55 on London in 1650: of the *c.*20,000 apprentices in London 1650, *c.*85% were migrants, many from nearby but also some from further away. The same situation already existed a century earlier.

[55] One of the oppositions on which Lucian's *Somnium* is structured is that between a highly localized job as a sculptor versus the very worldly outlook of a literary career; in fact, the workshop of the maternal uncle where the narrator is apprenticed is situated in the proximity of his own house. For short distances and external apprenticeships in Roman Egypt, see Liu (forthcoming).

[56] *S.G.O.* 16/05/02, referring to a stay in Alexandria by a smith of precious metals from Konana in Phrygia, possibly in the context of an apprenticeship.

[57] *S.G.O.* 08/08/06, for someone trained as a doctor in Rome, commemorated by his nurse at home in Hadrianoi, Mysia.

[58] Noy (2000) 94–7, also for some of the sources discussed here. For Greek intellectuals in Rome in the age of Augustus, see Bowersock (1965) 122–39.

[59] Plin., *Ep.* 1.10.1 (Rome as the centre of liberal arts).

[60] Noy (2000) 100; Solin (2007) 1366.

[61] Already in antiquity biographies were circulating, also of some lesser-known personalities. For series, see (the surviving parts of) Suet., *de vir. ill.* (showing the centrality of Rome) and

seem to have come from outside.[62] Some set up a school, acquiring a following of pupils. Others enjoyed the patronage of one of the members of the aristocracy by whom they were sometimes invited to come to Rome, or they took up a salaried post in such houses.[63] In the exceptional case of rhetoricians, they could occupy the prestigious and well-paid chairs in Greek or Latin rhetoric that were instituted by Vespasian.[64] Some came from very wealthy backgrounds, which obviated the need to provide a means of living. But others stemmed from much lower economic strata, and some were freedmen. It is here that we find one of the major areas in Roman society where social and geographical mobility could coincide: transferring to Rome could entail a move up the social ladder.[65] Although many intellectuals subsequently moved on to other places, the city was considered to hold prime rank, and many stayed there for prolonged periods.

The fifth type of migration concerns a form of permanent mobility. Rome was part of the itinerary of performing artists: gladiators, actors of various sorts, charioteers, Greek athletes (especially after Domitian established the Capitoline games), musicians, and reciters of poetry—anyone who mattered artistically visited Rome at one point or another.[66] Over time, an enormous infrastructure for their performances was created; even if not all of the stadia, amphitheatres, and theatres were permanently in use, their sheer size is enough to indicate the very high demand for such performers.[67] For some, Rome remained just one venue out of many; for example, in the case of the athletic competitions, Rome formed simply a part of a four-year cycle. But Rome had a particular resonance, and for some performers it formed their base. We normally know of their whereabouts because their victories were commemorated, either by themselves or by the cities where the competitions were held, or by their home communities.

A sixth type of migration was also cyclical in nature: seasonal and temporary labour migration. This will be discussed in more detail in Chapter 6, Section 5. There can be little doubt that it constituted an important form of migration, but the sources that refer to it are scarce, and in consequence its

---

Philostr., *V.Soph.*, for the itineraries of the intellectuals of the Second Sophistic. For the epigraphic context, see e.g. Ferrandini Troisi (1996).

[62] e.g. *C.I.L.* 6.9454 with Bonner (1977) fig. 8 for a statue of Epaphroditus, *grammaticus Graecus*, known to have come from Chaironeia; Lucian., *Nigr.*, which centres on a fictive Greek philosopher living in Rome.

[63] Lucian., *De merc.*

[64] Suet., *Vesp.* 18 (salary of HS 100,000).

[65] The potential for significant social advancement was already noticed by Suet., *Rhet.* 1. Statius' father forms a good example, see Simelon (1992) no. 36.

[66] Noy (2000) 117–19; Casson (1974) 136–7 for general description. See e.g. *A.E.* (1956) 67 for a pantomime mentioning his stays in Rome, in the rest of Italy, and in the provinces.

[67] See the overview of Coleman (2000).

exact importance cannot be inferred from the sources alone.[68] Particularly in the harbour (of Ostia and in Rome itself) and in the building industry there was a high demand for hired labour. This would apply to unskilled labour in the first place, but in the building industry semi-skilled and skilled labour would also be required. Part of this labour could be supplied by seasonal workers from outside Rome, though it should be borne in mind that it could also be performed by the local population.

Closely related to seasonal and temporary labour mobility is the seventh type of migration: immigration by the poor. In the former case, Rome's demand for labour acted as a pull; in the latter, people were pushed out of their homes by poverty, and as a last resort moved to Rome.[69] Just as with seasonal and temporary mobility, poverty-driven migration is not well documented. As the poor were the least likely to receive a proper burial, they have left no visible trace in the funerary record.[70] The movement of impoverished peasants who found, on their return from war, that their land was occupied or devastated forms one of the main narrative strands of the history of the Republic and offers the paradigmatic case of proletarianization.[71] Although this model is increasingly under attack as the single causative mechanism for the societal problems of the later Republic, and even if some of the underlying problems were solved at the start of the Principate, it is hard to believe that the process stopped completely in imperial times.[72] In addition, one can think of groups other than peasants, becoming lost in the anonymity of the city: people evading taxes, fugitive slaves, deserted soldiers, and prostitutes, for example.[73]

---

[68] The few references to seasonal labour found in literary sources concern agriculture and have little to do with the city of Rome: Suet., *Vesp.* 1.4, mentioning labourers coming each year from Umbria to Sabine territory to till the fields; *C.I.L.* 8.11824, the well-known Latin epigram of the Harvester of Mactar referring to his seasonal labour, see Hamdoune (2006) 1008 with further bibliography. Cf. Cato, *De agr.* 144 for gangs of 50 olive-gatherers led by a contractor. In Sall., *Catil.* 37.7 in the later Republic peasants flock to the city, preferring grain handouts to hard work on the land. See Erdkamp (2008) 426–7 for further discussion. Cf. for a late antique context Syn., *Ep.* 4 for peasants turned sailors, though not necessarily on a seasonal basis.

[69] See Holleran (2011) 160–5, showing that both models have been applied to describe the movement of Italian peasants of the late Republic. Obviously there is a thin line between them, but for the Principate there is much to be said to keep them, at least for analytical purposes, separate.

[70] For the likelihood that in the Principate the poor were cremated in mass pyres see Huttunen (1974) 43–5, Hope (2009) 158, and esp. Bodel (2000). See e.g. Mart., *Epig.* 8.75 (*accipit infelix qualia mille rogus*); cf. Mart., *Epig.* 9.2 (mentioning the *sandapila*, the pauper's bier).

[71] Hopkins (1978) 1–98; Morley (1996) 46. Moch (2003²) 7, 11 for European parallels.

[72] See Jongman (2003); the papers collected in De Ligt and Northwood (eds.) (2008); Holleran (2011) 161–3; note that part of the criticism is that imperial authors (Plutarch and Appian) projected back contemporary conditions on the Republic. For a peasant driven off his farm by a wealthy neighbour, see the story in Apul., *Met.* 9.35–8 (set outside Italy).

[73] For prostitution, see Noy (2000) 122–3 and in general McGinn (2004). For imagery of the city's rabble, see Sall., *Catil.* 37.5; Juv., *Sat.* 8.174–175 (though set in Ostia). For *fugitivi*, see e.g. *Dig.* 14.5.8; *Dig.* 21.1.1.1 (edict of the curule aediles, for which see also Aul. Gell. 4.2.1); Mart., *Epig.* 3.91 (accompanying a discharged soldier returning to Ravenna); Apul., *Met.* 6.8 (where

There are few direct sources describing the movement of these persons, and more generally very little is known about poverty in the Roman Empire.[74] But urban poverty and begging certainly are documented in Rome.[75] In addition, there are many references to street-sellers, who quite likely will have operated on the verge of destitution.[76] Such urban poor will not always have been immigrants, but many no doubt were.

The eighth type is migration by traders. In a sense, they might be regarded as the archetypical movers.[77] In the case of Rome under the Principate, specific trade networks have been charted, sometimes on the basis of epigraphic evidence or literary sources, sometimes on the basis of material evidence.[78] The trade consisted partly of the state-induced import of grain, and partly of free market trade in all kinds of products. Individual traders have been attested in great numbers, but it is not as easy to determine the extent to which such traders settled in Rome.[79] Given the seasonality in trading, ships certainly had

Mercury places an announcement for Psyche as fugitive slave); Petr., *Sat.* 97; brief discussion in Joshel (2010) 154, longer in Bradley (1994) 118–30 and, from the perspective of hunting for fugitive slaves, in Fuhrmann (2012) 21–8, with full refs. and bibliography, who notes that fugitives formed a virtual obsession to the Romans. The latter was already stressed by Finley (1980) 111–13. For the poor, the army may have formed an alternative to going to the city: see Tac., *Ann.* 4.4, where Tiberius complains that volunteers were scarce and consisted usually only of the destitute and vagrants (*inopes ac vagi*). But note that less and less Italians were recruited. Roaming vagrants could also turn into brigands; see Chapter 8, Section 5 for brief discussion.

[74] Cf. Mart., *Epig.* 3.14, for a joke about a hungry person travelling from Spain to Rome but returning just before he reaches the city on the Milvian bridge once he hears about the nature of the *sportulae*; no doubt the long travel distance is used for satirical effect. Whittaker (1993) for the poor in Rome; Harris (2011) for an overview of the many unknowns, including discussing the question whether poverty was structural or conjectural. In Harris' view, Italy and the cities were better-off than the provinces and the countryside, because of the taxation structure and the larger number of opportunities in urban environments. But notwithstanding these advantages (or perhaps even because of them), it seems very likely that many poor ended up in one of the larger cities of the empire anyway. See also Holleran (2011) 175–6.

[75] The works of the satirists are full of beggars. See e.g. Mart., *Epig.* 10.5.5 (used as metaphor); Mart., *Epig.* 12.32.25; Juv., *Sat.* 14.134 (begging at bridges). Begging Jews occur in Mart., *Epig.* 12.57.13, Juv., *Sat.* 3.12–16 (at the Porta Capena); cf. Juv., *Sat.* 6.542 with similar phrases, *Sat.* 8.160 for a Syrian Jew at the 'Idymaean Gate'. See also Lampe (2003) 56. Pers., *Sat.* 6.56–60 and Juv., *Sat.* 4.117–18 (carriages had to slow down at the hill near Bovillae at the via Appia, which offered opportunities for beggars. Here also the expressions *progenies terrae* and *filius terrae* occur, used for persons without known parentage (cf. Juv., *Sat.* 4.98); and 'Manius', a typical beggar's name). Further discussion of image and reality in Morley (2006) and Woolf (2006).

[76] e.g. Juv., *Sat.* 5.48; Holleran (2011) 174–5; full discussion in Holleran (2012) 194–231.

[77] For traders as 'first immigrants', see Wierschowski (1995) esp. 30–3.

[78] Noy (2000) 114–17; Dresken-Weiland (2003) 20–9 and Terpstra (2013) 127–70 for many examples: e.g. *A.E.* (1979) 75 for a clothes-dealer from Narbonensis or Cic., *In Verr.* 1.20 for Sicilian *negotiatores* in Rome. For traders from Syria arriving in Rome and spreading (incorrect) news about the recovery of Germanicus, see Tac., *Ann.* 2.82 with Solin (1983) 624 n. 59 for bibliography on Syrian traders; cf. Philo, *Leg.* 15–18 for news about Caligula travelling around the empire through trade networks.

[79] Huttunen (1974) 125–8 emphasizes that relatively few traders are attested in Rome itself. For temporary stays in Rome of sailors (not traders) of the Egyptian grain fleet, see *B.G.U.* 1.27.

to remain in a harbour during winter, and we know that many traders followed fixed itineraries.[80] Some traders or persons connected to traders will have probably moved on a permanent basis to Rome to act as facilitators;[81] there are many parallels for later trade networks in which some traders were moving around, while others were brokers who settled in the new places.[82] Most of the evidence for the collective activities of traders concerns the *stationes*, which will be discussed in Chapter 7, Section 5. Given the fact that Rome itself had no sea harbour, and much of the wares would be unloaded in Puteoli and Ostia and subsequently transported over land or via the Tiber,[83] it might be presumed that most foreign traders would be active there rather than in the city. That seems overly schematic, however. The presence of several *stationes* in Rome itself is certain. The presence of foreign traders living in Rome finds a parallel in the presence of *negotiatores, mercatores, pragmateutai*, and other Romans in the provinces. These groups might be regarded as somewhere between businessmen and colonizers (in the non-technical sense of the word). Official, state-organized colonization ceased under Augustus,[84] and only a small number of the Roman colonies contained inhabitants from the city of Rome, all dating from the time of Caesar.[85] Already from the middle of the second century onwards, Romans and Italians had moved to the east and the west voluntarily.[86] After conquests of the areas and their conversion into Roman provinces, the practice continued. Everything suggests they moved in significant numbers: their presence and their associations[87] can be detected in almost all provinces, following the expansion of the provinces, and in some

Permanent settlement is implied in *C.I.L.* 6.9677 in which a *q(uin)q(uennalis) corporis negotiantium Malacitanorum* builds *inter vivos* a grave monument for himself, his wife, his children, and their freedmen and descendants. Although other scenarios are also possible, it is likely that the trader in pork and sheep who came from Misenum and was commemorated in Rome by his sons had moved to Rome after having performed magistracies in his home-town, for otherwise one would expect that his ashes were transported back over the relatively short distance. See *C.I.L.* 6.33887 with *Terme* 8.14 (*M(arco) Antonio M(arci) filio Claudia (tribu) Terenti oriundo civitate Miseni omnibus muneribus et honoribus patriae suae perfuncto negotiatori celeberrimo suariae et pecuariae*). Cf. *C.I.L.* 8.152 for return home.

[80] Cf. Philo, *Leg.* 15 for traders returning home during winter.

[81] In the inscription concerning the *statio* of the Tyreans in Puteoli, which will be discussed in Chapter 7, Sections 4–5, a distinction was made between resident Tyreans and traders: *I.G.* 14.830 lines 3–4, 7–8 (οἱ ἐν Ποτιόλοις κατοικοῦντες), 16–17 (οὔτε παρὰ ναυκλήρων οὔτε παρὰ ἐμπόρων). The distinction is also visible in *Dig.* 5.1.19.2.

[82] Sanjek (2003) 324.

[83] For subsequent transport, see e.g. *C.I.L.* 14.4234 with *Terme* 8.12 (*M(arcus) Caerellius Iazemis . . . codicarius item mercator frumentarius . . .*), probably himself a freedman with a Cappadocian cognomen.

[84] Scheidel (2004) 11; Keppie (1983) for detailed discussion of the foundations.

[85] Bowersock (1965) 67 for some, not all equally certain. Corinth was repopulated by Caesar 'mostly with freedmen', presumably from Rome itself: Strabo 8.6.23.

[86] Wilson (1966); Müller and Hasenohr (eds.) (2002) with further bibliography.

[87] Verboven (2011) 338 with further bibliography.

cases even preceding it. There is also some evidence for their presence outside of the empire. These 'Romans' did not necessarily originate from the city of Rome itself.[88] One striking feature (and that is how we know them) is that they present themselves in inscriptions as 'Roman' or as 'Italian', as well-defined communities living amidst a host population, whose stays presumably were meant to be permanent.

The ninth is a major category: it is formed by the immigration of slaves, brought to Rome to work in households. Their names are known by the hundreds from *columbaria* inscriptions of the large households, as well as from epitaphs for families working in smaller workshops. Many of the slaves were by this period born in captivity, but there always remained a part of the slave population that was imported (either over longer distances or sold from one owner to the other), and who in that sense belonged to the migrant population. Those that were imported were a commodity like any other type,[89] and hence could be transported from one end of the empire to the other. Their forced displacements were not only a structural feature of Roman society, but they were also at a symbolic level emblematic for the depersonal-ization, disempowering, and uncertainty that was a central aspect of Roman slavery: the rupture with the place of origin was complete.[90] Slaves were not completely tied to one place: imported slaves could be resold, and even *vernae* were sold, and slaves could be transferred between different property-holdings.[91] They could also be sent out to work for their masters. The Roman urban slave system was essentially an open one: for many urban slaves, slavery was a transient state because high rates of manumission were combined with a remarkable degree of subsequent integration into society.[92] It seems that manumission did not have large effects on mobility.[93] It is telling that the jurists debated the question whether freedmen were obliged to follow their patrons

---

[88] See Adams (2003) 643, 651–8 in his study of the Roman traders at Delos.

[89] Famously demonstrated by Trimalchio's casual remark in Petr., *Sat.* 76: *oneravi rursus vinum, lardum, fabam, seplasium, mancipia*; 'I loaded again wine, lard, beans, perfume, and slaves'.

[90] The 'natal alienation' of slaves is a major theme of Joshel (2010), who at 94 aptly states that 'home was in a fundamental way lost'. See in similar vein Bradley (1994).

[91] Hor., *Ep.* 2.1–18 (a slave born at Tibur or Gabii put up for sale in a poetic metaphor); *C.I.L.* 6.21695 for a *vicaria* (female under-slave) who was transferred at least twice within twenty years, from Picenum to Rome to Praeneste (*nata Piceno nutrita Romae mortua Praeneste v(ixit) an(nos) XX*); *C.I.L.* 6.9124 (with comm. in Candilio and Bertinetti (2011) no. 20) for a servile *actor*, *domo Veronae*, commemorated in Rome at age 25; *Graff.Palatino* 1.332 for a graffito from the *paedagogium* in Rome of an imperial *verna* born in Africa (and named after Nikaia in Asia, to add to the confusion), *Nikaensis Af(er) Hadrimetinus v(erna?) d(omini) n(ostri)*.

[92] Temin (2003/4) 526. Wiedemann (1985) was hypercritical, though no one will deny that for most rural slaves manumission will have been a distant dream; the openness therefore only concerns a part of the Roman slave system.

[93] For a possible exception, see *S.G.O.* 08/01/36, probably presenting a case where a woman is enslaved in Athens, brought to Rome, subsequently manumitted, and then moves to Kyzikos.

when the latter travelled.[94] Given the ties of dependency, most former slaves remained caught in a web of social, economic, and affectionate relations with the household of their former master; some in fact even continued to live in the patron's household.[95] 'In effect ... the owner's authority was redefined rather than discontinued', as Henrik Mouritsen aptly summarized the effects of manumission.[96] Although for many slavery was a transient state, they do not seem to have returned to their place of origin. In their case, manumission brought mainly chances of social rather than geographical mobility.

The tenth and last type of migration is military migration. Unlike in many other periods of Roman history, most forms of war-induced mobility are absent in the city in the Principate.[97] Rome seems not to have received large groups of refugees fleeing from war violence. The city of Rome was itself involved in some wars, most notably when, in AD 69, serious fighting took place in the city, and the Temple of Jupiter on the Capitol was burnt to the ground.[98] At other times smaller disturbances broke out among the populace: food riots, fighting around the theatres, the lynching of political opponents.[99] But it seems that no major population upheavals took place: there are no reports of large groups of people fleeing from the city, or people seeking protection in the city. People were, of course, recruited for the army and hence moved into Rome or away from Rome. However, recruitment into the army of inhabitants of the city was a minor phenomenon,[100] and even Italy came over time to supply fewer and fewer recruits for the army.[101] Rome is relevant mainly for two groups: one is the small elite stratum that took up commands in the army to be posted in the provinces—some kept to a single temporary function; others, most notably among the equestrians, could have a full career. The other is formed by the soldiers that were stationed in the city: mainly those serving in the praetorian guard, the urban cohorts, and the imperial horse guard.[102] Compared to other immigrant groups, the soldiers

---

[94] *Dig.* 38.1.20–1.   [95] *Dig.* 33.2.33.1; Tac., *Ann.* 13.32. Mouritsen (2011) 148–50.

[96] Mouritsen (2011) 8.

[97] For the wider historical context, see Zerbini (forthcoming *b*).

[98] Barry (2008); Edwards (1996) 74–82 for its literary resonance.

[99] Barry (2008); Fuhrmann (2012) 124–30.

[100] See Bruun (1992) with refs. For an exception, see *C.I.L.* 13.1893 (Lyon). See also Tac., *Hist.* 5.1, for Romans and Italians joining Titus's troops for the war against Judaea. Furthermore, the Jews in AD 19 are reported by Tac., *Ann.* 2.85; Suet., *Tib.* 36; Jos., *A.J.* 18.63–84 to be partially enlisted to combat brigands in Sardinia instead of being expelled; cf. Chapter 3, Section 5. For an attempt to raise an army in an emergency, see Suet., *Nero* 44.1–2 (after the revolts of Vindex in Gaul and Galba in Spain).

[101] For the general trends, see Dobson and Mann (1973) 191–8 and Wesch-Klein (2007). For recruitment figures of Italians into the army in the first century AD, see Scheidel (2004) 13 and Roselaar (forthcoming), both with further refs.

[102] The literature is extensive; major publications include Durry (1938); Freis (1967); Panciera (1993); Ricci (1994); Speidel (1994*a*) and (1994*b*); Coulston (2000). See Fuhrmann (2012) 114–17 for a useful brief overview with further recent literature.

stationed in Rome are exceptionally well documented.[103] The relative lack of references in literary works is amply compensated by the fact that most of the units are epigraphically well covered. Several hundreds of funerary inscriptions survive, mainly from Rome, but also from outside the city, and in addition a substantial number of *diplomata* have been found. In their documentary texts they employed highly consistent naming patterns, with the consequence that we very often obtain standardized information about the soldiers' units, their age, the length of service, and their origin. It can be established that, apart from a few exceptions, soldiers originated from outside Rome. This means that the simple fact of membership of one of these troops is enough to ensure identification as a migrant. Somewhat ironically, they present the only epigraphic case where we could dispense with origin and still be certain of migrant status.

This brief survey of ten of the main forms of migration into and out of Rome is already sufficient to demonstrate the varied nature of migration. Many of the types in fact show various interlocking subtypes of mobility— the complex movements of aristocrats form a case in point. It is also clear that in any such categorization some types are put together under a single heading that may just as well be regarded as separate forms. The movement of traders into Rome and the settlement of Roman businessmen to the provinces show parallels, but are not completely equivalent. The movement of young elite males in order to receive an education is not exactly the same as that of apprentices. Within the relatively homogeneous group of soldiers stationed in Rome, praetorians and imperial horse guards exhibit different recruitment patterns. The list may thus easily be expanded by splitting categories and adding types; ten is merely a convenient and manageable number to demonstrate the variety without overly fragmenting the discussion.

What the inventory also brings out is the enormous disparity in the coverage by the sources (and in subsequent modern discussion). Some forms are dramatically better documented than others. In particular, the temporary mobility of hired labourers and immigration of the poor have left little trace. Conversely, the mobility of the aristocrats who participated in the administration of the empire is known in sufficient detail to keep prosopographers happy for the coming centuries. The soldiers are massively over-represented in the epigraphy. The relatively small unit of the *equites singulares* alone provides about a fifth of all DOC migrant inscriptions.[104]

---

[103] Speidel (1994*b*) preface also points out that more monuments survive for the *equites singulares* than for all the other cavalry of the Roman army together.

[104] Speidel (1994*b*) 16, table 14, lists 234 *equites* who state their province of origin. Noy (2000) 59–60, table 1 gives 568 military and 521 civilian provincial immigrants attested epigraphically in Rome. The balance becomes even worse if we take membership of any of the three military units in itself as a sufficient sign of immigrant status. In addition, given the higher propensity of civilian immigrants from Italy to omit their origin, the proportions would be even more skewed

The inventory also shows the complex nature of the Roman migration system.[105] Most types of migration consisted of different forms of movement, both in and out of Rome. Permanent resettlement was just one of the many forms of migration, and might in fact be regarded as one extreme on the spectrum of possibilities. Rome's position as central node in the migration system is clear, but it served just as much as a hub as a final destination. People not only came to Rome, they also left the city, used the city as a transit point, had to leave the city and subsequently returned, were brought to the city by force and subsequently stayed, and so on, in an almost infinite variety of forms.[106] An unruly phenomenon indeed.

3. GEOGRAPHICAL HORIZONS

Where did this mass of immigrants come from? What was the geography of their movements? Charting the streams is not easy, at least not when it comes to more specific analysis. Evidence for origins is not absent, but it is, again, unevenly distributed. It is not always certain that what we do know about particular groups is representative of what is missing—also because some of our best evidence concerns relatively small groups.

In fact, completely different evaluations have been given about the origins of Rome's immigrants. In the evaluation, three major dichotomies have been employed: East versus West, Military versus Civilian, and Provinces versus Italy. In classic interpretations such as those of Frank, foreigners, slaves, Orientals, and Greeks were all lumped together into one (Greek, debased, servile) whole. Immigrants came from the East, almost by definition. Even nowadays, when stripped of its Orientalist connotations, the question of the extent to which slaves predominantly came from the Greek East has continued to determine the discussion. In much more nuanced modern treatments of general patterns of immigration into Rome, quite different assessments have been given. Noy pointed to a major difference between provinces that supplied immigrants mainly for the army (the frontier provinces running from Britain along the Rhine and Danube frontier), whereas other provinces supplied

---

if the Italian migrants were included. For brief but similar observations in the case of Germania, see Kakoschke (2002) 6.

[105] See in a somewhat similar vein the remarks of Woolf (2013) 352 on the 'interplay of different migratory movements' in the Roman world in general.

[106] For an example at the level of a particular individual, see Suet., *V.Verg.* 1 and 7–8, for Virgil moving from Mantua to Cremona to Milan to Rome, with *V.Verg.* 35–6 for subsequent itineraries. Noy (2000) 55 for more examples of itineraries. Tacoma (forthcoming *c*) for the movements of Augustine.

mainly civilian immigrants.[107] As a consequence of the demarcation of his subject, Noy focused on provincials and ignored Italian migration. By contrast, Killgrove pointed to the likelihood that many of the migrants originated from within the Italian peninsula.[108] In fact, in some of her attempts to establish the origin of immigrants through isotopic analysis, she assumed as a default option that immigrants in her sample originated from within Italy and tried to locate their origins within the peninsula.[109]

All three approaches contain useful elements, but none is decisive. To the extent that Frank based his arguments on verifiable analysis, he relied on onomastic criteria that have proven to be dubious. Noy's distinction between primarily military and primarily civilian provinces might be valid: there can be little doubt that Germany and Pannonia were major suppliers of the *equites singulares*. However, the analysis is based on a comparison between numbers of inscriptions of military with civilian immigrants that seems fragile: soldiers stationed in Rome almost always mentioned their origin, but civilians did so only haphazardly.[110] It is likely that in terms of volume the latter greatly outnumbered the former, which means that comparing the figures for the two groups is not particularly meaningful. Determining origins through isotopic analysis has remained difficult: far too little is known about the geological and hydrological profiles to identify geographical origin with any reasonable degree of certainty.[111] Limiting the analysis to the Italian peninsula on *a priori* grounds has the virtue of pointing to that area as a potential major source of migrants, but seems otherwise cavalier.

In analysing the origins of Rome's immigrants we might conceptualize a series of concentric circles around Rome: firstly areas from outside the empire, secondly the provinces, and thirdly Italy itself. We might start at the outer circle, and work towards to the centre.

---

[107] Noy (2000) 57–60, also discussing a third category, that of late-antique Jewish and Christian immigrants.

[108] Killgrove (2010*a*) 28–30.

[109] Killgrove (2010*a*) 227–30, in determining origin through analysis of strontium isotopes, called at 230 a 'conservative assumption', cf. 281–5 for analysis for origin by combining strontium and oxygen values.

[110] The point is acknowledged by Noy (2000) 60, but he maintains that the analysis 'at least produces some plausible patterns'.

[111] The point is unwittingly demonstrated in Prowse et al. (2007) 517–18, noting as possible origins of the immigrants in the Isola Sacra sample the area 'north of the Italian landmass', 'the foothills and heights of the Apennine Mountains', and 'the Iberian Peninsula or Greece', among others. Likewise, Killgrove (2010*a*) 262, in the analysis of the oxygen isotopes, discusses the origin of two potentially non-local individuals: they could have come from Rome and its environs, but other possible homelands 'include Greece, Portugal, and the west coast of Turkey', which is a wide range indeed. Budd et al. (2004) 134 gives as possible origin for four individuals buried in mod. Winchester in England 'the western Mediterranean and North African coast'. See further Eckardt et al. (2010) 113, discussing origins in samples from Roman Britain: 'the suggested places of origin . . . are based on "best matches" with currently available data and do not represent secure attributions'; the same point in Leach et al. (2010) 142.

One element seems relatively clear. Almost all immigrants that we find in Rome came from within the empire's boundaries. Evidence for non-Roman outsiders is limited and normally concerns persons from client kingdoms and neighbouring states that had ties with the Romans, friendly or less friendly. Hostages and diplomats form the prime examples.[112] Only a handful of true outsiders, such as Parthians,[113] are known to have lived in Rome. Roman products could be traded beyond the confines of the empire,[114] and goods from outside the empire were imported, but this does not seem to have led to the presence of non-Romans in Rome.[115] So, despite the extensive and regular trade that was conducted with India, no Indian traders are attested in Rome. Roman businessmen travelled in slightly greater numbers outside the boundaries of the empire, though the extent to which these 'Romans' originated from the city of Rome or even from Italy remains unknown. In fact, it seems quite likely that at the edges of the empire there was much more movement across the frontiers; a strong case has been made to regard the frontiers as zones of exchange in which people from both sides of the border moved with relative ease.[116] Be that as it may, it remains striking how little such movement was visible in the city of Rome. The whole world may have ended up in Rome, but that world consisted mainly of Roman subjects.

There is, however, one category that merits separate discussion, also because the arguments about it have important implications for our understanding of Roman migration. One important potential category of external immigrants is that of slaves. Many slaves were acquired through wars with external enemies[117] or by trade with tribes on the other side of the frontier. In consequence, it might be expected that we find in Rome imported slaves who originated from areas that were neighbouring the Roman Empire, or from regions that were incorporated by the Romans. Some of these regions had, in fact, a longer tradition of supplying slaves when the Romans added them

---

[112] Ricci (1996).

[113] Listed by Noy (2000) 291. In addition, Solin (2003²) 671–3 lists a number of geographical personal names referring to areas outside the empire (Mesopotamia, Persia, Armenia, Colchis, India). Some of these may have been carried by people actually originating from these regions, but the number of relatively certain cases is very small.

[114] Wells (ed.) (2013) for a recent overview.

[115] I assume that the presence of Parthians, Indians, and Sarmatians in Mart., *Epig.* 7.30 (in which a *Romana puella* has sex with various foreigners but spurns Roman men) functions to emphasize the otherness and un-Roman character rather than as a statement of their actual presence in the city. Likewise, the occurrence of peoples from outside the empire in imagery of Rome as cosmopolis (e.g. in Athen. 1.20c or Mart., *De spect.* 3 cited in Chapter 1, Section 2) serves to emphasize its grandness.

[116] Whittaker (1994); see also Moatti (2000) 933–5 on the 'grand flux transfrontalier'.

[117] For the connection between war and enslavement, see e.g. Tac., *Agr.* 31. When the troops of the Britons are brought together on the eve of the battle of Mount Graupius, the speech of their leader Calgacus is based on the assumption that if they lose they will be sold into slavery and end up in private households.

to their empire.[118] It is, however, striking that slaves in Rome that were unequivocally from regions outside the Roman Empire are relatively few.[119] The absence of non-Graeco-Roman cognomina among slaves might perhaps be explained by practices of renaming and cultural preferences for Greek names,[120] but the number of attestations of external slaves is otherwise also very small. It seems that the majority of slaves were recruited internally. 'We find one important fact clearly revealed in the literary texts: Roman writers believed that most of the slaves they encountered, apart from *vernae*, derived from the provinces and not from outside the Empire.'[121] There is very little to suggest that the Roman writers were wrong. There certainly is evidence for peaceful slave trade over the frontier, but the volume of the traffic does not seem particularly high.[122] Nor is there much evidence for wars by third parties as a substantial source of slaves.[123] Moreover, it need not be forgotten that in the regions under consideration the demand for slavery might also have been high, and in consequence there might have been little surplus available for export.[124] There is certainly a possibility that we hear less about external slaves because they were more likely to be put to work in the fields and in the mines, and therefore remained anonymous.[125] Strong selectivity might be assumed precisely in cases where slaves were sold rather than born in households: for the type of household slavery that was predominant in Rome, linguistic abilities are likely to have been more important than for chattel slavery. To become a household slave some basic knowledge of Latin or Greek might in practice have been a minimum requirement, and this will have strongly

---

[118] Bang (1910); Gordon (1924) 93–4. Philostr., *Ap.T.* 8.7 for Phrygia as a region where people customarily sold their children into slavery.

[119] Bang (1910) for the argument, with references to the exceptions. Note further that among the many wares listed in the *Periplus maris Erythrae* slaves appear only a few times, *Periplus* 8, 13, 49 (cf. Strabo 2.3.4), suggesting that the slave trade of the Romans with East Africa and India was small (and went both ways).

[120] The onomastic evidence of Solin (2003²) 671–3 does not suggest that many slaves were given names pointing to origin outside the empire.

[121] Harris (1980; 2011) 70; cf. Harris (1999; 2011) 103–4.

[122] Harris (1980; 2011) 73–4 for discussion of the literary and epigraphic sources.

[123] Scheidel (2011) 296–7: 'Roman slave society stands out for the crucial importance of the direct link between Roman campaigning and slaving; to a much greater extent than other slave-rich systems, the Roman elite relied on their own military forces to procure a captive labour force.'

[124] Scheidel (1997) 159; this applies in particular to the Parthian empire.

[125] This might perhaps be the explanation behind the otherwise almost inexplicable finding of Prowse et al. (2010) that at the imperial estate of Vagnari, Puglia, out of ten individuals whose DNA was analysed one individual showed descent from Sub-Saharan African stock and one from Japanese stock, though this does not necessarily concern first-generation migration. Note that in his general model of the Roman slave supply Scheidel (1997) 159–60 assumes that one-third of the population from which slaves were drawn came from outside the empire, but as Scheidel himself explains, this estimate is quite likely too high and serves merely to strengthen his case. See 164 for a further exploration of different scenarios.

favoured slaves from within the empire.[126] If we assume that outsiders were imported in significant numbers as well, the corollary is that they would end up in great numbers as chattel slaves, outside Rome. Although such an argument would affect our understanding of Roman slavery in general, the possibility that chattel slaves might proportionally more often have come from outside the empire's boundaries does not matter much for the present subject, for it only reinforces the idea that in the city of Rome they predominantly originated from within the empire.

Almost all migrants that we find in Rome came from within the borders of the Roman Empire. Most of our evidence for this internal migration concerns immigrants from the provinces rather than Italy itself. At the same time, the sources do not cover all types of provincial immigrants into Rome equally well. For some of the ten types of migration discussed above, all we can say is that immigrants came from all over the empire, without having possibilities for further analysis. This applies for example to traders living in Rome; what we know about their origins shows a random scattering of places around the empire. In Rome *stationes* are attested from Anazarbos, Ephesos (implied), Heraclea (it is unknown which), Mopsuestia, Tarsus, Tyre, Nysa, Sardis, Tralles, Tiberias and Claudiopolis, Noricum (as a province), and nearby Tibur.[127] The geographical origin of the attested ones is biased towards the eastern half of the empire, but this is probably chance. If we add to it the evidence from the *stationes* from Ostia, which were after all involved in the food supply of Rome, the picture becomes much more balanced.[128] Yet (if it were ever in doubt) Monte Testaccio serves as a reminder that the volume of goods imported from particular regions shifted over time and it does not seem unreasonable to assume that such changing streams were reflected in changes in the origins of traders living in the city.[129] Likewise, in educational migration we should expect networks around certain teachers. Detailed evidence from the correspondence of Libanius in fourth-century Antioch shows the geographical horizons of such a network: Libanius attracted students from

---

[126] One particular but presumably numerically small category was formed by eunuchs, who became increasingly popular as luxury slaves in the elite households. As emperors tried, at least from the time of Domitian onwards, to ban castration (*Dig.* 48.8.3.4), it is likely that they were mostly foreigners. *New Pauly* s.v. 'Eunuchs', '*Castratio*'. See for such external origins e.g. *S.G.O.* 13/10/01 for a eunuch from Armenia, buried in Venasa, Cappadocia.

[127] See Noy (2000) 160–1 (based on Moretti (1958), cf. La Piana (1927) 260); further Ricci (2005) 57–60 and Verboven (2011) 337–8.

[128] Listed by Noy (2000) 162–3.

[129] For the underlying mechanisms of such shifts, see the comments of Shaw (2001) 434–5 in his discussion of Horden and Purcell (2000). See also the remarks of MacMullen (1988) 11–15. At a much more detailed level, such shifts are also implied in the famous letter of AD 174 concerning the *statio* at Puteoli, in which the Tyreans claimed that, due to their dwindled numbers, their *statio* was in difficulties; the claim is to be interpreted in the light of the diminishing importance of Puteoli relative to Ostia. See *I.G.* 14.830 with Sosin (1999).

a host of places, but despite his fame, the catchment area remained confined to Thrace, Asia Minor, and Syria.[130] Similar types of zoning may have been at work in the student followings of individual teachers working in Rome in the early empire.

In principle, more information is available about the origins of slaves who came from within the provinces, but the discussion must remain somewhat inconclusive.[131] For example, it is possible that specific regions of the empire obtained slaves from specific areas,[132] and there are some hints that not all slaves were transported over long distances.[133] But there is no way to verify these notions, and it may be assumed that such regional patterns would be less relevant to Rome. The origin of a slave had to be specified when he or she was sold: it was considered important because ethnic origin was associated with specific qualities, and because knowledge of origin helped to prevent ethnic bonding in the household.[134] The origin of slaves was thus known in some detail to their owners, but for us most of this information has been lost.[135] As we saw, most of the slaves ending up in Rome originated from areas that were part of the empire, or they were obtained in the context of conquest and war from neighbouring areas or areas that were in the process of being incorporated. Apart from stray references in literary sources,[136] we have two

[130] Cribiore (2007) 98–100 (with some areas producing more and others very few students, presumably the result of the haphazard formation of personal networks).

[131] Discussions include Bang (1910); Frank (1916) (for which see Chapter 1, Section 3); Gordon (1924); Harris (1980; 2011).

[132] Cf. Webster (2010) 46–8 on research on African–American slave flows.

[133] Tomlin (2003) with Woolf (2013) 359 for a female slave probably transported from western Gaul to London; *S.G.O.* 17/09/07 for a slave from near Sardis commemorated in Patara, Lycia. For attested long-distance transactions, see Scheidel (2011) 301–2. For Augustus purportedly stipulating that rebels and traitors sold as captives should not serve in neighbouring regions, see Suet., *Aug.* 28.2: *ne in vicina regione servirent*.

[134] For the importance of the *natio* see *Dig.* 21.1.31.21; and in agricultural slavery Varro, *De agr.* 1.17.5 (though as a source of conflict) and *Ling. Lat.* 9.93 (*in hominibus emendis, si natione alter est melior, emimus pluris*), Tomlin (2003) for an example in a contract of sale. The *natio* had also to be specified in census declarations, see *Dig.* 50.14.4.5. For the use of placards hung around the neck of slaves, see Prop. 4.5.51, *quorum titulus per barbara colla pependit*; cf. Sen., *Ep.* 47.9 Augenti (2008) 17–18 for ethnic stereotypes; e.g. Strabo 5.2.7 on Corsicans as almost worthless slaves, or Varro, *De agr.* 2.10.4 on Gauls as excellent herdsmen. Further Webster (2010) 45, and the observations (made in a different context) of Amory (1997) 19–20 on geographical determinism in ancient ethnography.

[135] As Gordon (1924) observed in her classic paper; e.g. Solin (1983) 722 (see also 613) thinks that Syria was 'das Herkunftsland der Sklaven par excellence', but then explains the relative paucity of sources indicating Syrian origin by arguing that, because of the relatively bad reputation of Syrians, such origin was normally not mentioned.

[136] e.g. Pers., *Sat.*, 6.77 for Cappadocians on the *catasta*; Mart., *Epig.* 6.77 for Cappadocian litter-carriers; Mart., *Epig.* 4.42 for an Egyptian boy. Needless to say, many of these references are part of moralizing discourses: see Finley (1980) 119 and e.g. Lucian., *De merc.* 10; 17; 27, for the intrusion of Syrian, Libyan, and Alexandrian slaves in elite households, and Garrido-Hory (1998) 201–4 for the ethnicity of slaves in Juvenal's satires.

types of information on slave origins in Rome:[137] a limited number of DOC inscriptions that stem mainly but not solely from the large elite *columbaria*[138] (which date to the earlier part of the Principate), and much fuller onomastic evidence of thousands of undated inscriptions with servile names that have an ethnic ring to them.[139] The identifications of origin in the *columbaria* are in themselves precise, but they are given only relatively seldom. The onomastic evidence of ethnic names is difficult to interpret. Owners were free in the choice of a name for their slaves, and only sometimes used precise ethnic names.[140] If anything, a century of scholarship has made it clear how difficult the slave cognomina are to use in determining origin.[141] The massive presence of Greek cognomina in Rome does not directly imply that all carriers of such names were of Greek descent. Many carriers of Greek cognomina were slaves, though not all.[142] Conversely, Latin names of slaves may not imply an origin of the western part of the empire.[143] Many slaves no doubt originated from the eastern parts. But there is enough evidence that also in households, slaves often originated from other provinces. On balance, it seems more likely that slaves did not come predominantly from the East, but rather formed what Gordon called 'a strange epitome of the *orbis terrarum*'.[144]

One way to approach the origin of provincial immigrants generally is offered by the epigraphic evidence assembled by Noy. He listed altogether 521 civilian (i.e. non-military) provincial immigrants below the elite; see Table 2.1.[145]

---

[137] Potentially also relevant are the origins of the slave traders active in Rome, as they might give clues about the structure of the trade networks; at least some of them came from the East. See Harris (1980; 2011) 83–4 with Bruun (1992), but there are far too few traders known to base firm conclusions on it. See also Scheidel (2011) 300–4, noting that in the late Republic and early Empire many had Roman citizenship, and some may have been of high status.

[138] e.g. *A.E.* (1916) 57 with Ricci (1993) no. A.24 for a Thermitarion Alexandrin( ), a slave (gender undetermined) from Alexandria from a *columbarium* near via Salaria and via Nomentana; *C.I.L.* 6.9719 for a separate grave monument for a Thracian slave and his wife; *A.E.* (1972) 14 of 47/46 BC showing a *familia* of freedmen and freedwomen of mixed origins: Greece, Phrygia, Smyrna, and Carthage are mentioned, while in addition a *verna* and a freedman whose origin is unspecified occur. Freedmen whose origin is specified (e.g. *A.E.* (1979) 75, from Narbonensis) may have been freed elsewhere and hence cannot be taken into account.

[139] In addition there are a couple of inscriptions from outside Rome, e.g. *S.G.O.* 08/01/36 (Athens), prob. 04/16/01 (Kouara, Lydia).

[140] Solin (1983) 635; Joshel (2010) 94. Cf. Varro, *Ling. Lat.* 8.21: a slave bought at Ephesus might be named after the seller, after the region where he was bought, or after the place where he was bought. As Mouritsen (2011) 124 n. 19 observes, the offspring of slaves may also have been given a name by the slaves themselves.

[141] Solin (1983) 633–51; Webster (2010) 50–1.

[142] Solin (2003²), in fact, most names belong to *incerti*; Mouritsen (2011) 123–9.

[143] Augenti (2008) 17.

[144] Gordon (1924) 95, cf. 98, and 101 for rejection of Frank (1916), who argued that Greeks dominated (discussed in Chapter 1, Section 3). Cf. Tac., *Ann.* 14.44, referring to whole slave *nationes in familiis*.

[145] Noy (2000) 57–60. Noy employed relatively strict criteria; for several of the areas other lists are available that produce slightly different figures, but they are unlikely to alter the picture.

Table 2.1. Origins of provincial immigrants

Area of origin	Epigraphically attested immigrants in Rome
Britain	0
Raetia	2
Sardinia and Corsica	3
Sicily	5
Dalmatia	7
Dacia	8
Noricum	9
Moesia	9
Mauretania	10
Pannonia	23
Germania	24
Africa and Numidia	36
Gaul	43
Hispania	60
LATIN WEST	239
Macedonia	3
Cyrene, Crete, and Cyprus	4
Lycia	7
Cilicia	9
Cappadocia	11
Galatia	12
Greece	18
Egypt	23
Bithynia	24
Thrace	27
Syria and Palestine	48
Asia	66
GREEK EAST	252

Source: Noy (2000) 59–60, table 1

It is not certain to what extent these figures reflect actual immigration streams. Several biases may have been at work. The population in the sending areas will have differed significantly in size, which may mean that some areas sent proportionally more immigrants than others. The epigraphic habits and traditions in the sending areas differed, though this need not necessarily have affected the epigraphic behaviour of immigrants in Rome. Moreover, the individual figures are all small, so not too much weight should be placed on them. With all due caution, some general observations can be made. Firstly, it seems that the Greek East and the Latin West contributed roughly equal numbers of immigrants. Secondly, immigrants did indeed come from all parts of the empire, but not in equal numbers from all provinces. Thirdly, geographical and cultural proximity seem important. So, Britain's absence from the list can be explained by distance and its late incorporation in the empire; it is in line with the general paucity of attestations of British migrants outside north-western Europe.[146] In the case of the western, Latin-speaking part of the empire, Gaul, Hispania, and North Africa all contributed a relatively large number of immigrants. In the case of the Greek East, the prominence of Asia Minor stands out: Asia, Bithynia, Lycia, Cilicia, Cappadocia, and Bithynia produced almost 60 per cent of all Greek immigrants.[147] The general prominence of Asia Minor may be explained by its large number of inhabitants, and its flourishing urban life, and the close connections of its western regions by sea with Rome. Fourthly, some of the provinces that formed major recruitment areas for the army (to be discussed shortly) also show relatively large groups of civilian migrants. Two explanations, not mutually exclusive, are possible: the group of civilians may have hidden a number of military immigrants who simply did not mention their profession, or those who were closely connected to them (wives of soldiers, for example); or the stream of military migrants may also have produced significant civilian migration (and vice versa).

An important additional perspective is offered by regional epigraphic studies of mobility patterns in various areas of the empire. All show strong patterns of zoning.[148] Most of the mobility is confined to the native cultural zone, and nearby, neighbouring areas. However, almost invariably Rome, and to a lesser extent Italy, were included in the migration streams. For example, a study of mobility attested in Hellenistic and Roman epigrams from the Greek East shows that, after its incorporation in the Roman world, Rome was added to the list of possible destinations, but this did not apply to other places in the Latin West.[149] A study of Roman Britons who emigrated to other provinces shows that most of the evidence for their presence is confined to the western, Latin-speaking half of the empire.[150] In another epigraphic study, 107 emigrants were identified who left Roman North Africa for other parts of the Roman Empire. The great majority went to the western, Latin-speaking provinces, with a heavy concentration moving to Italy, Rome in particular. The Greek part of the empire is almost completely absent from the list—and this includes neighbouring Cyrenaica.[151] Likewise, mobility patterns in Gaul suggest that the Gauls did not leave their area in great numbers, but that when they did their mobility was in the direction of neighbouring areas and Italy and

---

[146] Ivleva (2012).   [147] 129 out of 222 = 58%.
[148] Regionalism is also emphasized by Woolf (forthcoming *a*). For somewhat similar results from isotopic studies from various Romano-British sites, see Eckardt et al. (2010), though the variation between sites is larger, and the subject is less easy to analyse, since isotopic evidence is more effective in establishing the presence of foreigners than in determining their origin and does not distinguish between soldiers, slaves, and civilians. Cf. Leach et al. (2009), where it is claimed that in Roman York migrants came from all over the empire, and Leach et al. (2010), for the possible occurrence of a young female migrant from North Africa in Roman York.
[149] Tacoma and Tybout (forthcoming *a*).   [150] Ivleva (2012).
[151] Lassère (1977) 626–33.

Rome.[152] Lyon, as a large city, had a more mixed population that included some Greeks and Syrians, but even there the immigrants came predominantly from Gaul and the Rhineland.[153] Among the 715 attested immigrants in the Iberian peninsula, only 150 (18 per cent) came from outside.[154] Immigrants who settled in Roman Lusitania originated mainly from within the Iberian peninsula.[155] A study of Raetia suggests its immigrants came predominantly from areas immediately to the west of it, and only a few Italians are attested.[156] The regional studies clearly show Rome's central place in the migration system, but also its unique role. In structuring normal mobility patterns, physical proximity was very important, but in the case of Rome its central function overrode this. In consequence, the city connected parts of the empire that remained otherwise discrete.[157] Rome contained the whole world, but the whole world was not Rome.

In the case of two particular groups we know much more, and we can trace trends over time. The first is that of the senators. Not only did provincials become accepted in the elite in ever greater numbers, the regions from which they were recruited changed. As has been shown, westerners gave way to senators from the East and, to a lesser extent, North Africa. The proportion of western senators declined from 70 per cent in the time of Vespasian to 15.4 per cent in the third century, while the figures for senators from the East increased from 16.7 to 57.7 per cent, Africans from 10.0 to 22.9 per cent, with Dalmatians forming a small category that hardly changed in size (3.3 to 4.0 per cent).[158]

In the case of the soldiers, it is clear that those that came from the provinces were recruited mainly from a broad band of western provinces along the Rhine and Danube; see Table 2.2. The main suppliers were the Germanic provinces, Pannonia, and Thrace, with Raetia, Dacia, and Noricum also providing a fair share.[159] It needs to be kept in mind that specific types of troops had specific recruitment patterns. In particular, there were radical differences between the *Germani corporis custodes* and the *equites singulares* on the one hand

---

[152] Wierschowski (1995) 15–20.

[153] See Carroll (2006) 218–24; who correctly emphasizes the connections in the transport network rather than physical proximity per se as the main determinant.

[154] Haley (1991) with Woolf (2013) 358 and Holleran (forthcoming *b*).

[155] Stanley (1990): 70 epigraphically attested immigrants, of whom 12 (6 civilians, 6 soldiers) came from outside the Iberian peninsula.

[156] Dietz and Weber (1982); though note that it is possible that behind the Greek names that are occasionally attested hide immigrants from the Greek part of the empire.

[157] This may also have determined trade routes. It may be coincidence, but it should be noted that in *P. Bingen* 77, a register of cargo ships at Alexandria, the only ship that came from the western part of the empire was from Rome's harbour city Ostia.

[158] Hammond (1957) 77. There are some slight fluctuations over time, but the overall trend is clearly visible. See also Farney (2007) 237 n. 28 and 243 n. 49 and Eck (forthcoming) for further literature. Solin (1983) 667–70 for a list of Syrian senators and equestrians.

[159] Noy (2000) 57–60.

Table 2.2. Origins of provincial soldiers

Area of origin	Epigraphically attested immigrants in Rome
Sicily	0
Lycia	0
Cappadocia	1
Cyrene, Crete, and Cyprus	2
Britain	3
Cilicia	3
Galatia	3
Greece	3
Asia	3
Bithynia	4
Mauretania	8
Sardinia and Corsica	9
Dalmatia	11
Africa and Numidia	11
Macedonia	14
Egypt	14
Moesia	15
Hispania	19
Gaul	22
Syria and Palestine	22
Raetia	27
Dacia	30
Noricum	47
Thrace	72
Pannonia	109
Germania	112

Source: Noy (2000) 57–60, table 1

and the praetorians on the other: the former came from the frontier zones, whereas the latter were for a long time recruited from within Italy. The patterns therefore apply predominantly to the former groups. Given the fact that in their case otherness seems to have been a main determinant in recruiting, it is hardly a coincidence that they originated in large numbers from frontier provinces.

The most problematical issue in determining the origin of Rome's immigrants is to establish the relation between immigrants from within Italy and those from the provinces. Obviously, before the conquest of areas outside of Italy the peninsula had been the prime supplier of immigrants to Rome. It is likely that also under the Principate many immigrants still originated from areas within Italy.[160] However, the number of attested cases is not as

[160] Patterson (2006) 36.

large as one would expect, especially if the military inscriptions are left out of account.[161] The same result emerges from regional analyses of areas within Italy: for example, in a list of thirty-eight migrants who originated from or settled in Lucania, only one civilian is attested as having gone to Rome, and that is the father of Statius, whose movements are known through the poetry of his son, not through epigraphy.[162] In Italy itself, male migrants can sometimes be detected when they were inscribed in a *tribus* different from that which was normally used in the community, although the method is not infallible and the *tribus* was not often mentioned. In addition, if they are designated as *incolae* they are also immediately recognizable as outsiders. However, in Rome such criteria are meaningless, and in their nomenclature Italian immigrants were indistinguishable from people born in Rome: all were—in principle—Roman citizens, all used Latin, all used similar names.[163] Only when they chose to mention their origin in their inscriptions are we able to obtain information about it, and it seems highly likely that often they did not. Though technically they were provinces, the same phenomenon might in fact explain why there are relatively few migrants from Corsica, Sardinia, and Sicily attested in Rome.

In the absence of adequate evidence to analyse the migration from Italy, it is tempting to assume that distance and volume of migration were inversely correlated, as stipulated in one of the famous laws of migration formulated by Ravenstein at the end of the nineteenth century.[164] The patterns of zoning in the provinces discussed above suggest, after all, that most migration took place within a relatively confined area. This would then imply that Italy offered the greater share of Rome's migrants, and that within Italy the nearby regions and Rome's *suburbium* produced more immigrants. It should be kept in mind, however, that such a model is extremely crude and more likely to apply to some forms of migration than to others. For seasonal labour mobility it is likely that most people will have come from Rome's *suburbium*. For temporary labour proximity might also have mattered, and it seems likely that such labourers normally at least came from within Italy. Likewise, is likely that the destitute who were driven by poverty to Rome came primarily from within

---

[161] e.g. *C.I.L.* 6.13470 (Antium); *C.I.L.* 6.33887 with *Terme* 8.14 (Misenum); *C.I.L.* 6.9785 (Cortona); *C.I.L.* 6.1622 (Iulia Concordia, mod. Concordia Sagittaria, Veneto); *C.I.L.* 6.25678 (Altinum, mod. Quarto d'Altino, Veneto); *C.I.L.* 6.9124 (a servile *actor* from Verona); cf. *A.E.* (1956) 67 (a pantomime performing, among other places, in various parts of Italy).

[162] Simelon (1992) no. 36.

[163] Though cf. Salomies (2002) for the possibility of distinguishing between regions on the basis of onomastic profiles.

[164] For the laws, see Ravenstein (1885) 198–9; (1889) 286–8; with the reformulation in Lee (1966) 47–8; Zelinsky (1971) 226–7 added that it is not distance per se, but 'functional space' that matters. Pooley and Turnbull (1998) 19–20 place distance-decay models beside other models. For the importance of short-distance mobility also in the Roman world, see Woolf (forthcoming *a*).

Italy, not from overseas.[165] But these are specific groups, and in other cases the situation cannot be determined on *a priori* grounds. At the other end of the spectrum are the slaves, for whom we can assume that they normally did not originate from within Italy.[166]

The two groups of immigrants that offer reasonably clear information about the balance between provincials and Italians are again those of the senators and the soldiers stationed in Rome. Both groups seem to conform to the expected pattern: a significant number of the immigrants in these groups originated from within Italy. What is, however, more important is that in both cases the balance shifted dramatically over time. In the case of the senators, the percentage of Italians declined from over 80 per cent in the time of Vespasian to below 45 per cent in the third century, and the number of provincials increased correspondingly.[167] The case of soldiers also suggests that the balance between provinces and Italy shifted over time, though here the patterns are less clear, because the changes had also to do with particular imperial decisions.[168]

Although the analysis of the origin of Rome's immigrants is clouded by uncertainties, a number of general conclusions may be formulated. The first is the prominence of internal immigration: Rome's immigrants consisted primarily of people subject to Roman rule or who were in the process of being subjected, not of complete outsiders. This applied certainly to voluntary migrants and soldiers, but probably to slaves as well. As for migration from within the boundaries of the Roman Empire, immigrants did in fact come from all parts of the empire, though it seems likely that significant differences existed between the different provinces. No real distinction seems to have existed between immigration from the eastern and from the western parts. At the same time, Rome's position was peculiar: it held a pivotal role in the migration system. To some extent the mobility patterns of the feeder regions remained focused on regional mobility. Evidence for the composition of the senate and for military recruitment suggest (though do not prove) that

---

[165] Note in addition that for impoverished Italians, joining the army decreased over time as a viable alternative; see Roselaar (forthcoming) with further references to changing recruitment patterns.

[166] Or if they did, we may suppose that there is a higher chance that they were voluntarily slaves or were *vernae* who had been moved between different properties or had been sold by their first owners. For a list of slaves and freedmen originating from within Italy, see Bang (1910) and e.g. *C.I.L.* 6.9124 (with comm. Candilio and Bertinetti (2011) no. 20) for a servile agent, *domo Veronae*, commemorated in Rome.

[167] Hammond (1957) 77 (the figures for Italians include those from Rome itself).

[168] For recruitment of urban and praetorian cohorts being initially limited to Etruria, Umbria, Old Latium, and the ancient Roman colonies, see Tac. *Ann.* 4.5 (AD 23), with Farney (2007) 233–4. Cf. Roselaar (forthcoming) with refs. for corresponding changes in recruitment patterns of the legions; around the middle of the first century AD the share of Italians might have been in the order of 50%, but it declined sharply afterwards.

whatever the proportion between Italian and provincial immigrants had been earlier in the empire, the balance shifted over time in favour of the latter.

4. QUANTIFICATION

Just as difficult as establishing the origin of Rome's migrants is the question of numbers, although its importance is obvious. 'Just as any other elements of population history, the study of migration requires an appreciation of scale that must ultimately be grounded in some form of numerical analysis.'[169] How many immigrants were living in the city of Rome under the Principate? If we could dissect Rome's population at any instance in time, how many of the city's inhabitants were born elsewhere? No doubt the answer should be located somewhere between the 90 per cent of the population that, according to Frank, was tainted by Oriental blood and Noy's cautious estimate of 5 per cent for free provincial foreigners, but that is a wide spectrum of possibilities indeed.[170]

There are no textual sources that provide any real help. In a rhetorical argument Seneca tried to console his mother Helvia about his exile with the argument that he was hardly the only person to be living elsewhere: the greater part of the people of Rome were deprived of their country.[171] Seneca certainly had no intention of being precise: he meant 'many', not 'over 50 per cent'.

Estimates for the size of the Jewish community are of no help either. They are themselves of dubious quality. They are based on the figure of 8,000 resident Roman Jews who, according to Josephus, enthusiastically accompanied a Jewish embassy at the time of Augustus in Rome, and the figure of 4,000 Jewish freedmen who, according to Tacitus, were conscripted and sent to Sardinia to repress brigands there.[172] As both figures each comprise only a part of the Jewish community residing in Rome, they have been extrapolated in various ways, producing estimates running as high as between 30,000 and

---

[169] Scheidel (2004) 1.

[170] Frank (1916); Noy (2000) 15–29. See further e.g. Balsdon (1979) 14–15, who with some hesitation supports a high estimate; Scheidel (2004) 14, who uses Noy's estimate in his calculations, and Ricci (2005) 11–13, cf. 27, in line with Noy's low estimate. Note that part of the divergence is caused by the fact that different definitions of immigration are used (or not used at all).

[171] Sen., *ad Helv.* 6.2–3 (*maxima pars istius turbae patria caret* and *maiorem partem esse, quae relictis sedibus suis venerit*). Cf. somewhat similar rhetoric on the prominence of traders in Juv., *Sat.* 14.276–7.

[172] Jos., *B.J.* 2.80 (ἦσαν δὲ πεντήκοντα μὲν οἱ παρόντες, συμπαρίσταντο δὲ αὐτοῖς τῶν ἐπὶ Ῥώμης Ἰουδαίων ὑπὲρ ὀκτακισχιλίους) and *A.J.* 17.11.1 (καὶ ἦσαν οἱ μὲν πρέσβεις οἱ ἀποσταλέντες γνώμῃ τοῦ ἔθνους πεντήκοντα, συνίσταντο δὲ αὐτοῖς τῶν ἐπὶ Ῥώμης Ἰουδαίων ὑπὲρ ὀκτακισχίλιοι); Tac., *Ann.* 2.85 (*quattuor milia libertini generis*), not reported in the other sources about this expulsion, listed in Chapter 3, Section 5, Table 3.3. A large Jewish community is also implied in Jos., *B.J.* 2.105.

60,000 people.[173] The figures indicated by Josephus and Tacitus are relatively small compared to the total tallies, and can hardly bear the weight that is put on them. Josephus in particular is not known for his numerical accuracy, and there is a real chance that both authors simply meant to convey 'many' rather than give precise information.[174] In addition, a large Jewish community is difficult to reconcile with the almost complete silence of Jewish epigraphy in this period, and with the limited number of synagogues that have been attested.[175] A lower estimate of say 15,000–30,000 seems much more reasonable on general grounds.[176] What matters most for our purposes, however, is that even if the estimates could be trusted, they refer to a community that consisted only partially of immigrants in the definition used here.

It is with respect to the quantification of ancient migration that isotopic analysis has made a significant contribution. Isotopic analysis is capable of producing figures for total numbers of migrants within the population under consideration. In that sense it offers the type of quantitative evidence that is so desperately needed. An additional benefit is that isotopic analysis uses the same definition as that employed here: it identifies first-generation immigrants, independent of legal status.

The results of the strontium and oxygen isotopic analysis of two burial sites in the vicinity of Rome were published by Killgrove; see Table 2.3. The totals for these different burial grounds are reasonably close: 29 and 37 per cent of the individuals were of non-local origin. A similar figure of 33 per cent immigrants was produced by the analysis of Isola Sacra at Ostia/Portus. In itself there is no guarantee that the composition of Ostia/Portus would be similar to Rome (which is why the figures are not used here), but it seems comforting that the figure falls within the same range.[177] In the combined analysis of the two Roman sites, only individuals that were tested both for strontium and for oxygen were used, hence N(combined) = N(Oxygen). As Killgrove summarizes her findings: 'If the sample populations from peri-urban Casal Bertone and suburban Castellaccio Europarco are representative

---

[173] Solin (1983) 698–701 for an overview.

[174] Solin (1983) 699 places more trust in Tacitus than in Josephus, but this in itself would already be reason to lower the estimates.

[175] The names of eleven synagogues are attested, mainly in late-antique sources. If all synagogues went back to the early Empire (which is possible but not entirely certain), and on the assumption that each Jew frequented one synagogue, then either the synagogues were each serving rather large communities (2,700–5,500 people on average), or the number of missing synagogues is very high. Neither is very attractive. The former would imply that the synagogues functioned differently from the one known from Ostia. The latter is unlikely because the evidence from late antiquity itself seems relatively complete. Note also that no synagogues have been identified on the *Forma Urbis Romae*.

[176] Following Solin (1983) 698–701.

[177] Prowse et al. (2007), using the first molar data with the modified 'local range' established by Killgrove (2010a) 249. This produces 41 locals and 20 immigrants. For the problematic third molar data, see Chapter 4, Section 3.

Table 2.3. Immigrants in the isotopic evidence

	Strontium		Oxygen		combined	
	N	non-locals	N	non-locals	N	non-locals
Casal Bertone	79	5 (6.3%)	41	12 (29%)	41	15 (37%)
Castellaccio Europarco	26	2 (7.7%)	14	4 (29%)	14	4 (29%)

Source: Killgrove (2010*a*) 227 table 8.8, 255–258

of other non-elite urban burials, it stands to reason that well over one-third of the lower-class population of Imperial Rome was not born there.'[178] At the same time, it must be clear that the dangers of extrapolating the figures to the total population of Rome are great indeed: this is a world of small-number statistics. The figures are suggestive for general levels of immigration, but should not be used as the basis for major claims.

One other way to approach the problem is much less scientific but nevertheless worth trying. By this means, a series of 'guestimates' could be offered for the size of the different immigrant groups that were living in Rome. As will be clear by now, there is wide variation in what we know about each group. Consequently, for many we can do no more than try to establish a rough order of magnitude. Assigning such figures is in itself not particularly difficult, but at the same time it goes against the inbuilt caution of our discipline: it is deliberately speculative.[179] To make the exercise somewhat more palatable (and to capture some of the large margins of error involved) minimum and maximum estimates rather than single figures will be presented.

The following represents such an attempt at controlled speculation. The focus is squarely on immigrant *numbers*: the question is simply how many immigrants were living in Rome. Questions of age distribution, gender composition, marital patterns, return migration, and geographical origin of the immigrants are deliberately ignored: not because they are unimportant, but because they would complicate rather than augment our understanding. The same applies to fluctuations and changes over time, and to outbound movement. For the purposes of this argument the period of the Principate is regarded as a timeless universe, and the aim is to establish a notional average. Simplicity is the key.[180]

[178] Killgrove (2010*a*) 279.
[179] In defence, it should be noted that Noy's figure of 5% is also no more than a guess (though a cautious and informed one). For methodological considerations, see Scheidel (2005) 66, arguing (in his case about the slave population) that 'the best we can do is to simulate the aggregative procedure of deriving grand totals from their constituent elements, i.e. from the bottom up'.
[180] With the obvious exception of the ninth group, the estimates refer to the non-servile part of the immigrant population. However, some of the immigrant groups contained in reality not only freeborn people but also slaves and freedmen.

The first group of migrants is that of the aristocrats. We are well informed about senatorial composition, though much less so about the size of the rest of the elite living in Rome. We may posit, at a guess, that 2,000 members of the elite, senators and equestrians, resided in Rome, together with their families. If we may take the patterns of senatorial composition as a guide, it seems reasonable to suppose that the greater part of this group was born outside Rome (some in Italy, some in the provinces). Assuming that many more of their wives and children were born in Rome, 1,000–2,000 seems a good guess for the number of elite immigrants.

The second type of immigrants are those working in the state administration. As we have seen, most of this type of mobility concerned temporary emigration out of Rome rather than immigration. The administrative apparatus in Rome itself was composed of members of the elite and of imperial slaves and freedmen. Most of these people will have been included in either the category of aristocrats or slaves. In order to avoid overlap with these two groups, the figure may be set at a low 100–1,000 for those who fitted neither category, for example ambassadors who stayed for a prolonged period in Rome.

The third type concerns students. In late antiquity the evidence from Libanius suggests that successful teachers normally had some fifteen to twenty-five external pupils,[181] and that in a large city like Antioch there were several teachers active at any one time (who competed with each other for pupils). The level of detail in a late imperial ruling on the supervision of students staying in Rome is hardly credible if there were not a sizeable number of students in Rome as well,[182] and there is little reason to think of a much lower level of immigrant students in the Principate. The number of students might therefore be placed at a relatively high level of 5,000 to 10,000 persons.

As for the size of the fourth type of immigrants, the intellectuals, we should posit a wider group of much less successful and much less visible persons around those people that are attested in our sources. If we assume high numbers of students, we should match this by a high number of teachers: 5,000–10,000 students would imply 250–500 teachers if each had twenty students on average (and more if they were less successful in recruiting). We should add to these other, non-teaching intellectuals, including people with more dubious intellectual credentials such as astrologers. There can be little doubt that if such people are added, the size of the group greatly expands. At the same time, it seems difficult to assume that this group as a whole comprised more than 5,000 persons. A reasonable minimum would be 1,000.

---

[181] Cribiore (2007) 95–8; the highest attested number of pupils is 26. Actual numbers will have been higher, as there would be also pupils from local families (in the evidence from Libanius their numbers remain unknown).

[182] *C.Th.* 14.9.1 (AD 360).

The fifth type consists of performers. Although the number of performers that visited Rome will have been very high, they normally stayed for relatively short periods. The average number of those present in Rome at any particular moment in time would be relatively small: 1,000 to 2,000 seems a reasonable guess.

The sixth type is seasonal and temporary labour migration. In the absence of documentation, its extent remains unknown. Comparative evidence from early modern Europe suggests that the numbers of seasonal workers could be huge: annually tens of thousands of people were involved in temporary labour outside their own community, partly moving to do agricultural labour, partly moving as unskilled labourers to the large cities.[183] The crucial question in the case of Rome was whether there was enough employment at high-enough wages to attract them to the city—a question which will be addressed in Chapter 6, Section 5. Estimates for the numbers that must have been employed in the larger imperial building projects normally run into the thousands, and the same applies to the labour employed in the harbour. The number of labourers required will thus have been high. It is quite likely that tens of thousands of people would be employed at any one time. However, it is not all clear what proportion of such labour will have been performed by immigrants. In order to capture the uncertainties, we may employ a wide range, running from 5,000 to 50,000.

The knowledge of the seventh type, migration by the poor, is also slight. How many poor were living in Rome, and how many of these were born elsewhere remains unknown. Christian sources on charity by particular churches in late antiquity mention figures running in the hundreds. We may set the number of poor immigrants in the Principate at 1,000–10,000—the factor ten between the minimum and maximum again reflects the uncertainties involved.

The eighth type of migration concerns that of traders. In itself there will have been a very high number of traders originating from elsewhere that at one point or another came to Rome. At the same time, they were also highly mobile, and only a proportion would settle in the city. At a somewhat generous guess, we may assume that 5,000 to 10,000 lived in Rome on average.

Estimating the size of the ninth type of immigrants, the imported slaves and freedmen, forms a very complex issue. The literature is extremely large and this is not the place for in-depth treatment.[184] Three major issues need to

---

[183] Moch (2003²) 78 describes two seasonal migration systems in Italy, involving annually 50,000 and 100,000 labourers; Erdkamp (2008) 425.

[184] Major contributions include Harris (1980; 2011); Scheidel (1997); Harris (1999; 2011); Scheidel (2005); McKeown (2007) 124–40. See further Scheidel (2011) 288–92 for a general overview of the difficulties of quantifying Roman slavery. The evidence of the album of Herculaneum is also relevant: see de Ligt and Garnsey (2012), though how representative the findings are is not clear.

be addressed: the size of the slave population, the size of the population of freedmen, and the proportion of imported relative to home-born slaves. Each subject presents major difficulties. What we can do here is to establish rough orders of magnitude.

It is clear that slaves were present in large numbers in Rome.[185] Many were working in large, elite households, each of which may have employed hundreds of slaves.[186] The *familia Caesaris* consisted of thousands of slaves and freedmen, though only a part of them were employed in the city of Rome. The question of the extent to which slavery penetrated lower down the social scale continues to be debated, but there can be little doubt that many of the smaller but still well-off households owned a slave or two. Furthermore, slaves were also owned by institutions.

We may suppose there were 1,000 elite *domus* in Rome in which senators and wealthier members of the equestrian order lived. We may suppose further that 100 slaves lived in each: some of the wealthier senators will have owned many more, but there will be many with far fewer slaves. This produces the round figure of 100,000 slaves working in elite households. In reality the number of elite houses might have been larger, but logic dictates that the higher the number, the lower the average number of slaves will have been. As for the number of slaves working for owners below the elite, in the cities of Roman Egypt one in five households owned slaves. Applying the same ratio to Rome, some 40,000 households would own slaves (population of 1 million—family size of five). Assigning them on average 2.5 slaves, we again obtain the round number of 100,000 slaves. Although these figures seem plausible, it will also be immediately apparent that they are hardly more than educated guesses. The actual figures may have been higher also in view of the fact that some slaves worked outside the larger and smaller households. The total number of slaves living in Rome may then be estimated to be between 200,000 and 300,000.[187]

Freedmen formed the older part of the same biological cohort. The formal age at manumission for men was 30, but many slaves seem to have been freed even earlier. In consequence, Roman-style slavery pushed large numbers of

---

[185] See e.g. the famous passage in Sen., *De Clem.* 1.24.1, where a senatorial proposal to let slaves wear distinctive clothes is withdrawn on the grounds that it could be dangerous if slaves know how many they number.

[186] For literary references to large households of slaves, see Scheidel (2011) 288. The largest *columbaria* of elite households have over 400 inscriptions (some mentioning more than one person), covering several generations. See Hasegawa (2005) 4–29, with Table 2.1, and Borbonus (2014) 163–208 for a full list, but note also that the variation between *columbaria* is remarkably large—partly, no doubt, caused by accidents of preservation, but perhaps also an indirect reflection of differences in household size.

[187] I follow more or less the calculation of Scheidel (2005) 66–7, who arrived at 220,000–440,000 slaves, with a greater likelihood for the lower part of the range. De Ligt and Garnsey (forthcoming) opt for 200,000 slaves. Cf. Scheidel (2011) 289 for 600,000 urban slaves in Roman Italy as a whole.

people through the system. It is generally assumed that manumission was frequent but not universal.[188] Figures from the *columbaria* help to bypass the vexed problem of modelling manumission rates (which are age and gender specific). They suggest that the staff of elite households contained in the order of 30 to 45 per cent freedmen and -women.[189] As elite *domus* in the calculations would contain approximately half of all Rome's slaves, the figures for manumission in smaller households would have to be radically different to alter the balance.[190] If we apply the range of 30 to 45 per cent to all of Rome's estimated 200,000–300,000 slaves, we may add another 60,000–135,000 freedmen to the servile population.

Estimates for the number of slaves and freedmen that were born outside Rome and thus count as migrants are connected to general evaluations of the sources of slaves.[191] Most scholars accept the traditional argument that with the coming of the Principate warfare stopped being the main source of slaves, though it is also clear that episodically wars continued to lead to mass enslavements.[192] William Harris opted for exposure as the main source: unwanted

[188] For the extent of manumission, see e.g. Ross Taylor (1961); Harris (1980; 2011) 62; Wiedemann (1985), who doubted its frequency; the model presented by Scheidel (1997) (though his argument that manumission rates of female slaves were low is not compelling: low fertility reductions can go along with high manumission rates as long as the manumission occurs after menopause, which is what actually happened in Roman Egypt); McKeown (2007) 28; Mouritsen (2011), who argued that manumission had to be selective in order to work and is therefore sceptical of its frequency. The fact that slavery 'for life' could be used as a particularly severe punishment might imply that normally manumission could be expected at least as a theoretical possibility. See e.g. Suet., *Tib*. 36, where it is used against those Jews who are not complying with an order to leave the city. The evidence from the Roman Egyptian census records shows that universal manumission is more than an academic possibility, see Bagnall and Frier (1994). The presence of high numbers of freedmen in Herculaneum in combination with the small size of the city's population (5,000) implies high manumission rates, otherwise the implied slave population becomes far too large. See De Ligt and Garnsey (2012) 85–8, and (forthcoming), suggesting a manumission rate as high as 80%.

[189] Mouritsen (2013), tables 1 and 2 on the *columbaria* of the Statilii (*c*.30%) and of the Volusii (*c*.45%). Both figures are likely to have contained some deathbed manumissions (for which see Plin., *Ep*. 8.16). It is possible that the two different figures present variation in frequency in manumission practices in individual households. However, Mouritsen shows that the evidence from the Statilii is in itself more complete, but that more freedmen may have been buried outside the *columbarium*. In the case of the Volusii there seems to be an upward social bias, which suggests that freedmen may have been over-represented. The average figure for freedmen in elite households may therefore be somewhere between 30% and 45%.

[190] Mouritsen (2011) 205 suggests that for smaller households slaves performed much more vital economic functions, and manumission would therefore occur later and less frequently. This may be true, but if proximity and trust are the crucial determinants in manumission, then the chances of manumission would in smaller households actually be higher.

[191] Bradley (1987) for an overview of the sources of supply; likewise Bradley (1994) 32–8. Scheidel (1997) 156–7 for some further historiography, focusing on the reluctance to quantify.

[192] For wars as a diminishing source of slaves, see Harris (1980; 2011) 69–70; Scheidel (2011) 293–7. Cf. Bradley (1987). References to enslavement in war are very rare in epigraphy; see for an exception from Puteoli *C.I.L.* 10.1971 = *J.I.W.E.* 1.26 (Puteoli) *[Cl]audia Aster [H]ierosolymitana [ca]ptiva*. Cf. *C.I.L.* 11.137 (Classis, Regio VIII Aemilia, mod. Classe in Ravenna): *C(aius) Iul(ius)*

children who were taken and brought up as slaves.[193] Recently Morris Silver has made the case for voluntary slavery through self-sale, on the grounds that most slaves came from within the empire and that the freedom of movement that slaves exhibited is impossible to reconcile with the resentment captive slaves must have felt.[194] Although self-sale might have been more important than is usually acknowledged, it can only have concerned a small number of cases: the logic of the argument implies that such a risky strategy worked only when the positions slaves acquired were not open to freeborn people and brought evident advantages that compensated the risks.[195] Walter Scheidel has made a strong case for the dominance of self-reproduction through slave breeding, mainly on the grounds that the regions from which slaves came would not be capable of producing the required number of slaves.[196] Additional support for Scheidel's

Mygdonius generi Parthus natus ingenuus capt(us) pubis aetate dat(us) in terra(m) Romana(m). Silver (2011) 113 argues that in this case the capture that is referred to may not have been the result of war, but given the location of the inscription some sort of military context is very likely. See Joshel (2010) 78–81 for further contextualization.

[193] Harris (1980; 2011) with Harris (1994); though cf. Harris (1999; 2011) 105–6; see also Scheidel (2011) 298–9.

[194] Silver (2011), who sees this mainly as a form of migration to improve conditions rather than the result of dire poverty. See also Ramin and Veyne (1981), discussing a wider range of motives and forms of self-enslavement and Harris (1999; 2011) 104–5. Although arguments about the contractual nature of slavery are more common (see Temin (2003/4)), it should be clear that if Silver's arguments are correct they have major implications for our understanding of Roman society at large. Scheidel (2011) 300, for what can be regarded as the standard view: 'Genuine self-sales may arguably have occurred for the sake of upward mobility, with an eye to a career and later manumission. The quantitative weight of such events was presumably minimal.'

[195] It seems no coincidence that at least some of the probable examples of self-enslavement cited by Silver (2011) concern persons entering the imperial bureaucracy, and that some individuals might have become imperial freedmen immediately rather than slaves. See further Chapter 6, Section 2. Voluntary slaves would enjoy no particular protection and could be subjected, just like any other slave, to corporal punishment, including, ultimately, crucifixion in case of major misdemeanours (for which see *A.E.* (1971) 88 from Puteoli). This implies that the outcome of the transaction in self-sale had to be clear: household, occupation, and manumission had to be virtually certain in advance. In addition, there might also have been risks in buying self-sellers; as the comments of Crook (1967) 59–61 imply, such slaves might try at some point to reclaim their freedom.

[196] Scheidel (1997) 156: 'simple demographic models show that, for purely statistical reasons, natural reproduction made a greater contribution to the Roman slave supply than child exposure, warfare, and the slave trade taken together and was in all probability several times as important as any other single source'; 157: 'That reproduction does not meet total demand need not mean that other sources are more important than unfree birth or even come close to being as important.' Cf. also Scheidel (2005) 71 and (2011) 293: 'Logic dictates that, the larger a slave population becomes, the more difficult it is for capture to retain a dominant position in the slave supply, whereas the relative contribution of natural reproduction is bound to increase with overall size.' The difference in age at manumission between men and women attested in the census records of Roman Egypt is in itself a strong indication of the importance of slave breeding: female slaves were normally only manumitted on reaching menopause, male slaves already at around 30. See Bagnall and Frier (1994) 158. For an older argument about the importance of slave breeding, see Frank (1916). For the dominance of *vernae* among the *familia Caesaris*, see Weaver (2004), also referring to his previous studies.

arguments may be found in the fact that no slave-transport system developed to supply the Roman Empire with the enormous numbers of slaves it needed. The fact that we hear little about the transport of large groups of slaves may be due to the general silence of the ancient sources on chattel slavery, but we do not find slave ships either.[197] A percentage of 15 per cent of imported slaves may be taken to reflect Scheidel's model of the importance of slave breeding.[198] Critics of Scheidel have pointed to the difficulties for Rome's slave population to reproduce itself, mainly in view of gender imbalances.[199] The sources certainly suggest that slaves continued to be imported in significant numbers.[200] Such counter-arguments fail to fundamentally affect the logic of Scheidel's reasoning, though they might mitigate the overall preponderance of slave breeding some-what.[201] We may guestimate a maximum of 30 per cent imported slaves to do some justice to the criticisms. Combining the figures for the slave and freedmen population (260,000–435,000) with the percentages for immigrants among them (15–30 per cent), this would result in a number of 39,000 to 130,500 immigrant slaves and freedmen.

[197] Harris (1980; 2011) 62 estimated that half a million new slaves might have been needed *annually*; cf. 75–6 for discussion of the organization of the trade, partly small-scale, partly larger. Cf. Petr., *Sat.* 76 (quoted above) for slaves transported together with other wares.

[198] Scheidel (1997). Given the fact that Scheidel uses most of his figures to demonstrate demographic implausibilities, I opt deliberately for a percentage at the low side of those that are implied by Scheidel himself at 167–8. Harris (1999; 2011) 89 in his discussion of Scheidel's arguments uses a higher percentage of 20%; cf. also Silver (2011) 107, 111 for higher figures.

[199] Most notably Harris (1999; 2011), who adds lack of family structures among slaves, and higher levels of mortality among slaves. See prior Harris (1980; 2011) 62–3, though Harris' argument that self-reproduction implies an attempt by historians to soften the realities of ancient slavery is unconvincing: slave breeding surely can take on a highly exploitative and perverse character.

[200] In AD 6 gladiators and slaves for sale were expelled to alleviate the pressure of severe famine, see Cass. Dio 55.26 and Suet., *Aug.* 42.3.4, discussed in Chapter 3, Section 5. This may be taken to imply that the number of slaves for sale was relatively high. Note also that Augustus used the income from a sales tax on the purchase of slaves to pay the expenses of the *vigiles*; see Cass. Dio 55.31 and Tac., *Ann.* 13.31 with Harris (1980; 2011) 68–9 and Harris (1999; 2011) 107, which may again imply that the number of such sales was substantial. See further Tac., *Ann.* 14.44, where in the debate following the murder of the ex-urban prefect Pedanius Secundus a contrast is drawn between former times, when at least some slaves were home-born, and current ones, when 'our households comprise nations'—no doubt highly rhetorical, but again suggesting continuing imports. That buying slaves was a sign of elite wealth in the late Republic is implied by Nep., *Att.* 13, according to which Atticus had only home-born and home-trained slaves in his household, a sign of moderation: *Neque tamen horum quemquam nisi domi natum domique factum habuit; quod est signum non solum continentiae, sed etiam diligentiae.* For a small late Republican vignette of the composition of a *familia* see A.E. (1972) 14: among six freedmen and women, only one is a *verna*. Mouritsen (2013) 58 adds the argument that, as many occupations within elite households were very specialized and learning such skills would take time, owners would resort to buying slaves in case unexpected vacancies arose through death.

[201] Note that even Harris (1999; 2011) 107 concedes that 'something like Scheidel's model...must in the end have imposed itself'; see also his 2011 addendum, at 108: 'If I were to address this problem again, I would argue for an upwards curve in the proportion of Roman slaves who were born to slave mothers.' For a balanced discussion, see McKeown (2007) 126–40.

Moving Romans

Table 2.4. Guestimates for sizes of migrant groups

	Type of migration	Minimum	Maximum
1.	Elite	1,000	2,000
2.	Administrators	100	1,000
3.	Students	5,000	10,000
4.	Intellectuals	1,000	5,000
5.	Performing artists	1,000	2,000
6.	Seasonal and temporary labourers	5,000	50,000
7.	Poor	1,000	10,000
8.	Traders	5,000	10,000
9.	Slaves and freedmen	39,000	130,500
10.	Soldiers	4,500	24,500
	Total	62,600	245,000

The figures for the last type, military immigrants, are the easiest to establish. For the purposes of this crude calculation it seems legitimate simply to assume that all soldiers that were stationed in Rome were recruited outside the city. Excluding the paramilitary *vigiles*, their total numbers increased from 4,500 in the time of Augustus to perhaps as many as 24,500 under Septimius Severus.[202] Here, these two figures will be used as a minimum and maximum. The resulting figures can be seen in Table 2.4.

When these guestimates are added up, it emerges that something between slightly over 60,000 and 245,000 persons in Rome were immigrants. On a population of 800,000 to 1 million inhabitants, this would result in percentages of immigrants between 6 and 31 per cent.

It is important to understand the dynamics (and the dangers) of the calculation. Obviously, not too much significance should be attached to the individual guestimates; many of them are open to amendments. The wide range of 6 to 31 per cent is in itself telling of the uncertainties. However, it will also be immediately clear from the table that some groups are numerically insignificant. No matter how the figures for each of these are manipulated, this will not alter their relative importance, nor will such alterations affect the overall percentages of migrants within Rome's population as a whole. It is not entirely surprising, though it is rather sobering, that precisely the groups about which relatively much is known belong to that category. The corollary is that in those categories of immigrants about whom we know very little, the numbers start to really matter. These are in particular the seasonal and temporary labourers and the imported slaves.

It is remarkable that the range that is produced by the guestimates is on the low side (6–31 per cent) of the figures produced by the isotopic samples (35 per cent). Obviously, each of the guestimates might be adjusted, but it proves

---

[202] Coulston (2000) fig. 5.8, who emphasizes that some individual figures remain uncertain.

Table 2.5. Proportions of forms of migration according to guestimates

	Percentage according to minimum series	Percentage according to maximum series
Voluntary (nrs. 1–8)	31	37
Forced (nr. 9)	62	53
State-organised (nr. 10)	7	10

rather difficult to manipulate them such that the total increases significantly—in fact, some of the maximum estimates seem already on the high side. In that sense, the guestimates serve as a check: we cannot claim very high totals of migrants if we are unable to allot them space in any specific migrant group. Paradoxically, speculation fosters realism. Conversely, the isotopic evidence suggests that the natural and understandable caution in remaining on the safe side in assigning figures to immigrant groups might be unwarranted. We should not be over-cautious in detecting evidence for migration in inscriptions.

With regard to the balance between voluntary, forced, and state-organized migration, Table 2.5 shows roughly similar percentages in the series of minimum and maximum guestimates. Voluntary migration (nos. 1–8) hovers between 31 and 37 per cent, forced migration (no. 9) between 53 and 62 per cent, and state-organized migration (no. 10) between 7 and 10 per cent.

In itself the similarity in figures may not be very significant. If the figures from the two series are combined, the similarities quickly disappear and a broader range of possibilities appears. For example, we may combine the minimum guestimate for voluntary migration with the maximum guestimates for forced and state-organized migration in order to obtain a minimum percentage of voluntary migration. Repeating the procedure for each form of migration creates the outer contours of what was possible (see Table 2.6).[203] Of course, in reality it is not particularly likely that minimum and maximum figures occurred together, and in all likelihood the actual percentages were somewhere between the extremes.

Despite the uncertainties, the matrix shows some noteworthy characteristics. In the first place, the scale of Roman slavery was so large that, even if Scheidel is right that imported slaves formed only a small part of the slave population, they still constituted a major part of all of Rome's immigrants. If we combine maximum estimates for all other migrant groups with minimum estimates for imported slaves, forced migrants would still constitute a quarter of all migrants. It is quite probable that the actual percentage was higher, though it was unlikely to be higher than 60 per cent. It does strongly suggest

[203] In the case of forced migration, the calculated maximum percentage is 85%, but this is impossible to reconcile with the required minima for voluntary and state-organized migration, and has therefore been lowered to 100 − 39 − 2 = 59%.

Table 2.6. Proportions of forms of migration according to a minimum-maximum matrix

	Minimum guestimate	Total maximum immigration	Minimum Percentage	Maximum guestimate	Total minimum immigration	Maximum percentage
Voluntary	19,000	174,000	39	90,000	133,500	67
Forced	39,000	153,500	25	130,500	154,100	[59]
State-organised	4,500	225,000	2	24,500	82,600	30

that forced immigration remained very important in the Principate. It would take radically different assumptions about the structure of Roman slavery to argue otherwise. At the same time, it is also clear that the volume of voluntary migration was also high. At least four out of ten migrants came of their free will to Rome, and it is likely that the figure was higher. By contrast, it is clear that soldiers formed what might be called a significant minority among the immigrants, though it has been pointed out that, compared to other times and places, the number of soldiers serving in the city was actually very high.[204] Elsewhere in the empire the balance may have been radically different, but most immigration into the city will have been by civilian free and unfree immigrants.

But it might be possible to go further. If the precise evidence from the isotopic analysis is combined with the guestimates, the logical corollary is that the higher end of the guestimates is more likely to be correct. If it is accepted that only the upper part of the series is correct, it implies that the balance between voluntary, forced, and state-organized migration should be roughly in line with that sketched by the maximum series in Table 2.5. For general purposes, the round figures of 50 per cent forced, 40 per cent voluntary, and 10 per cent of state-organized migrants may then be used to describe the composition of Rome's immigrants. It goes without saying that such figures are approximations and depend on the acceptance of the general relevance of the isotopic figures.

5. OVERLAP AND INTERSECTION

Migration historians of other periods have faced similar problems to those that are at issue here: the number of forms of mobility is large, and even if they confine themselves to the more permanent forms that we call migration, the

---

[204] A point made both by Coulston (2000) and Fuhrmann (2012) 123–30.

variety still remains significant. The forms differ widely: the distances covered, the frequency of the moves, and the duration of the stays vary dramatically. Some forms are significantly better documented than others. Also, finding a way to quantify such movement is difficult.

In the case of Rome, one point is clear. The abundance of forms implies that it is not legitimate to privilege one group and regard them as the migrants par excellence: this does not apply to provincials moving to Rome, nor to traders, nor to stakeholders in the empire (no matter how they are defined), nor to any other group. Migration was not primarily an elite phenomenon, nor, conversely, confined to slaves. The issue is of importance, because radically different assessments have been made about the relation between status and mobility: according to some, it was a prerogative of the elite, while others have argued that the mobility of those without property tends to be higher.[205] Migration was not the preserve of particular groups; all kinds of status groups participated in it.[206]

Furthermore, it is hard to avoid the overall impression that levels of mobility were relatively high. If one looks for a single percentage of the immigrant population, 25 per cent seems a fair guess. But it is much safer to work with a range, and this might be put at 20–30 per cent immigrants on the total population.[207] As for the balance between voluntary, forced, and state-organized, a plausible set of working percentages may be (again in round figures) 40 per cent voluntary, 50 per cent forced, and 10 per cent state-organized migration. Such figures may be used for the purposes of modelling, but it should by now be abundantly clear that they must be treated with caution.

The figures might, for example, be employed to re-analyse the changes in the geographical origins of immigrants discussed at the end of Section 3. If it is assumed that slaves came from outside Italy but from within the empire, it follows that during the whole of the Principate at least half of Rome's immigrants originated from the provinces. Among the other half, consisting

---

[205] See Wierschowski (1995) 16, 21, on mobility as a prerogative of the elite, while the mass of the rural population remained fixed in its location, and 209–57 for detailed analysis on the basis of the epigraphy of Roman Gaul. But cf. Hin (2013) 216 for almost the opposite idea. Erdkamp (forthcoming) argues that moderately prosperous households are more likely to engage in seasonal mobility than the very poor. Taylor (2011) 119–20 stresses, in discussing mobility in classical Athens, that both poverty and wealth could be motives for migration. For early modern Germany, Hochstadt (1983) postulated an inverse correlation between class and mobility: the higher the status, both in cities and in the countryside, the lesser the propensity to move.

[206] Cf. Tacoma and Tybout (forthcoming *a*) for a somewhat similar argument on the basis of an analysis of mobility in Greek epigrams: despite the fact that these texts cover a relatively small part of urban society, moves of a surprisingly large part of the population are recorded in the texts.

[207] Cf. Killgrove (2010*a*) 29: 'once migration from other regions of Italy to Rome and the percentage of imported slaves in Roman society are accounted for, the total of the Roman population that was born elsewhere is closer to 40–50%.'

of voluntary immigrants and soldiers, the balance may have shifted from Italy to the provinces, and in consequence the percentage of provincial immigrants will have increased over time, to perhaps as high as 70 per cent. Some forms of voluntary migration, however, remained confined to Italy: seasonal migration, and migration by the poor.

Speculative calculations clearly have their use, because they help to delineate the spectrum of probabilities. At the same time, it is clear that they have their limits; there is indeed a thin line between probabilistic calculation and uncontrolled speculation. In fact, the problem goes deeper than that. Even if we had the hard quantitative data that the ancient sources have not given us, it would be hard to think of a methodology to measure all movement. Focusing on the figures for those living in Rome is surely a good starting point, but it captures only a part of what is by definition a fluid phenomenon. In reality, we should envisage a flexible population body: Rome breathed and changed its composition all the time.

The variety of migration forms raises issues about explanatory models. It must be obvious that no single causative mechanism will even come close to explaining the variety of the movements. There are simply too many factors involved in the moves. This might give rise to the idea that we should abandon all attempts at modelling. However, the answer should be sought in a systemic approach. Collectively, all these forms were part of a migration system of which Rome formed the centre. Many of the forms were related to one another. This occurs to such an extent that it is in fact hardly useful to consider them in isolation. Either the type of migration shows similarities in the distance covered, or in the duration of the stay, or because people with a similar profile were involved. For example, there is a natural tendency to think that the movements of the elite were unrelated to the mass movements of the rest of the population. Obviously, the social outlook of a young equestrian who moved to Rome to take up a career in the Roman administration was completely different from that of a foundling who was raised to be sold from the *catasta*. But both the equestrian and the slave may have gone the same route, they may have originated from the same region, and they even may have ended up in the same household. It is precisely this type of overlap and intersection that we need to come to terms with.

3

The Roman Migration Regime

Contemporary global immigration cannot be studied apart from the enormous legal apparatuses that define and channel it.[1]

1. THE INVENTION OF MIGRATION

Legal apparatuses or more generally state institutions are crucial to migration research of the modern, industrialized world. It was with the emergence of the nation-state that national identities developed fully. The formal demarcation of the citizen body almost automatically led to the exclusion of others, non-citizens, who were deemed to be undesirables. Such a demarcation gave rise to racial views of migration and the regulation of the immigration of unwanted groups. States placed much emphasis on the establishment of physical frontiers and attempted to control and monitor immigration. A bureaucratic apparatus came into existence alongside a system of control: the registration of the population and of immigrants, census-taking, passports all developed. Control led to the formulation of state policies with respect to migration, and this in its turn brought the issue of its effectiveness to the core of migration debates.[2]

It is obvious that this model of interrelated factors can only be indirectly relevant for the study of the Roman world. Conceptualized in this way, migration is essentially a modern invention, and is closely tied to the emergence of the modern nation-state and the development of a complex bureaucracy. It is no coincidence that there are only from the modern period onwards full sources available for the study of migration. It is also no coincidence that studies of modern migration often use a legal or institutional approach.[3]

---

[1] Sanjek (2003) 316.   [2] Moch (2003²) 10.   [3] Sanjek (2003).

At the same time, the model raises important issues about pre-modern migration regimes.[4] In the Roman case, migration occurred in the context of a strong and flourishing empire, with a relatively small bureaucracy. What was the relation between state control of mobility, definitions of citizenship, and politics of exclusion? Once again, Rome offers a window to study these relations before the advent of modernization.

The aim of this chapter is to analyse the extent to which Roman legal institutions fostered, controlled, or hindered mobility and the extent to which these institutions were related to each other. By way of introduction, a very concrete question will be posed: what was the legal status of the immigrants? The next section addresses the relationship between mobility and citizenship: did possession of Roman citizenship stimulate migration? In a subsequent section controls of mobility will be discussed. To what extent did a bureaucratic apparatus emerge that tracked population movements? Lastly an important aspect of state behaviour will be addressed: did the expulsions that took place from time to time offer *de facto* forms of migration control?

The primary focus in this chapter is on voluntary migrants, as their presence is most likely to have generated institutional attention. The state-organized movement of soldiers was not problematical precisely because it was supervised by the state. Slaves were classified as goods: as long as taxes were paid, and as long as slaves did not escape, no further institutional supervision was necessary. At the same time, the sheer massiveness and variety of immigration of all types is likely to have raised issues of control. If 20–30 per cent of Rome's population was born elsewhere, and came to Rome from all parts of the empire, it will have been hard indeed to keep track of population movement.

2. LEGAL STATUS

A good starting point is formed by a simple factual question: what was the legal status of the migrants that came to Rome?[5] The question is as basic as it is important. Naturally, legal status had different meanings to different groups of immigrants: for aspiring senators, Roman citizenship formed a necessary (though not sufficient) condition for entrance into the elite; for a trader, peregrine status might have produced hindrances for conducting business,[6]

---

[4] For the related concept of 'membership regimes', used to distinguish between different policies towards migrants and the variation in entitlements of new arrivals, see De Ligt and Tacoma (forthcoming), with further refs.

[5] For discussions see Noy (2000) 23–6; Ricci (2005) 28–9.

[6] Lawsuits between peregrines and Romans were, at least from Augustus onwards, the domain of the *praetor peregrinus*, for which see Daube (1951) on *Dig.* 1.2.2.28. For peregrine traders in the Roman East, see Henning (2001) 31–2.

whereas for a poor Italian immigrant driven by poverty to Rome, his citizenship would have hardly mattered, except that it might have made him eligible for the grain dole.

It should also be conceded that although the Roman legal principles for assigning status were in themselves straightforward, in practice confusion could arise.[7] Immigrants in particular might not always have been aware of their own legal status. Several legal rulings concern cases when Roman citizens had married in good faith partners who turned out to be *peregrini* rather than citizens.[8] The sources are in fact full of *incerti*, people whose legal status is unclear. It is debated whether their presence is merely the result of modern inability to determine their legal status or reflects ancient ambiguities.[9] It does suggest at least that legal status was not in all contexts equally important. But as much of the Roman institutional framework was based on legal status, it is certainly relevant to understand how the group of immigrants was composed.

We may safely leave aside the status of *hostis*. This term was originally used by the Romans for real outsiders who had no tie with Rome, but the term had shifted its meaning to 'enemy'.[10] As we saw in Chapter 2, Section 3, the number of immigrants from outside the empire that lived in Rome was small. The only group of possible significance brought from outside of the empire to Rome would be that of slaves. Their number seems to have been small, certainly in Rome, and as slaves they had a different status anyway. The only other visible presence of externals in Rome would be that of hostages and diplomats.[11]

As was argued in Chapter 2, Section 4, a significant proportion of Rome's immigrants consisted of slaves. Although the number of imported slaves remains unknown, even if minimalist scenarios are followed their presence among the immigrants must still have been large. It is important to emphasize that the mode of entrance into slavery was immaterial to the legal status of a slave: no legal distinction existed between imported slaves (immigrants in our definition) and *vernae* (local slaves born in the owner's house).

It was also argued in the same chapter that, given the high rates of manumission prevalent in urban slavery, there will have also been a substantial

---

[7] As Crook (1967) 36 emphasized, also because Roman citizenship itself was rather than a fixed category a bundle of rights whose actual contents could depend on (among other factors) gender and age. See for this theme Gardner (1993).

[8] e.g. Gai., *Inst.* 1.75; Cherry (1990) 256; Gardner (1993) 186; in general on the complexities Crook (1967) 38–41.

[9] For the prevalence of *incerti* in the epigraphic sources, see Huttunen (1974) 136–7; Solin (2003²); Hasegawa (2005) 54–5. For status confusion among children of (manumitted?) slaves, see the case from Herculaneum described by Crook (1967) 48–50 and Wallace-Hadrill (2011) 144–5. For a slave in the province who was unaware that he was set free by testament when his owner died, see *Dig.* 12.1.41; although the case is clearly exceptional, *Dig.* 45.3.34 suggests it might have occurred more often.

[10] Varro, *Ling. Lat.* 5.3; Cic., *De Off.* 1.12.   [11] Ricci (1996).

number of *liberti* among the immigrants. As is well known, the principle in such manumissions was that the *liberti* would take over the status of their manumitter; if the former owner was a Roman citizen, they would acquire Roman citizenship as well. There were some delaying mechanisms: the rights of freedmen were subject to some restrictions, and technically freedmen remained a separate, transient category, that of *liberti*, and only their children would acquire full Roman citizenship rights. Those who were not manumitted according to the formally prescribed procedures would obtain a lesser status of Latin citizenship, that of Junian Latins, which could be converted into the full Roman citizenship through various means.[12] Slaves owned by free persons without Roman or Latin citizenship would take over the manumitter's status and thus become *peregrini*. We may assume that there were only a few wealthy slave-owning *peregrini* living in Rome (see later in this section), and in consequence the number of peregrine freedmen is likely to have been small.[13] We may thus safely assume that the majority of manumitted slaves obtained either Junian Latin or full Roman citizenship.

In addition to the *liberti*, many of the immigrants were freeborn Roman (or Latin) citizens. Even before the coming of the Principate, citizenship had already lost its territorial connection, and it also could be held while maintaining local status.[14] We hear only occasionally of anything approaching a territorial concept of Roman citizenship.[15] Roman citizenship therefore did not imply residence in Rome, or Italy; nor, for that matter, did the acquisition of Roman citizenship imply a change of residence: it was first and foremost a change of legal status. In consequence, Roman citizens could be found in all parts of the empire, and many of them would never come to Rome at all.

Citizenship was passed to children born in a marriage of people with *conubium*, which first and foremost meant that both parents had to have Roman citizenship themselves. In cases of mixed marriages in which the right of intermarriage (*conubium*) was absent, children followed the lesser status.[16]

---

[12] Cherry (1990) 255. A possible case of a Junian Latin may be the commemorator of *C.I.L.* 6.13470 *C(aius) Baebius L(uci) f(ilius) Camilia Celsus domo Antio vix(it) annis XII fecit C(aius) Baebius Atimetus libertus patrono suo bene merenti.*

[13] Strictly speaking there was also a category of slaves manumitted by Roman (or Latin) owners that did not obtain Roman or Latin citizenship upon manumission. Slaves who had committed crimes and were subsequently manumitted became *peregrini dediticii*. See Crook (1967) 45–6; Gai., *Inst.* 1.13–15. As committing crimes will not have fostered the chances of manumission it is unlikely that this was a group of any significance.

[14] Mouritsen (2011) 89–90 with further refs.

[15] Suet., *Iul.* 42. SHA, *Pesc. Niger* 7.5 for a remarkable and no doubt highly unrealistic recommendation by Pescennius Niger in the late second century AD that no one should govern a province who was not a Roman of Rome, that is, born in the city: *nemo administraret nisi Romae Romanus, hoc est oriundus urbe.* For some other concepts of territoriality, see Crook (1967) 38.

[16] Cherry (1990).

Citizenship could only be obtained by outsiders on the basis of personal or collective grants.

As is well known, from the early days of Roman history onwards citizenship was awarded to outsiders.[17] The first two centuries AD witnessed a rapid spread of Roman citizenship, until the emperor Caracalla declared in AD 212 that all inhabitants of the empire were Roman citizens. Roman citizenship was awarded collectively to communities, and individually to slaves upon manumission, to members of local elites of Latin communities, and to soldiers. With respect to the latter, from Claudius onwards it was normally awarded to auxiliaries upon discharge. For the regular troops, citizenship was a requirement to be enlisted, though this could mean that it was sometimes awarded at the time of entry into the army.[18]

In principle, citizens can easily be identified in the epigraphic sources through their *tria nomina*, and a number of citizens can be found in the lists of epigraphically attested immigrants. However, origin was not included as a standard element alongside the *tria nomina*, even if the name was written in full, with *tribus* and filiation.[19] Only soldiers normally included their origin in their name. Civilian immigrants with citizenship might have had less reason to mention their origin, but would rather emphasize their citizenship and thus would remain unidentifiable as outsiders. There is thus a real chance that immigrants with Roman citizenship are under-represented in the sources.[20]

If we go through the list of the ten types of migrants discussed in Chapter 2, it quickly emerges that many of the groups will have consisted to a significant extent of Roman citizens. This applied not only to the elite or to socially privileged groups such as students, or to the soldiers stationed in Rome for whom citizenship was a requirement. In fact, if we assume that the destitute and the seasonal labourers originated predominantly from within Italy, it follows almost automatically that they must also have been in possession of Roman citizenship.

Continuing our speculative quantification started in the previous chapter, we may estimate the percentage of citizens (including *latini* and *liberti*) among the immigrants to obtain a sense of the scale (see Table 3.1). The figures for citizens among the servile population (no. 9) are taken from the calculations presented in the previous chapter about the number of freedmen. It was

---

[17] See in general *Brill's New Pauly*, s.v. 'Aliens, the position of'. Cic., *Pro Balbo* 12–13 for the principle that anyone can become a Roman citizen.

[18] Crook (1967) 47. For the closely related issue of name changes, see *B.G.U.* 2.423, concerning the Roman fleet.

[19] For exceptions see *C.I.L.* 6.6974 concerning a migrant from mod. Nîmes, *Q(uintus) Hortensius Q(uinti) f(ilius) Volt(inia) Secundus Nemausi(a)es*; *A.E.* (1982) 68 with Wierschowski (2001) no. 42 for a man from Elusa (mod. Éauze, SW France), *C(aio) Postumio C(ai) fil(io) Volt(inia) Silvano annorum XXIIII Elusati*.

[20] Cf. Noy (2000) 75–8.

Table 3.1. Guestimates for migrants with Roman and Latin citizenship (*incl. freedmen*)

	Immigrants	Total size	Citizenship (%)	Citizens
1.	Elite	1,000–2,000	100	1,000–2,000
2.	Administrators	100–1,000	90	90–900
3.	Students	5,000–10,000	50	2,500–5,000
4.	Intellectuals	1,000–5,000	50	500–1,000
5.	Performing artists	1,000–2,000	50	500–1,000
6.	Seasonal and temporary labourers	5,000–50,000	90	4,500–45,000
7.	Poor	1,000–10,000	90	900–9,000
8.	Traders	5,000–10,000	50	2,500–5,000
9.	[Slaves and] freedmen	39,000–130,500	30–45	11,700–58,725
10.	Soldiers	4,500–24,500	100	4,500–24,500
	Total	62,600–245,900	45–62	28,690–152,125

estimated there that there were 39,000–130,500 immigrant slaves and freedmen, of whom 30–45 per cent consisted of freedmen and hence can be supposed to have obtained citizenship (barring some slaves owned by *peregrini*). The other figures are obtained by assigning rough percentages to each group. Needless to say, some percentages are much more certain than others. It can be safely assumed that the elite (no.1) and the soldiers (no. 10) consisted completely of Roman citizens, and most administrators must surely have possessed citizenship as well. In the case of seasonal and temporary labourers and the poor (nos. 6–7) it might be assumed that the majority of them originated from within Italy, which automatically means that they were in possession of citizenship as well. For the remaining groups (nos. 3, 4, 5, 8), it is assumed that half of them were in the possession of Roman citizenship (a conservative estimate in the case of students and intellectuals, but in the case of traders more dubious).

It will be obvious that with each additional step in such calculations the margin of error increases further, and that the outcome simply depends on the input, the choice of the percentages. However, on *any* evaluation citizenship must have been widespread among Rome's immigrants. Half of all immigrants seems a good guess. In the present calculation, Roman citizens (including freedmen) will have comprised 45–62 per cent of the immigrant population. Moreover, it is not unlikely that the proportion of citizens increased over time, as citizenship itself became more widely distributed—though the effect might have been compensated by changes in the origins of the immigrants themselves if they increasingly originated from the provinces (see Chapter 2, Section 3).

The remainder of the immigrants will have been *peregrini*. Although the term could be used more loosely, denoting simply 'foreigner', technically it referred to free persons from within the empire without Roman (or Latin) citizenship who used their own laws.[21] From the perspective of the Roman jurists, the status of *peregrinus* might be seen as a negative category: the focus was on what people did not have, and peregrine status could apply to persons living in communities with widely different statutes. But the status of *peregrinus* also gave protection. As Moatti explains: '*peregrini* were in fact foreigners with whom Rome had established a negotiated relationship and who thus could travel safely in the empire.'[22] In Rome, lawsuits between *peregrini* and between *peregrini* and citizens could be brought before the *praetor peregrinus*.[23]

Just as was the case with Roman citizenship, peregrine status was not, or was not primarily, territorially defined. Though it has been argued that over time the difference separating the legal position of *peregrini* and citizens diminished,[24] there were no standard mechanisms by which *peregrini* could obtain Roman citizenship. In fact, whereas under Roman principles normally children born in marriages that were not governed by the right of intermarriage (*conubium*) followed the legal status of the mother, a special law was created in the later Republic to ensure that when a female Roman citizen married a peregrine husband without *conubium* the children would remain peregrine.[25] Ironically, it was much harder for *peregrini* to acquire citizenship than for slaves. In consequence, in Rome and other cities substantial groups of freeborn persons will have resided who did not have Roman citizenship and would have little chance of obtaining it.[26] Some of them may in fact have lived there for multiple generations.[27] Not all *peregrini* living in Rome were

---

[21] Cic., *De Off.* 1.12: *suis legibus utuntur*. For definitions of *peregrini* see esp. Gai., *Inst.* 1.79. For generic use of *peregrinus* as 'foreigner', see e.g. Suet., *Aug.* 42.3.4 who in his description of the expulsion of AD 6 (see Section 5) seems to use *peregrinos omnes* in a loose sense; Sen., *ad Helv.* 6.4, stating that every city has a large proportion of foreigners, *nulla non magnam partem peregrinae multitudinis habet*; or SHA, *Marc. Ant.* 11.8, where Marcus Aurelius allegedly uses the term *senatores peregrini*, though this might reflect late antique usage. See further also the brief remarks of Kakoschke (2002) 9. Note that whereas *peregrinus* as a legal status is not used as a marker of identity in epitaphs, Peregrinus/-a could be used as a personal name, also for slaves, see Solin (1996) 128–9 for examples from Rome.

[22] Moatti (2006) 119.   [23] See Daube (1951), the latter only from Augustus onwards.

[24] De Visscher (1958); see on this complicated issue Gardner (1993) 186–91.

[25] Cherry (1990).

[26] *Peregrini* are certainly attested in the epigraphy of Rome, but not in large numbers. An example can be seen in the recently published epitaph of a *Saturninus Dubnorigis f(ilius)* found at the Via Flaminia in Rome; the father's Celtic name Dubnorix can be linked to the tribe of the Aedui in Gaul. The son, despite being free and being in Rome, lacked Roman citizenship. Gregori (2012a) 162–3, no. 1 (2nd half 1st cent. BC). The different onomastic patterns stand out in *C.I.L.* 6.17171: *Dis Man(ibus) Epaeneti Epaeneti(s) f(ilio) Ephesio, T(itus) Munius Priscianus amico suo.* Examples of *peregrinae* in e.g. *C.I.L.* 6.10554, *Acteni filiae Soterichi*; *C.I.L.* 6.24339, *Plotiae Lesbi f(iliae)*. Many more peregrini may lurk among the *incerti*; the presence of a *praetor peregrinus* is itself an indication that they formed a sizeable group, cf. *Dig.* 1.2.2.28 (on an earlier period).

[27] Noy (2000) 1. Bruun (forthcoming) cites *Tribu* p.165 from Ostia, probably a membership list of an association of *fabri navales*. The list comprises *c*.90 names; almost all are Roman

therefore first-generation immigrants, nor were all immigrants *peregrini*. In fact, it is a distinct possibility that *peregrini* constituted only a minority of all immigrants living in Rome.

Although the observation is hardly novel, it remains important to emphasize that no specific legal status existed for immigrants.[28] *Peregrinus* was of course a status used to denote outsiders, but as territoriality was not a defining principle in it, the overlap with immigrants was very partial indeed. Many of the immigrants were slaves, and many others were in the possession of a form of Roman citizenship, either as freeborn immigrants with full Roman rights, or as freedmen, or with Latin rights.

The corollary is important. Compared with the local population of the city, the variety in legal statuses of the immigrants is likely not to have been all that different. As will be discussed in Chapter 5, several scholars have sought to distinguish within the population of Rome a static body of Rome-born citizens and a much more mobile envelope of others. It should be clear that from the perspective of legal status this is untenable: both groups contained the full spectrum of legal statuses. It is, in fact, not even certain that the Rome-born population contained proportionally more citizens and fewer slaves and *peregrini* than the immigrant population.

The arguments are also relevant for the gradual erosion of the value of citizenship in the first two centuries AD, culminating in the grant of the citizenship to almost all inhabitants of the empire in AD 212. The process is normally placed in the context of the wider dissemination of citizenship among the population of the provinces, but the situation in the heart of the empire is surely also relevant. If citizenship was widespread among Rome's immigrants and no legal distinctions separated the Rome-born from the immigrant population, Roman citizenship will have lost much of its distinctive value even in Rome itself. It can hardly be a coincidence that when, after AD 212, the term *peregrinus* lost its legal relevance, it gradually came to be redefined to denote 'foreigner', 'someone born elsewhere'.[29]

3. CITIZENSHIP AND GEOGRAPHICAL MOBILITY

With the rise of nation-states in the nineteenth century, citizenship acquired a new meaning based on a principle of territoriality and nationality. Various

---

citizens, but seven belong to *peregrini*. At least one of them, *Ostiensis Isidori filius*, was in view of his name in all probability not a first-generation migrant, but born in Ostia.

[28] Cf. also Noy (2000) 1–3, on the lack of a Latin term covering the full range of the English 'foreigner'.

[29] For some discussion of the concept in the later Empire, see Whittaker (2004) 52.

barriers were created for outsiders to obtain it. The Roman concept was clearly different, but it remains legitimate to ask to what extent the acquisition or possession of Roman citizenship[30] impeded or stimulated mobility, and more generally, to what extent legal status affected mobility and vice versa. As was argued in the previous section, there were, after all, many Roman citizens among Rome's immigrants, and they may have moved *because* of their citizenship. It is well known that migration can be self-selective. Scheidel argued that, under the Republic, 'one of the most essential characteristics of Roman citizenship was *mobility*', though in his model this mobility was primarily the product of imperialism rather than inherent in conceptualizations of citizenship itself.[31]

There were some historical precedents in which the wish to obtain citizenship had led directly to mobility. Livy relates how, in the not too distant past of the second-century BC Republic, Latins had caused problems for their hometowns by moving to Rome and registering themselves as Roman citizens.[32] That was the past. Especially after the Social War the situation had dramatically altered, because Italians had collectively acquired citizenship—though this need not necessarily have stopped migration to Rome.[33]

Latin citizenship was still known under the empire, and had a lower status than Roman citizenship. Latin status could be given to communities as a privilege; it implied that their magistrates would obtain Roman citizenship.[34] As we saw, manumitted slaves whose manumission did not meet certain formal requirements obtained a similar status: they became Junian Latins. Under certain circumstances Latin citizenship could be upgraded to the full Roman version: Claudius, for example, offered it to merchants of Latin status who transported grain to Rome for at least six years.[35]

By the time of the Principate citizenship itself had changed in character. Citizenship had become passive rather than active: old rights and obligations had disappeared.[36] It no longer entailed significant political rights. With the emergence of a professional army, there was no connection anymore—at least not directly—between citizenship and military service, apart from the fact that citizenship was a requirement for service in the legions.[37] Instead, citizenship offered practical advantages and status. It entailed use of Roman law. It offered

---

[30] The focus is here on Roman citizenship proper, as a legal status, not on the much wider issue of what it entailed to be a Roman. The two were studied in tandem by Sherwin-White (1973²); see for further discussion Gardner (1993) 1.

[31] Scheidel (2004) 20 (emphasis in the original).

[32] Livy 41.8.9 with Broadhead (2004). Cf. also Cic., *De Off.* 3.2.47.

[33] Cf. Scheidel (2004) 14: 'The expansion of citizenship across Italy and the introduction of food subsidies in the first century BC probably had the effect of accelerating migration to the capital.' The relation between the outbreak of the war and the eventual acquisition of citizenship is contested; see above all Mouritsen (1998).

[34] Crook (1967) 43–5; e.g. SHA, *Hadr.* 21.7.   [35] Suet., *Claud.* 18.2–19; Gai., *Inst.* 1.32c.

[36] Sherwin-White (1973²) 222.   [37] Sherwin-White (1973²) 266–7.

freedom from poll tax, but also privileges in penal law, such as freedom from being whipped—physical punishments were therefore symbolically charged.[38]

It is clear that, throughout the Principate, Roman citizenship remained valued. Several indications suggest that citizenship was an important status marker and that it was sought after.[39] We hear about sales of citizenship, presumably to *peregrini*.[40] A part of the anti-Claudian invective consisted of accusations that, at the imperial court, Messalina and Claudius' freedmen were selling citizenship.[41] We hear of people entering slavery voluntarily in order to become freedmen and hence acquire citizenship (discussed in Chapter 6, Section 2). We also hear of illegal usurpation of citizenship, both by slaves and by *peregrini*, a practice that was punished severely (normally by capital punishment).[42]

In itself, given the lack of territoriality, the acquisition of citizenship need not involve any movement. It was citizenship itself that was mobile, not its holders. Nevertheless, the relatively high proportion of citizens among the immigrants in Rome suggests that the acquisition or possession of citizenship fostered geographical mobility in a more indirect sense. The conversion of Latin to Roman citizenship, the (illegal) acquisition of citizenship by *peregrini*, and self-enslavement in order to become a *libertus* will have easily been accompanied by geographical mobility. The problem for us is that such a connection seems intuitively likely, but that it is a loose one. It does not lend itself easily to analysis, except for the obvious argument that such mobility will primarily have been directed to the city of Rome rather than anywhere else. The vagueness also increases because the connection between such movement and the acquisition of citizenship proper is lost: being Roman stimulated (though it did not require) going to or being in Rome, but this was culturally induced behaviour, not something automatically following from the acquisition of citizenship.

The most concrete connection that might be made between the acquisition of citizenship and mobility concerns the Roman grain dole.[43] There can be little doubt that citizenship was a condition for receiving grain, and that the grain was predominantly handed out to men. The age for eligibility was relatively low: it may have been 10 (earlier it had been 14). But beyond that there is much uncertainty. As citizenship was widely distributed over the whole

---

[38] Walters (1997).   [39] Sherwin-White (1973[2]) 313.

[40] Sen., *Apocol.* 9 for a god who is moneylender and sells citizenship in a small way, *vendere civitatulas solebat*. Crook (1967) 42–3; Sherwin-White (1973[2]) 246.

[41] Cass. Dio 60.5–6.

[42] Suet., *Claud.* 15.2, for a case about the question whether someone is a *peregrinus* or citizen; Suet., *Claud.* 25.3, for execution of those who had usurped Roman citizenship; Plin., *Ep.* 10.29–30, mentioning slaves passing as Roman citizens in order to enter the army; Epict., *Diss.* 3.24.41, where illegal assumption is severely punished. Crook (1967) 48; Reinhold (1971) 289–90; Cherry (1990) 256.

[43] For different ideas about the relation, compare Holleran (2011); Erdkamp (forthcoming); Bernard (forthcoming *b*); De Ligt and Garnsey (forthcoming).

of the Roman world, some requirement of residence in or near the city must have been formulated, though how this was effectuated is difficult to say—even apart from the problem that the boundaries of the city were ill-defined. Recipients must certainly have been physically present when the distributions took place, and this will have limited the recipients to those living on a more or less permanent basis in Rome. Physical presence and temporary inability to attend certainly form an issue for imperial policy.[44] The requirement of actual residence might be the background to the way revisions of the lists were made by Caesar: the lists were compiled street by street and with the help of the owners of *insulae*.[45] The requirement may then have been formulated in legal terms as one of *domicilium*: a place of residence that was officially entered in the registers. Assuming that both citizenship and residence were requirements for eligibility for the dole, it might have been tempting for the poorer among the Roman citizens to move to Rome in order to receive grain, just as the acquisition of Roman citizenship for those living in Rome may have been valuable because it would create the possibility of being entered on the grain lists. This may, in particular, have been attractive for immigrants originating from within Italy. Whether such immigrants will have been admitted to the dole is another question—we do not know enough about the procedure to know how this would have worked, though high mortality certainly will have created vacancies in the lists. It is not unthinkable that migrants were themselves not aware of the technical details and simply came on the basis of the expectation of free grain, unfounded or not.[46]

To sum up, it was primarily Roman citizenship that moved, not the citizens. Citizenship was an inclusivist rather than exclusivist instrument. In the absence of a territorial conceptualization of citizenship, movement was not in any sense restricted. As the likelihood of a relatively large presence of citizens among the immigrants suggests, acquisition of citizenship outside of Rome may have induced mobility to Rome for shorter or longer periods, or worked as a selective device in determining who left home.

4. SUPERVISING MOBILITY

To what extent did the Roman state supervise this mobility? Of course, the Romans had a reasonably well-developed fiscal system by which trade was

---

[44] In various ways: see Suet., *Aug.* 40.2, stating Augustus did not want the recipients to be frequently absent from their work to receive their rations; Philo, *Leg.* 158, mentioning Jews unable to receive grain on the Sabbath; Plin., *Pan.* 25.3–4, where Trajan's *liberalitas* is shown by the fact that those who are unable to be present are nevertheless allowed to obtain their share later.

[45] Suet., *Iul.* 41.3, cf. Suet., *Aug.* 40.2. Bernard (forthcoming).

[46] Holleran (2011) 164–5; 177; Bernard (forthcoming).

monitored. Tolls were levied at the frontiers of the empire, at provincial
boundaries, river crossings, mountain passes, roads, and cities. But this concerned goods, and although such goods could include slaves, other immigrants
were not subject to it. The question is to what extent voluntary human
mobility was also controlled.[47]

Imposing control does not only create physical obstacles to free movement
of people. In fact, such controls may in themselves be regarded as little
more than 'political and bureaucratic irritants than as serious impediments
to migration', as has been written about seventeenth-century emigration
control.[48] But nevertheless they are important, because they do also tell us
something about the way migration and mobility are perceived, about the
symbolic boundaries of the state, and about mechanisms of exclusion and
inclusion.[49]

To start with, it is important to note that freedom of movement was
considered a basic Roman right. 'Nobody stops anyone from walking along
the public road', as Plautus had already put it.[50] Unrestricted movement is, of
course, also suggested by the references in Greek and Latin authors about their
own extensive itineraries. In Greek and Roman novels movement through
space forms the dominant narrative thread, and again this movement does not
seem to be restricted.[51] The freedom of movement also applied to freeborn
non-Romans within the empire.[52] Conversely, the fact that slaves could be
moved around by others was a sign of their degradation.

Tying citizens to their community seems to have been exceptional. One
ancient worry was population decrease, and sometimes measures were taken
to encounter this. In one exceptional case described by Suetonius, Caesar
tried through several measures to stabilize Rome's population size, depleted
by the sending away of 80,000 colonists. One of his measures supposedly was
that Roman citizens aged 20 to 40 were not allowed to leave Italy for more
than three years.[53] Such measures, clearly taken on an ad hoc basis, are not

---

[47] The question has been discussed in depth in a series of studies by Claudia Moatti; the
present section owes a great deal to her work.

[48] Cressy (1987) 130.   [49] Moatti (2000) 927–8.

[50] Plaut., *Curc.* 35, *nemo ire quemquam publica prohibet via*, though placed in an ironic
context. Moatti (2000) 928.

[51] Knapp (1907) on travel in Greek and Latin comedy; Elsner (1992) on Pausanius' itineraries;
Millar (1981) on realism in Apuleius' *Metamorphoses*; Moatti (2000) 935–6.

[52] Moatti (2000) 925; Rebuffat (2004) 161, 173–4. Cf. Cic., *De Off.* 3.11.47, stating that
prohibiting foreigners (*peregrini*) from enjoying the advantages from the city was fundamentally
wrong (*inhumanum*).

[53] Suet., *Iul.* 42.1: *sanxit, ne quis civis maior annis viginti minorve quadraginta, qui sacramento
non teneretur, plus triennio continuo Italia abesset* (the reading '40' is very uncertain); in addition,
senator's sons should not go abroad (with some exceptions), those who made a business of
grazing should employ at least one-third of their staff freeborn, doctors and teachers obtain
citizenship. See on this *Auswanderungsverbot* also briefly Wierschowski (1995) 33; Moatti (2000)
938–9. For a distant (and utopian) parallel, see Plat., *Leg.* 12.950d, cited by Moatti (2000) 926.

encountered under the Principate, and are anyway unlikely to have been enforceable in a rigorous manner.

If freedom of movement was in principle unrestricted, the question then is to what extent and in what ways the movement was supervised by the state. It is well known that we do not have statistical information on migration in the Roman world. But was migration documented at all? Are we lacking sources about migration because they did not exist, or are we lacking the sources because they have not survived?

It is important not to approach the possibility of registration of mobility with exaggerated expectations. From a comparative perspective, it should not be forgotten that early modern registration systems of the population were never devised to register migratory movements[54]—hence the difficulties of historians to reconstruct quantitative aspects of migration before the modern period. It would be anachronistic to expect anything approaching a full apparatus monitoring immigration in the Roman case.[55] But some forms of control may have existed nevertheless.

Control is based on written documentation. In itself, sworn testimony rather than written proof might also have been used,[56] but precisely in the case of mobility the absence of other persons to confirm oral declarations will have necessitated writing.[57] Various terms are known for documents that allowed people to pass, suggesting that such documents were deemed necessary for travel.[58] At the same time, it is clear that there was no uniform procedure for the issuance and control of such *laissez passers*, let alone that anything even remotely approaching a passport system came into existence.[59]

Obviously, the major points for control were at the external frontiers of the empire. Controls were supposedly carried out by the army. It appears that even there control was not absolute;[60] in fact, a forceful argument has been made that the frontiers functioned more as contact zones than as barriers.[61] Some peoples from outside were allowed free movement into (and out of) the empire; others could do so under surveillance.[62] Sometimes

---

[54] Pooley and Turnbull (1998) 23: 'In Britain, there are no sources which were designed to collect direct information on population migration'; 24: 'Because all sources were designed for purposes other than research on migration, the amount of explanatory and contextual evidence relating to migration is always limited.'

[55] As Moatti (2000) 928 warns; likewise (2006) 119.   [56] Broadhead (2004) 324.

[57] Moatti (2006) 117.

[58] Casson (1974) 154; Moatti (2000) 941–3 on the various meanings of the term *diploma*; Moatti (2004) 5–6; Rebuffat (2004) 160–1, on terms used in North Africa, incl. Egypt: in Latin *tessera, littera, epistula*; in Greek *grammata, epistole, prostagma*.

[59] Balsdon (1979) 98; Moatti (2000) 928; Noy (2000) 46–7.

[60] Moatti (2000) 933–5; Moatti (2006) 123–4.   [61] Whittaker (1994).

[62] Moatti (2004) 3–4 and Whittaker (2004) 136.

specific days or places were set apart for contact.[63] Others will have passed illegally.

Among the higher strata, there were many regulations that limited the movement of Roman officials. When their term of office expired, governors had to return to Rome within three months.[64] Elite movement in general might be regarded by the state with suspicion. Tacitus tells a story about a Roman aristocrat who was accused of wanting to abscond to the Parthians because he was found near the Strait of Sicily and was unable to explain what he was doing there.[65] Geographically slightly bizarre, but telling of attitudes.

Controls had been tightened with the coming of the Principate: senators were forbidden to leave Italy without order or permission of the emperor. Even visits to their own estates in the provinces might still require imperial approbation.[66] It is telling that, in AD 6, to alleviate the pressure on the population during a famine, Augustus allowed senators to leave the city and go wherever they pleased—an exceptional measure.[67] In his capacity as censor, Claudius is said—in a hostile tradition—to have degraded men 'on the novel charge that they had left Italy without consulting him and obtaining leave of absence'.[68] Sicily and Narbonese Gaul would be exempted for those who had possessions there.[69]

Members of the elite were, of course, extremely visible. When they travelled, they would make use of the *cursus publicus*, armed with *diplomata*, and followed by large retinues, which made them easy to trace.[70] Tacitus relates how Julius Sabinus, after a failed attempt at revolt, managed to hide himself for nine years in a cave with his wife and two sons before he was found and executed.[71] The story, clearly regarded as exceptional, suggests that it was extremely difficult for members of the elite to escape detection without giving up the outward signs of their status.

Was there control at provincial boundaries within the empire? The sources from Egypt suggest as much,[72] but it is unclear to what extent they are representative for other areas, or rather, it seems that there was again no

---

[63] Tac., *Germ.* 41 on the Hermunduri, who travelled *sine custode*; Cass. Dio 72.11.3, where Quadi are refused right to attend markets under Marcus Aurelius in Pannonia; cf. 73.2.4 for restrictions on assemblies under Commodus.

[64] Cass. Dio 53.15.6.

[65] Tac., *Ann.* 6.14. For the allowance of free travel as a privilege and sign of trust, see SHA, *Marc. Ant.* 26.12; SHA, *Avid. Cass.* 9.3.

[66] Plin., *Ep.* 10.8–9.   [67] Cass. Dio 55.26 with Drogula (2011) 245, and see Section 5.

[68] Suet., *Claud.* 16.2 (trans. J. C. Rolfe, LCL): *notavitque multos, et quosdam inopinantis et ex causa novi generis, quod se inscio ac sine commeatu Italia excessissent.*

[69] Tac., *Ann.* 12.23; Cass. Dio 52.42.6–7, though note that according to Suet., *Claud.* 23.2 and Cass. Dio 60.25.6 up until the time of Claudius the granting of such requests was in the hands of the senate. Moatti (2000) 939–40 with further refs; Drogula (2011) 243–56.

[70] Drogula (2011) 245.   [71] Tac., *Hist.* 4.57.   [72] Sidebotham (1986) 79–82.

uniformity.[73] Given the control on elite mobility, the famous prohibition for senators and important *equites* to enter Egypt without imperial permission is unlikely to have been an Egyptian peculiarity.[74] The sources also suggest close monitoring of movement into and out of Egypt. Strabo stated that it was impossible to leave Alexandria without a *prostagma*: 'not only the harbour, but also all the other ways of issue from the city had always been kept closed under just as strong guard as I know is still kept up to this day (for I have lived a long time in Alexandria)—though at the present time, under Roman control, the watch is considerably relaxed.'[75] That controls existed is confirmed by rules in the *Gnomon of the Idios Logos* and the survival of papyri in which permission was sought to leave Egypt.[76] Similar types of control are suggested by stories about secret entrances.[77]

Within the provinces, travellers might be checked along the road, or within cities. In the early second century AD, Pliny discussed with the emperor the situation with regard to the safety and public order of Juliopolis. Byzantium had obtained a garrison to control the traffic passing through it. In the case of Juliopolis, the emperor refused a similar measure on the grounds that it would produce a precedent for other cities. It is not clear from the letters what the control would actually entail, though it is interesting to see that passing soldiers and persons returning to Rome are mentioned as creating problems.[78] In general, situations like those presented by Pliny point to the likelihood that soldiers stationed along roads or in cities checked those who passed them.

Within the provinces, the population was surveyed through censuses. Such surveys served multiple purposes. Apart from practical ones, the census also had symbolic overtones: being counted turned people into subjects.[79] In Egypt, the census declarations were used for levying poll tax, and found an indirect use in claims to access to particular status groups. At any rate, they served as a way of registering the population. One of the census rules was that people had to go home to declare themselves in the census; this is (famously) how it was in the New Testament, and likewise in the census of Roman Egypt. From the perspective of mobility this is a very interesting rule: on the one hand it was based on the premise that people should not leave their home-town, on

---

[73] Moatti (2006) 125: 'We could say therefore that the Roman empire lacked not control, but unity and regularity.'

[74] Tac., *Ann.* 2.59.3–4; Cass. Dio 51.17.1–2 with Drogula (2011) 244.

[75] Strabo 2.3.5 (trans. H.L. Jones, LCL): τοσαύτῃ φρουρᾷ κεκλεισμένου τοῦ λιμένος καὶ τῶν ἄλλων ἐξόδων, ὅσην καὶ νῦν ἔτι διαμένουσαν ἔγνωμεν ἡμεῖς ἐπιδημοῦντες τῇ Ἀλεξανδρείᾳ πολὺν χρόνον, καίτοι τὰ νῦν πολὺ ἀνεῖται, Ῥωμαίων ἐχόντων.

[76] e.g. *P.Oxy.* 10.1271 (AD 246). Moatti (2000) 950–3; Rebuffat (2004) 160.

[77] Philo, *In Flacc.* 27–8 (Agrippa).   [78] Plin., *Ep.* 10.77–78, with Moatti (2000) 936–7.

[79] For (strong) resistance to being registered, see Jos., *B.J.* 7.253; registering is seen as sign of submission to Rome.

the other, it also admitted that reality was different; it expressed a social pressure not to stay away for too long.[80]

The principles with respect to the performance of the civic *munera* are similar. From the late Republic onwards the legal idea developed that one could change residence without leaving the Roman community. A distinction developed between a *domicilium* that was changeable and that could differ from an *origo* that was fixed. In principle there was freedom of choice of domicile, but one had to register it.[81] The concern of the jurists (and no doubt of the local governments) was with the question where the *munera* were to be performed. Members of the local elites were not so much restricted in their movements, but they remained under the obligation to perform their duties. Initially this had to be in their hometown, but later this changed to their *domicilium*, or, especially in late antiquity, to both *origo* and *domicilium*.[82] Not all the duties related to *munera* may have required their physical presence, but the principle can nevertheless be regarded as an impediment to their movement.

At Rome itself there seems to have been no formal control over entering and leaving the city. People entered Rome by road or by ship. As Rome had outgrown its old walls significantly, the boundary of the city was not marked by walls until Aurelian would build a new set in the later third century AD. Nor, in fact, was it clear where exactly the city started.[83] Some controls are attested, but just as elsewhere, what was primarily controlled was the movement of goods. At least from later on in the first century, there were guards posted at the entrance roads whose task it was to levy tax on goods that were imported and exported. They are likely to have kept an eye on who entered.[84]

---

[80] See Moatti (forthcoming) for the wider ancient idea that physical presence is required for certain acts.

[81] e.g. *Frag.Vat.* 203, implying that *munera* are to be performed in the *domicilium*; *Dig.* 50.1.31, anyone can take up a *domicilium* of his choice; *Dig.* 50.1.27.2, anyone with two residences in both of which he lives can mark one of them as his official domicile; *Dig.* 50.16.203 for criteria to determine where is one's *domus*; *Dig.* 50.1.5 for the possibility to have multiple *domicilia*. Cf. *Dig.* 50.1.22.6, senators who are free to reside where they wish retain their domicile in Rome. Cf. also the late Republican *Tabula Heracleensis* (ed. Crawford 1996) l. 157–8. *Dig.* 9.3.1.9 draws a distinction between domicile and staying somewhere as a traveller.

[82] e.g. *Dig.* 50.2.1pr. decurions should be returned to their place; *Suppl. It.* 13.5.1 from Vardagates for *munera* to be performed both in the old and the new community; *Dig.* 50.1.38.3 for the position of women. Moatti (2000) 932–3 (with refs to the late antique laws concerning young students mentioned in Chapter 2, Section 2); Sherwin-White (1973²) 312; Avraméa (1995) 14–15.

[83] For ill-defined city boundaries under the late Republic, see *Tabula Heracleensis* (ed. Crawford 1996) l. 20; for full discussion of city boundaries, see Stevens (forthcoming).

[84] As is suggested by Philostr., *Ap.T.* 39.1 in which Apollonios of Tyana and followers approach the gates—the guards ask no question but look in amazement at their clothes, which do not look like those of beggars. Moatti (2007) 82–3; see Stevens (forthcoming) on boundary crossing.

Within the city of Rome there was some registration of the population. The way it worked is not known in full, but it is clear that it was not primarily directed at distinguishing immigrants from the Rome-born population.[85] Citizens were certainly registered in one way or another, for it is hardly conceivable that the grain dole could function without some form of underlying population register.[86] It is known that a system of birth declarations for citizens was in use. Since the time of Augustus, the birth of new Roman citizens everywhere was registered; a wooden diptych was handed out which served as proof.[87] It seems likely that the death of citizens was to be declared as well.[88] It may be that a registration of domicile was introduced in connection with Augustus' administrative re-division of the city into fourteen quarters and 265 *vici*, headed by *vicomagistri*. In addition, the establishment of the *fiscus Judaicus* under the Flavian emperors later in the first century must have been based on some form of registration of the Jews, but this will have functioned independently of their legal status.[89] Whether separate registers of *peregrini* existed is more open to question. Although we saw that changes of domicile had to be registered, we do not know how this was effectuated, and there is no evidence for the existence of such registers under the Principate.[90] In late antiquity, students coming from the provinces to Rome had to hand in a full dossier, including proof that they were allowed to leave their province, but the rulings seem designed specifically for students and may not have been in place in the earlier period.[91]

The extent to which the population of Rome was actually subject to identity controls is equally unclear. In itself the number of troops in and around the city was relatively large.[92] At the same time, a police force in the modern sense was absent, and law enforcement was selective.[93] In Petronius there is a story of a house search taking place in a lodging house in

---

[85] Cf. Holleran (2011) 156.

[86] That the grain dole itself used registers is certain, but the actual procedures are unclear. A relief with a *Beambtenszene* on the *Ara degli scribi* may perhaps depict the registration of someone for the grain dole: *Terme* 6.47. Crook (1967) 46–8 for general discussion of the registration of Roman citizens.

[87] Schultz (1942–3); e.g. in SHA, *Marc. Ant.* 9.7–8: Marcus Aurelius decrees that freeborn children are to receive a name and be declared within 30 days; a similar system is set up in the provinces.

[88] Virlouvet (1997).

[89] Solin (1983) 698 with n. 698 suggests tentatively that the lists might have been compiled by the Jewish community itself, which previously organized the Temple tax.

[90] Moatti (2000) 931 believes that *peregrini* must have been registered for fiscal reasons. She also points to the registration of prostitutes (as *infames*). Noy (2000) 46–7 is more sceptical.

[91] *C.Th.* 14.9.1, with brief discussion by Moatti (2006) 122–3; additional sources are cited in Chapter 2, Section 2.

[92] Griffin (1991) 40; MacMullen (1966) 163–4, who adds that by contrast the situation in other cities is very obscure; Coulston (2000); Fuhrmann (2012).

[93] Nippel (1995).

Campania.[94] We may suppose that such searches could take place in Rome as well. Although there are occasional references to the idea that foreigners were easily recognizable through their physiognomy, at the same time it must have been rather difficult to determine the status or origin of someone on the basis of his or her outward appearance.[95]

What is, at any rate, quite clear is that the major concern in all such controls was status, not origin. Roman literature abounds with stories of status usurpation, for example, of freedmen pretending to be knights.[96] Down the social scale, there was particular concern for runaway slaves.[97] In the event of sale, one of the things that had to be stated was whether the slave had tried to escape.[98] Some slaves tried to get into the army, passing as free citizens.[99] Fugitives of all sorts must have had some possibilities of disappearing in the mass of the population living in the city.[100]

On balance, it is fair to say that in the Roman case government interference with regard to mobility was relatively low. A general form of migration control was absent, and the controls that existed did not impose insurmountable hurdles.[101] The provincial census system was in itself impressive compared to pre-industrial standards, but did not focus on migrants—in fact, and somewhat ironically, the requirement to register in the home-town erased such traces in the Roman documentation. It is among the elite that we find the most evidence for control. It was their movement that mattered most to the state, rather than that of the general population.

5. EXPULSIONS FROM ROME

As early as in the early modern period, states had already started to formulate migration policies, or had at least taken coherent sets of long-term measures with regard to specific groups. After the Reconquista in Spain in the late fifteenth century, Jews and Moors were collectively expelled from the country.

---

[94] Petr., *Sat.* 97, presented as a search for a fugitive slave (though actually for a lover); note the combination of private initiative (of the supposed owner, who promises the reward) and municipal authority (a *praeco* and a *viator* do the searching). See further Fuhrmann (2012) 37–8.

[95] Moatti and Kaiser (2007) 14 on the 'fragilité du processus d'identification'. Cherry (1990) 256 remarks on the lack of formal proofs of Roman citizenship; Wallace-Hadrill (2011) 144–5 for a court case in which contradictory claims are made.

[96] See Reinhold (1971); e.g. Mart., *Epig.* 5.35, for a doorkeeper posing as a wealthy property-owner; cf. Mart., *Epig.* 9.59 for someone who is too poor to own slaves pretending to want to buy luxury products.

[97] Bradley (1994) 118–21.   [98] Aul. Gell. 4.2.1 on the edict of the *aediles*.

[99] Plin., *Ep.* 10.29–30 for a possible case.

[100] Apul., *Met.* 8.23; Suet., *Rhet.* 1; Petr., *Sat.* 97, and, for branding, 103.

[101] Moatti (2000) 928.

The Dutch offered tax relief and citizenship to immigrant French Protestants in the seventeenth century.[102] Such wider-ranging decisions based on a coherent view of how the population should be composed were not made by the Romans.

But the Romans did have a number of concrete measures at their disposal to control the population of Rome. These measures ranged from various types of punishments for criminal offences, including stipulations for offenders to remain at a certain distance from the city, to colonization programmes in which a part of the populace would be resettled (under Caesar and Augustus), and interdictions by which certain groups were forbidden to practise their profession in public.[103] Then there were measures in the religious sphere, such as the straightforward prohibition of cults,[104] or persecutions, the prohibition to congregate,[105] or, more subtly, the relocation of foreign cults outside the *pomerium*.[106] Nevertheless, under the early Empire expulsion was no doubt the major mechanism used by the Roman state to control the population of Rome.

It is certainly tempting to see these expulsions as responses by the authorities to the tensions caused by the presence of outsiders. Isaac writes, for example: 'When Rome developed into the capital of an empire, many representatives of the subject peoples came to settle there, causing various forms of tension. From time to time, such tensions became threatening enough for the authorities to expel minorities from the city.'[107] Although there was no doubt a link between the cosmopolitan character of Rome and the expulsions, the extent to which expulsions served as a mechanism to control immigration deserves further scrutiny, for, as we have seen in the previous sections, in other respects state control of mobility was relatively slight and haphazard.

As the expulsions share a set of characteristics, they should be analysed together, independent of the question whether they concerned ethnic, cultic or professional groups.[108] The details of the expulsions are listed in Table 3.2.[109] Seventeen expulsions are known in greater or lesser detail. The list starts just

---

[102] Moch (2003[2]) 10 (with both examples).
[103] Philostr., *Ap.T.* 4.47 (philosophers under Nero), Suet., *Dom.* 7.1 (actors under Domitian).
[104] Cass. Dio 67.14.1–3 on those drifting into Jewish ways under Domitian: capital punishment in the case of some, confiscation of property in the case of others.
[105] Cass. Dio 60.6.6 (Claudius with regard to the Jews).   [106] Orlin (2008).
[107] Isaac (2004) 235; similarly Noy (2000) 39; Moatti (2007) 87–8.
[108] So, somewhat similarly, Kelly (2007) 152–5, in interpreting urban riots.
[109] As always, there are some borderline cases. Domitian may have expelled the actors, but the references are so vague that they are not helpful; see Plin., *Pan.* 46.1; cf. Suet., *Dom.* 7.1. When troops stationed in Rome were disbanded by emperors there were some parallels to expulsions, but only some. So, Augustus' disbanding of his bodyguard in AD 9 after the Varus disaster (Cass. Dio 56.23.4; Suet., *Aug.* 49.1 with Speidel (1994*a*) 18–19) differed too much in aims and vocabulary to be included in the list. The same applies to Galba's disbanding of the bodyguard (Suet., *Galba* 12.2) and to Septimius Severus' treatment of the praetorians (Cass. Dio 54.1.1; Hdn. 2.13.4f; cf. SHA, *Sept. Sev.* 6.11).

Table 3.2. List of attested expulsions in the Principate

	Date	Expulsion	Source
1.	33 BC	Astrologers and magicians	Cass. Dio 49.43.5
2.	AD 6	Gladiators and slaves for sale (Cass. Dio and Suet.), and of all foreigners (*peregrinos omnes*) except physicians and teachers (Suet.)	Cass. Dio 55.26 Suet., *Aug.* 42.3.4 Oros., *Hist. adv. pag.* 7.3.6
3.	AD 16	Astrologers and magicians	Suet., *Tib.* 36 Tac., *Ann.* 2.32 Cass. Dio 57.15.8–9 *Collatio* 15.2 (Ulpian)
4.	AD 19	Practitioners of Jewish and Egyptian rites	Suet., *Tib.* 36 Cass. Dio 57.18.5a Tac., *Ann.* 2.85. Jos., *A.J.* 18.63–84 cf. Philo, *Leg.* 160 cf. Philo, *In Flacc.* 1 cf. Sen., *Ep.* 108.22
5.	AD 23	Actors and leaders of the factions	Suet., *Tib.* 37.2 Tac., *Ann.* 4.14 Cass. Dio 57.21.3 cf. Cass. Dio 59.2.5
6.	Caligula	Male prostitutes	Suet., *Cal.* 16.1
7.	AD 49 (or 41)	Jews	Suet., *Claud.* 25.4 *N.T. Acts* 18.2 (cf. 18.18–19 and 26) cf. *Schol. on Juv.* 4.117 Oros., *Hist. adv. pag.* 7.6.15–16 Eus., *H.E.* 2.18 cf. Cass. Dio 60.6.6
8.	AD 52	Astrologers	Tac., *Ann.* 12.52
9.	AD 56	Actors and their factions	Suet., *Nero* 16 Tac., *Ann.* 13.24–25 cf. Tac., *Ann.* 14.21
10.	Nero	Philosophers	Philostr., *Ap.T.* 4.47
11.	AD 69 (Vitellius)	Astrologers	Suet., *Vit.* 14 Cass. Dio 65(64).1.4, cf. Zonaras 11.16 p.47, 7–13 D. Tac., *Hist.* 2.62
12.	AD 70	Astrologers	Cass. Dio 66(65).9.2
13.	Vespasian	Philosophers	Cass. Dio 66(65).13.1
14.	Domitian	Philosophers (and astrologers?)	Cass. Dio 67(66).13.3 Aul. Gell. 15.11.3–4 Tac., *Agr.* 2 Plin., *Ep.* 3.11 Suet., *Dom.* 10.5 Jer., *Chron.* s.a. 88 Suda s.v. 'Dometianos' cf. Philostr., *Ap.T.* 7.4

15.	AD 99–100	Actors	Plin., *Pan.* 46.2–5
16.	Commodus	Actors	SHA, *Comm.* 3.4
17.	Alexander Severus	Male prostitutes	SHA, *Sev.Alex.* 34.2, 4

before the onset of the Principate with the expulsion of astrologers and magicians by Agrippa as aedile in 33 BC, and runs to the expulsion of male prostitutes by Alexander Severus. Most evidence stems from the first century AD; the sources for second-century expulsions are markedly poorer. It is also noteworthy that, barring one exception, all the evidence stems from literary sources. Both seem to be due to chance. The actual number of expulsions may have been higher,[110] for the sources about collective expulsions are scanty and scattered. In a couple of cases, there is only one source available to describe the event—sometimes in works composed centuries after the occurrence. Many of the passages are extremely short and frustratingly lacking in relevant details. Predictably, Tacitus wins the prize for brevity, with a three-word sentence about an expulsion ordered by Vitellius: *pulsi Italia mathematici.*[111] Expulsions from the city of Rome are also attested earlier and later.[112]

The sources in the list concern the city of Rome, but expulsions are also attested in other large cities of the empire, though we hear less about them. In Alexandria threats of expulsion were used in the almost continuous conflicts between Greeks and Jews.[113] Later, at the beginning of the third century, the Egyptians were banished from the city by Alexander Severus.[114] In Antioch, the Greek part of the population tried to convince Titus to expel the Jewish part (which he refused to do).[115] There is also evidence for expulsions in Constantinople in late antiquity.

In a general sense, the historicity of the expulsions from Rome in the Principate cannot be in doubt. The sources show clearly that from time to time certain groups were driven from the city. In general, their authors seem not to be very much interested in the reasons behind these expulsions. Most are merely recording the expulsion without further comment, often amidst a series of other measures. Precisely the fact that they are normally mentioned in passing, in a matter-of-fact way, is suggestive of the records' veracity. 'The available evidence is enough to indicate that expulsions were normally more than symbolic gestures', as Noy writes.[116] They were real.

---

[110] Note that Cass. Dio 57.15.8–9, when discussing the expulsion of astrologers and magicians in AD 16, refers to a previous edict. This may be an ineffective one of the same year (so Cramer (1951) 24), but may also refer to a previous lost regulation.

[111] Tac., *Hist.* 2.62.   [112] Noy (2000) 37–47 for an overview.

[113] For some analysis of the background, see Cracco Ruggini (1980).

[114] Moatti (2007) 90.   [115] Jos., *B.J.* 7.103–111.

[116] Noy (2000) 47. Cf. Isaac (2004) 236.

However, it is noteworthy that there are numerous conflicts between the sources over the details of individual expulsions.[117] Sometimes distinct events which somehow referred to expulsions were lumped together in the sources: different groups expelled in different years were presented together,[118] or banishments of individual senators were discussed almost in one breath with collective expulsions.[119] As a rule, the more sources available for a particular expulsion, the greater the number of contradictions, omissions, or inconsistencies. As an example, the expulsion of astrologers in AD 16 is described in four testimonia. All seem in themselves reliable and sketch in broad outlines the same events. But they vary considerably in their details: there may have been two expulsion orders (of uncertain chronology) instead of one; magicians might also have been banned; some sources mention executions which others omit.[120] Even if we leave aside the many problems about the exact dates at which the expulsions took place,[121] there are still numerous contradictions and omissions. In the case of a relatively well-documented expulsion under Domitian, only two late sources state that, apart from the philosophers, astrologers were also expelled.[122] About the expulsion of AD 6, Suetonius and Cassius Dio are essentially in agreement. However, Suetonius adds to the account of Cassius Dio that, apart from the gladiators and slaves for sale, '*all foreigners* with the exception of physicians and teachers' were also expelled. The inclusion of 'all foreigners' makes quite a difference in our evaluation of what happened.[123] The expulsion of the Jews under Claudius in AD 49 is attested by many authors, but Cassius Dio flatly contradicts their evidence by stating explicitly that Claudius did *consider* expelling the Jews, but instead merely ordered them not to hold any meetings.[124] The same applies to the

---

[117] Cf. somewhat similarly Kelly (2007) 154, observing that in descriptions of urban riots there is much variation in key details.

[118] Cass. Dio 57.18.5a, where the expulsions of AD 19 and 16 are described just one after the other.

[119] Tac., *Ann.* 2.85.   [120] See the discussion of Cramer (1951) 21–9.

[121] In the table I have simply followed the standard chronology. However, it should be noted that some individual passages drift in a chronological vacuum and can only be dated on the basis of the assumption that they refer to securely dated events attested in other sources. In the case of the expulsion of the Jews that, according to Suet., *Claud.* 25.4, occurred *impulsore Chresto* the dating of AD 41 or 49 has wider implications for the earliest history of the Christian community in Rome; see Lampe (2003) 14–15 with further refs.

[122] Jer., *Chron.* s.a. 88; *Suda* s.v. 'Dometianos'.

[123] Suet., *Aug.* 42.3.4, *peregrinosque omnes exceptis medicis et praeceptoribus*. By contrast, Cass. Dio 55.26 mentions a distance (100 miles) not mentioned by Suet., and does not list the 'greater part of the household slaves' as part of the expulsion proper. Oros., *Hist. adv. pag.* 7.3.6, certainly not based on independent sources, adds a Christianizing causality for the famine that led to the expulsion, and includes 'all the foreigners', *omnesque peregrinos*, but omits the 'slaves for sale'.

[124] Cass. Dio 60.6.6, placed by most scholars in AD 41 (well before the expulsion), see e.g. Lampe (2003) 15, but note that Dio's phrasing suggests a general ruling.

causes for the expulsion. In the case of the expulsion of actors in AD 23, Suetonius reports that this followed an incident in the theatre ending in bloodshed, whereas Tacitus and Cassius Dio refer to the actors' depraved behaviour with regard to women.

It is possible, of course, to resolve such contradictions. In fact, a great deal of the historiographical attention paid to the expulsions has been devoted to ironing out the inconsistencies. For example, 'Augustus may originally have wanted a general expulsion but decided to settle for a more limited one, or a general expulsion which was feasible in Augustus' time no longer seemed plausible to Dio', as Noy explains the contradictory accounts of the expulsion of AD 6.[125]

Perhaps—but also perhaps not, and there is no way of telling. Although it would be rash indeed to abandon source criticism altogether, it is legitimate to wonder to what extent it really helps. Excessive focus on particular details of individual expulsions therefore easily leads to over-interpretation. It seems more productive to start from the assumption that the ambiguities in the accounts are in themselves of importance. The fact that the details did not matter is in itself significant.

The sources show that expulsions were considered to have a more or less fixed pattern, in which the details were to some extent interchangeable. The motive, the issuing authority, the group that was expelled mattered little. Certainly, the interchangeability was not absolute. There is some historical specificity to some of the events. But only some: the fact that an expulsion took place seems to have been more significant than what exactly happened.

Given the high degree of interchangeability, it is no coincidence that what exactly happened during particular expulsions is not entirely clear. But by combining the details occasionally preserved in the sources it is possible to make a reconstruction of the broad characteristics. Ironically, expulsions turn out to have been, to some extent, non-events: they were passive administrative measures. At the same time, they were clearly symbolically charged and thereby obtained a meaning that extended widely beyond the victimized groups.

It is clear that expulsions were ad hoc measures at a local level. They did not form part of a larger policy regarding specific groups, and should not be interpreted as such.[126] So, it is noteworthy that the Jews were *not* expelled

---

[125] Noy (2000) 40.

[126] The question of the existence of wider policies has received a great deal of attention in the case of the Jews, also in view of the claims made by Jewish writers, such as in Philo, *Leg.* 155–8. See in particular Rajak (1984) and Rutgers (1994; 1998).

from Rome after the Jewish War and the destruction of the Temple.[127] The
expulsions attested in Rome that occurred at other moments were not paral-
leled elsewhere.

Expulsion was a matter of decree. The emperor and/or the senate issued an
administrative order in which it was stated that a certain group had to leave.
A story about the expulsion of the astrologers by Vitellius contains the detail
that such a proclamation was put up in public.[128] We may assume that this
was the normal way to publicize the order. In the sources the particulars
of the operation were left vague, and the vagueness seems deliberate. How it
was effectuated and where the expelled went was of little concern. They were
removed from the community, and that was what counted.

In none of the sources do statements occur about the application of force.
Perhaps part of the explanation is to be sought in the imperial reluctance to
employ violence unless absolutely necessary.[129] But it also seems quite likely
that expulsions were passive administrative measures: those expelled were
not physically transferred by force, but were ordered in a decree to depart
before a specific date.[130] The relatively passive procedure was, at any rate, in
line with standard Roman administrative practices. Only non-compliance
with the expulsion order would create a criminal offence.

That the expulsions were primarily administrative in character is corroborated by the absence of any ritualistic elements. There is no known social
ritual attached to expulsions: there were no collective meetings, no scenes at
the theatre, no religious rituals, no rituals of separation in which the populace
could distance itself from the expelled.[131] The absence is noteworthy, given the
fact that ancient religion abounded with expulsion rituals, scapegoat or otherwise, and that public humiliation and sadism were standard ingredients in
public executions.[132] The expulsions were not marked in such ways.

Identifying all members of a group that would be expelled might have
been difficult. 'It was quite common for the Roman authorities to expel
easily identifiable groups from Rome in times of political turmoil', writes

---

[127] Cf. however Philo, *Leg.* 330, where King Agrippa, after writing a letter to Gaius (Caligula)
opposing the erection of his statue in the Temple, fears it might lead to expulsion of the Jews
everywhere.

[128] Cass. Dio 49.43.5. Cf. Dion. Hal., *Ant. Rom.* 8.72.4–5 (set in 486 BC) for a proclamation in
the streets.

[129] See Kelly (2007), though in Kelly's case the reluctance concerns the use of violence against
the urban population during riots.

[130] As is attested in the expulsion of the astrologers by Vitellius. Likewise Dion. Hal., *Ant.
Rom.* 8.72.4–5 (set in 486 BC). Cf. App., *Mac.* 11.9 for immediate expulsion from the city (171 BC)
and the chaos it produced.

[131] Cf. Tac., *Ann.* 2.32 for executions of individuals accompanying an expulsion, but they
hardly qualify as social ritual and are not mentioned in other expulsions. For rituals of
separation, see Barry (2008).

[132] Coleman (1990); Barry (2008).

Rutgers (my emphasis),[133] yet although such groups may have been easily *targeted*, actual identification must in many cases have been problematical.[134] In cases where ethnic groups were expelled, it must have been almost impossible to identify them.[135] Philosophers might be distinguished by their dress and general appearance, but the upshot was that these could be changed just as easily.[136] Seneca gives an unexpected detail when he writes that when some foreign rites (which must refer to the Isis cult and Jewish rites) were forbidden, abstinence from certain kinds of animal food was seen as proof of allegiance and was therefore regarded with suspicion.[137] But one can hardly imagine the state keeping an eye on what the general populace did not eat. Nor should it be forgotten that mechanisms for policing the city remained rather rudimentary.[138]

The effectiveness of the expulsions can therefore be questioned.[139] Tacitus, in the case of the astrologers in AD 52, explicitly states that the senatorial decree was 'drastic but ineffective'.[140] We hear very little of groups actually leaving the city. We do hear occasionally of *individuals* leaving Rome, sometimes more or less of their free will after the promulgation of an edict.[141] It is quite striking how often groups that were banished previously turn out to be quite large at their next expulsion.[142] At the same time, the decrees cannot have been completely without effect. It seems quite likely that punishments in the case of non-compliance could be severe. In the case of the expulsion of the Jews in AD 19, Suetonius states that those Jews that were expelled rather than conscripted were threatened with slavery for life if they did not obey.[143] If such draconian measures were standard practice, it stands to reason that many of the persons to be expelled complied voluntarily with the measure.

---

[133] Rutgers (1994; 1998) 64.   [134] Cf. Moatti (2000) 932.

[135] Noy (2000) 44. Cf. Broadhead (2004) 325–8 for difficulties in the identification of Latins who had migrated to Rome in the earlier second century BC.

[136] As Philostr., *Ap.T.* 7.3 actually states. Moatti (2006) 120.   [137] Sen., *Ep.* 108.22.

[138] Nippel (1995); also the brief comments of Reinhold (1971) 276.

[139] Balsdon (1979) 98, 'it is difficult to see how . . . the expulsion order can have been carried out effectively'; Moatti (2007) 84.

[140] Tac., *Ann.* 12.52 (*atrox et inritum*); cf. Tac., *Hist.* 1.22 for astrology always being forbidden and always being retained. Cramer (1951) 10 writes that: 'Tacitus failed or refused to see that such decrees were meant to be emergency measures only.' This might have been their intent, but it is not how they were phrased.

[141] Acts 18:2 (cf. 18:18–19 and 26) and Eus., *H.E.* 2.18 (Jews in AD 49); Philostr., *Ap.T.* 4.47 (philosophers under Nero); Philostr., *Ap.T.* 7.4 (philosophers under Domitian).

[142] Explicitly stated by Cass. Dio 60.6.6 in the case of the Jews. Cf. also Cass. Dio 67(66).13.3. Cramer (1951) 29 points to Tac., *Ann.* 4.58: ten years after their expulsion, a host of astrologers, evidently residing in Rome, predicted that Tiberius would never re-enter Rome alive.

[143] Suet., *Tib.* 36, *sub poenae perpetuae servitutis nisi obtemperassent*, Jos., *A.J.* 18.63–84 reports, furthermore, that 'a good many' of those Jews that were conscripted into the army did not want to serve for fear of breaking the Jewish law and were subsequently punished. Marasco (1991) emphasizes the harshness of the measures.

In many sources the motive for the expulsion remains unmentioned. The lack of specificity suggests that expulsions hardly needed explanation or legitimation; they were self-evident.[144] Of course the astrologers (magicians, Isis-worshippers, actors, etc.) would have to be expelled! In the cases where explanations are given, the list contains no surprises: the threat of a famine, public disturbances, crimes, too great an influence on society, a bad influence on women, the corruption of the youth, as a precautionary measure, unspecified rumours. Again there are also conflicting accounts, and again the causes seem to some extent interchangeable.

The major (and obvious) characteristic of an expulsion was that those expelled were sent away. But away *from where* is less clear. The expelled were told to leave, but not where to go: expulsions had no destination. It is often not even entirely clear *what territory* the expelled exactly had to leave. Where information is given, the groups are usually expelled from the city of Rome.[145] In one case the expelled were probably sent away 100 miles from Rome.[146] Sometimes they had to leave Italy,[147] or both the city and Italy.[148] Again, it seems that the details did not really matter. The lack of clarity implies that removal was considered more important than the subsequent itinerary. The act of expelling stopped just after the expulsion from the community. The fact that the expelled went elsewhere within the empire was of no concern, and the expelled were never driven over the border of the empire. The fact that Romanness was expressed in terms of membership of the population of Rome may seem unsurprising, but it remains remarkable that in an age in which Roman identity was expressed throughout the vast empire the focus remained so much on the capital. The city still mattered.

What applies to the spatial dimension also applies to the temporal dimension. The sources contain no statements at all about the duration of the expulsion. The implicit suggestion is, of course, that the expulsion was meant to be permanent. At the same time, it is equally clear that the reality was different. The simple fact that the same groups are repeatedly expelled

---

[144] Likewise on urban riots Kelly (2007) 156.

[145] Suet., *Tib.* 36. (AD 19); Suet., *Claud.* 25.4; Acts 18:2, also in Philo, *Leg.* 157, where expulsion of the Jews is mentioned as an option; all sources about the expulsion of philosophers (and astrologers?) under Domitian, except Aulus Gellius.

[146] Cass. Dio 55.26 (750 *stadioi*); 100 miles was the area of jurisdiction of *the praetor urbanus*.

[147] Tac., *Ann.* 2.32 (AD 16.); Tac., *Ann.* 2.85 (AD 19); Tac., *Ann.* 4.14 (AD 23); Tac., *Ann.* 12.52 (AD 52); Tac., *Hist.* 2.62, and Cass. Dio 65(64).1.4 (AD 69).

[148] Suet., *Vit.* 14; Aul. Gell. 15.11.4, *eiecti atque urbe et Italia interdicti*, 'they were driven from the city and forbidden Italy'; cf. also Suet., *Aug.* 45.4 for an individual actor expelled *urbe atque Italia*. Acts 18:2 (cf. 18:18–19 and 26, and Eus., *H.E.* 2.18), one of the very few cases where we can follow the effects of an expulsion at an individual level, is not really helpful. All sources uniformly state the expulsion was from the city of Rome, but the couple actually left Italy and moved to Corinth and subsequently to Ephesus. This might mean that the expulsion was indeed from Italy as well, but it also might simply mean that the couple left Italy out of their free will, after being expelled from the city.

shows that they returned (or that some members never left). There might have been some additional measures to ensure that the expelled stayed away, but we hear of these only in a few instances. So, in the case of the actors that were expelled by Tiberius in AD 23, Cassius Dio states that after their expulsion Tiberius would allow them no place to practise their profession.[149] Something similar seems to have happened in the case of their expulsion in AD 56.[150] Recalling a group or revoking a decision was possible, though we hear very little about this. In the case of the expulsion of the actors in AD 23, Tiberius could not be induced by any entreaties of the people to recall them (which suggests in itself that that was deemed possible), but Caligula, upon his accession, immediately revoked the decision of his predecessor.[151]

It is clear that in the expulsions legal niceties were passed over, not only because no time would be lost in establishing a justification for the expulsion, but also because the legal status of the expelled was hardly ever a subject of concern. Only in two instances was a differentiation made between groups of different legal status. In the expulsion of astrologers and magicians of AD 16, Cassius Dio and Ulpian report that foreigners were put to death, whereas citizens were banished and lost their property, and from the former source we learn that the treatment of citizens was a source of concern to the senate.[152] In the expulsion of the Jews of AD 19 a difference was made between freedmen of military age and the rest.[153] That is all.[154]

There can be little doubt that among the expelled there were people of different legal statuses: there will have been Roman citizens among them, *peregrini*, freedmen, and slaves. What clearly must have prevailed over their legal status is the fact that they were regarded as outsiders. It is tempting to see this as deliberate strategy. Ignoring their legal status emphasized their un-Romanness, which in turn legitimized their removal from the community.

The absence of legal distinctions might perhaps be placed in the context of developments in penal law. A distinction had gradually developed between the elite and the rest of the population that at a later stage would be formalized in the distinction between *honestiores* and *humiliores*. By the end of the Republic a system of courts was in existence, with juries, in which the accused could be

---

[149] Cass. Dio 57.21.3.

[150] In the case of the philosophers under Nero, there is no evidence for an expulsion, but Nero forbade them, according to Philostr., *Ap.T.* 4.47, to practise their profession.

[151] Suet., *Tib.* 37.2 and Cass. Dio 59.2.5, resp.

[152] Cass. Dio 57.15.8–9; *Collatio* 15.2, with Cramer (1951) 26.

[153] Tac., *Ann.* 2.85. See Marasco (1991) with further literature. Solin (1983) 687 in his discussion of the expulsion of the Jews in AD 19 points out that only *peregrini* could be sent away without process, and that therefore conscription was used for the others. However, in other expulsions such subtleties do not occur.

[154] I take it that Suet., *Aug.* 42.3.4 in his description of the expulsion of AD 6 uses *peregrinos omnes* in a loose sense, 'all foreigners'; if not, it would present another instance of legally based distinctions.

defended by a lawyer. Punishments were relatively mild. Under the Principate this system remained in use, but became more and more the preserve of the aristocracy, which in addition had the privilege of judging its own members. In parallel with this, a system emerged by which magistrates in the provinces pronounced decisions on the provincials and had great liberty to do as they saw fit. This system also came to be used in Rome for the general populace, independent of their legal status.[155]

The expulsions may be interpreted at different levels, and these interpretations are not mutually exclusive. At a practical level, law and order in the city needed to be maintained. In a large city such as that of Rome, disturbances arose from time to time, and targets needed to be found—independent of the question whether the target groups were responsible for the upheaval.[156] Secondly, from a functionalist perspective, driving out certain groups can be seen as a way of releasing tensions in society. Expelling a part of the population may have helped to release conflicts in society and to re-establish social norms.[157] Thirdly, MacMullen has placed the expulsions in a context of opposition. Perceived enemies of the Roman order were removed.[158] Lastly, at a more symbolic level, expulsions can be regarded as a way of establishing the boundaries of the community by defining who did not belong to it. Roman society was essentially open, but that in itself invited discussions about the boundaries of acceptability. The boundaries between what was considered foreign and what belonged to one's own culture were subject to continuous renegotiation.

Who belonged to Rome? What was considered foreign? If expulsions are regarded as negative community definitions, and were used to draw boundaries and to establish who belonged to the community and who did not, it is striking that the list of expelled groups cut through normal social taxonomies. The groups that were targeted were all regarded with suspicion, and were all seen as outsiders, but the expelled did not consist solely or even predominantly of immigrants in the strict sense of the word.

The groups that were expelled formed a rather odd collection: Jews, worshippers of Isis, astrologers, philosophers, magicians, gladiators, slaves for sale, male prostitutes. Some of the expelled groups were quite large, while others must have been numerically insignificant: the Jewish community might have numbered 15,000–30,000,[159] but astrologers are unlikely to have formed a

---

[155] Coleman (1990) with further refs.
[156] Rutgers (1994; 1998); Isaac (2004) 11, quoted above.   [157] Hoffmann (1986) 1–23.
[158] MacMullen (1966); Kudlien (1991) 30–3.
[159] Cf. Cass. Dio 60.6.6, where size is an issue. For the argument that in the expulsion of the Jews/Christians in the late 40s only their leaders were expelled, see Lampe (2003) 13–14. In view of the fact that such a notion is absent in any other expulsion and is not supported by the sources, the idea seems untenable. For the size see Chapter 2, Section 4; note that part of the estimates are based on the figure of 4,000 expelled Jewish freedmen reported in Tac., *Ann.* 2.85.

large group. All groups have some claim to outsider status, but it is also clear that the overlap with immigrant groups is very partial indeed. Also in numerical terms they will have formed only a small fraction of the total immigrant population.

It is noteworthy that specific groups were under attack, whereas before and after the early Principate sometimes simply 'all foreigners' were expelled. In AD 6 gladiators and slaves for sale apparently constituted large enough a group to alleviate the pressure in response to a severe famine.[160] The astrologers and magicians and suchlike were a continuous target:[161] in AD 16, in AD 52, and in AD 70 they were expelled. Jews were targeted in AD 19 and AD 49, in the former case in combination with worshippers of Egyptian rites (by which the Isis cult must have been meant); actors and leaders of the factions in AD 23 and again in AD 56. Philosophers were expelled by Vespasian and Domitian.

The groups that were expelled did not only form a rather odd collection. It is also noticeable that some categories are lumped together. MacMullen has observed that words for philosophers, diviners, magicians, and astrologers came to be used almost interchangeably.[162] The fact that Jews and 'worshippers of Egyptian rites' were expelled together has caused so much—implicit—embarrassment that their expulsions have normally been studied separately.

Nor is there a significant overlap with large immigrant groups. Not only are there no Italians expelled in this period; more exotic and visible ethnic groups are also not expelled. It is striking how many other groups simply remained untouched, such as the Syrians, or the Spaniards, or in fact almost all of the epigraphically attested ethnic groups living in Rome. In fact, some ethnic groups that were targeted in the Republic do not reoccur.[163] Jews and Egyptians might, of course, be regarded as ethnic categories, but in their expulsions it is religion rather than ethnicity that plays a prominent role. Many groups that are targeted in the literary sources do not occur in the list of the expelled. Jews and Egyptians do figure in invectives, but a significant discrepancy still exists between the dystopian universe sketched by Juvenal and Martial and the groups that are actually targeted. The Orontes may have emptied itself in the Tiber, but expulsions did little to stem the tide.

The expulsions can, therefore, only in a limited and indirect sense be regarded as a form of immigration control. The act of expulsion was highly symbolic. Noy was right to emphasize the historicity of the expulsions, but negative community definition was the main aim. The community was cleansed, and unwanted elements had to be got rid of. Expulsions were

---

[160] Cass. Dio 55.26; Suet., *Aug.* 42.3.4.   [161] As much is stated by Ulpian in *Collatio* 15.2.
[162] MacMullen (1966) 110 and 124, 128–9, 141–2, also commenting on a correspondence between philosophy and Judaism.
[163] Polyb. 27.6; Livy 42.48.3 and App., *Mac.* 11.9 (Macedonians in 171 BC); Plin., *N.H.* 29.8.15 (Greeks at an unknown moment).

not directed at migration as a phenomenon, nor targeted at specific migrant groups. If regarded as an instrument to curb or control migration, it was extremely blunt.

6. A LIBERAL MIGRATION REGIME?

The aim of this chapter was to address firstly the question of the extent to which a series of specific institutions stimulated or impeded mobility, and secondly to what extent these institutions were related.

There was no such thing as a migrant status, and hence the concept of illegal immigration, which is so dominant in modern thinking, was absent. As much of the Roman effort towards population control was directed at status, it is of importance to know the status of the immigrants that were living in Rome. Although precise information is lacking, there can be little doubt that in terms of legal status the immigrants formed a mixed bag. There were certainly many slaves and freedmen among them. But it also seems highly likely that many were freeborn persons in the possession of Roman or Latin citizenship. Only a proportion of them will have consisted of *peregrini*. By implication, there was no specific legal status attached to the immigrants as group.

With regard to citizenship, instead of narrowing or defining more precisely who belonged to the citizen body, citizenship was increasingly distributed, both in the provinces and in Rome. The disappearance of a territorial concept of citizenship became even more clearly demonstrated by the phenomenon of free persons without Roman citizenship who lived in Rome and other Roman communities. Thus, citizenship itself did not entail mobility: its acquisition and possession were not connected to residence in Rome. Indirectly, its acquisition might have stimulated mobility, and this will, at least in part, have been focused on the city of Rome. But the connection remains a loose one.

State controls of mobility were relatively weak, which is not entirely surprising in a state without a well-developed bureaucratic apparatus. The primary focus of population control was status, not origin, and it was social mobility rather than geographical mobility which the state sought to control. Obviously in some cases the two coincided. But movement was in itself unproblematic—though it could raise suspicions, as it could imply status usurpation. Freedom of movement was a fundamental principle: for free persons it was seen as a hallmark of their identity; conversely, the fact that slaves could be moved around by their owners was a sign of their loss of autonomy. Some restrictions nevertheless applied: registration in the census required returning to the *origo*, and in the performance of *munera* care was taken that obligations were fulfilled in the home-town. Elite movement was subject to more controls. Members of the elite often travelled over long distances—both in a private and an official capacity—and their movements were at least potentially more dangerous to the interests of the state.

Expulsions from Rome took place on an ad hoc basis and were not primarily directed at migrant groups. Expulsions were certainly not based on a coherent migration policy. They rather served both symbolically and in practice to establish the boundaries of the community by negative definition: by getting rid of undesirables. The boundaries of who belonged were not fixed, and were subject to negotiation. Expelling groups in times of perceived crisis helped to re-establish the boundaries of the acceptable. What is remarkable is that the expelled did not comprise the major groups of immigrants.

Citizenship thus did not fence off the population from foreign intrusion, but moved itself over wide stretches of territory. Many of Rome's immigrants held citizenship prior to moving. Population control was mainly aimed at status control, rather than control of movement. Expulsions were intended to keep the population pure, but foreign elements were not necessarily equated with immigrants.

As will be discussed in Chapter 7, studies of collective identity have increasingly emphasized dynamic aspects of identity formation: the boundaries between what was considered foreign and what as one's own culture were subject to continuous renegotiation. Demarcations of belonging and exclusion were negotiable and subject to contestation. If being Roman meant participating in an insider debate about what was considered to be Roman, boundaries were permeable and they could change. There were several ways to draw the lines.

The Roman migration regime might be described as liberal, or one of laissez faire, but both terms are somewhat misleading in that they imply a conscious response to something that was perceived as a problem. The Roman state had no migration policy. The key in state behaviour or even general attitude is that origin was not seen as a primary marker of identity. Indirectly, migration and mobility raised many questions about what it meant to be Roman, about the symbolic boundaries of the Roman community. But in itself, migration was relatively unproblematic.

4

Migration and the Family

The heightened propensity to migrate at certain stages of the life cycle is important in the selection of migrants.[1]

1. HOUSEHOLD COMPOSITION

Over the past decades migration historians have emphasized the importance of the family and the life-cycle in structuring migration.[2] Marriage patterns and household composition created conditions which made migration possible for some members of the family and inhibited the mobility of others. Some people remained tied to their kin, others became, at certain points in their life, available for the labour market or sought an education outside the home-town and moved permanently or temporarily out of the house of their birth family. In particular, marriage was an important occasion. It functioned both as a point in time at which individuals settled down and as a time when people might move out of the house to set up a new household.

In consequence, household composition and marriage patterns can be used to contextualize migration. In itself such an approach is indirect, because the availability of potential migrants does not mean that people actually move. But household formation can be used to analyse the conditions that make migration possible. At a general level, it may also help to understand why many of the decisions to move are not taken by individuals, but are rather made in the context of family dynamics.[3]

This general idea calls for further exploration with respect to the Roman case.[4] There is, after all, an abundant scholarly literature on the Roman family. Over the past decades an immense amount of work has been done on precisely

---

[1] Lee (1966) 57.   [2] Manning (2013²) 192.
[3] Cf. Taylor (2011) 125–7 on classical Athens.
[4] Cf. Erdkamp (2008) 433–7 for brief but important exploration in the case of the Roman Republic.

those issues that are of importance for the subject of migration: patterns of marriage, mortality patterns, household composition, and the position of women both within and outside the family.[5] Moreover, there is an added advantage in approaching migration through the family, in that it almost automatically forces us to think about gender. Men and women might have radically different migration patterns.[6] The subject has only gradually been finding its way onto the agenda of ancient mobility studies.[7] In the Roman evidence it is not difficult to find travelling women attested in inscriptions and in the isotopic evidence, but the question is how their movement should be interpreted. In early modern Europe female migrants played a large role as servants. Given the dominance of household slavery, it is likely that this route was blocked for free women moving to Rome, but how should we conceptualize Roman women's movement? What was, to use two of Woolf's expressions, the 'female horizon', and which 'social cages' constrained their movement?[8]

This chapter explores the relation between migration and the Roman family. I start with a general model, combining ideas formulated for modern European history with general knowledge about the Roman family. In subsequent sections this general model will be applied in more detail to the city of Rome. To what extent are the expectations met by the evidence? To what extent does the evidence refine the predictions of the model?

2. A GENERAL MODEL

Some decades ago the historical demographer Hajnal published two articles which together presented a theory which in later years has been termed the Hajnal hypothesis. He postulated a unique pattern of marriage and of household composition that prevailed for a long period in recent European history and that was not found elsewhere or in earlier periods of history. It was this Western pattern, Hajnal argued, that led to large streams of migration.[9]

---

[5] The bibliography is vast; key publications include Rawson (ed.) (1986); Bradley (1991); Dixon (1992).

[6] Manning (2013[2]) 192.

[7] See in particular Woolf (2013) for discussion and an overview of the available data in the Roman West. For the closely related subject of female travel in the Roman world, see Foubert (2013), noting at 391 that '[r]esearch on women's travels in the Roman world is almost nonexistent'. See also Foubert (forthcoming) on female mobility in Roman Egypt and Parker (2008) for representations in literature. For female mobility in the Hellenistic world, see Loman (2004), discussing at 20–7 the almost complete absence of previous historiography. See now also De Ligt and Tacoma (forthcoming) for some remarks.

[8] Woolf (2013).

[9] Hajnal (1965) and (1982); the latter has also appeared with minor alterations as Hajnal (1983). Hajnal in his turn was quick to point out that his focus on the importance of

It is clear that Hajnal's model was framed in a way to explain the rise of the West, and that the model—again—connected migration to modernization. World-historical approaches have shown modes in which non-Western family forms may also lead to migration.[10] Yet Hajnal's work remains an excellent starting point for present purposes. He formulated explicitly a causal relationship between migration and family forms. His work has been extremely influential among historians of the family, and has formed the basis of subsequent discussion of family typology and marriage patterns, including Roman debates.

The Western marriage pattern as described by Hajnal had two characteristics: marriage occurred late both for women and for men, and there existed a substantial group of persons who never married. Men and women delayed their marriage up to the age of 30, and some 10 per cent of the population remained single for the whole of their life. The actual ages and figures differed from country to country, but the general pattern was remarkably consistent. The pattern can be found west of the line from Petersburg to Trieste and can be traced from the 1940s all the way back to about 1740. Hajnal argued that the demographic evidence for marriage *before* that period was so sparse that it was difficult to be certain about earlier periods, but he considered it likely that at some point in time between the late Middle Ages and 1740 the Western marriage pattern came into existence, as both medieval and ancient evidence suggested a different pattern. The modern European pattern was also unique in a geographical sense: it was not attested outside Europe. Furthermore, such marriage patterns are typified by a specific type of household: what Hajnal called the 'simple family'. This household was characterized by the fact that the married couple were in charge of their own household, that few relatives lived in such households, and that instead lodgers and servants lived together with the family. Marriage was delayed because wealth had to be acquired in order to set up a separate household.

By contrast, the pattern found elsewhere showed early marriage for both men and women, and a situation in which marriage was universal. Hajnal termed this pattern 'Eastern European', but perhaps it is more appropriate to term it 'non-Western', as Hajnal's main contention was that it prevailed in all societies outside Europe west of the Petersburg–Trieste line. He also found it in various African and Asian societies at different periods in the nineteenth century. Within Europe itself the non-Western pattern was probably the norm before the rise of the Western pattern at an undetermined moment before the 1740s. The joint household belonged to this pattern. This is a relatively

late marriage was not new; it was already a major theme in Malthusian thought: Hajnal (1965) 130.

[10] See Moch (2007), discussing Chinese patterns in the nineteenth century.

complex type of household, where two or more related couples lived together. Marriage did not have to be delayed because the couple moved into an existing household: wealth was not a necessary condition for marriage.

Although Hajnal's main point was to discuss the patterns in marriage and household formation, he also discussed their implications for migration patterns. For Hajnal, the crucial group was formed by persons aged 15 to 30, not yet married. These men and women formed a labour force of people at the peak of their physical capacity but not yet caught in a web of familial obligations. Their presence gave rise to a system of temporal migration in which young men and women moved out to work for a significant period in their lives. In his typology, it was the Western model of late marriage and nuclear families that formed a stimulus for migration, and, by implication, the non-Western model did not.

Given the binary nature of Hajnal's typology, the two different patterns can be summarized as shown in Table 4.1. The question is how the Roman family fits into such a scheme.

According to Hajnal's reasoning, the Western family only came into existence somewhere between the late Middle Ages and the 1740s. The logical corollary was that the Roman family belonged to the non-Western pattern, and this is in fact what Hajnal argued. Following Hajnal's argument, the possibilities for migration will have been severely limited.

The current consensus among ancient historians about the nature of the Roman family is otherwise. One of the central contentions in the debate on the nature of the Roman family has been that it was of the nuclear type, similar to the modern Western simple family. It consisted of a husband, his wife, and their children. This idea was most forcefully formulated by Saller and Shaw on

Table 4.1. Hajnal's typology of marriage, household, and migration

	Pattern of Marriage	Household	Migration
'Western' pattern • pre-1740 to 1940s • W. of Trieste – Petersburg line	Late • late male marriage • late female marriage • a significant minority never marries	Simple • only one married couple • couple in charge of own household	Large • young men and women before marriage
'Non-Western' pattern • all other periods • everywhere else	Early • early male marriage • early female marriage • universal marriage	Joint • Two or more related married couples • Newly married couple starts in a household in which an elder couple is in charge	Negligible

the basis of a massive study of Latin epitaphs.[11] In the thousands of relationships that Saller and Shaw recorded, there turned out to be a very heavy emphasis on nuclear family relationships. Everywhere we see wives setting up epitaphs for their husbands, fathers setting up inscriptions for their children, children setting up inscriptions for their parents. By contrast, dedications in which siblings or other members of the extended family occur are rare. The paternal grandfather—*the* symbol of the Roman extended family—is conspicuously absent in the epitaphs.[12] Phrased in the terms of Hajnal's model, Saller and Shaw moved the Roman family from the non-Western into the Western type.

Although most scholars would probably still adhere to Saller and Shaw's argument about the nuclear composition of the Roman family, important adjustments have been made to their thesis.[13] In the first place, their method of analysis was itself heavily biased in favour of the nuclear family. In the second place, scholars have argued that more than two household forms can be distinguished in the Roman evidence, and the problem must thus be rephrased somewhat. In the third place, scholars have pointed to the fact that family forms evolve over time; in itself this is obvious, but it may imply that the supposed distinction between nuclear and extended may be more apparent than real. This may cast renewed doubt on the place of the Roman family in Hajnal's typology.

Be that as it may, a discussion of Roman patterns of marriage shows without any doubt that the Roman family does not fit into Hajnal's categorization at all. Using Roman data for female marital ages, Hajnal categorized the Roman pattern as non-Western, because the ages at marriage of women were low, normally well below 20.[14] Hajnal was certainly right about early female age at marriage,[15] but he ignored the evidence for Roman males.[16] Roman males

---

[11] Saller and Shaw (1984).

[12] Saller and Shaw (1984) 136, emphasizing further that there are far fewer paternal grandfathers than predicted by mortality models, and that even in dedications in which grandparents figure, the paternal *avus* is under-represented.

[13] Martin (1996) 40 with n. 1, and Gallivan and Wilkins (1997) 240 n. 3 for further references to endorsement of Saller and Shaw's thesis. Bradley (1991) and Martin (1996) for important objections.

[14] Hajnal (1965) 120–2, concluding that '[t]he population whose deaths the tombstones record had a marriage pattern of "non-European" type. The same conclusion emerges from an entirely different type of data, the "censuses" of Roman Egypt.'

[15] Hopkins (1964/5) on Harkness (1896). There has been much subsequent debate about the question how 'early' female age at first marriage is exactly; for present purposes that question is unimportant. See among others Shaw (1987); Lelis, Percy, and Verstraete (2003); Hin (2013) 175–9.

[16] At the end of his discussion, Hajnal (1965) 122 did observe that Egyptian men married substantially later than women, but he did not discuss the possible implications for his classification. Hajnal did not analyse the non-Egyptian Roman data presented by Harkness (1896) for males, although he based his analysis of female marriage precisely on that article.

married relatively late, normally between 20 and 30, in a pattern that is similar to their later European counterparts.[17] As there are no grounds for privileging either the evidence for female ages at marriage (as Hajnal did) or male ages of marriage, the conclusion is inescapable that the Roman marital pattern does not fall into either of Hajnal's categories. A third pattern exists, with early female and late male marriage.[18]

The implications for migration patterns are obvious. In the Roman pattern late marriage existed, but it was confined to men. Male marriage was delayed, and this created a large time-span between adulthood and marriage. Following the logic of Hajnal's arguments, the conclusion must be that Roman migrants should be primarily located among young unmarried males. Their marriage occurred late, which implied that they were free to move around. Young Roman men between, say, the ages of 15 and 30 would have a long period for training, education, work, travel, and combinations of these.[19]

For similar reasons, the mobility of women will have been much more constrained. Women married straight out of the parental home at a very young age, which left them little room for movement afterwards. It thus seems probable that much of their mobility was marital mobility. To what extent this marital mobility would involve travel over significant distances is difficult to predict. On the one hand, one would think that recruitment pools would be severely restricted socially and geographically, especially if men returned home and subsequently married. On the other hand, a situation in which their prospective husbands travelled and thus might come from further away also might imply that the marriage market would open up.

A second moment at which such female marital mobility might be posited was at the termination of marriage. Because of the high mortality rates, many marriages terminated at an early stage, and here the difference in marital age is of relevance. As men were older than women, many husbands will have died before their wives. This will have resulted in a large pool of once-married women. As women married young, they might still have a long life ahead of them when their husbands died. Some women moved into new households through remarriage. Such a move will undoubtedly have also contained some element of geographical mobility, but the extent of this could vary significantly. In many cases, remarriage will have meant a double move: a woman moved first back to her parents (or other relatives), and from there into the household of her new husband. Women not remarrying might have stayed in their

---

[17] Saller (1987).

[18] Hin (2013) 179–81 explains the age-gap as an adaptive strategy minimizing the risk of underproduction and increasing the chances that men had sufficient wealth to establish a household.

[19] Cf. Moch (2007) on Chinese history, where (especially but not solely in the nineteenth century) imbalances in the sex ratio due to female infanticide and government encouragement of migration gave rise to very substantial long-distance migration systems by young males.

deceased husbands' house, but it needs to be realized that in many cases she will not have inherited the house and hence might have moved to property of her own. Much movement consisted of circulating around the family households. A woman might move back to her parents, or move into her son's household, which might be taken over from his father. If she were to set up her own household, she would do so presumably near the place where she had lived, or where her parents had lived or were still living.

Indirectly, marital mobility also structured the patterns of male migrants. At some point during their stays elsewhere they would have to face the question of marriage. They could settle in their new place and start a family there, or return home and find a bride there. The model thus allows both for permanent migration and for temporary migration.

To sum up, Hajnal ignored the possibility of a third marital pattern consisting of early female marriage and late male marriage. We may posit the existence of a large group of people not yet caught in a web of new ties, just as in modern Europe. The crucial difference is that in the Roman case this group consisted entirely of males. By contrast, women will have moved essentially in the context of their marriage: either at the beginning or at its termination. The model does not exclude the possibility of family migration, but does not accord a central role to it.

Further economic dynamism may be added to the model. Temporary emigration may have served to remove excess labour from the family in times when there was less work, and this type of migration might thus be seen in the context of adaptive family strategies that people used to cope with fluctuations in the economy.[20] In addition, whereas in a system of primogeniture the children who were born after the first son were almost automatically forced out of the house, arguably in the system of partible inheritances that was prevalent in the Roman world there was not so great an incentive to remain, but rather to return upon the death of the parent, especially if the inheritance consisted of landed property. This may have encouraged return migration at some point.

Important though such additions are, a fundamental point needs to be investigated first. The model is a general one: it is applicable to all periods in which the observed demographic characteristics occurred. In consequence, it is important to establish to what extent the actual demographic profile of migrants coming to Rome fits with the model, and to what extent the model can be refined. We should therefore shift the focus from the sender families to the receiving society.

---

[20] For excess labour Erdkamp (2008) 433–7; explored in more detail in Erdkamp (forthcoming); for the concept of adaptive family strategies (in a different context) Groen-Vallinga (2013).

In testing the applicability of the model, it needs to be taken into account that the nature of migration to Rome was rather diverse. To what extent is it legitimate to apply a unitary model? The model is implicitly focused on voluntary movement. It may certainly be relevant to recruitment patterns of soldiers, but it seems to be less directly applicable to the servile population: in enslavement, family dynamics might have played some role, but hardly in a straightforward fashion. To what extent, then, is the model also applicable to forced migration? In order to obtain a sense of the variability in patterns without fragmenting the discussion too much, it seems best to concentrate on the three major forms of immigration distinguished before: soldiers, voluntary immigrants, and slaves.

3. A DEMOGRAPHIC PROFILE

The model sketches the availability of family members for migration. On this basis we expect that single individuals were more prone to move than family groups, that young adult males dominated migration streams, and that the mobility of women was restricted to the context of marriages (either when they were concluded or when they were terminated).

It seems best to start with counter-arguments. On the basis of analysis of oxygen-stable isotope ratios of series of teeth in a sample of sixty-one individuals from Isola Sacra in Ostia, it has been argued that there were a substantial number women and children among the immigrants. It has been claimed that their presence vitiates the male-based migration model, and rather points to family movement.[21] However, several interpretations might be used to explain the presence of women and children: while it is certainly feasible that children moved as part of a family together with their parents, they could also have been brought as slaves, or, in the case of women, as brides, or have moved independently. Depending on their exact age and economic position, they may also be classified as 'sub-adults' rather than as children.[22]

In addition, the data on which the claim for child migration is based are problematical. The analysis used oxygen isotopes from first and third molars to determine local and non-local origin. The first molar is formed before birth and completed around age 2.5–3.0; the third starts to form at age 7–12 and is completed at age 10–17.5. The time-gap between the first and the third molar allows the moment of migration to be determined. People with a non-local

---

[21] Prowse et al. (2007), e.g. 510 (abstract): 'This study demonstrates that migration was not limited to predominantly single adult males, as suggested by historical sources, but rather a complex phenomenon involving families.' Likewise Prowse et al. (2010).

[22] Bruun (2010); Hin (2013) 234–7; Tacoma (forthcoming c).

Table 4.2. Isola Sacra data

M1	M3	N	Interpretation
Local	Local	33	Locals
Non-local	Local	13	child immigrants
Non-local	Non-local	7	adult immigrants
Local	Non-local	8	??

(*source*: Prowse et al. (2007))

first molar and a local third molar can be thought to have migrated in their youth; people with non-local first and non-local third molars, to have migrated as adults. The analysis of the Isola Sacra data found, among sixty-one individuals, thirteen child immigrants and seven adult immigrants; see Table 4.2.[23] This produced a remarkable and unexpected pattern, with almost twice as many children as adults. However, what on closer inspection also emerges from the data is that there is an additional group whose migrant history is less easy to explain: those with a local first molar and non-local third molar. This group consists of eight persons. According to the logic of the argument, they must have been born in Ostia, moved elsewhere in their teens (before the formation of the third molar started, at age 12 at the latest), and then returned after their third molar was completed. Although it is certainly possible to come up with scenarios,[24] it is very difficult to think of a coherent pattern that can explain such movements. It is disconcerting that this group was ignored in the original publication of the research, particularly in view of the claims about the importance of child migration. In fact, and somewhat strangely, this group of young 'remigrants' was silently subsumed under the local population.[25] The point would be of minor academic interest, were it not for the fact that the claim of child migration rests precisely on these third-molar data. If the third-molar data are left out of consideration, most of the

[23] The figures are based on the recalculated 'local range' of Killgrove (2010*a*) 249, of −5.8 to −3.7%. This does lead to slight adaptations of the figures (including a lowering of the problematical category of 'remigrants' from 10 to 8), but does not significantly affect the results.

[24] Bruun (2010) 122 hypothesizes in two of such cases either step-wise migration (an individual had grown up in a region with a similar isotopic signature as in Ostia/Portus, then moved elsewhere, and finally settled in Ostia/Portus) or return migration (a child of a mid-ranking official, for example). Another possibility could be temporary movement to Rome. Hin (2013) 237 takes the pattern to support the 'model of a spectre of migration, with people moving back between urban and rural areas'. Perhaps so, but the connection between such a model and the findings is rather tenuous.

[25] Prowse et al. (2007) refer consistently in their figures for immigrants to the first-molar data only. The presentation in their table 4 of local and non-local values for first and third molars obscures the problem. The table might easily give the impression that the number of new immigrants declines over time: first molar shows 33% non-locals, third molar only 25%. In fact, among the 25% there are a significant number of individuals who had a local first molar.

case for child migration is lost: we are left with twenty immigrants who came to Ostia at an unknown point in time after their first molar had formed.[26]

Given the present state of the evidence, too large claims cannot be based on the isotopic analysis alone. At the same time, the arguments about the importance of family migration surely invite further scrutiny and need to be compared with epigraphic evidence.[27] There are, in fact, several elements that should be discussed: the age at immigration, the sex ratio, and the family composition of the immigrants.

Let us start with the age at immigration. For one group, the information we have is extremely precise. In the case of soldiers, the age at which they came to Rome coincided with the age of their recruitment. The latter can be established with precision because epitaphs normally state both length of life and length of service. For praetorians the age of entry was normally between 18 and 20 years, but other ages are attested as well.[28] Likewise, soldiers serving in the urban cohorts went to Rome between the ages of 18 and 20, though again other ages are known, running from a very early 13 years to a very late 32 years.[29] The *equites singulares* were recruited from the best horsemen who had already served three to seven years in the *alae*; their ages of entry among the *equites singulares* thus start somewhat later, from age 23 onwards.[30] Both because of the irregularities and because the recruitment age of *equites singulares* was delayed, the complete age-range at which soldiers came to Rome covers a somewhat wider spectrum than one might think at first sight, but it still forms a relatively narrow band.

Obviously, in the case of voluntary immigrants the age-range at which they came to Rome is likely to have been much wider than that of soldiers: they were not bound by formal recruitment criteria. Most of the information we have is imprecise: age of death in migrant inscriptions serves as *terminus ante quem* for the moment of the move of civilians (see Table 4.3). In themselves these ages can only give rough approximations, because they might simply replicate the tendencies to favour certain age-groups in the epitaphs in general.[31] Yet they can be compared to the epigraphically attested ages at death of soldiers whose age at recruitment is known. In the analysis it needs to be kept in mind that only a fraction of all civilian migrant inscriptions include ages,

---

[26] See Bruun (2010), who arrives through a different route at a similar conclusion. Given the fact that what constitutes the 'local range' is disputed, it seems a real possibility that many of the third-molar values are actually local, not non-local. Hin (2013) 236 n. 93 observes that only four cases in the problematic group of 'remigrants' are relatively far removed from the local range.

[27] See Tacoma (forthcoming *c*) for comparison with the epitaphs from Isola Sacra.

[28] Durry (1938) 262.

[29] Freis (1967) 47, who points out that this variety is similar to the recruitment ages of the legions.

[30] Speidel (1994*a*) 86–90; based on ages in epitaphs. Note that technically *equites* were 'chosen', *allectus*, not recruited.

[31] So Hin (2013) 237, 244.

Table 4.3. Ages of death of provincial civilians and soldiers (*in %*)

	Civilians (N = 111)	Soldiers (N = 360)
0–9	3	
10–19	22	1
20–29	35	23
30–39	21	47
40–49	8	22
50–59	4	4
60–69	3	–
70+	3	–

(*source*: Noy (2000) 63–65)

and that all kinds of biases might have distorted the patterns: for example, young children were less likely to be commemorated anyway, and migrants might in later years be less prone to mention their origin, and might therefore have disappeared from the radar. And the figures allow for multiple interpretations: the fact that migrants also appear in some numbers in the 30–9 age-group would in my view point to prolongation of some stays (to be discussed below) rather than late arrival. What the table shows is that the bulk of deaths (78 per cent) fall in the 10–19 (22 per cent), 20–9 (35 per cent), and 30–9 (21 per cent) age-groups. A comparison with the military population shows that the civilian population has a younger profile, with markedly more immigrants dying in the 10–19 age-group. In itself the contrast is not surprising, given that before the age of 18 hardly any soldier in Rome entered the army. But it certainly does suggest that civilian immigrants also came to Rome at younger ages. At the same time, it is noteworthy that in the inscriptions there are only very few deaths below 10 years old.[32] We also hear little about children as migrants in other contexts. It therefore seems best to regard the members of the age-group of 10–19 as sub-adults, rather than as children proper.

We are less well informed about the ages at which slaves came to Rome. Using the age of death of the *columbaria* populations as a *terminus ante quem* does not seem a viable option, because the *vernae* are normally not distinguishable from the imported slaves, of whom only a limited number explicitly state origins.[33] No doubt the age-range at which slaves were brought to Rome also covered a wider spectrum than that of the soldiers. This age-range was no doubt also slanted towards the younger ages of the spectrum. We know that slaves could be and were purchased at younger ages as well, and it therefore seems likely that in the case of slaves we should also find significant numbers of children in the 0–9 age-group. At the same time, it seems likely that beyond

---

[32] Likewise Ricci (2005) 30, who discusses the relative lack of children in migrant inscriptions, and suggests that the most likely explanation is that people moved to Rome without children.

[33] e.g. *A.E.* (1916) 57 for an Alexandrian slave dead at 23.

age 40 the value of slaves decreased, and sales and imports of older slaves on a significant scale seem much less likely. Again, the preference will have been for the younger age-groups, although this time the group will have included children as well.

To sum up: although the ages at which migrants came to Rome cannot be determined with precision, everything suggests they were predominantly young adults aged 15–30. Somewhat different characteristics apply to the three groups. Soldiers show a much narrower range of ages at recruitment, civilians cover the full range, and slaves probably exceeded the predicted age-limits. Taken together, the ages still conform to the model, though the presence of somewhat older children and sub-adults is larger than one would expect on the basis of the model alone.

Next, sex ratios of immigrants. The sex ratios in the isotopic evidence show biases in favour of men. Hin, with all due caution, analysed the sex ratio in the three isotopic samples from Isola Sacra, Ostia, and Casal Bertone and Castellaccio Europarco near Rome together, finding eighteen males, twelve females, and ten adults of unknown gender.[34] Not too much can be inferred from this, however. Even if one is allowed to lump the three samples together, the resulting totals remain extremely small, and given the difficulties in determining gender, the category of unknowns remains rather large. More-over, the evidence should be corrected for the gender bias in the samples as a whole.[35] What these and other isotopic studies suggest in a more general sense, however, is that there were usually also some women who migrated.[36]

For obvious reasons, the sex ratio of soldiers is not very interesting: the group consisted solely of males. The actual figures depend somewhat on demarcations: as we will see, some soldiers married imported brides, and these might, with some justice, be considered to have belonged to the military population[37]—also because it is becoming increasingly clear that elsewhere in the empire soldiers could be accompanied by wives and families.[38] But given the limited number of marriages of soldiers stationed in Rome, even if

---

[34] Hin (2013) 235.

[35] For Casal Bertone, see also Catalano et al. (2013) 8–9: there are slightly more than twice as many men than women in the necropolis, whereas the average of all their sites around Rome is only 1.13.

[36] Leach et al. (2010) for the general picture. I take it that the absence of female migrants in some samples is due to chance, particular circumstances, or small sample size. Dupras and Schwarcz (2001) found in the Dakleh Oasis in Egypt no female and two male migrants on a sample of 109 individuals (of which 26 males, 37 females, and 46 infants and juveniles). Leach et al. (2009) found in Roman York three male migrants and one migrant of uncertain sex in a sample of fifty individuals.

[37] e.g. *C.I.L.* 6.2734, for a Thracian wife of a *beneficarius*. It should be noted that Noy (2000) has listed in his epigraphical appendix such wives of soldiers in the civilian, not the military, category.

[38] Foubert (2013) 393; Woolf (2013).

these family members are taken into account the gender balance of soldiers remained heavily biased in favour of males.

The epigraphic evidence for civilian immigrants suggests that these individuals were predominantly male. Predominantly, but not solely. In Noy's sample of provincials in Rome, 76.7 per cent are men and 21.0 per cent women (with 2.3 per cent undetermined).[39] The pattern is confirmed by his later Jewish and Christian inscriptions (men 69.2 per cent; women 19.0 per cent; unknown 11.8 per cent resp.).[40] Remarkably similar percentages can be found in samples elsewhere:[41] 18 per cent women in the inscriptions from Gaul;[42] about 20 per cent in the epigrams of the Greek East.[43] Such patterns also seem to underlie many of the smaller data-sets that cannot in themselves claim any statistical relevance: of six civilian migrants attested in Lucania, one is a woman;[44] of sixteen civilian immigrants epigraphically attested in Raetia, none is female.[45]

However, notwithstanding their uniformity, the proportions might be biased. The patterns should be corrected for the heavy gender bias in the inscriptions in general.[46] As is well known, women are heavily underrepresented in the epigraphy. If we take this into account, the dominance of men among the migrants becomes less marked, though it is still visible. For example, in the case of Gaul the 18 per cent of female migrants should be set against the occurrence of 33 per cent of women in general.[47]

The gender of the imported slaves poses the most problems. The sources suggest that urban slavery was dominated by men, but the question is to what extent the sources can be trusted. A relatively small proportion of the slaves working in elite households were women.[48] The best evidence for the gender

---

[39] Noy (2000) 61, table 2 (N = 521). No significant variation between regions can be observed. Noy warns that there is a slight possibility that some male immigrants might have been regarded incorrectly as civilian because they omitted military status, which would lower the male percentage somewhat.

[40] Noy (2000) 62, table 3 (N = 195). No significant variation between regions can be observed.

[41] The Olle di San Cesareo containing what is possibly a late Republican community of Campanian immigrants shows a higher presence of 35% of women, see Shaw (2006) 95, table 4.2 (108 men, 60 women). But its interpretation is very uncertain, and the women need not have been immigrants too. Cf. further, from late antiquity, the small vignette offered in Syn., *Ep.* 4, where one-third of over fifty passengers on a ship are young women.

[42] Frézouls (1989) 129 and Wierschowski (1995) 262–6.

[43] Tacoma and Tybout (forthcoming *a*): 30 women in 146 epigrams.

[44] Simelon (1992) nos. 33–8; the woman occurs as part of a couple in *C.I.L.* 14.1723.

[45] Based on Dietz and Weber (1982) List A, omitting the military examples. In a few inscriptions wives occur, but it remains unclear whether they were locals or immigrants.

[46] The point is ignored by Woolf (2013) 360: 'There is some reason then to trust the indications that repeatedly represent female migrants as outnumbered by male ones by a ratio of roughly 1:4.'

[47] Wierschowski (1995) 262–6.

[48] Treggiari (1973) 248, noting that in Livia's household out of eighty individuals with occupations, only seventeen were women; with on 246 the question 'what *did* they [i.e. the Romans] do with female slaves?' Some more discussion in Treggiari (1979*a*) 189–92.

bias is formed by the inscriptions of the *columbaria*, where only 36 per cent of the names are those of women.[49] The proportions rise somewhat in the cases where owners were themselves women, but even there male servants dominated. In itself there is sufficient reason to regard the *columbaria* as mirroring closely the composition of elite households, but the problem is that the epigraphy in general shows a heavy over-representation of males, and the *columbaria* may to some extent simply replicate the same commemorative practice. This will have mitigated the strong bias in favour of men, yet given the 'closed' nature of the *columbaria*, it remains difficult to think that there is not some accuracy in the gendering, and that this is an expression of higher demand for male slaves.[50] Systems of natural reproduction would in principle almost automatically lead to more or less equal proportions of male and female slaves at birth. If we assume that a large part of the slaves were the product of slave breeding (see Chapter 2, Section 4), a partial explanation to explain gender imbalances may then be sought in boy preference, resulting in female exposure and infanticide.[51] A further explanation is to assume that the male predominance in the *columbarium* inscriptions is caused by the fact that the *imported* slaves were predominantly male.[52] Although it has to be admitted that the arguments remain somewhat fragile, on balance it seems difficult to think of a reverse scenario in which female imports would dominate slave streams and at the same time would produce inverse sex ratios in the *columbarium* inscriptions. With some caution, we may then assume that males dominated among the slave immigrants.

Lastly, there is the question to what extent migrants moved as families. In the isotopic evidence, the case for family migration would have been strengthened if there were clusters of individuals of different ages with exactly the same non-local profile. On the reasonable assumption of viri-local marriage (the practice by which women upon marriage moved into the household of their husband), it can be expected in the case of family migration that children had the same isotopic profile as their fathers. Such evidence has not (yet) been produced.[53]

---

[49] Hasegawa (2005) 65–9 (on slaves and freedmen together).

[50] Harris (1999; 2011) 95–6. Cf. Scheidel (2005) 73.

[51] Treggiari (1979a) 201: 'The question which still worries me most is "If slave-breeding produced roughly equal numbers of boy and girl babies, what did slave owners do with the girls?"' Harris (1999; 2011) 100: 'it is quite possible that the mortality of slave-born girls was much worse than that of slave-born boys.' See also Harris (1980; 2011) for the predominance of male slaves, also because of the exposure of female slaves. The prices of Diocletian's Price Edict suggest female slaves were valued less than male slaves, see Groen-Vallinga and Tacoma (forthcoming).

[52] Harris (1999; 2011) 100: 'Males were probably in the majority both among the external recruits to the slave population (slaves imported across the frontiers) and among the internal recruits (foundlings and the "self-sold"). Male war prisoners are likely to have been more numerous than female.' Mouritsen (2013) 58. Cf. Scheidel (2005) 72–8 for counter-arguments.

[53] Prowse et al. (2007), though it needs to be kept in mind that in Isola Sacra only a small sample of skeletons was used. It seems that physical proximity (enhancing the likelihood that

In the inscriptions there are very few certain cases of immigrants who came to Rome *en famille*.[54] Movement of families is epigraphically a marginal phenomenon, and there is also little in the literary sources that points in another direction. Also in cases not well covered by the sources—temporary migration and migration by the poor—individual movement seems more likely than movement by families. The inscriptions overwhelmingly suggest that the majority of migrants moved individually and not as a family. In fact, there are even cases where it is clear that people who did have a family still went on their own to Rome.[55]

Admittedly, it is possible that inscriptions under-represent family movement. By their very nature, inscriptions focus on individuals. It is a standard pattern in migrant inscriptions that the origin of only one person is mentioned (normally the deceased). If a deceased migrant is commemorated by spouses and/or children who do not explicitly state that they originated from elsewhere, the safer assumption is that the family was only created in Rome, but this may not always be correct.[56]

A similar lack of family movement can be observed in the epigraphically attested mobility patterns elsewhere. In a study of the mobility patterns of 146 epigrams from the Greek East, twenty-four cases *might* concern the migration of families, but many are rather uncertain and allow for multiple interpretations, while there was only one case in which the text of the epigram itself explicitly and unambiguously referred to a migration *en famille*.[57]

Of course, this does not rule out the possibility that *some* migrants came as a family to Rome. In fact, some certainly did. One such case is formed by a couple from North Africa who did (unknown) business in Rome for what seems to be a prolonged period; when they returned, the wife died in Carthage and was buried in their home-town further south. It may be significant that no

individuals would come from family graves) has played no role in the selection, cf. Prowse (forthcoming). Likewise, no positive evidence for family migration was found at the imperial estate in Vagnari in southern Italy, see Prowse et al. (2010).

[54] Noy (2000) 67–75; also for the sources discussed below.

[55] *C.I.L.* 3.9713 for a 22-year-old male who apparently died in Rome but was commemorated at home by his wife in Dalmatia; *C.I.L.* 8.8501 for a 17-year-old man who died as a *notarius* at Rome, but was commemorated at Sitifis by his father, who the next year buried his daughter, aged 8—both clearly had remained at Sitifis. For a vignette from literature, see Min. Fel. 2.1: a visitor entering Rome for business, leaving his wife and children at home.

[56] Cf. outside Rome *C.I.L.* 2.900 from Caesarobriga (mod. Talavera de la Reina, Spain) for a relatively certain case where only the man is styled as immigrant, but his family (mother, sister, maternal uncle, wife, son) probably migrated with him. The case of Augustine serves as a warning. When Augustine moved around the Roman world of late antiquity, he did so as an unmarried male. But he did have a concubine and a son, who accompanied him. See Tacoma (forthcoming *c*).

[57] *S.G.O.* 18/01/16. See Tacoma and Tybout (forthcoming *a*). Among the twenty-three other possible cases, two involve movement to Rome: *S.G.O.* 08/01/36 and poss. 10/02/32.

children were mentioned on their grave monument.[58] A somewhat similar case is presented by a commemoration set up in Rome for a woman who was praised for having followed her husband abroad.[59] There are also some indications of movement by families with children. In inscriptions found in Rome where both parents and children are said to originate from outside the city, it is almost certain that the family had moved as a unit to Rome.[60] Likewise, cases in which parents occur next to a child who is stated to have been born elsewhere may also be explained by family movement.[61] However, such relatively certain cases are rare, and in a number of others that hint at movement *en famille*, alternative interpretations cannot be excluded: a marriage may have been concluded after arrival in Rome,[62] family members may have reunited later,[63] or relatives who appear in migrant inscriptions may simply have travelled to Rome to bury their children.[64] That such alternative

---

[58] *C.I.L.* 8.152, for the mausoleum of Urbanilla, who is described as *comes negotiorum*, with Hamdoune (2006) no. 8. Cf. *C.I.L.* 14.1723 from Ostia, in which a couple from Lucania occurs; see Simelon (1992) nos. 33 and 38. For another trading couple, buried in York, he from Gaul, she from Sardinia, see *R.I.B.* 1.678 and 1.687, with Foubert (2013) 393 n. 11. Somewhat similar is *C.I.L.* 13.1988, an epitaph in Lyon set up by a husband from Trier for his wife from Vienne; the son that is mentioned in the text may have been born after the move to Lyon. Cf. Tozzi (2014).

[59] *C.I.L.* 6.17690.

[60] *A.E.* (1992) 154 (father, mother, and son all originating from Hispania; the son is at least 22 years old).

[61] *A.E.* (1992) 155 for a father, mother, and a son who is from Hispania. As this is a slave family (with the mother possibly a freedwoman), it is likely that the family was as a whole enslaved in Hispania and brought to Rome. Alternatively, if *natio* could also be applied to second-generation migrants, the slave marriage took place in Rome and the inscription has no bearing on the present discussion; *C.I.L.* 6.24162 for a father, mother, and a young son from Hispania; *C.I.L.* 6.27441 for a father, mother, and a young son from Cantabria in Spain; *C.I.L.* 6.20012 for a dedication for a father by a son who describes himself as *Liburnus*, Liburnian, i.e. from the Dalmatian coast; *C.I.L.* 6.29694 for a father who builds a grave for himself and his son, who is *legatus Bosporanorum*—the grave and the fact that both have Roman citizenship plead in favour of permanent settlement in Rome rather than a short-term embassy/business trip; *I.G.U.R.* 2.326, in which a father commemorates a son from Laodicea, dead at 9; *I.G.U.R.* 2.508, in which a father commemorates a son from Crete, dead at 24; *I.G.U.R.* 2.610, where a mother commemorates her son from Alexandria, dead at 26; *N.S.A.* (1916) 109 for a father who commemorates his son from Cologne.

[62] *C.I.L.* 6.1625a, testifying possibly to movement together by a couple from Trier, but the marriage might also have occurred afterwards, with a spouse from the same region; *A.E.* (1979) 78 for two hostages (*obses*) from Parthia who built a tomb for themselves and their daughter— possibly the husband and wife had been brought to Rome as a couple; *C.I.L.* 6.21569, for a dedication by a husband for his wife, deceased at 19. At least one of them, and possibly both, were from Spain. Given the young age of the wife, it is possible that they married before coming to Rome; *C.I.L.* 6.34466, for dedication by a Phrygian for his 'brother'; the monument is also for his wife, who may or may not also originate from Phrygia, and may have emigrated together with the dedicator to Rome.

[63] In the cases discussed above in which one rather than two parents commemorate or are commemorated by a child, this is in fact a serious possibility.

[64] *C.I.L.* 6.3303 with the comments of Speidel (1994*b*) no. 345. In such cases obviously proximity will have mattered, but see Tybout (forthcoming) for travel over substantial distances to bury dead relatives. See also Mart., *Epig.* 9.30 for a woman bringing the ashes of her deceased

explanations have some force is clear from those cases where soldiers commemorate or are commemorated by parents or other relatives.[65] Although we know surprisingly little about actual processes of recruitment, it seems most unlikely that potential soldiers moved with their families to the place of destination,[66] and they were normally too young to be married already when they enlisted.

There is no noticeable difference in the lack of family movement between servile, civilian, and military migrants. Slaves could be moved in groups, as chattel, but normally not as part of a family. Splitting up of families upon enslavement was in fact part of the dehumanizing process. Nevertheless, contrary to what one would expect, some of the cases of possible family movement seem to concern slaves rather than freeborn families.[67]

However, rather than movement of complete families at one point in time, Noy has pointed to the possibility of family reunion: first one person who would go to Rome, who would be followed by other family members. Such a scenario would suggest family networks of migration. The epigraphy shows among commemorators of migrants a significant number of brothers, to a much smaller extent also sisters, and parents (either alone or together).[68] The major problem for the argument is that we are dependent on patterns of commemoration. In almost all attested cases there exists a serious possibility that family members only came over for the burial and commemoration of their relatives. It is, in fact, becoming increasingly clear that people could travel for hundreds of kilometres to repatriate the remains of their beloved

husband back from Cappadocia to Rome; it is unclear whether she had accompanied him or came over to receive his ashes.

[65] *C.I.L.* 6.3236, for an *eques singularis* from Dacia who is described as *nepos*, nephew, by at least one of the two male dedicators; *C.I.L.* 6.2714, for a dedication by a mother for her two soldier sons; if the sons died at the same time (which seems likely), they enlisted at different moments, suggesting they did not come together to Rome; *C.I.L.* 6.36324, a father for his son, *natione Frisao*, with *C.I.L.* 6.36325, in which the father of 36324 also erects an inscription for someone else who comes from a different region. Though this is not explicitly stated in the text, both the son and the other person commemorated may be soldiers.

[66] For recruits coming to Italy on their own, see *B.G.U.* 2.423, *P.Mich.* 8.490, and 491, all concerning the fleet at Misenum. Note, however, that in the papyri the liberal use of kinship terminology hinders the analysis, see e.g. *P.Mich.* 8.487, in which the writer upon his arrival in Rome finds his 'brother' departed. Cf. for a presumably highly exceptional story *Sent. Hadr.* case no. 12, with Lewis (1991) 274, in which a father petitions the emperor to be allowed to accompany his two sons who have enlisted in the army so that they may not do something stupid; he is even prepared to enlist as their servant. He is made a centurion over his sons instead. The case need not necessarily refer to Rome. Some further discussion in Noy (2010*b*).

[67] *A.E.* (1992) 155; *C.I.L.* 6.13328, for two brothers from Madauros and a mother from Theveste; the latter might have been married to a man from Madauros before the family moved to Rome. The fact that at least one of the sons is an imperial slave and the mother is freeborn (or freed, but in that case not an imperial *liberta*) may perhaps be explained by voluntary enslavement rather than that the whole family was enslaved in Africa.

[68] Noy (2000) 67–75. Cf. *R.I.B.* 1.184 for a fragmentary funerary inscription for a man, possibly an imperial freedman, commemorated by his *soror*, both *domo Roma*.

ones, and the evidence suggests strongly that such practices were not confined to the upper strata of society.[69] Some caution is therefore needed. The options are not mutually exclusive, and the epigraphy fits both.

In terms of demographic profile, the evidence is congruent with the expectations of the model. In fact, the profile of immigrants is relatively uniform and the differences in the demographic composition between free civilians, slaves, and soldiers seem relatively small. Mostly we are dealing with young adult males. The soldiers conform completely to the profile predicted by the model, but in view of what we know about military service this can hardly be surprising. In the case of free civilians, the ages at which immigrants came to Rome are more varied and partly also on the low side of the predicted range, and somewhat more women than expected seem to be present. What is perhaps most remarkable is that the profile of slaves fits relatively well with that of the other immigrants.

4. THE MARRIAGE MARKET

If the bulk of the immigrants had roughly the same demographic profile, with a predominance of young adult males, the structure of the urban population of Rome as a whole will have become imbalanced. The effects might have been mitigated somewhat if the people moving out of Rome also had the same demographic profile. But it seems rather unlikely that counter-streams completely compensated for the imbalances produced by immigration. A highly skewed sex ratio will have been the result, and this raises questions about the way the marriage market functioned. De Vries argued, with regard to the early modern period, that in cases where there was an excess of men (due to the presence of male migrants), all women 'had' to marry, and immigrant men often turned to widows.[70] This is, of course, just one scenario out of many possible options, and we need to investigate what the situation in Rome was.

Imbalances in the sex ratio will have created friction on the marriage market. Demographers of the Roman world assume that marriage was universal: under normal conditions everyone would be married at some point in his or her life. Whether this marriage was officially recognized (as a Roman *conubium* marriage) or not (for example, as a slave *contubernium* partnership) does not matter for our purposes. If we assume that in the Roman world men normally married between the ages of 20 and 30 and the age of entrance into Rome of male immigrants normally was between *c.*12 and 30, marriage would at some point inevitably become an issue.

---

[69] Tybout (forthcoming).   [70] De Vries (1984) 196.

Friction on the marriage market through a shortage of marriageable women might have led to a number of responses, not mutually exclusive. Firstly, it might have led to an adaptation of marital ages, with women marrying earlier and men delaying their marriage, thereby widening the age-gap between spouses. Secondly, there is a possibility that some men never married (contrary to the assumption of universal marriage). Thirdly, the lack of available marriage partners might have forced migrants to return home, where a larger pool of women would remain available.

In itself there is an abundance of evidence that marriage was common in Rome. A quick perusal of inscriptions suffices to show that marriage was a routine phenomenon. The survey by Saller and Shaw of commemorators showed that in the city of Rome members of the nuclear family were the primary commemorators, just as elsewhere in the empire.[71] We can safely assume that in Rome marriage was a societal norm as much as it was anywhere else in the Roman world.

There is also much evidence for marriage among migrants of various sorts.[72] In some cases it is not marriage itself that is attested, but the presence of children that tells of marriages (or unions). Noy's analysis of patterns of commemoration shows that marriages are frequently attested among the provincial civilian and military immigrants. In total, 110 marriages are attested directly or indirectly because the deceased was commemorated by spouses or children.[73]

That marriage was common both among the general population and among Rome's immigrants is thus not in doubt. The more difficult point is to establish to what extent marriage was truly universal in Rome. Of course, the majority of the population married, but did they all?

Evidence for singlehood among the voluntary immigrants is difficult to find, but it is also difficult to think of a way to detect such singles. In itself, it seems sensible to assume that some of the poorer immigrants that came to Rome were not particularly well positioned to find a spouse, also because of their precarious ability to sustain a livelihood, but the argument quickly becomes circular.

The wide availability of burial associations in the city has been adduced as indirect evidence for the relative absence of family relations among the population of Rome. They compensated for lack of kin. Strictly speaking, such

---

[71] Saller and Shaw (1984).

[72] e.g. *A.E.* (1979) 78, for Parthian hostages who built a tomb for themselves, their daughter, and their descendants; *A.E.* (1992) 154 for a father, mother, and two children from mod. Portugal; *C.I.L.* 6.1625a, for a couple from Trier; *C.I.L.* 6.21569, for a couple, at least one of whom came from mod. Spain; *C.I.L.* 6.24162, for a couple whose son is said to be *Hispanus*; the parents may have come from the same area; *C.I.L.* 6.34466, for a dedication by a Phrygian for his 'brother'; the monument is also for his wife.

[73] Noy (2000) 69, table 7 and 72–3, table 8.

an argument is not completely correct. Burial associations primarily provided a savings mechanism to meet the cost of burial, independent of the question whether one had a family or not. Membership did not exclude the possibility that families were involved. Although the burial clubs thus do not necessarily imply lack of family relations, the associations could still offer compensation for those who lacked conjugal companions. The fact that they seem to be male dominated reinforces the picture.[74]

For soldiers the situation is somewhat clearer. From the time of Augustus soldiers were subject to a legal ban on marriage during active service. In Rome the ban was enforced more strictly than elsewhere, and it was only from the third century onwards that soldiers in Rome started to marry in larger numbers.[75] Although service in Rome was shorter than elsewhere, soldiers might still be well past the normal age of marriage before they would be discharged. It is therefore conceivable (though it certainly does not directly follow) that some soldiers never married at all. In cases where older veterans were commemorated by (former) comrades rather than by wives or children, it is possible that these are among such bachelors (though other explanations cannot be ruled out, such as a wife having died earlier).[76] However, on general grounds it seems unlikely that there were many such unmarried veterans. The dynamics were rather different, since there would be many reasons to enter a marriage at the end of the period of service—it should not be forgotten that soldiers stationed in Rome belonged to elite troops, and because of their relatively high status and wealth will have been attractive marriage partners. And many left Rome anyway.

A group that is more likely to include singles is that of slaves. Although a slave union was also beneficial to the master, as any offspring would be of servile status, the possibility of entering into stable relationships was likely to have been subject to the control of the owners.[77] Although we do not know of fixed rules, it seems possible that there was a tendency to confine such unions to the slave *familia* of the own household. If so, it will have imposed severe restrictions on the pool of available partners.[78] There is therefore a distinct possibility that some slaves never found a partner. Although it remains uncertain whether the sex ratio of the slave population was as skewed as the inscriptions from the *columbaria* suggest, it is likely that this type of

---

[74] Hopkins (1983) 213–14. Hasegawa (2005) 85; Perry (2011) 507 with further refs.; see Chapter 7, Section 5 for further discussion of associations.

[75] Phang (2001).

[76] e.g. *C.I.L.* 6.3311 = *Terme* 6.52 for a veteran *eques singularis* from Cologne commemorated in Rome by two male heirs who were likely fellow soldiers, while two of his *liberti* took care of the erection of the stele.

[77] Likewise Mouritsen (2011) 145.

[78] Cf. Plin., *Ep.* 8.16 and Sen., *Ep.* 47.14 on the *familia* as the basic social unit for his slaves. Flory (1978) for slave marriages in elite households.

singlehood will primarily have concerned male slaves. In a system of slave breeding, the pressure on female slaves to produce children will after all have been high.

There are thus some hints that marriage may not have been completely universal in Rome. These indications locate singlehood primarily among men, not among women. It is harder to state the extent to which singlehood could especially be found among immigrants, though it is to be noted that the two groups most likely to have contained singles, consisted partly (slaves) or wholly (soldiers) of immigrants.

Rather than complete avoidance of marriage, there may have been some adjustment in marital ages: delays for men, and an acceleration of female marriage at younger ages. In a society in which marriage was at least ideologically the norm, it is to be expected that such adjustments were commoner than complete avoidance of marriage.

One way to approach the question whether ages at marriage were adapted is to look at the exactly recorded ages at marriage found in inscriptions. As is well known, these data show that among the inscription-erecting population of Rome women married early, men married late, and that the age-gap between husband and wife was considerable.[79] A similar pattern emerges from the analyses by Saller and Shaw of shifts in commemoration. Shifts from parents to spouses as commemorators show indirectly the approximate age at which men and women started to marry. This method is less precise, but it uses many more sources than the inscriptions in which age at marriage is stated with exactitude. Again, the shifts in Rome occurred for women relatively early and for men relatively late.[80]

However, it is more difficult to determine whether in Rome marriage of women was earlier and that of men later, and whether the age-gap was wider than elsewhere in the Roman world. This has to some extent to do with the nature of the sources, but also with the question how the expectations are formulated: do we expect other cities to have a different but coherent marital profile? The countryside remains outside our field of vision, and it may be here that the largest differences with Rome occurred.

Data from elsewhere in the Roman world allow for an argument that Rome's marital ages were adjusted, though they do not offer absolute proof. The data on exact age at marriage stem to a large extent from Rome. The data from outside Rome are much fewer (and geographically also much more widely dispersed); hence a comparison is difficult.[81] A more promising line is found in the research on shifts of commemoration from parents to spouses. According to Shaw, the ages in Rome were different from the population

---

[79] Harkness (1896); Hopkins (1964/5); Shaw (1987); Lelis, Percy, and Verstraete (2003); Hin (2013) 175–9.

[80] Saller (1987); Shaw (1987).   [81] Hopkins (1964/5).

elsewhere in the Latin West. This would indeed suggest that marital ages in Rome were adjusted downwards in the case of women and upwards in the case of men.[82]

The second question is whether the patterns applied to the whole population or to the migrants only. Both scenarios are certainly feasible. There is, in fact, significant comparative evidence that migration increased the age-gap between husbands and wives.[83] In the case of voluntary migrants, in view of the exiguous nature of the data it is impossible to make a distinction in the age at marriage between the immigrants and the Rome-born population. Far too few exact migrants' ages at marriages are preserved to allow for a serious analysis of migrant marriage patterns.[84] The same applies to slave marriages, where there is an additional difficulty that normally no distinction is made in the sources between imported slaves and *vernae*.

Soldiers' marriages are much better documented. The age patterns from Rome fit with those found elsewhere among soldiers in the empire: male marriage occurred late.[85] It has been observed that in Rome the marriage ban seems to have been more strictly enforced than among other troops. Although the incidence of marriage increased over time, the process was slower than elsewhere, and it was only in the third century that soldiers stationed in Rome started to marry in significant numbers.[86] Some marriages were only concluded after discharge; consequently, we find dedications by veterans for relatively young wives.[87] But especially in the third century many other marriages were clearly concluded during service—as the commemorations by wives for soldiers who died in service testify. The ages of death of such soldiers provide a *terminus ante quem* for male marriage among soldiers. In the case of the *equites singulares*, the earliest age of commemoration of a married *eques singularis* is 28, and most ages are significantly higher, well above 30. In some of these cases there are young children mentioned as well, suggesting that the marriage had been concluded recently. Likewise, an analysis by Sarah Phang of shifts in patterns of commemoration among praetorians showed that when, in the third century, praetorians started to

---

[82] Shaw (1987). [83] Erdkamp (2008) 434 with n. 59.

[84] e.g. *C.I.L.* 3.9713, for a 22-year-old male who apparently died in Rome, commemorated at home by his wife, and thus already married—though probably not in Rome; *I.G.U.R.* 3.1161, for a woman from Laconia, dead at 14, already married; *C.I.L.* 6.21569, for a dedication by a husband for his wife, deceased at 19, and thus married at or before that age.

[85] Phang (2001) 142–96.

[86] Speidel (1994b) 22; Phang (2001) 159–64. *C.I.L.* 6.3194 = Speidel (1994b) no. 318 is the only possible case of a marriage prior to AD 193 among the *equites singulares*. For a *coniunx* from Aquitania of a praetorian in active service see *C.I.L.* 6.2497, but the inscription is undated.

[87] *C.I.L.* 6.37271, for a woman from Pannonia, dead at 19, commemorated by her veteran husband. Given the relatively young age of the deceased wife, if the marriage was not concluded after discharge it will have been concluded at the end of the term as soldier; *C.I.L.* 6.3454, for a veteran who commemorates his wife from Aquincum, dead at 23, and his son, dead at 2.

marry in significant numbers, most of them did not marry before the age of 30, and none before 20; in consequence, she opts for marriage in the mid- to late thirties as the norm,[88] well beyond the already late marriage of civilian males.

Differences in the ages at marriage of immigrants are thus only directly observable in the case of soldiers. All other things being equal, the delayed marriage of soldiers would still imply that male marriage of immigrants would be pushed backwards, but it is clear that the late soldier's marriage had more to do with the fact that they were soldiers than with the fact that they were immigrants. Moreover, soldiers constituted a relatively small group compared to all immigrants; hence the effects would only be small. Among servile and civilian immigrants, adjustments of marital ages are impossible to establish. This does not rule out that they occurred, but it is also possible that immigrant patterns in general did not differ greatly from those of the Rome-born population.

A further question still needs to be answered. In those cases where immigrants married, where did they find their spouses? If we start from the perspective of male immigrants, a series of possibilities might be envisaged. One is that immigrants married women born in Rome, and thus competed with Rome-born males for partners from the same pool. Another is that they married immigrant women who came from other parts of the empire than they did themselves. This would imply that immigrants *as a group* created a second pool. Another is that they married women from their own region. Another is that they took manumitted female slaves as wives. Obviously these patterns are not mutually exclusive: we may find a mixture of all of them. It also needs to be taken into account that the marriage market might have functioned differently for different groups of immigrants.

The patterns of the soldiers are the best-known, and therefore form the natural starting point. As we saw, soldiers' marriages were delayed: soldiers married late, perhaps some did not marry at all, and many did so only after discharge, when it was officially allowed. When they married, soldiers often married within the soldier community, that is, with female relatives of other soldiers.[89] These may or may not have originated from the same region.[90] It is also possible that soldiers often obtained their wives by manumitting their

---

[88] Phang (2001) 153, with tables 10–12: in the third century, out of forty-two commemorations by wives or children, only two concern praetorians aged between 20 and 29. Earlier the proportions are slightly different, but that seems to be due to the small numbers involved: in the first century one out of two, in the second century three out of seventeen. For the general pattern of commemorative shifts in all military epitaphs, see Phang (2001) 170, table 2: even in the age-bracket 30–5 the birth family still dominates; only from 35–9 onwards do wives and children take over.

[89] Phang (2001) 224–8 (mainly discussing the evidence from Egypt).

[90] Cf. *C.I.L.* 13.1893 for a husband and wife both originating from Rome, the wife buried by her husband in Lyon; *C.I.L.* 6.2497 for a wife from Convena, Aquitania, but the origin of the praetorian soldier is unknown. Noy (2000) 71–2 has pointed out that another possible

own slaves. Among praetorians, Phang found 7 per cent of wives who were explicitly identified as slaves who were manumitted by their owners, and more may have been hidden under *duo nomina*.[91] In the cases where soldiers or veterans married their own slaves, it should still be taken into account that buying such a slave was not a particularly cheap option.[92] The fact that relatively few slaves are mentioned in the epitaphs of the rank-and-file is surely relevant.

Female slaves who were manumitted for marriage had probably little option but to obey their masters' wishes, and every incentive to do so. In other cases, however, freedwomen married freedmen, or, more probably, converted already existing unions into marriage. It cannot be determined to what extent a shared origin played a role in finding a spouse, but there can be little doubt that servile status rather than ethnicity was the primary factor. In addition, there was a high likelihood that spouses originated from the same household. Given the mixed composition of the slave households (both Rome-born and immigrant slaves, and slaves with different ethnic origins), the servile marriage market seems to have been open and closed at the same time.

The marriage patterns of free civilian immigrants are least clear. In almost all of the recorded immigrant marriages attested in the funerary epigraphy of Rome, the origin of only one of the spouses is given.[93] This might be interpreted in different ways. One is that the marriage market was open, and that regionalism or immigrant status played no role in finding spouses. However, there is another interpretation that cannot be excluded, namely, that the foreign origin of the second person was implied, or simply not thought important enough to be mentioned. In some cases ethnic names suggest an ethnic origin, usually from the same region as the husband.[94] In the few cases where a wife's origin is stated, it is striking that many of these marriages are concluded with wives from the same region.[95] If marriages were

explanation for the prominence of Greek names of soldier's spouses is that they used Graecized names to replace their foreign ones.

[91] Phang (2001) 193–4: nine out of 132 women married to praetorians. If possible cases are included (women with same nomen as husband, or Greek cognomen), the percentage rises to 35%, but Phang is rightly cautious. The percentages vary significantly between various troops.

[92] Phang (2001) 194: in the provinces about two years' salary for a legionary.

[93] Noy (2000) 71; e.g. *A.E.* (1984) 121 for a woman from Autun commemorated in Rome by her husband.

[94] e.g. *C.I.L.* 6.10781, in which the names of husband and wife suggest that both originated from Egypt.

[95] *A.E.* (1979) 78, for a couple from Parthia; *A.E.* (1992) 154, for a wife from Salacia (mod. Alcacer do Sal, district Setúbal, Portugal), husband from Meidubriga (not localized, perhaps region of Meda, district Guarda, Portugal); *C.I.L.* 6.1625a, both husband and wife from Trier. Cf. *C.I.L.* 14.1723 with Simelon (1992) nos. 33 and 38: a husband buries his deceased wife in Ostia; both come from Lucania (the wife from Potentia, the husband's origin unknown). A contrasting case may perhaps be visible in *I.G.* 14.830, where a certain Laches, a Tyrean resident in Puteoli, is described as son of Preimogenia and Agathopous, which may imply that Laches' father was a

contracted with people from the same region, the implication is that some segmentation in the marriage market occurred, but far too little is known to be certain.

This is the context in which much of the mobility of women should probably be placed. There remains a risk of interpreting all female movement as marriage mobility for the simple reason that it concerned women, but in the cases where more can be inferred, movement in order to marry is at least a distinct possibility.[96] It is surely significant that, in Rome, immigrant women are almost never commemorated by parents but almost invariably in the context of their marriage, by husbands or children.[97] Somewhat paradoxically, the imbalances in the sex ratio thus may have generated marital mobility.

5. RETURN MIGRATION

One other possible response to the skewed sex ratio and to the resulting congestion on the marriage market was that people would be forced out of the city. Male immigrants who were unable to find a bride might have left after some time. This would have produced a pattern of return migration. Such a pattern may not necessarily have been phrased by the participants themselves in terms of the marriage market, and marriage itself may not have been a motive for return. Mobility might rather have been perceived in terms of temporary stays and subsequent return.

As the focus in modern research has been to establish the presence of migrants in Rome itself, return migration has not received the attention it deserves. There is, to be sure, ample evidence that at least some migrants remained in Rome for prolonged periods, and some certainly had the intention to settle there. But did they all? The possibility that much migration was of a temporary nature is often acknowledged but has not been taken fully into account.[98]

Tyrean who had married a Roman woman from Puteoli (note that she was mentioned first, suggesting higher status). Although the distances involved are large, a certain amount of regionalism may still be visible in *C.I.L.* 3.4869 from Virunum, Noricum (mod. St Veit an der Glan, Austria) in which a couple with children appears, he from Rome, she from Aquileia.

[96] Similarly Tacoma and Tybout (forthcoming *a*). Cf. for other possible motives the observations of Foubert (forthcoming).

[97] Noy (2000) 72–3, table 8: 39 out of 50 (78.5%) commemorations are by members of the nuclear family (husband and/or children), against 2 out of 50 (4%) by parents.

[98] Cf. Taylor (2011) 129 for somewhat similar remarks on classical Athens: 'permanent resettlement is not necessarily the best model for fourth-century Athens.' For ancient reflections, see Artemid. 1.36, on dreaming that one's head is turned around, which signifies for those abroad that they will return (but for those who plan to migrate means that obstacles will impede their movement).

As was discussed in Chapter 2, migration historians of other periods have warned that permanent resettlement is just one extreme in a series of migration patterns. Much more irregular patterns have in fact been postulated in some conceptualizations of the functioning of diaspora communities, suggesting that substantial movement between origin and destination could occur. And some of the ten types of migration discussed in Chapter 2 also seem to suggest substantial movement between the place of origin and Rome.

That return migration has been neglected is understandable, given the severe problems of identification. Finding foreigners is one thing, identifying temporary stays and return migration quite another. We normally only see people at the point of their death, and at the place where they died. Every immigrant commemorated at Rome had become a permanent immigrant by definition, but that does not mean that all migration to Rome was intended to be permanent. And if a returned migrant was buried in his home-town, there was simply less chance that an intervening stay somewhere else would have been recorded. Especially, simple gravestones are unlikely to be of help, for there would be no inherent reason to mention a stay elsewhere in a short text. Likewise, isotopic analysis is usually unable to shed light on such return migration: if someone returned to his home region and was buried there, his migrant history would remain chemically invisible.[99]

Once again, it is useful to differentiate. The opposite phenomenon, that of permanent settlement in Rome, can be observed most clearly in the case of slaves. As was discussed in Chapter 2, Section 2, manumission of slaves was frequent, and some of the freedmen had been born outside Rome. One might thus expect significant return migration, yet there is a striking absence of references to slaves moving elsewhere after manumission. For example, in Roman legal discussions of ungrateful freedmen, no mention is made of freedmen who escaped from the obligations to their patrons by moving elsewhere. It remains theoretically possible that some freedmen left the place where they had lived as slaves and subsequently disappeared in the local population, but given the enormous amount of attention paid to slaves, it is hard to see why we do not hear about such a phenomenon had it been significant.[100] It is telling that many freedmen were buried in the *columbaria* of their former masters.

On closer consideration, the absence of return migration among freedmen is easy to understand. After manumission, centripetal forces remained much stronger than centrifugal ones. As we saw, enslavement often occurred within the territory of the Roman Empire. Not infrequently it will have been the result of sale by parents, or of exposure, and often poverty will have been the reason. In such cases there would be little reason to return. Return would also pose practical obstacles—even in those cases where the original family was still alive and could be traced. Within the new household in Rome, social pressures ensured that former slaves remained within the orbit of the house of the former master. In fact there was much that militated against return: social ties to the *patronus*, the possibility of benefiting from his patronage, financial dependency, a long life already spent in the city, the rupture of ties with the original family, and—quite likely a very strong factor—the existence of family ties with slaves who remained within the household.[101]

A more common pattern of mobility after manumission was to be sent out as freedman by the patron on some business venture; the relatively large room for manoeuvre that freedmen had as business agents was reflected by their relatively high degree of geographical mobility. Obviously, such mobility did not constitute return migration, though in cases where such stays were of a more permanent character it could function to some degree as structurally equivalent. The same applies to imperial freedmen who were assigned to places outside Rome. But there was normally an expectation that they would return home after a number of years, and there does not seem any tendency to send freedmen to the places they had originated from. Although the geographical mobility of slaves quite likely increased after manumission, it seems reasonable to assume that the import of slaves essentially entailed a form of permanent immigration, even if they were manumitted after some time.

Soldiers clearly occupy the other part of the spectrum of possibilities. Everything suggests they normally left Rome after discharge, and that their stays were thus temporary.[102] Discharged soldiers were well placed to return; they had received relatively high pay during service, and received additional money and privileges upon discharge. The relative wealth of their grave monuments and the frequent mention of heirs suggest that many of them managed to save some money. Their discharge formed a particular moment in time that forced them to think about the second half of their lives. If they had not married yet they would have good reasons to look for a spouse. If they had already entered into a stable relationship, they still might opt to return home—especially if their brides had come from their own region of origin. The legal rulings about soldiers' marriages at the very least posed no obstacles to returning or moving somewhere else, and in fact seem to have facilitated such moves by elevating the marriage with peregrine wives to *conubium* status.

---

[101] One of the main arguments of Mouritsen (2011), e.g. 146–59, who stresses the continuing relations between freedman and patron, and 152 for evidence for mixed slave/freed families.

[102] In the army as a whole there was a variety of return patterns; see Roselaar (forthcoming) for further discussion and refs.

Geographical horizons had no doubt been widened during their stay in Rome. During their service, the primary point of reference would be the army camp, and here soldiers interacted with others who were recruited from different areas. Even in the case where recruitment was confined to particular parts of the empire, they would still have interacted with men originating from places that could be hundreds of kilometres apart.

Long stays in Rome are likely to have altered the ties between the soldiers and their family at home. Altered, but not severed. Soldiers who served in Rome remained in contact with home.[103] It is well known that many commemorations for soldiers who died in service were made by fellow soldiers; the army units clearly functioned to some extent as surrogate families in a situation in which the birth family lived far away. At the same time, occasionally family members do appear as commemorators on the soldiers' gravestones. They had probably travelled to Rome to see that the deceased received a proper burial. Often this would have involved travel over significant distances. There are also a significant number of grave monuments for soldiers serving in Rome that are found outside Rome. Ricci found 335 such epitaphs, of which 70 per cent seem to have concerned commemorations in the region of origin, and normally in a familial context.[104] The soldiers who were commemorated were still in active service, which implies that under normal circumstances they had died in Rome, or at least not in the region of origin. Their ashes might have returned home, or they received a cenotaph, or the monument was built *inter vivos* (there are some examples of family graves). The practice testifies to an ideology in which the soldier was supposed to return home.[105]

It is impossible to say exactly how many soldiers left Rome after service, but it was certainly a very common practice. The fact that almost all military *diplomata* for soldiers who had served in Rome have been found outside the city might support such an argument. Some veterans stayed in Rome, but the number of attested cases is quite small. In the case of the *equites singulares*, it is known that some remained in service and stayed with the troops.[106] By contrast, outside Rome some 200 inscriptions for veterans have been found, mostly epitaphs. Basing estimates on a comparison of surviving numbers of inscriptions at Rome and outside Rome is hazardous, because there are many factors influencing survival patterns. But the indications all suggest relatively large numbers of returnees. The case of the *equites singulares* is more complicated, because veterans simply disappear from the epigraphic record altogether, but the most likely explanation is that they left Rome and returned to their home regions in the frontier zones which had a less well developed epigraphic tradition.[107]

---

[103] Contacts with home are best visible in the soldiers' letters found in Roman Egypt; see from Italy *B.G.U.* 2.423, *P.Mich.* 8.490, and 491.

[104] Ricci (1994).   [105] Tybout (forthcoming).   [106] Speidel (1994*a*) 93 on *retenti*.

[107] Speidel (1994*a*) 93–4.

We cannot determine proportions with precision, but we can analyse where veterans went who left Rome. It is not surprising that many former soldiers simply returned home. There are a few inscriptions in which veterans mention an origin which coincides with the find spot of the stone, but this is in fact rare, as the mention of *origo* in one's own place of origin would not be particularly meaningful. Much more often, we can trace return migration because in an epitaph the birth family occurs alongside the veteran. Less precise are ono-mastic indications: we find veterans that have names that belong to the region in which the inscription is found.[108]

The best evidence for return migration of soldiers is offered by the military *diplomata*.[109] Over 100 military *diplomata* have been found that pertain to discharged soldiers who were stationed in Rome.[110] The thirty-three cases where both the place of origin has been preserved in the text and the find spot of the *diploma* is known allow an analysis of resettlement patterns.[111] (See Table 4.4) A few have been found in the city of Rome itself. Often (and unsurprisingly) origin and find spot are identical: many of the veterans returned to the place of origin.[112] However, there are only few *diplomata* where origin and find spot are *exactly* identical. More often, the distance between origin and find spot is relatively small. In such cases there are two possible explanations. One is administrative practice: soldiers normally regis-tered a large city as place of origin, but they may have actually come from a village in the surrounding territory; thus, although the stated origin and the find spot of the *diploma* do not coincide exactly, they still may have simply returned to their native village. But it is also possible that small-scale mobility had taken place, within the own region—this is for example more likely in those cases where the find spot of the *diploma* is nearby, but outside the official territory of the stated city of origin. Medium-scale mobility is visible in a significant number of cases. Then there are also a remarkable number of real discrepancies between origin and find spot. In some, veterans settled some-where in Italy. Others concern clear forms of resettlement in another province.

---

[108] Ricci (1994) 22–5.

[109] A good general discussion, summarizing a copious bibliography, in Phang (2001) 53–85.

[110] I have taken as my basis the data up till *R.M.D.* 5, and after some consideration decided not to harvest subsequent publications. Although the number of finds and publications of diplomas has been increasing steadily over the past decades due to the use of metal-detectors, returns are diminishing: they often concern small fragments, often of unknown (or disputed) origin. The chances that they would significantly alter the conclusions are small.

[111] The evidence is not watertight, of course. *Diplomata* are much more easily transported than stone inscriptions. Discharged soldiers may have lost a *diploma* en route, they may have had additional military duties after the diploma was issued, the children or other heirs may have transported the diploma somewhere else after the death of the owner, or they may have been bought (or stolen) by a third party because of the value of the metal. Also, due to illegal excavations, find spots may be incorrectly stated. But the overall patterns can hardly be in doubt.

[112] Lieb (1986) 327, 'Fundorte ausserhalb Italiens entsprechen im engeren oder weiteren Sinne der Herkunft der Entlassenen', is, however, overstated.

Table 4.4. *Diplomata* with known find spot of Roman soldiers with stated origin

	Reference	Date	Stated origin	Unit in Rome: P(raetorian guard) / U(rban) C(ohort) / E(quites) S(ingulares) A(ugusti)	Find spot diploma
1.	*C.I.L.* 16.18	AD 85	Savaria, Pannonia superior (mod. Szombathely, Hungary)	UC	near Sirmium, Pannonia inferior (mod. Sremska Mitrovica, Serbia)
2.	*C.I.L.* 16.21	AD 76	Aquae Statiellae, regio IX Liguria (mod. Acqui Terme, Piemonte)	P/UC	Tomis, Moesia inferior (mod. Constanța, Rumania)
3.	*C.I.L.* 16.25	AD 72?	Clunia, Hispania Tarraconensis (near mod. Coruña del Conde, Spain)	P	Rome (*in alveo Tiberis prope pontem Palatinum*)
4.	*C.I.L.* 16.81	AD 122	Augusta Taurinorum, Regio XI Transpadana (mod. Turin, Piedmonte)	P	Vindonissa (*in castris prope praetorium*?), Germania superior (mod. Windisch, Switzerland)
5.	*C.I.L.* 16.95	AD 148	Nuceria, regio III Bruttium et Lucania (mod. Nocera Inferiore, Campania)	P/UC	Paestum, regio III Bruttium et Lucania (mod. Capaccio, Campania)
6.	*C.I.L.* 16.98	AD 150	Aguntum, Noricum (mod. Lienz, Austria)	P/UC	same as origin
7.	*C.I.L.* 16.124	AD 161 or 166	Teate, regio IV Samnium (mod. Chieti, Abruzzo)	P/UC	Anxanum, regio IV Samnium (mod. Lanciano, Abruzzo)
8.	*C.I.L.* 16.134	AD 194	Faventia, regio VIII Aemilia (mod. Faenza, Emilia-Romagna)	UC	Humagum, regio X Venetia et Histria (mod. Umag, Croatia)
9.	*C.I.L.* 16.137	AD 216	Faventia, regio VIII Aemilia (mod. Faenza, Emilia-Romagna)	UC	same as origin
10.	*C.I.L.* 16.139	AD 221	Trimontium (Philippopolis), Thracia (mod. Plovdiv, Bulgaria)	P	same as origin
11.	*C.I.L.* 16.142	AD 225	Poetovio, Pannonia superior (mod. Ptuj, Slovenia)	P	Aquincum, Pannonia inferior (mod. Budapest, Hungary)
12.	*C.I.L.* 16.143	AD 226	Nicopolis ad Istrum, Moesia inferior (mod. Nikyup, Bulgaria)	P	same as origin

(*continued*)

Table 4.4. Continued

	Reference	Date	Stated origin	Unit in Rome: P(raetorian guard) / U(rban) C(ohort) / E(quites) S(ingulares) A(ugusti)	Find spot diploma
13.	*C.I.L.* 16.144	AD 230	Malva, Dacia (near mod. Reşca, Rumania)	ESA	near Naples, Campania
14.	*C.I.L.* 16.145	233 AD	Acamantia Dorylaeum, prob. Dorylaeum, Phrygia (near mod. Eskişehir, Turkey)	P	mod. Fantanele, Moesia inferior (Rumania)
15.	*C.I.L.* 16.146	AD 237	Serdica, Thrace (mod. Sofia, Bulgaria)	ESA	mod. Prodanovtsi, Thracia (mod. Bulgaria)
16.	*C.I.L.* 16.147	AD 243	(Teanum) Si<d>icinum, regio I Latium et Campania (mod. Teano, Campania)	P	Lugdunum, Gallia Lugdunensis (mod. Lyon, France)
17.	*C.I.L.* 16.151	AD 246	Aelia Mursa, Pannonia inferior (mod. Osijek, Croatia)	P	*in agro Pedemontano*, regio XI Transpadana
18.	*C.I.L.* 16.153	AD 248	Mantua, regio X Venetia et Histria (Mantova, Lombardia)	P	same as origin
19.	*C.I.L.* 16.155	AD 254	Poetovio, Pannonia superior (mod. Ptuj, Slovenia)	P	Industria, regio IX Liguria (mod. Monteu da Po, Liguria)
20.	*C.I.L.* 16.156	AD 298	Sirmium, Pannonia inferior (mod. Sremska Mitrovica, Serbia)	P	Gnathia, regio II, Apulia et Calabria (mod. Egnazia, Apulia)
21.	*C.I.L.* 16.189	AD 224	Philippopolis, Thracia (mod. Plovdiv, Bulgaria)	P	mod. Karlovo, Thracia (near Plovdiv, Bulgaria)
22.	*R.M.D.* 1.75	AD 222	Serdica, Thrace (mod. Sofia, Bulgaria)	P(/UC?)	mod. Planinica (within territory of Serdica)
23.	*R.M.D.* 1.76	AD 224	Pautalia, Thracia (mod. Kyustendil Bulgaria)	P	mod. Leshko (within territory of Pautalia)
24.	*R.M.D.* 1.77	AD 236	Serdica, Thracia (mod. Sofia, Bulgaria)	P	mod. Sohace, Moesia inferior (northwestern Bulgaria)
25.	*R.M.D.* 1.78	AD 306	[Italy]	P	mod. Campagnatico, regio VII Etruria (mod. Tuscany)

26.	*R.M.D.* 2.132	AD 228	Nicopolis ad Istrum, Moesia inferior (mod. Nikyup, Bulgaria)	P	Butovo, near Nicopolis ad Istrum
27.	*R.M.D.* 2.135	AD 223/235	Savaria?, Pannonia superior (currently Szombathely, Hungary)	P	mod. Niederleis, Pannonia superior (Austria)
28.	*R.M.D.* 3.163	AD 90/140?	Interamna (Nahars), Regio VI Umbria (mod. Terni, Umbria)	P	near mod. Pegognaga, regio X Venetia et Histria (Lombardia)
29.	*R.M.D.* 3.188	AD 206	Poetovio, Pannonia superior (mod. Ptuj, Slovenia)	P	Brigetio, Pannonia superior (mod. Acs, Hungary)
30.	*R.M.D.* 4.303	AD 206	Mogentiana (location unknown, poss. eastern Pannonia superior)	P	mod. Inotapuszta, Pannonia inferior (Hungary)
31.	*R.M.D.* 5.453	AD 205	Serdica, Thrace (mod. Sofia, Bulgaria)	ESA	Moesia inferior (mod. Pelovo/Iskar, Bulgaria)
32.	*R.M.D.* 5.454	AD 207	Antioch, Syria	ESA	Moesia inferior (mod. Pelovo/Iskar, Bulgaria)
33.	*R.M.D.* 5.473	AD 247	Serdica, Thrace (mod. Sofia, Bulgaria)	P	Moesia inferior (mod. Pelovo/Iskar, Bulgaria)

If the *diplomata* are anything to go by, they suggest that return to the place of origin was only one of several options available.

The most interesting cases are those where soldiers did not return home. Individual decisions are beyond recovery, but a plausible general explanation is intermarriage between military families, in which co-*milites* served as brokers. Arrangements would have been made in Rome, at the end of the term of service. As sisters of fellow soldiers would normally be too old to serve as brides (and would have been married long ago), choices must have been made in the wider family. The veteran would then move to the new destination and set up a household near the house of his wife's family.

Such a pattern would be consistent with what we know about the cases in which soldiers married during service. In such cases, it is also likely that co-*milites* served as brokers, and that women from their family were married to fellow soldiers. One important clue about marital patterns is that roughly 30 per cent of gravestones for soldiers who died during service but were commemorated outside Rome were erected elsewhere than in their region of origin.[113]

The hardest part is to determine the frequency with which free civilians returned home or elsewhere after a stay in Rome, but it seems likely that their patterns should be placed somewhere between the extremes posited by slaves and soldiers. In contrast to manumitted slaves and soldiers, there was no particular moment in time that forced them to think about the rest of their lives. Decision-making was a fussier process, and probably much more embedded in wider family considerations.

Some migrants clearly intended to stay in the city. There are some examples of people who built a tomb *inter vivos*.[114] Also, in those cases where we find epitaphs for migrants who reached old age, we can be relatively sure that their stay in Rome had been intended to be permanent.

We can offer a counterweight to these permanent stays. As we saw in Chapter 2, Section 2, there were many persons who came to Rome with the intention of returning home. Ambassadors, tourists, athletes, students, teachers, doctors—some remained for prolonged periods in the city, but many left again after some time. Likewise, itinerant traders might return home at some point in their life. In itself there is nothing surprising about the phenomenon, but it is of some relevance for the return patterns of those people who stayed for a prolonged period in Rome and then decided to leave the city. Such patterns of temporary stays in Rome paved the way, or created a template, for others who stayed for longer periods in the city. Leaving the city was not exactly something unheard of.

---

[113] Ricci (1994) 10–11 with n. 2.   [114] For references see Chapter 2, Section 1.

As most of the sources consist of epitaphs, evidence for such return patterns is usually not found in Rome itself.[115] There are somewhat more texts from the provinces that mention temporary stays in Rome. For example, among the epigrams of the Greek East we find an architect from Mylassa who had worked in Rome; an ambassador to Rome from Kyme; someone who died in Rome while being trained there as a doctor, commemorated by his nurse at home in Hadrianoi; and someone who was a member of a collegium of *summarudes* in Rome.[116] It is not always clear whether Rome was merely a transit station, or had been the place where the migrant had stayed a number of years, but it seems likely that in such cases there was an intention to stay only temporarily and then return home.

As commemorations make clear, in the case of civilians too contacts with the homeland were not severed. Sometimes people travelled to Rome to erect a gravestone for a deceased relative. In other cases they erected gravestones at home for those who died in Rome, sometimes as cenotaphs, sometimes with the ashes that were transported back. It is especially this funerary ideology that suggests that returning was a normal phenomenon, if not in life, then in death.[117]

The evidence presented in Table 4.3 for the age structure of provincial migrants who died in Rome is in line with the idea that a substantial part of them returned home. Out of 154 recorded ages at death, only 10 per cent concerns people above 50, and another 8 per cent concerns the age-group 40–50.[118] All others died earlier. Obviously there are biases at work: we may, perhaps, suppose that younger persons had a higher chance of being recorded. Foreign origin may also have been mentioned more frequently at the early stages of a person's stay in Rome. It is, however, remarkable that the strong decline in numbers after age 40 follows the same pattern as that of soldiers, who are known to have left Rome in large numbers. At the same time, the 30–9 age-group figures relatively largely in commemorations of migrants, suggesting prolonged stays for many. Moreover, somewhat differently from the case of the soldiers, the later age-groups (over 40) are still present, though in relatively small numbers.

---

[115] Cf. from Rome itself *C.I.L.* 6.17690, in which a woman is praised for having followed her husband *in provinciam*; the fact that the stone was set up in Rome implies return migration. What the scenario is behind *I.L.L.R.P.* 826, a dedication found in Ithaka, Greece, remains unclear. This text states that an *Epaphroditus Novi ung(u)entarius de sacra via hic fuit* in 35 BC. The mentioning of the *sacra via* and the fact that the text was written in Latin suggest strongly Epaphroditus came from Rome. Perhaps a mere visit?

[116] Tacoma and Tybout (forthcoming *a*), referring to *S.G.O.* 01/15/03 (architect); 05/03/03 (ambassador); 08/08/06 (doctor); 15/02/03 (member of collegium of *summarudes*).

[117] Tybout (forthcoming); e.g. *S.G.O.* 04/16/01 (a cenotaph commemorating in Tabala, Lydia, a girl who went to Rome to work at the imperial court).

[118] Noy (2000) 64–5 for data and discussion; the argument about return migration is mine.

As regards return migration, it seems clear that slaves and soldiers present two extremes in the spectrum of possibilities: in the former case migration to Rome normally meant permanent resettlement; in the latter, it meant a temporary stay for the duration of service. The patterns of free civilians should in all likelihood be located somewhere between these extremes. It seems likely that many free immigrants also returned home after a longer or shorter stay, but there is also some evidence for permanent resettlement. For obvious reasons, the patterns are likely to show much more variation. That a substantial part of them returned cannot be in doubt, however.

6. VARIATION AND SIMILARITY

In general, the patterns seem to follow those predicted by the model sketched in Section 2. Immigrants were mostly individuals rather than families. They were mainly young adults, and mainly male. Female mobility primarily occurred in the context of marriage.

But there are also some refinements to be made. The group of sub-adults seems relatively large—the age composition may have been more slanted towards the younger ages than the model may in itself suggest. Female mobility appears to have been relatively large. Although the most likely context is that of marital mobility, the volume is higher than one would perhaps expect on *a priori* grounds. Migration of families seems a relatively unimportant phenomenon, though family reunion remains a possibility. There was a significant degree of return migration. Leaving Rome may also have meant going somewhere else than the place of origin: not all movement constituted return migration in the strict sense of the word.

Distinguishing between military, slave, and voluntary immigrants adds some nuance to the model and allows the spectrum of possibilities to be charted without inhibiting the possibility for generalization. It is likely that differences existed between the groups in terms of age composition, sex ratio, and patterns of return. Wittgenstein's famous notion of family resemblances is helpful: rather than a fixed set of shared characteristics, the groups share a series of overlapping similarities.

Continuing the crude calculation offered in the previous chapters, we may model the average properties of the three groups as shown in Table 4.5.

Once again, it should be emphasized that the outcome is simply a consequence of the input, and does not in itself prove anything. All figures are open to emendation. Although some of the figures are relatively certain, others are hardly more than guesses. However, the resulting totals do help to make the argument explicit. Following the logic of the calculation, we can assume that most migrants were male and young, and that return migration was substantial.

Table 4.5. A model of demographic properties of the three immigrant groups

	% of all immigrants	% of males	Average age at entrance	% of return migration
Imported slaves	50	80	15	5
Voluntary migrants	40	70	18	50
Military migrants	10	90	20	95
Total	100	77	16.7	64

At the same time, the fact that the findings for the three groups are similar (though not the same) is in itself remarkable. Especially in the case of slaves, it was certainly not self-evident that the predictions of the model applied, since enslavement had in itself little to do with the dynamics of family formation. Nevertheless, the profile of imported slaves seems relatively close to those of the other immigrants. The similarities between the groups point to the fact that, for all its variation, the groups to some extent formed a single pool, not only geographically but also demographically. They were, to adhere to Wittgenstein's metaphor, members of the same family.

5

Migration and Urbanization

[I]t is tempting to speculate, as several ancient historians have, that in terms of mortality, early modern cities may profitably be compared with republican Rome: that the high-risk urban environment dominated the demographic experiences of the citizens making them comparable despite the intervening 1,500 years.[1]

1. URBAN MIGRATION THEORY

In all urbanized societies, many of the streams of migration are directed to the city. Peasants move to nearby towns—temporarily or permanently. From smaller towns people move higher up in the urban hierarchy. Large cities attract high numbers of migrants. When a large part of the population lives in clustered settlements, a network of streams of migration comes into existence in which the cities form the nodal points. As Pooley and Turnbull state, a map of all migration origins and destinations should be very similar to a map of population distribution in general.[2] The relation between migration and urbanization is thus in itself relatively straightforward.

As was briefly discussed in Chapter 1, it is a well-known characteristic of the Roman world that it was highly urbanized. The Roman urban system was also strongly hierarchical. We know very little in terms of details, but crude categorizations are certainly possible.[3] Most inhabitants lived in some form of nucleated settlement. Depending on definitions, many of these settlements were villages or small towns, some consisting of several hundreds of inhabitants, others of several thousands. There were also larger centres, with populations well over 10,000 inhabitants. At the apex of this system stood some extremely

---

[1] Woods (2007) 393.   [2] Pooley and Turnbull (1998) 53 on Britain.
[3] For Roman Italy, see e.g. Morley (1996) 182 and Patterson (2006) 38–9, both emphasizing wide variation in urban population sizes even when Rome is left out of account. A large research project on the Roman urban network in general is currently being conducted by L. de Ligt and J. Bintliff; see De Ligt (2008) for a pilot study.

large cities: Alexandria, Carthage, and Antioch, each with several hundreds of thousands inhabitants, and, largest of all, Rome, with an estimated population of 800,000 to 1 million inhabitants. At a general level, we may assume that the growth of cities and the integration of the cities of the Roman Empire into a very steep urban hierarchy also led to an increase in streams of migration. Peasants moved to towns, townsmen sought their luck elsewhere, members of the elite flocked to larger cities, and so on.

The well-known phenomenon of migration to the city raises the question how exactly we should perceive the relation between migration and urbanization in the case of Rome. In itself, urbanization and migration clearly often belong together, but this leaves unexplained the mechanisms behind the relationship. As we now know so much more about the demographic profile of Rome's immigrants, more precision can be obtained.

The best starting point from which to analyse migration to cities is the body of urban migration theory that has been formulated with respect to the cities of early modern Europe. According to this theory, early modern cities with a stable or growing population received streams of migrants. The theory comes in two versions. The classic formulation, which is usually called the urban graveyard theory, is based on the idea that cities experienced natural decrease. Urban populations were unable to reproduce themselves because of the very high levels of mortality that prevailed in the cities. According to this argument, cities functioned as urban graveyards, or as population sinks. The alternative version might be called the depressed fertility theory.[4] It is based on a reversal of the causative mechanism behind the observed prevalence of deaths over births in the urban population statistics. In this version, a distinction should be drawn between a core population of permanent residents and an envelope of immigrants. Whereas the core population had a more or less normal demographic regime, the immigrant population had a lower rate of marriage and hence a lower rate of fertility. In consequence, it was unable to reproduce itself, but by contrast, it did offer a significant contribution to urban mortality. In both theories, large streams of migrants were the result, siphoning off the surplus from the countryside.

Given the high rates of urbanization, it seems *a priori* likely that urban migration theory is applicable to the Roman world. The theory has in fact been applied by a number of ancient historians, mainly to analyse the growth of the city of Rome under the Republic. Yet its applicability also needs closer scrutiny. The theory has been formulated for early modern Europe, a society with very specific conditions. It is not completely self-evident that it can be

---

[4] My terminology differs somewhat from that which is normally employed. I use 'urban migration theory' as an umbrella term for both theories, whereas that term was used by Sharlin to describe his own theory. Migration is, however, central to both.

applied to other societies. For example, in the Roman case the fact that a substantial part of migration to Rome was forced might be relevant.

In this chapter the applicability of the urban migration theory to the city of Rome under the Principate will be discussed, as a way of offering a more general approach to conceptualizing the relation between migration and urbanization. Firstly the historiography of the urban migration theory will be discussed in more detail, both for early modern Europe and for the Roman world. Then a series of factors that are relevant to its application will be discussed one by one: the size and composition of the population, urban mortality levels, and fertility levels. By way of conclusion, an evaluation will be made of how the theory may help to understand migration patterns.

2. ONE THEORY, TWO VARIANTS

Before we discuss how far the urban migration theory is applicable to the city of Rome during the Principate, a *status quaestionis* should first be provided. This is of importance because it might show both the possibilities and the risks of borrowing concepts from other periods.

The classic version of urban migration theory, the urban graveyard theory, is best known from an important article by Wrigley published in 1967.[5] In this article, he formulated a model to understand the characteristics of the spectacular and exceptional growth of London between 1650 and 1750. At the basis of Wrigley's model were differences in rural and urban mortality: although variations occurred over time, the crude death rate in London was significantly higher than in the countryside. In London, deaths exceeded births by a wide margin, whereas in the countryside the reverse was true. But despite London's natural decrease, the city grew at a spectacular rate. The only possible explanation was that the high urban mortality was compensated by even higher levels of immigration. The migrants consisted of the excess population from the countryside. Hypothetical calculations suggested that London absorbed about half of the population increase from the country.

It is important to realize that the urban graveyard theory is based on two different arguments. Firstly, it postulates urban natural decrease: within the city, death rates are higher than birth rates, due to which the population would contract without external supply.[6] Secondly, we find differential mortality between city and countryside: rural levels of mortality are lower than in the city. It is thus relative rather than absolute levels of mortality that are important.

---

[5] Wrigley (1967), esp. 45–9.
[6] Cf. Van der Woude (1982) 55 on relatively low urban birth rates; note, however, that it is death relative to births rather than birth rates in absolute terms that are at issue.

Whether the urban population remains stable, grows, or even declines depends on the actual levels of these two differential rates. Urban growth can occur in situations where there is a surplus of births in the countryside that can be siphoned off to the city, and where this surplus exceeds the urban birth deficit.

Wrigley applied his theory to London in the period 1650–1750, during which time London was in many respects a highly exceptional city. But elements of the model could be found elsewhere. In fact, the theory of urban natural decrease has a long pedigree.[7] '[T]he implied inability of cities to sustain themselves by natural generation constitutes what is easily the single most widely noted demographic feature of early modern cities.'[8] Birth deficits were observed in the data of many larger cities of early modern Europe, whereas the countryside showed in general an excess of births.

Given the generic nature of the model, it is hardly surprising that the theory of urban graveyards has found application far beyond London. It has been applied to the whole urban landscape of early modern Europe, and has become a standard tool of modelling the urban world in this period.[9] In a handbook published in 1969, Wrigley sketched a theoretical demographic contour map of areas with equal mortality conditions.[10] Mortality is density dependent: as levels of pre-industrial mortality were mainly determined by the spread of diseases, one of the major factors influencing levels of mortality was how close people lived to each other.[11] In Wrigley's general model, settlement size functioned as a proxy for density, and thereby for mortality levels. In this way we can imagine a settlement landscape in which the largest settlements had the strongest natural decrease, and, conversely, that smaller settlements were relatively healthy. The flows between the net producers and net consumers determined the basic pattern of migration. At some point in the settlement hierarchy an equilibrium was reached; cities had to reach a threshold population and threshold density for the graveyard effect to apply.[12]

The theory has found wide application to the urban world of early modern Europe, but its applicability to other periods and regions is open to question. Is it justifiable to speak of a law of urban natural decrease, and if so, how universal is this?[13] It is obvious that its applicability is limited to the *pre-industrial* period, since with the onset of industrialization the relationship was

---

[7] For historiography, see Sharlin (1978) 126–7, De Vries (1984) 179, and Galley (1995) 448–9.

[8] De Vries (1984) 178–9.

[9] De Vries (1984) 180, where it is called a 'venerable orthodoxy' and 'the only child' of historical urban demography.

[10] Wrigley (1969) 98–9; see also Galley (1995) 449. [11] Finlay (1981*a*) 172.

[12] Given the fact that many of the cities of early modern Europe were relatively small, the question where equilibrium was reached forms a problem of real importance. See Sharlin (1978) 128 n. 5 and De Vries (1984) 202 for a population size of 10,000 as threshold; higher figures are also offered. Woods (1989) 81–2 for an instructive series of equations.

[13] Van der Woude (1982) 74; De Vries (1984) 182.

reversed, and cities began to experience urban natural increase.[14] The general applicability of the law of urban natural decrease even within early modern Europe has been questioned, as there are a number of cases where the urban natural population grows, and many of the cases of urban natural decrease concern the demographically unfavourable period of the long eighteenth century.[15] As Van der Woude has argued forcefully, it is not unthinkable that the situation was different in the preceding period: at least some cities might have been capable of urban natural increase.[16] With regard to its applicability outside early modern Europe, Woods has pointed out that the evidence for differences between urban and rural mortality from East Asia is in fact equivocal.[17] He has also placed the idea of a differential urban mortality regime in the context of the development of the early modern city as a fenced-off entity: because it was separated administratively, socially, and economically from the countryside, it could also develop a different mortality regime.[18]

A major attempt at revision of the theory was made by Sharlin in 1978. Sharlin did not deny the 'overwhelming importance of migration' for urban growth, but suggested a different underlying structure and reversed the causative mechanism.[19] According to him, the key lies in fertility, not mortality. He distinguished between two groups: a resident core population and an envelope of migrants. The core population might be said to have had normal demographic characteristics: no excess mortality occurred among this group, and some slight population growth might even have been possible. The migrants, by contrast, had a very different composition: they were mostly young and single. Due to institutional impediments to marriage, their fertility lagged behind and they were hence unable to reproduce. Even in the case that their mortality patterns were the same of the rest of the urban population, migrants provided a fair share of the levels of mortality, but hardly contributed to fertility.[20] In consequence, cities were able to grow thanks to the influx of

---

[14] Galley (1995) 451 n. 21: 'By the mid-nineteenth century much of the rise in urban populations was due to natural increase.' See also Van der Woude (1982) 55, 59 on the modern reversal.

[15] Galley (1995) 451.

[16] This is the central argument of Van der Woude (1982), based on the evidence of the western parts of the Netherlands. He also points out (at 59) that at least in some cases the reversal to urban natural increase at the end of the eighteenth and nineteenth centuries took place in cities in which living conditions were at least as bad as in the preceding period.

[17] Woods (2003) 33 f.   [18] Woods (2003) 29.

[19] Sharlin (1978) (with quote at 126 n. 2); for a different formulation of Sharlin's principal argument, see Woods (1989) 89: Sharlin focuses on 'the interaction produced by age- and sex-selective migration which is likely to influence nuptiality and thus both overall fertility levels and also the pattern of age at death'.

[20] De Vries (1984) 181 offers an instructive parallel with a retirement community: old pensioners are not registered as being born in the community, nor are their children registered there, but they do die in the community. Hence they greatly increase mortality figures, whereas the community's own population may have a completely normal mortality pattern.

migrants, but at the same time the migrants also produced a much higher overall level of urban mortality. Migrants were therefore both cause and solution to the problem of population decrease. In aggregate statistics the distinctions are lost; if migrants form a substantial part of the urban population, deaths will automatically exceed births.

Sharlin's article has been hailed as a turning point in the debate in all the subsequent literature. But the debate itself has remained unresolved.[21] Whereas both theories present internally consistent models,[22] the problem is that empirical data to verify (or falsify) either theory are lacking.[23] One important additional element is that although they are normally taken as such, there seem to be no good grounds to assume that the theories are mutually exclusive.[24]

There are a number of problems in verifying the theories. Firstly, there is no doubt that urban mortality levels could be very high. But this does not mean that they could not be compensated by even higher levels of fertility. It has proven difficult to verify the point with the help of data. The point is not merely an academic one: as we have seen, examples have been found of the reverse, of cities experiencing urban natural increase.[25] Secondly, it is possible that the distinction made by Sharlin between the mortality of the immigrant population and the core population is in reality rather a difference in mortality levels between different classes, with the poor having the highest levels of mortality. If so, immigration is immaterial to the hypothesis.[26] Thirdly, it is difficult to distinguish between permanent residents and temporary migrants in the data; even Sharlin himself had to use proxy data to make his argument. It has been pointed out that migrants were in many cases able to settle down and start a family. There are numerous cases of cities where at least a part of the migrant population married, and, to complicate matters further, there are also examples where there was a great deal of intermarriage.[27] As migrants form by their very nature a very volatile group, it is unlikely that the required data ever surfaced.[28] 'Sharlin's model of urban migration is not discredited, merely not proven', as Woods summarizes the discussion.[29]

---

[21] See Finlay (1981*b*) vs. Sharlin (1981).

[22] Though note that Van der Woude (1982) 71 observes that if Sharlin's theory is taken to its logical extremes, the implication is that urban growth can only exist due to urban natural increase—something which is manifestly contradicted by much of the evidence.

[23] Woods (2003) 29, emphasizing that uncertainties in the analysis of urban–rural differences in mortality lie in 'description, measurement and interpretation'. For a general overview of the difficulties of urban demography, see De Vries (1984) 175-7.

[24] See for the early modern world Galley (1995), for a situation in which both theories may sequentially apply.

[25] Galley (1995) 449–50, summarizing a part of the subsequent debate between Finlay (1981*b*) and Sharlin (1981) and citing examples of urban natural increase (Breslau 17th cent., some English cities in the 16th and 17th cents.).

[26] De Vries (1984) 184.   [27] De Vries (1984) 186–90.

[28] This is the principal point of Woods (1989) 89–92; see also Galley (1995) 450.

[29] Woods (1989) 93.

Migration is central to both theories, but in a different vein.[30] In Wrigley's theory, the migrants are, as it were, the product of a calculation. It is urban growth that matters. The fact that this is due to migration is important (also because of its social consequences), but the nature of the migration itself is irrelevant. Even the demographic composition of the migrants is not important to its application: all the migrants needed to do was come to the city. From the viewpoint of migration history, Sharlin's attempt at revision had one important beneficial effect: it turned the focus on the migrants themselves. Sharlin's theory dissected the population into two groups, with different characteristics. It was the migrants' composition in terms of age and gender, their demographic behaviour (marriage and fertility), and the social institutions preventing marriage which were central.[31]

The important question remains, to what extent the theory helps to chart migration. The theory belongs to the field of urban demography, rather than to that of migration history itself. It is, in fact, striking how little the findings from migration historians have been taken into account, and vice versa, how little migration historians have been interested in the theory. The implicit criticism of migration historians seems to be that the theory is unable to capture the complexity of mobility patterns. Both varieties of the theory proceed from the assumption that migration is a straightforward process of moving from the countryside to the city.

> The victory of the city is neither complete nor simple. Although it seems to have pulled masses of people from the countryside to permanent urban lives, the history of labor demands, urban geography, and demography all indicate that migration to the city was complex, entailing far more than a one-time rural-urban move for most people.[32]

In applying the urban graveyard theory to the Roman world, several points are to be taken into account. To begin with, it is important to realize that there are two main theories, not one. Secondly, there is an ongoing debate about their applicability. For the Roman world, urban natural decrease is not to be taken for granted, because it can hardly be considered a universal property of all pre-industrial cities. Thirdly, levels of urban fertility should also be discussed—establishing high levels of mortality is not enough. There may have been differences in fertility regimes between a core population and an envelope.

---

[30] De Vries (1984) 200.
[31] Likewise Galley (1995) 450: 'Clearly the demographic characteristics of these migrants and the factors governing their ability to settle permanently are crucial to an understanding of early modern urban demography.'
[32] Moch (2003[2]) 12.

3. APPLICATIONS TO THE ROMAN WORLD

Urban migration theory is well known among Roman historians and has been used repeatedly. Wrigley's model seems to have been introduced into ancient history by Hopkins,[33] and more extensive applications were subsequently offered by Jongman and Morley, who have both applied the urban graveyard theory to construct demographic models for the spectacular growth of late Republican Rome.[34] In a later paper Jongman argued that slaves, rather than impoverished Italians from the countryside, were the immigrants: the demand could not be met from the Italian countryside, as the surplus of births was too small, and in the light of revisions of Republican history it has become less likely that the migrants consisted of impoverished peasants.[35] Scheidel has made important qualifications to the calculations, arguing on the one hand that excess mortality was higher than previously thought, but on the other, that the number of immigrants required to compensate for the deficit was lower.[36] Erdkamp added the important point that if most immigrants were young males, this will have important consequences for the model and its calculations.[37] Lo Cascio has raised some important objections against its applicability, and substituted his own revisionist version, based on Sharlin's alternative model.[38] He has also argued that migrants contributed to further growth of the city under the early Empire rather than compensated an urban deficit.[39] Noy argued that in the Principate Rome's birth deficit was pre-dominantly compensated by immigration from free provincials rather than impoverished peasants or imported slaves, as was the case in previous periods.[40] Patterson, while endorsing the application of the urban graveyard theory in general, pointed to the difficulties of determining whether peasants moved directly to the major centres or whether stepwise migration occurred.[41] Hin has stressed that the complex nature of Roman migration mitigated some of the mortality differentials.[42]

Many of these ancient historians have concentrated on the application of Wrigley's model for London to Republican Rome. The reason for the use of Wrigley's model is not difficult to see. Not only was the parallel between the growth of London and the growth of Republican Rome difficult to miss, it is also the coherence and simplicity of Wrigley's model that has made it so

---

[33] Osborne (2006) 7 draws attention to an unpublished paper by Hopkins based on Wrigley (1967). In his published work Hopkins did not offer a neat and coherent version of the urban graveyard theory, though the idea seems to inform many of his discussions of urban demography. It is interesting to see that in Huttunen (1974) 28 the applicability of the theory was still denied.

[34] Jongman (1990); Morley (1996).

[35] Jongman (2003), cf. Hin (2013) 223 n. 50 for qualifications.   [36] Scheidel (2004) 17.

[37] Erdkamp (2008), in particular 442.   [38] Lo Cascio (2000).

[39] Lo Cascio (forthcoming).   [40] Noy (2000) 18–19.   [41] Patterson (2006) 38.

[42] Hin (2013) 210–57.

attractive. In many of the earlier applications, the subsequent debate has been downplayed. Sharlin's analysis usually receives short shrift—a passing reference as an alternative of no real value. If Sharlin's model is applied at all (as by Lo Cascio), it is his distinction of an urban population into a core and an envelope rather than fertility itself that has attracted most attention.

It should also be noted that ancient historians have mainly legitimized the application of Wrigley's urban graveyard model by pointing to the very high levels of urban mortality in the city of Rome. Although this is certainly an important element of the model, high mortality itself is not a sufficient condition for the theory to apply.[43] Conversely, counter-arguments against such high mortality do not in themselves invalidate the application of urban graveyard theory.[44]

There is an inherent difficulty in the application of urban migration theory to the Roman world. The theories are demographic ones, based on observations about early modern Europe. They are almost always couched in empirical observation based on specific demographic data of specific cities in specific periods. Such data are absent for the city of Rome. However, this has not deterred scholars from offering calculations. These calculations are presented as 'reasonable' (and they might well be), but this usually means that Wrigley's figures of the London birth deficit are simply transferred to Rome. Demographic models based on the fragmentary survivals of statistically useable information from the Roman period have proven resilient to finding mortality or fertility differentials.[45] If the theory can be applied at all to the Roman world, the application will be qualitative, not quantitative. Such data as we have can only be proxy data; they are of our own making.

The main advantage of the theory seems to have been that it bypassed the inadequacies of the Roman sources. However, while testing the applicability seems out of the question, it certainly would be reassuring if the theory could be brought closer to the sources. But this is difficult. Skeletal evidence is only for a very limited part relevant—the study of migrant's diseases and standards of living impinges only indirectly on one part of the theory. Literary sources are also of little help. For example, a statement of Sallust that around 70 BC young men preferred idling in the city to labouring on the land is in itself interesting as it points to rural–urban migration by young males, but even apart from the fact that for Sallust the phenomenon was connected to a specific moment in late Republican history, and even if it would be legitimate to separate his alleged fact from the moralizing context in which he places it, it would be difficult to infer much more from the passage.[46] The potential

[43] Cf. Scheidel (2003).   [44] Cf. Kron (2012).

[45] Bagnall and Frier (1994); Tacoma (2012); Adams (forthcoming).

[46] Sall., *Catil.* 37.7, *iuventus, quae in agris manuum mercede inopiam toleravat, privatis atque publicis largitionibus excita urbana otium ingrato labori praetulerat.* App., *BC* 2.120 makes the

bearing of documentary sources on the theory is certainly larger, but even in that case there are clear limits. For example, in our study of mobility in the epigrams in the Greek East, Tybout and I observed much more random movement between urban settlements than movement upwards into the urban hierarchy (though there was a trickle of migrants to Rome), but this impression cannot be converted into hard data.[47]

To the extent that sources have been used, there is also a problem of selectivity. Applications of the urban migration theory are based on a negative evaluation of urban life in Rome. As an embodiment of the city par excellence, Rome attracted both praise and invective. In applying the urban migration theory, it is tempting to privilege the negative side and to take the negative statements in the ancient sources as a fact. But it has been pointed out that, in a way, this continues the ancient moralizing discourse in a scholarly objectifying fashion.[48] This need not necessarily mean that the ideas are wrong. But the question is how we get to such *realia* if our sources are so biased. Juvenal is a case in point. Negative statements made in his *Satires* are often taken literally. Even apart from conventions of genre, the fact that we find the same *topoi* over and over, and the fact that we do not hear Juvenal speaking but his fictitious *personae*, suggest that Juvenal's Rome is simply different from our ancient Rome. For example, one of the factors that negatively impacted on living conditions in Rome was the repeated flooding of the Tiber.[49] Flooding is known to have been a continuous problem in Rome, but does not loom large in Juvenal's *Satires*. His argument about Rome's living conditions is also couched in moral terms which no one nowadays would like to use. Often sexual politics mingle in ways that are bewildering. Can we select some of Juvenal's statements simply because they match with what we think?[50]

All these concerns do not necessarily suggest that the application of the theory is not warranted. But they clearly show that there are also risks in borrowing concepts from other scholarly disciplines. De Vries has warned against the risk of applying a 'mechanistic "law" based on assumed "natural"

---

same argument for the period around the assassination of Caesar. For somewhat similar moralizing vignettes about the dichotomy between countryside and city, see Hor., *Ep.* 1.7 for a barber who becomes a small landowner, but has to work far too hard and wants to return to his normal life; Varro, *De agr.* 2 pr.3; Suet., *Aug.* 42.3 for easy life in the city.

[47] Tacoma and Tybout (forthcoming *a*).

[48] This is the major argument of Laurence (1997), but see already briefly Morley (1996) 41.

[49] Aldrete (2007) 3–4, emphasizing that even in the modern world flooding is more damaging than any other natural disaster, and that the problems in ancient Rome were structural because 'the Romans chose to build it squarely in an area that nature had designated as a floodplain'.

[50] Scheidel (2003) 160 is overstated: 'for every sardonic aside in Juvenal . . . we have access to independent data from archaeological surveys to legal provisions and medical observations that are fully consistent with the bleak picture painted by Scobie.' Cf. Morley (2006) 26 and esp. Woolf (2006).

conditions',[51] and it is hard to avoid the impression that this is precisely what has happened in the application to the Roman world. Let us therefore take a closer look at the factors relevant to its application.

4. SIZE AND COMPOSITION OF ROME'S POPULATION

Applications of the urban migration theory for the Roman world start with the size and composition of the urban population of Rome. In the theory of urban natural decrease, size functions as an indirect indicator of population density, and density forms an index of levels of mortality. The large size of Rome therefore functions as legitimation for the employment of urban graveyard effects. In Sharlin's migration theory, it is not so much the size of the urban population itself but its composition that is of importance, especially the balance between the core of Rome-born residents and an envelope of immigrants. In both cases the well-known calculation for the size of the Augustan population plays a major role. Without going into too much detail, it is worth considering the logic of the argument.

In a general sense, there can be no doubt that Rome was an extremely large city. The sheer size of its infrastructure and amenities (baths, aqueducts, theatres with enormous seating capacities, public buildings, and so on) suggest that the city was enormous. Rome was extremely large by ancient standards, and equally huge by pre-industrial standards.[52]

But Rome presents a conundrum. Much of our knowledge about Rome's population size is inferred. On the one hand there is no doubt that Rome had a population running into the hundreds of thousands of people; on the other, there is immense uncertainty about the particulars. The size and composition of the Roman population has been debated over and over, but unless new evidence turns up, it is most unlikely that the discussion can be advanced.[53] However, in view of the fact that the urban migration theory is in the end a demographic, quantitative one, and given the fact that size is the one aspect about which quantitative statements (no matter how imperfect) can be made, it still is necessary to offer some discussion. It seems, therefore, best to concentrate on the methods of the calculation rather than on the figures themselves.

---

[51] De Vries (1984) 183. Cf. also Lo Cascio (2000) 43 on 'una ferrea legge di natura' and Van der Woude (1982) 74: 'As always in good history there is no law.'

[52] The large size of Rome under the early Empire also stands out when placed in the context of its own population history. See for a convenient graph charting 2,600 years of Roman population history Aldrete (2007) 78, fig. 2.7.

[53] Hopkins (1978) 96–8 is brief but remains fundamental. An overview of the subject with further references can be found in Morley (1996) 33–9; see also De Ligt and Garnsey (forthcoming).

Frustratingly enough, there would have been some demographic information available in Roman times. In the case of Rome the ignominious truth is not, to paraphrase A. H. M. Jones' famous dictum, that there are no ancient statistics, but that they are lost.[54] The surviving aggregate totals of Roman citizens known from the Roman census cannot be used, for the obvious reason that Roman citizens were not confined to Rome. The census registers (or, in any case, the individual declarations) will certainly have specified to what city a person belonged; but it is only the aggregate figures that have survived.[55] As we saw in Chapter 3, a system of birth and death declarations was in use in Rome, suggesting there were population registers. It is likely that if their information had survived they would still not have provided all the details we need to know, but it is obvious that they would have helped.

The fact that a significant part of Rome's population will have consisted of migrants (many of them only residing there temporarily) will have made the population unstable. The chances that this large and fluctuating immigrant population was accurately recorded are not very large.[56] Although this does not mean that it is impossible to discuss the urban population size at a theoretical level,[57] it remains somewhat ironic that size is used as an index of migration, but that migration hinders estimates of size.

The population of Rome is traditionally estimated at 800,000–1 million inhabitants around the reign of Augustus. Although the general order of magnitude is not in doubt, there are immense uncertainties about the particulars. The figure is based on attested numbers of recipients of the grain dole and cash handouts. A multiplier is used to obtain the families, and then additions are made to take the groups into account that were excluded from the dole. The uncertainties concern the question which groups did receive grain, who were excluded, and in what numbers.

The starting point is provided by the figures of recipients of the grain dole (and in some cases cash handouts) attested under Augustus and shortly before his reign.[58] The grain dole figures cover a period from 46 BC to AD 14/15.

---

[54] In a similar vein Lo Cascio (2000) 22. But see Morley (1996) 34 for some consolation ('[n]o ancient writer offers an opinion on the size of the city, sparing us the problem of deciding whether such a figure could conceivably be relied upon').

[55] Kolb (1995) 448.

[56] Holleran (2011) 156, 'it is doubtful that there was ever any accurate means of recording a large and fluctuating urban population'; in a similar vein also Morley (1996) 33: '[u]pon close examination, the concept of "the population of Rome" becomes increasingly elusive.'

[57] Contra Horden and Purcell (2000) 382: 'Hence we find it theoretically impossible to talk of "the population of a city"—such as Rome in Antiquity, for example.' It is precisely in theory that we can talk of 'the population of Rome'.

[58] It is generally agreed that two other procedures, using the territory of the city and using disparate figures in literary sources about grain imports, have serious defects and are only of limited value. See e.g. Lo Cascio (2000) 23–6, 42. But see Kolb (1995) 453–7 for a more optimistic evaluation. For the difficulties inherent in a fourth method, using the figures for *insulae* and

Table 5.1. Grain dole and *congiaria* figures

Date	Recipients	Source
46 BC	320,000 of grain reduced to:	Plut., *Caes.* 55.3
45 BC	150,000 of grain	Cass. Dio 43.21.4
		Suet., *Iul.* 41.3
46 BC	(implied) 150,000, 400 HS each	Cass. Dio 43.21.3
44 BC	unknown, 300 HS each	R.G. 3.15
29 BC	250,000, 400 HS each	R.G. 3.15
24 BC	250,000 or more, 400 HS pp	R.G. 3.15
23 BC	250,000 or more, of grain	R.G. 3.15
12 BC	250,000 or more, 400 HS each	R.G. 3.15
5 BC	320,000, 240 HS each	R.G. 3.15
2 BC	to those 200,000 (or slightly more) who received grain,	Cass. Dio 55.10.1
	240 HS each	R.G. 3.15
AD 12	unknown, 300 HS each	Suet., *Tib.* 20
AD 14 or 15	(implied) 150,000, 260 HS each	Suet., *Aug.* 101
		Tac., *Ann.* 1.8.5
		Cass. Dio 57.14

The series starts with a reduction from an earlier figure of 320,000 to 150,000 by Caesar and varies subsequently between 150,000 and 250,000 recipients. In addition, there are some comparable figures for cash handouts (*congiaria*) from the same period, fluctuating between 150,000 and 320,000. Though the *congiaria* were one-time events and might not in all cases have been given to the same part of the population that received grain, there is a clear connection between the two.[59] It therefore seems safest to take the *congiaria* figures into account as well. The figures have been listed in Table 5.1.

These figures have been debated over and over again, without much result. Inasmuch as the ancient sources offer explanations at all, the explanations are contradictory.[60] In the absence of major catastrophes, it is hard to believe that fluctuations in the population size itself can account for major changes. As the modern discussions have shown all too clearly, there are many administrative factors that may have influenced the individual figures. The minimum age for eligibility may have changed,[61] residential requirements may have changed, freedmen may have been included or excluded, and so on.

---

domus reported in the fourth-century AD regionary catalogues, see above all Hermansen (1978). See also Holleran (2011) 156–8 for scepticism about all methods.

[59] For *congiaria* that are explicitly said to be given to the grain receivers, see Cass. Dio 43.21.3 (46 BC), Cass. Dio 55.10.1 (2 BC), Cass. Dio 50.25.7 (AD 45) and, much later, Cass. Dio 77.1.1 (AD 202). Cf. Cass. Dio 55.26 (AD 6, additional grain to those who already receive); Philo, *Leg.* 158 (where the reference to monthly distributions of money and grain suggests equal status), *C.I.L.* 6.10228 (testifying to a registration procedure for receiving a *congiarium* that is analogous to if not the same as the one used for receiving grain), Plin., *Pan.* 25–8 where *congiaria* and grain distributions seem at times almost interchangeable.

[60] Contrast Cass. Dio 43.21.4 with Plut., *Caes.* 55.3.   [61] e.g. Lo Cascio (2000) 40.

However, what is not in doubt is the suggested order of magnitude. In that sense it obviates the need to go into too much detail. At the beginning of the Principate the part of the population receiving grain and cash handouts consisted of 150,000 to 320,000 persons. The problem that the difference between these two figures is rather large is mitigated somewhat once it is realized that, by definition, the higher figure is simply more inclusive and the lower one more exclusive. This means that the gap between the two need not necessarily widen with further multiplications.

The monthly ration of grain was more than was needed to feed a single person, and was clearly meant to support a wider number of family members. As the grain was handed out predominantly to men, and only from a certain age onwards, a crude calculation can be made to obtain the number of family members that were attached to the recipients. Normally a multiplier of 2.5 or slightly higher is used to obtain this wider *plebs frumentaria*.[62] It seems legitimate to use a somewhat lower multiplier of 2.0 for the more inclusive high figure of 320,000 grain recipients, precisely because it is more inclusive.[63] This would result in a wider *plebs frumentaria* of 375,000 to 640,000 persons.[64]

The major unknown is how this wider *plebs frumentaria* was composed, or rather, who was excluded from it. It is clear that not everybody was eligible.[65] Who exactly was excluded is not only unknown because of a lack of data, but we also need to realize that part of this population was more transient and unstable.

It is possible that there was a *numerus fixus*. The sources suggest that the lists were closed at least twice, and that new persons were only admitted when others had died.[66] The problem is that a *numerus fixus* is difficult to reconcile with the other fluctuations in the attested figures. At any rate, if there was a closed register the group of persons who were eligible for the grain dole is likely to have been larger than the *plebs frumentaria* proper.[67]

Although it is clear that the dole was directed at the masses, poverty formed no criterion in itself. In fact, eligibility was irrespective of wealth.[68] At the other side of the economic spectrum, there is no evidence that the elite participated in the dole. It may be that aristocrats were barred officially,[69] but it is just as likely that they chose not to enlist for the handouts.

---

[62] Hopkins (1978) 97; Morley (1996) 37, Scheidel (2004) 14.

[63] Cf. Scheidel (2004) 14. One possibility is that the sex ratio of the groups that are additionally included might be skewed.

[64] 150,000 * 2.5 = 375,000 or 320,000 * 2.0 = 640,000.

[65] Bernard (forthcoming) for the tension between exclusivism in practice and inclusivism in ideology.

[66] Suet., *Iul.* 41.3 with Rickman (1980) 177–9; Cass. Dio 55.10.1.

[67] Whittaker (1993) 1; Kolb (1995) 452.   [68] Whittaker (1993) 20–1.

[69] Whittaker (1993) 20–1; Rickman (1980) 182. Some enigmatic phrases in the Late Republican *Tabula Heracleensis* (ed. Crawford 1996) ll. 1–19 may be relevant for this issue, but see the comm. ad loc., and Rickman (1980) 241–3.

There can be little doubt that Roman citizenship was a condition for receiving grain. This will have led to a dual exclusion: both slaves and *peregrini* could not participate, irrespective of how long they had lived in Rome. It is debated whether the freedmen who obtained Roman citizenship upon manumission could be included; some scholars argue that the large fluctuations in the numbers of recipients can only be explained by the inclusion and exclusion of this sizeable group.[70] It seems certain that those freedmen who did not obtain Roman citizenship and became Junian Latins instead were excluded.

The uncertainties about the sizes of the excluded groups are thus large. At the same time, it is clear that at least some of these groups numbered in the tens of thousands of persons. The number of slaves will in fact have been even larger—200,000 to 300,000 in the calculation used in Chapter 2. Notwithstanding the considerable uncertainties, it is therefore highly probable that we have to add several hundreds of thousands of persons to the wider *plebs frumentaria*, and this is how the conventional figure of 800,000 to 1 million persons is arrived at.

In fact, it is not completely unthinkable that Rome continued to grow after the time of Augustus.[71] The continued monumentalization of the capital and the continuous improvements of the infrastructure of the city do not in themselves offer proof, but it should be noted that in the case of other Roman cities historians normally have no difficulties in inferring population growth from such indicators. The one element that curbs expansionist fantasies in the case of Rome is that the figure of 800,000 to 1 million already implies very high urban densities. Although we do not know exactly where the city ended, the space to accommodate additional people is relatively small.[72] In consequence, either one adopts a lower starting-figure at the time of Augustus in order to allow for modest growth, or one assumes a population of 1 million that did not expand significantly after the time of Augustus.

The calculation on which the estimate of 800,000 to 1 million inhabitants is based is also of interest for the Sharlin model of depressed fertility of migrants. The calculations are based on a distinction between a core of grain-receiving families and a remainder of the population that was excluded from the dole.

---

[70] They were sometimes included in the gifts of money: Suet., *Aug.* 42.2, where Augustus removes them from the lists. A century or so later, the *Sententiae Hadriani* contain three cases of disputes over *congiaria* (cases 2, 10, and 11); in case no. 2, a patron of a freedman who is condemned to the quarries petitions for his *congiarium*, which is refused by Hadrian; see Lewis (1991) for description. Morley (1996) 36–8, following Virlouvet (1991), assumes freedmen had been removed when the dole was reformed in 46 BC. Whittaker (1993) 21 (those who had been removed must at any rate have been freedmen, 'if only because they were the majority of those eligible'). Note that somewhat later in the first cent. AD Pers., *Sat.* 5.73–79 still seems to be based on the idea that manumission leads to entitlement to distributions of grain: 'Not that freedom which entitles any Publius, once he is enrolled in the Veline tribe, to possess a little voucher for old grain', *non hac, ut quisque Velina Publius emeruit, scabiosum tesserula far possidet.*

[71] Lo Cascio (forthcoming).   [72] Frézouls (1987).

Some ancient historians have readily seized upon this distinction in order to apply Sharlin's model of a home-born core population and a transient and volatile population of migrants. The equation is tempting, but can only be justified in part. As we saw in Chapter 3, Section 2, a part of the free foreigners will no doubt have consisted of recent migrants. But the category of *peregrini* will also have comprised foreign residents who might have lived in Rome for many generations. With respect to the slaves, it should not be forgotten that in the Principate most of the slaves were probably home bred and therefore arguably would belong to the core population rather than to its envelope.

The size and composition of the population of Rome can therefore be seen to have played a large role in the application of the theory, but they create difficulties of their own. The size has been used to legitimize the application of the graveyard theory, but it has at the same time been used to claim Rome's uniqueness. Its composition has been used to distinguish between a resident core and a more unstable envelope. Although such a distinction is certainly useful, it cannot be based on the calculation for Rome's population size. It is far from certain that the calculation can carry the enormous weight that is placed on it. We therefore need to consider the two most important elements in more detail: mortality and fertility.

5. MORTALITY

The role of mortality in both models is quite different. In Wrigley's model of the urban graveyard, two conditions should be met: mortality should be higher than fertility, and mortality in the city should be higher than elsewhere. For Sharlin's model, mortality levels are not really of importance. The core population is able to replace itself or might even grow slightly, whereas the excess mortality is mainly found among the immigrant population. The urban excess mortality is not the product of a different mortality regime, but of a skewed age composition and a lack of fertility. It is rather the fact that a large stream of migrants enters the city that creates an excess of deaths over births in the urban statistics.

In the context of urban migration theory, an additional argument is sometimes made. Migration itself is in some instances thought to contribute to mortality. Immigrants may both be more susceptible as a virgin population to particular diseases, and they may at the same time import other diseases from their home region to which the resident population had not yet developed immunity.[73] That such a scenario is not completely unthinkable is shown by a

---

[73] Morley (1996) 44–5; Gowland and Garnsey (2010) 131: 'Rome required a constant flow of immigrants in order to sustain its population at existing levels, and such immigration had to be

short vignette in Tacitus, who reports that when Vitellius brought new troops of Gauls and Germans into the city they died in great numbers. They were unaccustomed to the climate and the heat, and made things worse by drinking water from the Tiber.[74] But Tacitus clearly considered this an exceptional event. Given the geographical background of migrants, with most of them coming from within the empire, the large variety between the migrants, and the fact that a substantial part of them returned after some time, it seems unlikely that many immigrant groups can be regarded as virgin populations.[75] Skeletal evidence is not unequivocal: the two populations of Casal Bertone and Castellaccio Europarco showed no clear distinction in skeletal and dental diseases between immigrants and locals.[76] In the present state of the evidence, the issue of different mortality of immigrants cannot be settled and should be approached with caution.

As for mortality differentials in the population at large, it will be obvious that we have very little empirical data at our disposal.[77] We do not have sufficient evidence to establish precise levels of mortality, let alone evidence to establish differences between Rome and elsewhere. When the data are fully published, the skeletal evidence from various sites around Rome might help to give us a better grasp of mortality patterns, but at first sight the age-at-death profiles of the sites seems to vary so widely that it is difficult to come up with an explanation.[78] Elsewhere in the empire, it should be noted that in the Egyptian census declarations, despite strong hints of rural–urban migration, there appeared to be no significant differences in mortality between town and country—perhaps even there due to a lack of quality in the documentation, or

continuous because new arrivals would have been vulnerable to diseases to which they had not previously been exposed.'

[74] Tac., *Hist.* 2.93–4.   [75] Cf. Erdkamp (2008) 438–9; Hin (2013) 210–57.

[76] Killgrove (2010*a*) 294–9, concluding at 299 that 'neither immigrants nor locals appear to have been differentially affected by skeletal or dental diseases'.

[77] The possibility of establishing urban–rural mortality differences through anthropometrical analysis of body height is mentioned by Komlos and Baten (2004) 195 with respect to later periods of history. The discussion of the Roman material has up till now mainly been focusing on the controversial issue of whether stature in the Roman period increased or decreased relative to preceding and succeeding periods and its implications for standards of living; see Gowland and Garnsey (2010) 150–2, and Harris (2011), both with further references. Catalano et al. (2013) for very brief discussion of stature at six different sites around Rome, giving average male height as 167 cm, average female height as 156 cm. However, it seems safer to approach differences in average stature as the result of ecological adaptation strategies rather than as straightforward reflections of living standards, let alone as the product of levels of mortality per se.

[78] Gowland and Garnsey (2010) 139–40 for an overview on the basis of the already published materials from via Collatina, Osteria del Curato and Vallerano. Catalano et al. (2013), esp. 8 for a brief overview of the larger project data; the project will eventually allow comparison of a significant number of burial grounds around Rome. None of the sites seem to fit the predictions of standard mortality tables, suggesting—unsurprisingly—strong cultural preferences in burial. Note also that a (small) part of the graveyard population was cremated and hence falls outside the analysis.

because the difference between town and country was not that large in the nomes of middle Egypt: most of the villages where the documents originated were themselves quite large.[79]

In itself, most indicators that we have point in the direction of very high levels of mortality in the city of Rome.[80] The substantial fluctuations in seasonal mortality that are attested in the city point to a demographic regime with low life-expectancy, in which infectious diseases play a very important role.[81] In addition, one may point to the low standards of hygiene and sanitation, to the bad standards of housing, especially for the poor,[82] and to the possibility that structural undernourishment of the population occurred,[83] and then add episodic disasters like flooding and fires.[84]

However, all the above points are controversial and have been debated at great length. It might well be that Roman historians have been too pessimistic in their evaluations. Perhaps they have also been too simplistic, as the analysis of skeletal evidence which is beginning to appear produces rather ambiguous results with respect to living standards and pathologies.[85] Even apart from the fact that the arguments in favour of very high levels of mortality can only be suggestive and cannot establish exact levels of mortality,[86] the inquiry is to some extent misleading, as it is not high mortality itself that is important, but the differences in mortality between Rome and elsewhere. It is not particularly difficult to claim that Roman mortality must have been high, but one must go beyond that if one wants make a plausible case for the application of urban graveyard theory.

---

[79] Bagnall and Frier (1994), Tacoma (2006); Adams (forthcoming).

[80] Gowland and Garnsey (2010) 132–3 for a brief overview.

[81] Shaw (1996); Scheidel (2004); Shaw (2006); Hin (2013) 103–4.

[82] The works of the satirists are full of references to substandard accommodation and speculation by the wealthy with cheaply built *insulae*; e.g. Mart., *Epig.* 3.30, a *fusta cella* as living quarter; 3.48, a *cella pauperis*, first built for fun, then becoming real; 3.52, speculation with real estate; 4.37, high income from *insulae*; 7.20, for a *cella* 200 steps high. For further references, see Holleran (2011) 179 n. 127.

[83] Garnsey (1991).

[84] e.g. Mart., *Epig.* 3.52, for a building set on fire, possibly deliberately. Ramage (1983) for further references and Aldrete (2004) 93–7 for introduction. For fires Capponi and Mengozzi (1993) 7–13; for floods Aldrete (2007), estimating at 14–15, 81 that every few years a flood would occur, and every twenty years a major one.

[85] See Killgrove (2010*a*) 7, summarizing her own research on Casal Bertone and Castellaccio Europarco. Notwithstanding some variation between the two sites, 'the human remains indicate a surprisingly healthy life, or at least one without diseases that took a toll on the skeleton. The assumption that urban life had a demonstrably ill effect on the health of the lower classes is therefore questioned.' But compare Gowland and Garnsey (2010) 149, summarizing their discussion of evidence from via Collatina, Osteria del Curato and, somewhat further out from Rome, Vallerano: 'The skeletal evidence supports the hypothesis that Rome was an unhealthy place in which to live.'

[86] Hin (2013) 104 points out that in a regime of high mortality $e_{(0)}$ can still be somewhere between 20 and 40.

The best approach is through the study of the infectious diseases that were responsible for mortality.[87] The levels of high mortality that occurred in the Roman world are, after all, generally believed to have been caused by infectious diseases. In the absence of adequate medicine, populations were relatively unprotected to whatever disease came around. Of course there were other causes of death, such as warfare, famine, and natural disasters, but infectious diseases structured the basic patterns.

Obviously we cannot chart their occurrence in any detailed way. Although great advances have been made in identifying diseases in skeletal material, the fundamental problem remains that *infectious* diseases hardly leave traces in bones.[88] But by studying the general mechanisms for transmission we can obtain a better sense of potential mortality differentials. It has been argued that the fact that much migration was temporary will have mitigated such differentials.[89] Although enhanced connectivity is certainly something to be taken into account when thinking about disease pools, the fact that diseases could spread rapidly does not imply that differentials would be nullified: endimicity thresholds, for example, would only to a very limited extent be affected. It also needs to be taken into account that not all diseases will have been transmitted by humans; malaria is a case in point.

The disease environment of Rome shows a variety of diseases—endemic, epidemic, or both. 'Rome was a doctor's dream.' '[E]very contagious disease known to its empire was bound to enter it sooner or later', as Scheidel writes. He also points to the damaging effects when they interacted with each other.[90] Rather than discussing the whole cocktail, we may focus on three major diseases. It is generally agreed that malaria, tuberculosis, and typhoid fever were three great killers in Rome,[91] but it is also clear that they differed from each other in major respects.

If infectious diseases are the main killers, the crucial determinant is how diseases were spread. Major differences existed in the transmission of diseases. At least three factors seem important.[92] Malaria is locus specific: geography holds the key. In the case of typhoid, lack of hygiene is the crucial determinant for its spread. Tuberculosis is transmitted through proximity to someone who sneezes or coughs, which means that it is the degree of social interaction and more generally population density that determines its spread. The question is

---

[87] For what follows, see Oerlemans and Tacoma (2014) with full references.

[88] Catalano et al. (2013) 18: 'Le malettie infettice che provocano la morte raramente lasciano tracce evidenti sullo scheletro.' Though see Gowland and Garnsey (2010) for indirect indications of malaria in skeletal material.

[89] Hin (2013) 210–57.   [90] Scheidel (2003) 158, 169. See also Morley (1996) 41–3.

[91] Scheidel (1994) 156; Shaw (1996) 133; Morley (2005) 195.

[92] Temperature is a fourth variable, but though its importance for malaria is very large indeed, it is for the present discussion of less relevance.

to what extent the situation with respect to these three factors (geography, hygiene, population density) differed between Rome and elsewhere.

Malaria is a highly localized disease; its transmission depends on particular types of mosquitoes that feed on malarious humans.[93] Although the hills of Rome will have offered protection and significant variation will have occurred even within the city itself, it is clear that the lowlands of Rome formed ideal breeding grounds for the mosquitoes. The exact degree to which malaria occurred may be debated, but we may safely assume that malaria was endemic in Rome. It is also likely that Rome belonged to the more malarious areas of the Roman world. At the same time, it should be realized that if we were able to draw a distribution map of the disease's prevalence, this map would bear little relationship to the urban hierarchy. Mosquitoes are not known for their capacity to distinguish between city and village. Some places, Rome included, would offer good breeding grounds, others would not. Rome was certainly at one end of the spectrum, but so might be other regions, both rural and urban.[94]

Hygiene is the second variable. Typhoid is spread by drinking polluted water or eating polluted food. Cesspools, street food, the lack of separation between drinking-water and sewage systems, all form risks. The quality of sanitation has direct repercussions for the spread of diseases. In an often-cited article, Scobie argued that hygienic conditions were horrendous in Rome.[95] Sewers, latrines, and baths were all extremely unhygienic. The Roman infrastructure and public amenities that made life in the city attractive must also have contributed greatly to mortality.

Scobie's assessment formed a healthy (?) antidote against overly optimistic assessments of Roman hygiene. Scobie based himself to a large extent on ancient literature. Subsequent research by archaeologists has, at least in two respects (hygiene in toilets and waste disposal), vindicated Scobie's arguments.[96] With respect to housing, the picture is more ambiguous: the existence of slums (in the proper sense of the word) may be questioned,[97] and the few surviving *insulae* turn out to be of relatively high quality, similar to those in Ostia,[98] though of course one may argue that that is precisely the reason why they were the few that survived.[99] However, in the ensuing debate about

---

[93] Sallares (2002).   [94] Cf. Lo Cascio (forthcoming).

[95] Scobie (1986); contrast the much more positive evaluation of Kolb (1995) 568–81; Aldrete (2004) 97–103 for an overview.

[96] Thüry (2001) on waste; Jansen (2011) on toilets.

[97] Aldrete (2007) 112–13 provides some good discussion of the possible dwellings of the urban poor, but admits that much remains speculative. The problem is not only that these dwellings have left no trace in the archaeological record (which is only natural), but that ancient literature, though certainly mentioning beggars, never does refer to slums.

[98] Laurence (1997).

[99] See Aldrete (2007) 105–12 with further refs, for a pessimistic assessment of the quality of most *insulae*. For the notion that standards were improved after the great fire of Nero, see Tac., *Ann.* 15.43.

Scobie's arguments, the question has been raised which yardstick we use. Was life in Rome that bad by pre-industrial standards? It is not inconceivable that, in comparison with other major pre-industrial cities, Rome performed moderately well.[100] Lo Cascio argued that, from Augustus onwards, the involvement of emperors with the basic infrastructure of the city resulted in improvements in hygiene and sanitation.[101] Others, however, have been less optimistic. 'In no other period was Rome ever as big and as unhealthy as in antiquity. For this reason, comparative evidence capable of conveying an adequate impression of the scale of mortality and morbidity in the ancient metropolis simply does not exist.'[102]

For our purposes, the crucial question is *not* how Rome performed compared to other pre-industrial metropoleis, but rather how it performed relative to other Roman settlements (urban and rural). In itself the cities outside Rome can hardly be thought to have been more hygienic. But if public amenities and street food were the main contributors to lack of hygiene, then the sheer scale of Rome is likely to have made conditions worse.

The situation with respect to the last variable, population density, is clearest. It is here that some data are available. We need not go as far as Farr, who formulated a statistical law relating density to mortality: the twelfth root of the density of the population. The law certainly applies to the cities of Victorian England, but for other periods exact proof is lacking.[103] The crucial point about imperial Rome is that population density was extremely high in comparison to that of other, smaller Roman cities. We might use the Augustan population figure and the area covered by the Augustan *regiones* to calculate population density. Assuming the estimated 800,000 to 1 million inhabitants lived on 1,783 ha, population density was in the order of 450–560 pers./ha.[104] The calculation is obviously of a rough order. Within the area, large variations must have existed. The figures will have been much higher in specific areas, particularly in the heart of the city.[105] Moreover, perhaps only as little as half of the area of Rome was available for housing, while the rest was occupied by public buildings, imperial palaces, open spaces, roads, and aristocratic

---

[100] As Scobie (1986) 400 himself already acknowledged. This is one of the central arguments of Lo Cascio (2000) 43–56. See Morley (2005) and Jansen (2011) for further discussion with bibliography. Cf. also Scheidel (2003) 159–60 on the Blissful Dinosaur Fallacy: 'the assumption that dinosaurs could not be harmed by an asteroid impact because they did not know the first thing about astronomy.'

[101] Lo Cascio (2000) 48–9.   [102] Scheidel (2003) 174.

[103] De Vries (1984) 179; Woods (1989) 85.

[104] For refs to comparative data, see Morley (1996) 34–5. Lo Cascio (2000) uses 400–500 pers./ha. The calculation is affected by notions of how densely Rome's *suburbium* was populated and where the built-up area of the city ended; see for some discussion Killgrove (2010*a*) 20–4.

[105] Aldrete (2007) 213. For wide variation in density figures, also in comparative evidence, see Hin (2013) 222.

horti.[106] Furthermore, many low-lying areas were less suited for housing because of the risks of flooding by the Tiber, though this was in itself not an impediment to building cheap *insulae* in such locations.[107]

Be that as it may, the average population density of the city of Rome was certainly much higher than anywhere else. The figure that is often used for medium-sized cities is 200 pers/ha. Also with regard to density, Rome was at the apex of the urban hierarchy. The many small cities that dotted the empire not only had much smaller populations but also much lower population densities. Although it has sometimes been assumed that they functioned equally as urban graveyards, it is much more likely that they were at or below equilibrium levels, and were capable of producing a surplus population.[108]

Even within the contours of a relatively simple model of three variables, a varied landscape of mortality will have existed, in which the rural–urban divide was not as clear-cut as it has often been taken to be.[109] However, no matter how we weigh the various factors, it seems unavoidable to assume that Rome was also at the apex of mortality regimes. It is clear that Rome performed badly with respect to all of the three main factors that determined the spread of disease. Firstly, Rome was certainly extreme in its population density. With respect to geography, it also clearly belonged to the more malarious parts of the peninsula. And finally, the immense scale of the public amenities might have affected hygienic conditions adversely. It thus seems very likely that there were substantial differences in mortality between the city of Rome and the rest of the Roman world.

6. FERTILITY

Fertility is the other element that is relevant for urban migration theory. Just as is the case with mortality, marriage and fertility play a different role in each model. In Wrigley's model, differences in the levels of mortality are the cause of migration. There is, however, one important condition that should be met, and that is that the high levels of mortality are not compensated by equally high or higher levels of urban fertility. In Sharlin's model there are *differences* in the level of fertility between the resident core population and the migrant population. The key for these lower levels of fertility lies in mechanisms preventing marriage among immigrants. If we want to investigate the applicability of either theory, we should therefore devote some discussion to these

---

[106] Hermansen (1978) 146–7, 152, and 166–7, where there is a warning against a too rigid division between private and public space.
[107] Aldrete (2007) 211–17.   [108] Jongman (1990). Cf. Hin (2013) 223 n. 50.
[109] In a similar vein Hin (2013) 227.

factors. Is there evidence for relatively high levels of fertility among the urban population? Should we posit a separate fertility regime for the immigrant population, with lower incidence of marriage?

Even for the early modern world these questions have received less attention than they deserve. Much of the discussion for early modern Europe centres on the interpretation of insufficient empirical data. For a long time fertility was also hardly discussed when the urban migration theory was applied to the Roman world.[110] Scheidel devotes no more than a footnote to it (though admittedly an important one).[111] Other authors are even less forthcoming.[112] Again, the lack of empirical data is obvious; the discussion can only be conducted in a qualitative way.

The answer to the first question, whether the high mortality of Rome was compensated by equally high levels of fertility, must on general grounds be negative. Fertility levels are likely to have been high, but the likelihood that they were so high that they compensated for mortality is dim. The arguments have already been discussed in Chapter 4, Section 4 from a somewhat different perspective in the discussion of marriage patterns and skewed sex ratios. Whether we locate the responses to the friction in the marriage market specifically among the migrants or in the population at large does not seriously affect the argument. The likelihood of male singlehood and the delay in male marriage are difficult to reconcile with a scenario of high fertility.

There is only a need to discuss some additional arguments. On general grounds one may perhaps assume that poverty led to lower fertility rates, but it has been argued that poverty does not necessarily lead to smaller families.[113] By contrast, a reverse argument has been put forward. It has been pointed out that the fact that female age of marriage was so low in the city (starting when women reached puberty) will have led almost automatically to high fertility.[114] But the question remains to what extent really low ages at marriage actually contribute to fertility: women will not yet have been at full reproductive capacity for a long time. The very early age of female marriage is primarily the product of scarcity of available female marriage partners. In fact, early pregnancies are more likely to have contributed to female mortality than to anything else. There can be little doubt that the pressure on women to produce children was high, but there is little reason to assume that it was so high that births exceeded deaths.

---

[110] Likewise Hin (2013) 211: 'the role of fertility has not been studied in sufficient depth.'

[111] Scheidel (2003) 175 n. 74: 'Although correspondingly higher birth rates are possible in theory, in this context they would seem improbable for a number of reasons including a high incidence of stillbirths owing to malaria infection, below-average nuptiality and fertility among first-generation immigrants, and the possibility of male-biased sex-ratios'—note that Scheidel discusses the two problems simultaneously. Cf. also brief remarks by Morley (1996) 44–5.

[112] Though cf. now Hin (forthcoming) on migrant fertility in Roman Athens.

[113] Hin (2013) 172–209.

[114] Hin (2013) 252–3; likewise De Ligt and Garnsey (forthcoming).

Table 5.2. Children as commemorators of soldiers

Sample	Source	N	Children	%
1. Soldiers commemorated in Rome	Noy (2000) 69 table 7[1]	364	14	3.8
2. Soldiers commemorated outside Rome	Ricci (1994) 29 table 2[2]	315	8	2.5
3. Veterans commemorated outside Rome	Ricci (1994) 29 table 2[3]	183	28	15.3

Notes: [1] Soldiers with stated origin outside Rome. Categories 'wife and children' (4), 'children' (10). Presumably the totals include veterans as well (few in number). [2] *Milites* category *filii/filiae*. [3] *Veterani* category *filii/filiae*.

Sharlin's migrant fertility implies that proportions married are different in town and country, and that immigrant fertility was much lower than that of the Rome-born population. Again, many of the issues have been discussed in the previous chapter. Following the arguments presented there, there can be little doubt that immigrants lagged behind in the incidence of marriage. It does not matter much whether we postulate substantial return migration of men seeking brides in their places of origin, or hypothesize a rather cramped urban marriage market leading to substantial delays in marriage of migrants. The resulting lower incidence of marriage will almost automatically have led to decreases in migrant fertility. Overall fertility in the population of the Roman world may not have been affected, as returning migrants might have fathered children at home rather than in Rome.[115]

In the case of the soldiers, we can observe some of the patterns, though it is strictly speaking not fertility itself but paternity that can be analysed. Given the delays in marriage discussed in the previous chapter, it seems extremely likely that soldiers produced few children when they were in active service. The patterns can be analysed by comparing various epigraphic samples in which children act as commemorators of soldiers and veterans (see Table 5.2). The figures themselves are of little significance; what matters are the differences between the samples. The percentage of children who commemorate soldiers who died in active service in Rome (sample 1) is very low. The percentage is similar to that of commemorations of soldiers who were commemorated outside the city (sample 2). Percentages increase drastically for veterans outside Rome (sample 3), which suggests strongly that children were normally only produced after service, and after discharged soldiers had left Rome.[116] The findings conform to the patterns discussed in the previous chapter and

---

[115] Hin (2013) 245–50.
[116] What does not appear from the table, but has been confirmed by other research, is that most of the commemorations by children date from the third century AD, after the lifting of the marriage ban. The implication is that the percentages for the first two centuries will have been even lower.

suggest (unsurprisingly) that fertility patterns were directly related to the peculiar marital patterns of soldiers. Within the city they will have produced relatively few children. The patterns of fertility and paternity are certainly related to their return migration.

Fertility patterns of slaves were probably different. In all probability, overall levels of fertility among slaves (both within and outside stable relations) were relatively high. In the prevailing system of slave breeding, a clear relation existed between fertility and manumission: manumitted slaves compensated their owners with new slaves—their own children. But the argument for relatively high levels of slave fertility is based on slave-breeding systems, which rests on the assumption that most slaves are Rome-born. The logic of the argument is important. The more emphasis is put on higher slave fertility, the more it is implied that slave breeding was the dominant source for new slaves, and the less we consider them as immigrants. Freedmen fertility should also be taken into account. Freedmen couples had every incentive to produce children after their manumission, as these children would count as freeborn and would have full legal rights. But female manumission often occurred relatively late, at the end of the reproductive period. The late timing of female manumission was certainly quite deliberate: in this way the high frequency of manumission did not lead to high numbers of descendants of freedmen. It has been pointed out that, despite the fact that freedmen figure very prominently in the epigraphy of Rome, there are relatively few freeborn children mentioned by them.[117] The servile population might have offered a relatively high contribution to fertility, but this produced mainly additions to the slave stock, not to the citizenry. Particularly high levels of fertility should not be considered a property of the unfree *immigrant* population.

The arguments in the previous chapter concerned marriage rather than fertility itself. One question that remains to be discussed is the extent of extramarital fertility. Augustan marriage laws indicate that the problem they attempted to address was in creating legitimate offspring, not necessarily in increasing overall levels of fertility. Prostitution, extramarital affairs, and sexual relations with slaves will all have produced children in addition to those produced in wedlock. However, given widespread practices of infanticide and exposure, and the fact that often such children will not have been welcome, the likelihood that they made up for fertility deficits seems slight. Again, such an argument can only be suggestive, but it would take a radically different understanding of Roman society to argue otherwise. Extramarital fertility will certainly have existed, but is unlikely to have remedied the low incidence of marital fertility.

---

[117] Morley (1996) 45.

If the composition of migrant groups was as unbalanced as was argued in the previous chapter, the conclusion is almost inescapable that migrant fertility was relatively low. Migrants delayed their marriage, some may perhaps have never married at all, whereas many left Rome. Many of the children that migrants may have had will thus have been born outside Rome. It therefore seems very likely that Sharlin's scenario of depressed immigrant fertility does apply to the case of Rome.

7. MODELLING ROMAN IMMIGRATION

We may, then, posit that *both* Wrigley's and Sharlin's models applied to the city of Rome.[118] If so, it would also imply that all ancient historians who have employed varieties of the urban migration theory have been right. This may not be an earth-shattering conclusion, but we should realize that it may form an important contribution to urban migration theory, for the two models have not been combined simultaneously for the early modern world.

A new model might be tentatively formulated. The model does not distinguish between free, forced, and state-organized migration. It operates independent of agency; whether migrants are moved, or move out of their own volition, does not matter. What does matter is the fact that these three forms of migration show similar patterns in terms of geography and demography, for this legitimizes a unitary approach.

Due to the living conditions and disease structure, the population of Rome experienced natural decrease, with deaths exceeding births. An outside supply was necessary to keep the city at a stable size. Migrants came to the city, but a significant part only stayed there temporarily. Also, because of their skewed gender composition, with men dominating the migration streams, migrant fertility within Rome was low. Many migrants were unable to find a marriage partner, or died before they had found one, or returned home and married there.

On the basis of the London data, an annual deficit of 10 persons per 1,000 inhabitants has been postulated for Rome: the number of deaths per 1,000 per thousand persons was 10 higher than the number of births (say 40 to 30 per 1,000).[119] With a population of 800,000 to 1 million this would lead to an annual birth deficit of 8,000 to 10,000 persons. If this is regarded as an annual cohort of missing people, and standard model life tables are applied, the deficit

---

[118] For a similar conclusion for the Roman Republic, see Erdkamp (2008) 446; cf. Morley (1996) 40.

[119] Morley (1996) 44; Scheidel (2004) 16; cf. Scheidel (2003).

for the total population that is thus created consisted of 215,000 to almost 270,000 persons, or 27 per cent of the population.[120]

How many immigrants would have to come on an *annual* basis to Rome to compensate for this birth deficit depends on their age structure and their return patterns—migrants are the survivors of a birth cohort.[121] Attempts to analyse the age and gender composition have been made in the previous chapter. However, the *total* number of immigrants that must have been living in the city to compensate for the missing births is simply the same as the total deficit population. Irrespective of gender, mortality, and fertility regime, the total number of immigrants produced by the calculation must have consisted of 215,000 to almost 270,000 persons, or 27 per cent of the total population.

This figure of 27 per cent is, of course, only the outcome of proxy data for the birth deficit. It may or may not be correct. But it is remarkable that it is closely in line with the estimated range of 20–30 per cent of immigrants among Rome's population argued for in Chapter 2, Section 4. Although each of the figures (the guestimates, the isotopic evidence, and the urban graveyard figure) is in itself not particularly trustworthy, the figures can be used to support each other.

A last issue remains. As for immigration itself, the theory might offer only a partial approach. In his original article Wrigley warned: 'all the calculations made above are based on figures of net immigration into London. The gross figures must certainly have been considerably higher since there was at all times a flow of migrants out of London as well as a heavier flow inward.'[122] But the warning seems to have been lost in the subsequent discussion.[123] Actual levels of migration could be higher than that of the net migration postulated by urban graveyard theory.

In fact, one of the famous migration laws of Ravenstein stipulated that for every stream of immigration a counter-stream comes into existence.[124] It is important to realize that the counter-stream does not consist of migrants who are returning, but of people who are born in the city and subsequently emigrate. The size of the counter-stream varies, but often it can be very significant. In fact, in London Ravenstein has shown that in a later period very significant counter-streams of London-born persons migrating to other

---

[120] With Model West Level 3 females a missing cohort at birth of 8,000–10,000 would result in a missing total population of 215, 394–269, 242.

[121] Cf. Scheidel (2004) 15–17.

[122] Wrigley (1967) 49; cf also Pooley and Turnbull (1998) 24 in a more general sense: 'A strictly demographic approach focuses attention on the net impact of migration in changing the distribution of population and the size of settlements . . . Such analysis clearly demonstrates the extent to which population increase or decrease in particular regions was due to migrational change or natural change, but concentration on the net balance of migration flows seriously underestimates the total impact of migration.'

[123] Though cf. De Vries (1984) 209–12, and, for the Roman world, Erdkamp (2008) 441.

[124] Ravenstein (1885; 1889); Pooley and Turnbull (1998) 11–12 for discussion.

English cities existed. The focus on net migration obscures both qualitative and quantitative appreciations.

It is impossible to use urban migration theory to calculate the gross rates of immigration and emigration. At the same time the fact that in the calculation the level of net migration is already high is of real importance. If it is really within the same range as the estimates presented in Chapter 2, which do concern crude immigration, it means that the room for any additional immigration and emigration was very limited. If we assume that net immigration was close to crude immigration, the important implication is that, in the case of Rome, the theory actually does function relatively well to describe actual migration streams.

6

Migration and Labour

The working stratum, as opposed to a class in the purely economic sense, includes Romans who manage small businesses, those who own them, and those who labor in them as slaves or wage-workers; skilled artisans working for themselves and for others and professionals such as doctors and teachers must also be included here. Thus, for the Roman world, workers are proletarian, slave, artisan, professional, petit bourgeois and low level bureaucrat. Foreigners as well as citizens belong in this group too.[1]

1. FINDING MOTIVES

In a pioneering study of female labour in Ostia, Kampen described the composition of the Roman workforce. As the quotation makes clear, it was a mixed bag. This chapter addresses a seemingly simple question: to what extent did migrants come or were they brought to Rome looking for work?[2] How did Kampen's 'foreigners' fit into her workforce? More generally, the chapter analyses the relation between migration and Rome's labour market. That relationship is potentially complex. Not only do the available opportunities for work determine the volume of migration, the type of labour opportunities might also structure migration streams: if mainly casual labour is available, migration might remain largely of a temporary nature attracting unskilled labourers; if it was easy to set up independent workshops, craftsmen from other urban centres might be tempted to come to Rome. Conversely, migration itself may structure the labour market or induce changes: if large groups of unskilled workers are seeking a living, projects might be created to provide an income for them. To complicate matters further, at a personal level

[1] Kampen (1981) 28.
[2] This chapter incorporates material from Tacoma (forthcoming *a*). Much of the subject matter is treated in more detail by the dissertation on the labour market of Roman Italy by my colleague Miriam Groen-Vallinga; some of our combined views on labour-related subjects can be found in Groen-Vallinga and Tacoma (2015) and (forthcoming).

migration might involve a change of livelihood:[3] it might, for example, turn a peasant into an unskilled worker unloading ships in the harbour.

The subject is important, for more than one reason. If voluntary and forced migration are regarded to some extent as structurally equivalent, the question what governs the choices between the employment of free and slave labour becomes all the more acute. Moreover, in Chapter 3 it was argued that the particular form of the Roman family favoured the immigration of young males. Ultimately, however, the arguments only concerned the availability of potential migrants rather than actual migration. And once we assume that the potential labour of young adults is diverted outside the home, it is still not necessarily the case that this labour is employed in Rome: a young adult male peasant in search of work might also work as farmhand elsewhere.[4] Likewise, the urban migration theory discussed in Chapter 4 might easily suggest a causality that is not there. Cities may need migrants in order to remain at a stable size, but that does not mean that migrants move to Rome because the city needs them.[5] Need or motivation must be established, not assumed.

Finding in the written sources motives—establishing need—for moving to Rome is less easy than it might appear at first sight. There are very few ancient sources giving reasons for migration.[6] Migrant inscriptions are usually confined to bare basics, and motivation normally cannot be inferred from the lapidary information they contain. Admittedly, an often-quoted passage from Seneca does discuss the motives of free migrants. Beautiful though it is, it goes too far to use it as an explanatory framework for the motives of the thousands of migrants that lived in Rome. The text is too isolated, the context too rhetorical, and it is too obviously written from an elite perspective.[7]

> But look at this mass of people, for whom the number of houses of the immense city hardly suffices: the largest part of this crowd lacks a fatherland. From their *municipia* and colonies, from the whole world they have streamed together. Some have been brought by ambition, some by the requirements of public office, some

---

[3] Erdkamp (2008) 418.   [4] Cf. Erdkamp (forthcoming).
[5] Morley (2003) 150; likewise Holleran (2011) 158, who wryly remarks that 'rather Rome would have functioned better with fewer people'.
[6] Noy (2000) 85–7, noting that the only (and rather late) case in which the process is described in any detail in ancient literature is Aug., *Conf.* 5.8.14, cf. 4.7.12 and 5.12.22–13.23, where two of his other moves are motivated. However, Augustine's wish to be able to teach in a stricter environment than Carthage can hardly be taken to be representative even of ambitious teachers. See in general Holleran (2011) 161 n. 35: 'in any case, every migrant testimony may be different, with personal accounts too individualistic to allow generalisations to be drawn.' For the importance of the *Confessiones* for other aspects of Roman migration, see Tacoma (forthcoming c). For a satirist's joke about reasons for coming to Rome, see Mart., *Epig.* 3.38, 14: 'if you are a good man, Sextus, you can live by accident', *si bonus es, casu vivere, Sexte, potes*.
[7] For brief but pertinent remarks, see Holleran (2011) 161. It is unclear to me how seriously Noy (2000) 85–139 takes the passage; on the one hand he makes a number of qualifications, but on the other, he uses the passage to structure his lengthy analysis.

by an embassy that was imposed upon them, some by luxury, searching for a convenient and richly furnished place for their vices, some by the wish to study, some by the spectacles; others are drawn by friendship, others by zeal, finding ample opportunity to display virtue; some have brought beauty for sale, some eloquence for sale.[8]

Despite its limited role in Seneca's passage, it seems obvious to assume that labour formed a major motive for Roman migrants to move to the city.[9] In modern forms of migration there is a direct link between migration and labour: much—though certainly not all—migration is related to work.[10] To be sure, it is often the Industrial Revolution that is held responsible for the creation of an open labour market (or vice versa) that in its turn created large waves of labour migration.[11] But precisely in the absence of mechanization that was the hallmark of pre-industrial conditions, the demand for human labour was immense.

In the case of the ten types of migration described in Chapter 2, it is clear that for some types labour-related migration motives will have been more important than for others. For the elite it did not matter—or rather, the absence of having to work formed a necessary condition for belonging to the real aristocracy both in a practical and symbolic sense. Some other migrants came to Rome in order to work, not because they were looking for it. But for almost all migrants below the elite, their moves were at least to some extent connected to labour. The assumption that most migrants were young adults reinforces the idea.

---

[8] Sen., *ad Helv.* 6.2: *Aspice agedum hanc frequentiam, cui uix urbis inmensae tecta sufficiunt: maxima pars istius turbae patria caret. Ex municipiis et coloniis suis, ex toto denique orbe terrarum confluxerunt: alios adduxit ambitio, alios necessitas officii publici, alios inposita legatio, alios luxuria opportunum et opulentum uitiis locum quaerens, alios liberalium studiorum cupiditas, alios spectacula; quosdam traxit amicitia, quosdam industria laxam ostendendae uirtuti nancta materiam; quidam uenalem formam attulerunt, quidam uenalem eloquentiam.*

[9] There is some room for interpretation. Basore, in the Loeb edition of 1922, translates the *industria* phrase rather freely with 'some, seeing the ample opportunity for displaying energy, by the chance to work'. Cf. in the same text Sen., *ad Helv.* 7.4, stating that different people have been impelled by different reasons to leave their homes, *alios alia causa excivit domibus suis*, but where finding work is not mentioned at all among the motives. For the importance of labour as a migration motive, see De Ligt and Tacoma (forthcoming).

[10] In many studies the role of labour as a motive for migration is seen as self-evident. Already Ravenstein based his Migration Laws on this assumption; see Ravenstein (1885) 198: 'the call for labour in our centers of industry and commerce is the prime cause of those currents of migration which it is the object of this paper to trace. If, therefore, we speak somewhat presumptuously of "laws of migration", we can only refer to the mode in which the deficiency of hands in one part of the country is supplied from other parts where population is redundant.'

[11] Sanjek (2003) 325 on the relation between proletarization, the development of wage labour, and the emergence of rural–urban labour. See Moch (2003) 60–101 for proto-industrialization and proletarization after 1750. Holleran (forthcoming *b*) makes a plausible case for linking in the Iberian peninsula many migrant inscriptions to the mines that were ubiquitous there, despite the fact that none of the persons involved mention an occupation.

Such labour migration is usually studied in the context of push-and-pull theory.[12] Migrants were either pushed from their homes because of adverse conditions, or pulled to their new destination by opportunities to improve their lot; or, in fact, by the relative difference between the two, and the number of intervening obstacles. Opportunities for labour are usually considered to be the main pull factor, and the research is then directed to the question to what extent and in what ways this pull factor operated. Even apart from the fact that it reduces migrants to passive victims of outside forces who are unable to take their own decision,[13] in the Roman case we have to add forced migration, which locates the motivation at the point of destination rather than origin, and adds an external agency to something which is usually regarded as voluntary. In applying the analysis to the Roman world, it is furthermore important to keep in mind that in a way the causation is almost reversed: as the volume of migration is difficult to determine, the question to what extent labour demands generated migration streams also helps to evaluate the volume of migration, rather than the other way around.

The commercial landscape of Rome can best be seen as an enormous, amorphous mass of small and medium-sized workshops. It is telling that even a grand structure like Trajan's Market consisted of small offices. The conceptual distinction between *opifices* who worked in workshops and *tabernarii* who worked in shops or inns was in practice blurred.[14] Some of the workshops were populated by the servile population, some by the free, and most by a combination of the two. Many artisans worked *and* sold their goods in their own workplace annex shop. They often lived in their own shops (though these would normally be rented), that consisted of one room with an opening at the front and a rear area that could be used for storage, production, and accommodation.[15] In the case of luxury items, the artisans may not have had a great stock, but probably produced on demand.[16] Most production remained small-scale and occurred within the context of the Roman *familia*, though larger production sites employing tens of workers have also been identified.[17] Larger workforces were of course employed in, for example, the imperial building projects, but even there work seems to have been contracted out and divided up into smaller units.

[12] Manning (2013[2]) 198–9. Holleran (2011) 160–1 for its application to the Roman world; De Ligt and Tacoma (forthcoming) for some general remarks.
[13] Jackson and Moch (1989; 1996) 63.   [14] Treggiari (1980) 52.
[15] For a well-preserved example from Rome, see the *insula* on the slope of the Capitol near the S. Maria in Aracoeli, Coarelli (2007) 41. Further e.g. Zimmer (1982) no. 114. DeLaine (2005) 32–6 on Ostia.
[16] Kolb (1995) 468.
[17] Examples include the bakery depicted on the tomb of Eurysaces, see Coarelli (2007) 204–5, and the *fullonica* of Casal Bertone, for which see Musco et al. (2008). For the relative lack of economies of scale, see Mouritsen (2011) 216.

Notwithstanding (or precisely because of) its fragmentation, the economy of the city of Rome must have been of an immense complexity. This is particularly evident from the ownership of workshops. We find almost every imaginable form of property relation. Some workshops were owned by the people who worked there. Others were in the ownership of a somewhat wealthier stratum who owned a number of such shops.[18] Many workshops were owned by members of the elite; these were normally situated in small front rooms in their own *domus*, or were located on the ground floors of the *insulae* that they owned. They could set up their freedmen there,[19] but such workspaces could also be leased out—and not necessarily to people who wanted to work there themselves.[20]

Most of the production will have catered for the needs of the population of Rome itself. This applied both to the general populace, which needed to be fed, clothed, and housed, and the elite, whose appetite for luxury products was endless. Although Rome is often regarded as the archetypical consumer city, Rome did not just consume—there is also evidence of exports.[21] This concerns not only the small objects that people bought when they visited Rome,[22] nor the loads of bricks that were used as counter-freight for the returning ships.[23] Bronze strainers produced in the Circus Flaminius have been found in Noricum and modern Romania;[24] glass and jewellery from the city of Rome can be found all over the empire.[25] The general tendency in art history to automatically ascribe works of very high quality to ateliers located in Rome is certainly not unwarranted.

Given the high volume of production, there can be little doubt that in Rome the demand for labour was very high. At the same time, Rome's labour market will also have been rather crowded.[26] Not only was there a high demand for labour, the availability of labour was also large. Also, in view of the fact that there is hardly any evidence suggesting that migrants occupied particular

---

[18] See Juv., *Sat.* 1.103–111, for an invective against a freedman from the Euphrates, who owns five shops generating an income of HS 400,000. For five shops in a row owned by a woman and associates see the *Forma Urbis di Via Anicia* (*Terme* 1.27): *Corneliae et soc(iorum)*.

[19] See e.g. the *Sententiae Hadriani* case no. 7, with Lewis (1991) for a conflict over income derived from a *taberna* between freedman and patron.

[20] Implied by Juv., *Sat.* 7.3–5, where due to lack of finances, well-known poets are said to be driven to apply for the lease of a bathhouse at Gabii or a bakehouse at Rome.

[21] For general discussion, see Pleket (1993). For ancient imagery of Rome as the city where all goods arrive, see Ael. Arist., *Or.* 26.13.

[22] Petr., *Sat.* 70, where Trimalchio gave his cook a present: 'I brought him back from Rome some knives, made of steel from Noricum.'

[23] Lo Cascio (2000) 20; Martelli (2013) 102. For an exceptional use of the river ships to transport rubble after the fire of Rome in AD 64, see Tac., *Ann.* 15.43.

[24] *A.E.* (1939) 277; Kolb (1995) 467.   [25] Kolb (1995) 467, 469.

[26] Holleran (2011) 173. This probably explains why we do not hear of the employment of convict labour or the labour of soldiers in Rome.

niches of the urban economy, it is legitimate to ask to what extent immigrants could be absorbed by the labour market.

Phrased in this way, the opportunities for migrants may seem slight, but caution should not necessarily lead to pessimism. The problem might be less severe than it may seem. It has been repeatedly emphasized that it is not so much labour per se that attracts migrants, and not even the *differences* in income between the place of origin and Rome (vital though they are), but rather the *expectation* of being able to improve one's situation. Not all potential immigrants will have been well informed about the situation in Rome. In such conditions, migration can remain strong even if a proportion of the migrants are unable to find work, or wages turn out to be lower than expected.[27] Such a situation is of course well known from contemporary Third World megalopoleis.

The problem might be rephrased: it is the openness of the labour market that is crucial for migrants to be able to find work. In order to speak of a labour market in which supply and demand of labour meet, workers (or in the case of slaves, their owners) should have freedom of choice in economic activity and locality. It is here that migration comes in, for the crucial point is that enough mobility must take place for a labour market to function.[28] This mobility may take different forms. It may involve the possibility to switch jobs, but it may also involve physical mobility. The question how much access migrants (free *and* unfree) had to the labour market therefore strikes at the heart of the matter.

In pre-industrial economies perfect market conditions are unlikely to have been fully met, because market forces could not work unimpeded.[29] In the case of Rome, it is the presence of the grain dole (also discussed in Chapter 5, Section 4) that formed the largest distortion. Whatever other reasons there were for distributing grain, there can be little doubt that the massive handouts of free grain and, occasionally, cash imply that many people had difficulties acquiring an income through other means. Although the criteria for eligibility remain hotly contested among scholars, it is clear that a significant part of the free population was entitled to substantial monthly quantities of free grain. However, it is also clear that only a part of the population was included in the distributions (and not necessarily those who needed it most, since it was not a form of poor relief). Although the distributions offered a substantial source of income, they were insufficient to feed a family.[30] Their main function must have been to create a stable, regular base which served to cushion the

---

[27] Holleran (2011) 177–8; Bernard (forthcoming *b*); cf. Erdkamp (forthcoming), emphazising that migration decisions may be taken independently of wage levels.

[28] Temin (2003/4) 515; Holleran (forthcoming *a*); Holleran (forthcoming *b*).

[29] Temin (2003/4) 515–17; Bang (2007) 23–4 emphasizes the importance of transaction costs.

[30] Brunt (1980) 94–5; Bernard (forthcoming), both with further refs.

variabilities in income and food supply, not to alleviate the need to work at all.[31] But the income will have been large enough to create a distinction between the recipients of the dole and those parts of the free population that were excluded from it, and it may, in fact, have lowered general wage levels.[32]

Migrants are in themselves not very visible in our sources about the labour market.[33] In order to know how open the labour market was we need to analyse labour relations from several perspectives and discuss four basic dichotomies that structured labour. The discussion will start with the relation between slave and free labour, then move on to the differences between skilled and unskilled labour, then to the gendering of the labour market, and finally focus on permanency and seasonality. It is only by this indirect route that migrants in the labour market can be located.

2. SLAVE AND FREE LABOUR

It is often assumed that the servile population dominated urban labour in Rome.[34] Such a dominance may have had important economic repercussions. According to this reasoning, it impeded the emergence of a labour market that was dependent on the availability of free labour.[35] It may have blocked important avenues to free migrants looking for work.[36] An open, integrated market where supply of labour and demand for labour would meet through price-setting mechanisms would have been absent. Although the prevalence of slaves in Rome is not in doubt, in recent years this cluster of ideas has come under attack.

The dominance of the servile population in labour is often thought to be visible in the epigraphy of Rome, where freedmen seem to dominate. However, there are two major problems with this type of argument. One is that there are clear epigraphic habits which meant that freedmen put up inscriptions in disproportionate numbers.[37] The other is that the supposed prominence of freedmen in the evidence is more problematic than is often acknowledged:

---

[31] This is also implied by Suet., *Aug.* 40.2, in which it is stated that Augustus rearranged the distributions in such a way that they interfered as little as possible with the work of the recipients.

[32] Noy (2000) 88.

[33] Though see Schörner (papers presented at a conference) for archaeological evidence of mobile artisans.

[34] e.g. Frank (1916), Frank (1927²) (e.g. at 208: Rome 'had no industries not in servile hands'); Rostovtzeff (1926) 168 ('[t]he labour employed both in small workshops and in large concerns of the factory type was chiefly, though not exclusively, slave labour'); or Ross Taylor (1961) 131 ('[t]he freeborn of Rome were also, in the main, shut out of the crafts and the professions'). Bradley (1994) 13 for discussion of similar more recent statements.

[35] Temin (2003/4) 513–14 and Bang (2007) 9 for some historiography; e.g. Hopkins (1978) 14 ('a society which had no labour market') and 111.

[36] Noy (2000) 88–9.   [37] See McKeown (2007) 24–6.

although the Roman onomastic system was in theory exceptionally clear, in practice people omitted crucial status indicators from their names almost at random—which may, incidentally, imply that the status distinctions were for them less important than we tend to think. The number of *incerti* in any data set is extremely high.[38] Moreover, in most analyses the possibility that some persons without *tria nomina* were *peregrini* is simply left out of consideration. The difficulties in interpretation are so great that the conclusion that the servile population dominated the urban labour force cannot be drawn directly from the sources.[39]

If inscriptions cannot solve the issue, the problem might also be approached in a quantitative way. The extent to which servile labour dominated the economy was dependent on the prominence of the servile population within the urban economy: put simply, the size of the group. As we saw, the proportions of slaves, freedmen, and free persons among the population of Rome can only be guessed at, but by any estimate the servile part of the population was large. Slaves formed a substantial part of the population. In line with conventional estimates, in Chapter 2, Section 4 the size of the slave population was estimated at 200,000–300,000 persons, to which freedmen need to be added, at a guess another 60,000–135,000. Out of Rome's 800,000 to 1 million inhabitants, the servile population consisted of 26 to 54 per cent. The logic of the argument suggests precisely the opposite from what is normally argued. Although the servile population formed a sizeable group, in all estimates the free population was very large as well. Only if we combine the maximum numbers of slaves and freedmen with a relatively small population of 800,000 did the servile population form the majority. If the hundreds of thousands of free persons had to make a living, it seems likely that many of them did so on a permanent basis, no matter how precarious such a basis might be. The former were protected by the fact that they were fed by their masters, the latter (at least a part of them) by the grain dole, but in neither case did that obviate the need to work.

It may be that slaves and freedmen dominated the inscriptions, but the sources also clearly show freeborn people in significant numbers at work. Zimmer, for example, found at least 32 per cent of free workers in a series of occupational reliefs.[40] Whatever the proportions, the labour force will have

---

[38] e.g. Kampen (1981) 108 on *incertae* among female workers. In the catalogue of *griechischen Personennamen* of Solin (2003²) *incerti* form the majority (see xxxviii).

[39] Kampen (1981) 27; Silver (2011) 103–4. Cf. Mouritsen (2011) 206–7, who emphasizes the first argument, but downplays the difficulties of identification.

[40] Of the 200 reliefs showing occupations (dating from the first two centuries AD, not from Rome only) analysed by Zimmer, 107 have an inscription that allows analysis of status, of which 34 bear a *tria nomina* with filiation, 36 belong to freedmen, 7 to *seviri*, 2 to slaves, and 28 are *incerti*. Even if all others belong to the servile population (which is uncertain), there would be at least 32% freeborn Roman citizens. Zimmer (1982) 6, however makes the reverse argument, that

consisted of both significant numbers of freeborn and significant numbers of slaves and freedmen.

The most important argument that is based on the analysis of the inscriptions is that slaves and free persons performed the same types of work. Not only did slaves, freedmen, and freeborn work side by side in workshops, in many respects there was no clear distinction between employer and employee.[41] They also did the same work. Occupations attested in the inscriptions or in other written evidence appear to have been held by the servile and free population indiscriminately.[42] This applies also to skilled and relatively high-ranking occupations, such as those of architects.[43]

The functional equivalence of slave and free occupations squares ill with the notion that slaves dominated the urban economy. The similar occupations of the servile and freeborn population have led not only to the rejection of the idea that the servile population dominated the economy, but also to the broadening of the argument to include the notion that slavery should *not* be regarded primarily as an economic institution. Although slave and free labour can (and should) analytically be separated, there was much more interaction than one would expect. As Peter Temin rightly observes, '[t]he question is not how many slaves were present . . . but rather how slavery operated'.[44] As both he and Keith Bradley have emphasized, the distinction between slavery and freedom is primarily of a social and legal rather than an economic kind.[45] One may add Mouritsen's argument that manumission, though of real importance in other respects, changed little in the economic activities of an ex-slave: freedmen, in other words, did not perform other jobs than slaves.[46] In consequence, slavery might be regarded merely as a specific (though rather peculiar) type of labour relation, an extreme form on a spectrum of possibilities.

Although in a general and abstract sense the observed equivalence between servile and free labour seems correct, it merits closer analysis. Precisely to what extent and in what ways were free and slave labour similar in the city of Rome?

most are of servile origin. Cf. Maxey (1938) 8, who emphasized the prominence of slaves, but then wrote that '[t]he small freeman, on the other hand, appears in sufficiently large numbers to convince one that not all poor freemen lived on the dole'.

[41] Treggiari (1980) 52.

[42] Bradley (1994) 65. Likewise Forbes (1955) 326. Groen-Vallinga and Tacoma (forthcoming) on the absence of specifically servile work in Diocletian's *Prices Edict*.

[43] Brunt (1980) 82; DeLaine (2000) 120.   [44] Temin (2003/4) 516.

[45] Bradley (1994) 65 'Nothing indicates . . . that there was a strict separation of slave labour from free labour, or indeed that there was necessarily any competition between the two. In a society where slaves were primarily a social, not an economic category, any such notion would have been alien to the prevailing mentality'; see also Temin (2003/4) 515: 'ancient slavery was part of a unified labor force', and 529 'hence, most Roman slaves, particularly urban slaves, participated in a unified Roman labor market'. In a similar vein already, Crook (1967) 58. Finley (1980) 100–2 stressed the ambiguity it produced in the slave's position.

[46] Mouritsen (2011) 206–47, though note that because of the selectivity of manumission, freedmen are likely to have contained proportionally more skilled than unskilled workers.

There are two approaches: one is to study the exact degree of overlap between slave and freeborn occupations, and the other is to investigate the extent to which servile and freeborn labour relations worked in practice in similar conditions.

The sources certainly show that the freeborn and servile population served in similar economic roles in the city of Rome, but some separation can also be surmised. Domestic servants in close personal service serving masters and mistresses in elite *domus* are likely to have consisted exclusively of slaves and freedmen.[47] Though theoretically possible, it is difficult to imagine a *nomenclator*, a *ministrator* ((table-)servant) or a *pedisequus* (attendant) as freeborn. Physical proximity and trust demanded dependency.

The argument can also be extended to other positions in which trust played a large role. Members of the elite frequently used freedmen in informal arrangements to oversee parts of their personal and business interests. Theoretically this could just as well be done by others, but precisely the fact that freedmen were caught in a web of obligations and patronage made them the ideal candidates to look after their patron's interests.[48]

In that respect the figure of the *institor* is also of importance, a person who was in charge of a business owned by someone else.[49] The concept of indirect agency was widely applied and could comprise practically any economic activity. It was not only used for the wealthier people, but also at quite modest economic levels of society.[50] Although *institores* could be slave, freed, and free alike, in practice it seems that normally slaves and freedmen were employed.[51]

Somewhat similarly, it might also explain why slaves and freedmen were so prominent in the lower ranks of the imperial bureaucracy. The imperial bureaucracy had grown out of elite households. There was a relatively strict division between the salaried posts of the higher echelons and the lower-ranking positions, which seem to have been the preserve of the servile population.[52] The fact that there is some evidence (to be discussed later in this section) that the positions could be obtained (bought?) by outsiders who voluntarily entered slavery is telling.

Slaves in trusted positions in elite households and the imperial bureaucracy were obviously well off—though proximity and trust would produce dangers as

---

[47] Maxey (1938) 5.   [48] Mouritsen (2011) 214–16.

[49] Aubert (1994) for a full study.

[50] Aubert (1994) 7–8 on the occupations mentioned by Ulpian in *Dig.* 14.3.5.1–15. See further e.g. *C.I.L.* 6.10007 for an *institor unguent(arius)* (one of the rare occurrences of *institores* in epigraphy). For the possibility that apprentices are turned into *institores* by a *fullo* who leaves his workplace, see *Dig.* 14.3.5.10.

[51] Treggiari (1980) 53; Bradley (1994) 75; Mouritsen (2011) 216–17. For an example of a slave *institor* at Rome, see *Dig.* 5.1.19.3; for slaves and freedmen conducting business overseas, see *Dig.* 40.9.10.

[52] For a moralizing vignette of the imperial household, see SHA, *Sev.Alex.* 42.2–3: Alexander Severus employs slaves rather than freeborn, and only one of his physicians receives a salary.

well. Yet as is well known, the fortunes of Roman slaves could vary dramatically. At the other end of the spectrum of urban slavery, there is evidence of
slave gangs being used for regular maintenance tasks in state projects. In the
case of the aqueducts, new building projects would presumably be contracted
out, but there were also two maintenance gangs consisting in total of 700
slaves;[53] similar gangs may perhaps be surmised for other state projects. More
generally, dirty, dangerous, or laborious tasks were presumably carried out by
slaves.[54] For example, people turning the millstones in a bakery or the individuals depicted on the treadmill of the crane on the monument of the Haterii
are unlikely to have been anything but slaves.[55] It is also telling that other
mechanical devices that needed muscle-power could be driven both by
humans and animals interchangeably. In all such cases, it seems most unlikely
that free persons would voluntarily sign up for such jobs. As such work was
hardly subject to positive self-identification, it has left few traces in the sources,
at least not by the actors themselves. The types of work might have been used
as a direct punishment for unruly slaves, or been given to slaves thought unfit
for other work, or to slaves specifically bought for the purpose. As examples
such as those of the aqueduct gangs also show, the numbers of slaves involved
in such degrading tasks could be large. It thus seems likely that the bottom of
the occupational ladder remained reserved for servile labour. These areas may
be considered marginal (in more than one sense), but the numbers involved
were not.

It is also significant that all of these examples concern the servile population. The free population seem to have had no separate niches that were
reserved for them, at least not in the civilian sphere. We even find free persons
performing functions that we might, in a Roman context, intuitively associate
with servile labour, such as nursing or teaching.[56] The army is the sole
exception: neither the elite troops stationed in Rome nor the army in general
employed slaves or freedmen.[57]

---

[53] Front., *De aquis* 98, 116–18 for a *familia* of about 240 slaves, originally of Agrippa, passed
on by inheritance to Augustus, and thence to the state, plus a *familia Caesaris* of 460, added by
Claudius. Previously the care for specific aqueducts would be let out to *redemptores*, who also
would employ slaves, *De aquis* 96.

[54] Though note that even a *cloacarius* could apparently also be hired: they occur in Diocletian's *Prices Edict* (7.32), which may imply that also free persons were involved. Thüry (2001) 8
for brief discussion of the organization of the workforces cleaning the sewers; Jansen (2011)
161–2 for the dangers.

[55] For the Haterii, see Zimmer (1982) no. 83; Galli and Pisani Sartorio (eds.) (2009) 93. Vitr.
10.1.3 mentions machines driven by 'multiple workmen' (*pluribus operis*) without specifying
their legal status. For an exception see Suet., *Tib.* 51, where an equestrian is consigned as a
punishment to an *antlia*—no doubt the condemnation of a free Roman of high status to a slave
task served as a double humiliation.

[56] Bradley (1991) 13–75.

[57] Bradley (1994) 65. Suet. *Aug.* 25.2, for the exceptional use of freedmen in the army by
Augustus. They were freed before being enrolled, and kept apart from the freeborn troops. For

The second argument is that slave and free workers operated in daily life in conditions that were very similar. It is a well-known characteristic of Roman slavery that many urban slaves were not completely dependent on the whims of their master, but had considerable room for manoeuvre. Many sources testify to a remarkable degree of freedom for urban slaves.[58] This room for manoeuvre could take diverse forms. The fact that many slaves were skilled is in itself already significant, for it often created knowledge that was outside the control of the owner.[59]

Slaves often had considerable leeway in their dealings, but it is equally remarkable that freedmen, who by definition had much more room for manoeuvre than slaves, very often remained circling around their former master, as was already pointed out in a different context in Chapter 2, Section 2. There is a natural tendency by modern observers to see manumission as the major event in the life of a Roman slave, since it led to the subsequent integration of the freedman into the citizenry. But it seems that in many cases a change of legal status implied little socio-economic change. It is improbable that many freedmen changed their occupation upon manumission, and some will simply have remained in the service of their former master. Nor do we hear of former slaves starting a new life elsewhere. As Henrik Mouritsen puts it: 'manumission did not mark the end of a process but represented a point on a broad continuum of incentives that covered the entire working life of the slave/freedman.'[60] It is telling that the *columbaria* of the *domus* were occupied by slaves and freedmen alike, and that freedmen and their descendants were commonly included in the graves of the wealthier parts of the urban population. In some cases the obligations to the former master were formalized in claims to *operae libertorum*, days of work for the master, but normally the claims remained implicit. In a more general sense, an ideology of loyalty pervaded the relation between freedman and patron— loyalty was expected through *obsequium*, but inscriptions set up by grateful freedmen for their deceased patrons show that it was also internalized.

Slaves and freedmen also worked outside the houses of their owners. Many of the occupations mentioned in the *columbaria* are so specialist that it is unlikely that they only catered for the needs of the *domus* itself. Many of the slaves or freedmen who held them will have worked in workplaces. But in

another exceptional case, see SHA, *Marc. Ant.* 21.6, where slaves and others were enrolled to fight in the Marcomannic War, due to the shortage of manpower created by the Antonine Plague. The only real exception to the exception was the enrolment of freedmen in the *vigiles*, the paramilitary night watch and fire brigade.

[58] e.g. *Dig.* 14.5.8, discussing the case of a slave lending money and taking pledges and engaging in a wide range of related economic activities; likewise *Dig.* 12.1.41.

[59] Though cf. Sen., *Ep.* 27.5–8 for a wealthy slave owner who regards slaves who memorize the literature that he is unable to learn as an extension of his own brain.

[60] Mouritsen (2011) 152.

addition, there is also some evidence that slaves could and did work as hired labourers elsewhere. Either they were hired out or they hired themselves out.[61] They worked under exactly the same conditions as other labourers (though the wage might have gone to the master). This might also apply to the unskilled slaves, and the slaves who worked within smaller households. They will have assembled in one of the fora or other well-known spots. We may imagine that such slaves for hire would assemble in the same place where free labourers could be hired, and one may even imagine that this would also be the place where slaves were sold.[62]

Next there is the evidence for self-sale (or sale by parents), by which free persons entered voluntarily into slavery. It is clear that at least in some cases this was done to obtain coveted positions,[63] and not merely as a desperate move in conditions of dire poverty.[64] Although the scale of the phenomenon

---

[61] Brunt (1980) 89. External slave labour is implied in *Dig.* 7.1.25.2; 9.2.27.34; 13.6.5.7; 19.2.42; 19.2.45.1; 32.73.3. Holleran (forthcoming *a*) points in this context to the definition of Chrysippus of a slave as a *perpetuus mercennarius*, cited in Sen., *De Ben.* 3.22.1.

[62] This might be a possible interpretation of Suet., *Claud.* 22, in which Claudius recites a supplication from the rostra at the forum, 'after all day laborers and slaves (*operariorum servorumque*) had been ordered to withdraw'. See also Plaut., *Aul.* 280–3 and *Pseud.* 790, 804–7. For the location of slave markets in Rome, see Mart., *Epig.* 9.59, in which luxury products, including special slaves, can be found in the Saepta Julia; Sen., *De Const.* 13.4, referring to *qui ad Castoris negotiantur nequam mancipia ementes vendentesque*, i.e. at the temple of Castor and Pollux in the Forum Romanum; cf. Plaut., *Curc.* 481–2, *pone aedem Castoris, ibi sunt subito quibus credas male. in Tusco vico, ibi sunt homines qui ipsi sese venditant*, seemingly referring to male prostitution, but self-sale into slavery is also a possibility. Treggiari (1980) 50–1; Holleran (forthcoming *a*) for in-depth discussion; further Corbier (2001) 62–3 on the *columna lactaria* in Rome, which may have been the place where nurses could be contracted, rather than the place where children were abandoned.

[63] The evidence is discussed in full by Silver (2011), see also Ramin and Veyne (1981) and Crook (1967) 59–61 for the legal ramifications. The legal sources include *Dig.* 1.5.5.1, for persons selling themselves to share in the price, *ad pretium participandum*, likewise *Dig.* 40.14.2pr. *ut pretium ad ipsum perveniret*; also *Dig.* 28.3.6.5, with self-sale in order to engage in the business of the buyer as an alternative motive, *ad actum gerendum*; *Dig.* 48.19.14, where soldiers who allow themselves to be sold into slavery are punished by capital punishment; by implication, civilians who do so are only lightly punished or not all. Other sources include Sen., *De Ben.* 4.13.3, where it is somewhat curiously stated that 'the slave trader renders service to slaves', *prodest . . . mango venalibus*, which seems to imply voluntary self-sale; Petr., *Sat.* 57, where the alleged son of a king explains *ipse me dedi in servitutem et malui civis Romanus esse quam tributarius*; *1 Clem.* 55.2, where selling oneself into slavery is placed in the context of self-sacrifice for the community; Dio Chrys. 15.23, cf. 15.13, where it is claimed in a dispute that many people sell themselves into slavery by contract, δουλεύειν κατὰ συγγραφὴν, though note that the dispute is set in classical Athens. Possible cases of voluntary slavery include *C.I.L.* 6.13328, in which at least one of the sons is an imperial slave and the mother is freeborn (or freed, but in that case not an imperial *liberta*), and *S.G.O.* 04/16/01, where a girl who went to work at the imperial court in Rome is commemorated by her parents at home in Tabala, Lydia; *P.Oxy.* 46.3312, for a person who has gone to Rome and has become an imperial freedmen in order to take up offices, Ἑρμῖνος ἀπῆλθεν ἰς Ῥώμ[ην] καὶ ἀπελεύθερος ἐγένετ[ο] Καίσαρος ἵνα ὀπίκια λάβ[η].; despite the reservations of Weaver (2004) the phrasing seems to imply that he became an imperial freedman straightaway.

[64] Silver (2011) sees self-sale essentially as a betterment strategy; e.g. 74: 'in antiquity free persons faced grave difficulties in borrowing against future earnings to finance training, and,

remains unknown (and is variously interpreted by scholars),[65] the fact that such stories were circulating of people voluntarily selling themselves into slavery in order to advance in society is telling. It is obvious that in such cases the benefits must have outweighed the risks, and it seems likely that the possibilities to be manumitted after a number of years must have seemed relatively certain. It is probably no coincidence that most of the known attestations concern the imperial bureaucracy—precisely one of the high-status areas that were difficult to enter for the free population.[66] It suggests again that the boundary between slavery and freedom was blurred.

The boundary was also crossed from the other side. Lucian's *On taking salaried posts* sketches a situation in which a scholar takes up a position within an aristocratic household. That we hear of hired labourers who lived in the houses of their employers is telling. This could, for obvious reasons, apply to nurses, child-minders, and teachers, but there are also other cases.[67] It seems that they also occasionally ended up in the *columbaria* of the elite, amidst their slaves and freedmen—at least, this is one possible explanation for the occasional appearance of outsiders in the graves.[68] Living and dying together will have blurred the lines between slave, freed, and free.

In that sense, the aristocratic equation of hired work with slavery was to some extent justified.[69] 'Hiring oneself out, selling one's time and labour (*operae*), becoming, however temporarily, the dependent of an employer, perhaps living in his house, perhaps taking orders from his slaves, all this can be seen as limiting a man's freedom of action and reducing his dignity as an individual.'[70] It is likely that many people, both slave and free, did in fact work in the service of others in similar roles.

To sum up, economically the boundary between slave and free was blurred, though not completely absent. Servile and free labour only partially overlapped and are best seen as *imperfect* economic substitutes. The servile population dominated some areas of economic life, but these were relatively few. In

---

especially migration'; self-sale into slavery thus offered a possibility which was otherwise out of reach. Ramin and Veyne (1981) at 488 stressed that both poverty and improvement could be motives, and argued that the distinction might be visible in the expressions *ad pretium participandum* and *ad actum gerendum* which occur in the legal sources.

[65] See Mouritsen (2011) 10 and Scheidel (2011) 300 for doubts about its prevalence. Ramin and Veyne (1981) for a claim that it was common (though in their view exposure was the main source of slaves); Silver (2011) argues that it was widespread.

[66] In this respect SHA, *Elag.* 6.2 might also be relevant, where the emperor is accused (*inter many alia*) of selling positions at court.

[67] Treggiari (1980) 50. Although *Dig.* 48.19.11.1 differentiates between slaves and freedmen living in the house of their masters or patrons and *mercenarii* whose labour is hired, the fact that both are placed within the same domestic context may be significant.

[68] Mouritsen (2013) 46.

[69] Cic., *De Off.* 1.150; cf. 1.13. For general disdain of hired workers, see e.g. Juv., *Sat.* 8.43.

[70] Treggiari (1980) 50.

many others employers had free choice between various types of labour. This raises the question as to why and how choices were made by those who employed them. Individual choices are beyond recovery, and, given the fact that in many areas free and servile labour can be found in equal measure, no easy answers should be expected. The relative costs of purchase and hire, training, investment, upkeep, permanency, flexibility, productivity: all would be relevant.[71]

3. SKILLED AND UNSKILLED LABOUR

A second categorization can be made: that between skilled and unskilled labour. The dichotomy between skilled and unskilled labour is to some extent an analytical one, for in reality a spectrum running from completely unskilled labour to extreme specialization rather than a strict dichotomy will have existed: within the group of skilled workers there was a very large variety of skills and experience; there was also a grey area of people we should call semi-skilled workers, and people might themselves move through the spectrum, by learning on the job.[72] At the same time, it is clear from what we know about remuneration that some conceptual distinction was made between skilled and unskilled jobs: the former paid at least twice as much.

It is important to emphasize that the distinction between skilled and unskilled did not coincide with that between slaves and free.[73] Both could be found in both categories. In the case of the free population, there is enough evidence that both skilled and unskilled work was done. Although some sources about Roman slavery seem to suggest an equation of urban slavery with skilled, specialized work,[74] in practice also many urban slaves will have been working in generic tasks for which little to no special training was required. This applies not only to the cases where smaller households owned one slave, who was likely to have performed all kinds of odd jobs, even if working alongside the owner in a particular craft or trade. It has also been observed that, of the population in the *columbaria* inscriptions, only a quarter mention an occupation. It may be that the rest simply omitted their job, but it

---

[71] Hawkins (forthcoming), discussing the reasons for employing slaves; see also more briefly Silver (2011) 88. Cf. Varro, *De agr.* 1.16.4, who discusses the relative benefits of hired and servile labour on estates.

[72] See e.g. *Dig.* 9.2.27.34, where the distinction between skilled and unskilled was made in the case of a slave hired to lead a mule. For general discussion of the legal framework, see Martin (2001).

[73] Cf. Casson (1978) 45 claiming that unskilled work 'was done totally by slaves'.

[74] Cf. (implicitly) Tac., *Germ.* 25, where slaves among the Germanic tribes, unlike the Roman ones, have no specific duties allotted to them.

is also possible that they formed an unskilled workforce of a more flexible nature, doing whatever task was asked of them.[75]

Unskilled workers are certainly encountered in the sources—and they encompass more than slaves who did not mention an occupation. But much of the written evidence we have for labour is biased towards the skilled part of the labour force. The occupational inscriptions and reliefs in particular are heavily biased towards the arts and crafts.[76] Unskilled work will not always have resulted in a demarcated occupation that lent itself easily to recording; some unskilled work will have been of a temporary nature and therefore was less prone to be etched in stone, and unskilled work provided much less a marker of identity.

The fact that the unskilled are heavily under-represented in the sources makes quantification of proportions of skilled to unskilled work difficult.[77] As we have just seen, in household service too, some (and possibly even many) jobs required little or no training. The two main sectors which needed unskilled labour in large quantities were building and transport. Both also generated a great deal of additional labour through the supply industries, and much of this was again unskilled.

The building industry required labour on a massive scale; enormous numbers of people were involved, though not necessarily all of them unskilled.[78] The major projects were instigated by the emperors, who seem to have had in the back of their minds that this would provide an income for the people, as the all-too-often cited anecdote about Vespasian's rejection of a new labour-saving device shows: he had to feed his *plebicula*.[79] In addition, private projects were instigated at various scales: also private *domus* and *insulae* needed to be built, rebuilt, or renovated. As much of this was financed by the aristocracy, it played a role somewhat similar to that of the emperor in providing employment. In

[75] Hasegawa (2005) 30.
[76] Lo Cascio (2012) 472. Cf. Groen-Vallinga and Tacoma (forthcoming): also in Diocletian's *Prices Edict* unskilled work is mentioned much less frequently than skilled, which implies that epigraphic habits alone cannot explain the biases. For representations of unskilled workers, see Martelli (2013) on clay figurines of *saccarii*.
[77] Temin (2003/4) 517 states that 'the great mass of workers in the early Roman empire were illiterate and—by modern standards—unskilled'. This might be true (taking into account the fact that many people lived in rural areas), but it does raise the question how many people entered the apprenticeship system.
[78] Kolb (1995) 482–5; Holleran (2011) 170–2.
[79] Suet., *Vesp.* 18. For discussion see, among others, Casson (1978); Brunt (1980); Mrozek (1986) 706; Pleket (1988) 273; Kolb (1995) 478–80; Lo Cascio (2012) 475; Erdkamp (forthcoming). See also, in a somewhat similar vein, Suet., *Vesp.* 19.1, where Vespasian gives dinner parties, 'to help the marketmen', *ut macellarios adiuaveret*. Brunt (1980) discusses Plut., *Pericl.* 12.5, who states that the aim of Pericles' building projects was to give the common people a share of the revenues without them becoming lazy; this is regarded as anachronistic and therefore all the more relevant. Casson (1978) 50 n. 27 cites Jos., *A.J.* 20.219–22, in which, after the rebuilding of the great Temple in Jerusalem, the *demos* urges Agrippa II to keep the 18,000 workmen employed.

addition, there were related activities, such as road building and maintenance, which also required the employment of large numbers of workers.[80]

It is the sheer scale of the imperial *grands traveaux* that indicates the large amounts of labour required. Moreover, the fact that many of the projects were built over very short time-spans implies the mobilization of huge labour forces on a short-term basis.[81] Much of the unskilled labour went in the not-easily-visible parts of such buildings. Many of the large imperial building projects were built on artificially created terraces, for which enormous amounts of earth was moved without mechanical aid—wheelbarrows were absent, and baskets were used instead.[82] And before the ground could be levelled, existing buildings and other structures needed to be demolished.[83] The creation of foundations alone already required enormous amounts of building material.[84]

Little is known about the organization of the building industry. Under the late Republic, major-scale operations were contracted to *redemptores*, who for small works contracted individually but for large projects might have formed collectives.[85] It is probable that the practice continued under the empire, both for the large imperial projects and for the smaller private ones.[86] The contractors may have been men of intermediate wealth, who might bring in some workmen (slaves) of their own but needed to hire the rest from outside.[87]

For some particular buildings, scholars have produced estimates of the labour that must have been involved. Calculations for Ostia suggest that if *insulae* were built in four years, only a small team of sixteen-to-seventeen persons would be needed, though that would still imply that in the period of intense building that occurred in Ostia in the early second century AD at least 1,000 men, both skilled and unskilled, would be employed in buildings its

---

[80] Laurence (1999) 69–77.

[81] DeLaine (2000) 129; e.g. the pyramid of Cestius, one of the largest surviving private tombs in Rome, was built in 330 days; see van Aerde (2015) 381 with *C.I.L.* 6.1374. The truly massive Baths of Diocletian were built in eight years, between autumn AD 298 and July 306; see Coarelli (2007) 249 on *C.I.L.* 6.1130.

[82] DeLaine (2000) 129–31.

[83] The dedicatory inscription of the Baths of Diocletian mentions the purchase of 'buildings sufficient for a work of this magnitude', *coemptis aedificiis pro tanti operis magnitudine, C.I.L.* 6.1130. Subsequent excavation has laid bare a part of what was a densely populated quarter that was demolished to make way for the artificial platform of 356×316 metres on which the bath complex was built. See Coarelli (2007) 251–2.

[84] Kolb (1995) 483 on the Colosseum.

[85] Polybius 6.17 with Brunt (1980) 84, for the early practice of using *redemptores*.

[86] Brunt (1980) 84; DeLaine (2000) 121–4. For road-building and maintenance, see e.g. Cass. Dio 59.15.4 and Tac., *Ann.* 3.31, with Laurence (1999) 46. For *redemptores* used for aqueduct maintenance, see Front., *De aquis* 96. For use of *redemptores* by *curatores operum publicum* in the provinces, see *Dig.* 50.10.2.1. For wider use of contracts, see Juv., *Sat.* 3.31–3, where Umbricius inveighs against people who easily take on contracts for temples, rivers, harbours, for draining floods, and transporting corpses to the pyre, *quis facile est aedem conducere, flumina, portus, siccandum eluviem portandum ad busta cadaver.*

[87] Brunt (1980) 86–8.

apartment blocks.[88] In building Rome's large temples, even something as simple as carving cannelures in columns might alone have involved the employment of numerous persons.[89] For one of the truly large projects, the Baths of Caracalla, some 6,000–10,000 workers might have been used, half of them unskilled and semi-skilled, and we may add another 1,000 persons engaged in the production of the raw materials.[90]

The other sector requiring massive numbers of unskilled labourers was the transport sector. It was concerned mainly but not solely with the food supply[91]—the other major task concerning (again) the supply of raw materials to the building industry.[92] We find, for example, *saccarii* (carriers of sacks)[93] and amphora carriers.[94] Occasionally unskilled labour in the transport sector is also mentioned in literary sources. Suetonius mentions *geruli*, carriers, Propertius refers to the towing of ships on the Tiber, and Vitruvius describes *phalangarii*, porters, who worked in teams of four or six people to carry very heavy loads that were balanced in the middle of carrying-poles.[95] It is quite clear that much of this unskilled work was physically demanding; for example, even when empty, amphoras were very heavy.[96] The transport sector provided employment all the way from the harbour in Ostia/Portus to the *horrea* in Rome. It has been estimated that hauling the ships from Ostia to Rome may have provided work for some 4,000 persons, while unloading them at the Tiber quays would involve at least another 3,000 persons.[97]

It has been guestimated that the building industry employed 3–6 per cent of the population, or 15 per cent of adult males, though this proportion included the skilled workers.[98] More general evaluations of the total need for unskilled labour are hindered by other considerations: there is somewhat more evidence for lifting devices than is often admitted, and the immense difficulties of moving monolithic columns in later periods imply the extensive use of cranes;[99] some of the required muscle-power was supplied by animals rather than humans;[100] and the concept of labour-saving practices was not completely

---

[88] De Laine (2000) 126–8.   [89] Kolb (1995) 484.   [90] DeLaine (2000) 131, 135.

[91] Kolb (1995) 485–8.   [92] De Laine (1995).

[93] e.g. *C.I.L.* 6.5356; Martelli (2013).

[94] Meiggs (1973²) pl. 26 and Casson (1994) 103, fig. 76 for a relief from Portus depicting how a ship is unloaded.

[95] Suet., *Cal.* 40; Prop. 1.14.1–4; Vitr. 10.3.7.

[96] See Casson (1994) 102–3 on the weight of an amphora; Martelli (2013) 104 on the weight of sacks filled with grain.

[97] Kolb (1995) 486 on hauling; Aldrete and Mattingly (1999) 197 on unloading requiring 3,000 *saccarii*, an estimate considered by Martelli (2013) 102 as too low.

[98] DeLaine (2000) 135–6; Holleran (2011) 171.

[99] Galli and Pisani Sartorio (eds) (2009); DeLaine (2000) 130–1 argues that the crane that is depicted on the monument of the Haterii could lift 10–12 tons, whereas the large columns used in the Baths of Caracalla weighted *c.*100 tons.

[100] For mules complementing human labour of porters see Laurence (1999) 124–6, citing Hor., *Ep.* 2.2.72 and Suet., *Cal.* 39. Further Erdkamp (forthcoming).

alien to Roman minds.[101] Furthermore, even in sectors where large workforces were required, many of the workers appear to have been skilled: even the slave gangs mentioned by Frontinus that were employed in the maintenance of the aqueducts included some skilled men.[102]

In trying to conceptualize the other end of the spectrum, that of skilled labour, the first element to note is that skill clearly paid off. Normally, skilled labourers would earn at least twice as much as unskilled workers, and it is also clear that, depending on the type of skills that were involved and the status of the occupation, the wage difference could become more marked.[103]

In that respect it is also significant that some of the occupational reliefs depicting tools show very clearly defined occupations, while others depict a much broader range of occupational activity.[104] There are also cases of slaves serving in more than one capacity.[105] We should perhaps envisage a spectrum of specialization in which some persons performed highly specific tasks and others more generic ones within one branch of economic activity. At the upper end of the occupational ladder people were not only expected to be highly skilled, but also to be well educated in general. Thus, Vitruvius stated that architects were expected to be schooled in a much wider set of disciplines than architecture alone, including philosophy, music, medicine, law, and astronomy.[106]

Occupational inscriptions and reliefs form a relatively good guide to the skilled part of the occupational spectrum. They have survived by the hundreds. Some simply state in what job someone was working, others are much more elaborate, and some also contain depictions. The people who commissioned them clearly identified with their labour.[107] They were not confined to craftsmen but concerned all kinds of workers—we find very similar inscriptions for soldiers. Although the elite looked down upon menial labour, the occupational inscriptions and reliefs were not necessarily put up in direct opposition to elite values, but rather emphasized one's place in society.[108]

It is a well-known feature of Roman urban society that an enormous range of different jobs existed. In the city of Rome there are some 160 different

---

[101] Brunt (1980) 83, again on Suet., *Vesp.* 18.   [102] Front., *De aquis* 117.

[103] The best evidence for the differential comes from Diocletian's *Prices Edict*, see Groen-Vallinga and Tacoma (forthcoming); see also *Dig.* 17.1.26.8, in which a *faber* buys a slave, trains him, and sells him for double the price. Hawkins (forthcoming) cites some additional evidence and argues that a skill premium of a factor 2 or more implies that skilled labour in the city of Rome was scarce. However, as Bernard (forthcoming *a*) shows, the Roman skills premium seems in comparative perspective a normal one, and we have no evidence for the exact differential in Rome itself.

[104] Zimmer (1982) no. 161.

[105] *Dig.* 32.99.4 for a cook and litter-bearer, the latter presumably requiring little skill.

[106] Vitr. 1.3; DeLaine (2000) 120 points out that that such well-educated architects are not unknown.

[107] Joshel (1992); McKeown (2007) 27.   [108] Lis and Soly (forthcoming).

occupations mentioned in the inscriptions.[109] The range of jobs was endless. In the household of Livia, the wife of Augustus, we find a furniture-polisher (*colorator*), a wool-weigher (*lanipendus*), and a pearl-setter (*margaritarius*). In total, almost fifty different jobs are known from her *columbarium*, and this certainly does not constitute a complete list. Similar patterns of high specialization appear elsewhere, both inside and outside elite *domus*.[110]

The high degree of occupational differentiation has been noted by many scholars, but it has led to divergent interpretations. On the one hand, it has been interpreted as a sign of specialization and—by implication—of economic complexity.[111] On the other hand, given the fact that many of the occupations belong to the servile population of elite households, it is often interpreted as a sign of conspicuous consumption, connected to the elite ideal of self-sufficiency and the social imperative to display wealth.[112] These explanations are not mutually exclusive.

For our purposes, the precise interpretation of the high degree of specialization matters less than the question who had access to training and in what form. It is often thought that slaves were in a better position to obtain a training, and that this is part of the explanation of their ambiguous position: on the one hand they had the lowest status in society, while on the other, they could experience real social mobility thanks to the skills acquired during slavery. However, if we assume that manumission was a selective process, and given the fact that freedmen dominate the epigraphic record,[113] it is not surprising that the inscriptions easily give the impression that skilled work was predominantly performed by the servile population. In reality, it seems more likely that both slaves and freeborn had access to training in equal measure.

People, both free and unfree, started to work from early on. The value of a slave was reckoned from age 5 onwards, which was apparently the moment he or she was thought to become productive.[114] There are quite a number of epitaphs for children with an occupational title.[115] Many occupations were inherited from father to son, even in the case of slaves. There are epitaphs for young children with depictions of the tools of the job of their father, or

---

[109] Treggiari (1980) 56 with appendix, counts 225 urban jobs for the Latin West, for Rome itself 160.

[110] The classic analysis is that of Treggiari (1973); Bradley (1994) 61–5 added some further comments; further analysis of the *columbaria* occupations is available in Hasegawa (2005) 30–51. The composition of an elite *domus* can also be seen in the will of 'Dasumius' of AD 108, see *C.I.L.* 6.10229.

[111] Kolb (1995) 466–8.   [112] Joshel (1992) 74; Holleran (2011) 167.

[113] Both central arguments of Mouritsen (2011).

[114] *Dig.* 7.7.6.1, clearly set in the context of work.

[115] e.g. *C.I.L.* 6. 9213 for a 9-year-old *aurinetrix*, gold-spinner. Bradley (1991) 115–16; the fact that Hasegawa (2005) 31 found no persons with job titles in the *columbaria* under 16 seems a coincidence.

representations of tools that do not refer to specific members of a family.[116] Although it does not exclude the possibility of subsequent apprenticeships, in many such cases the training of the children is likely to have been informal. Children would start by helping their father and gradually acquire the necessary skills. In the case of young slaves, we may infer that experience was often acquired on the spot; within slave families of elite households, children may have been working in the same area as their parents.[117]

Some of the training might be formalized. In the imperial household there was a *paedagogium* where large numbers of slaves were trained.[118] Outside of it, a normal route would be through the apprenticeship system, also discussed briefly in Chapter 2, Section 2.[119] There is no intrinsic reason to assume that the apprenticeship system attested in Egypt, described in Lucian's semi-autobiographical work *The Dream*, and attested to a more limited extent in other sources, did not function in a similar way in Rome.[120] The apprenticeship system shows some similarities to those known from early modern Europe, with two exceptions. Firstly the Roman form concerned both freeborn and slaves alike—and this is, of course, an additional argument to equate the economic roles of slaves and free persons.[121] Secondly, it was not tied to the operation of *collegia*: it does not seem to have been subject to regulation or control. Apprenticeships appear to be based on personal relations, often between family members. Apprentices started at around the age of 12 to 14, an age at which it can be assumed that children did not make their own choices.[122] Apprenticeships could take anything from six months up to six years. Even in cases where fathers/owners held the same occupation, children and slaves could still be apprenticed outside their own household.[123] The system operated both in villages and in cities, and also concerned semi-skilled

[116] e.g. Zimmer (1982) no. 13 (son), no. 105 (family).

[117] Hasegawa (2005) 56–7 on the Euticus family; but the number of cases that lend themselves to analysis is extremely small. Cf. Nep., *Att.* 13 for home-trained slaves in a late Republican household, *domique factum habuit*.

[118] See Forbes (1955) 334.   [119] Bradley (1991) 107–12; Liu (forthcoming).

[120] Brunt (1980) 84 seemed to think that an apprenticeship system in Rome was absent, and hence that skilled labour was performed by slaves who were trained by their masters. Forbes (1955) 328, 333 assumed it was universal. Both Forbes (1955) 333–4 and Bradley (1991) 115 n. 64 and 75 cite evidence for *discentes* in *CIL* 6; these may be apprentices in the formal sense of the word. For Lucian's *Somnium* see Treggiari (1980) n. 4 and Bradley (1991) 112–13. For apprentices in the *Digest*, see 9.2.5.3 with 19.2.13.4; 14.3.5.10; 21.1.7.3; cf. 17.1.26.8. See further Sen., *Ep.* 27.5–8 for a wealthy parvenu who bought slaves to memorize poetry for him—if he did not find them, he had them made to order, *non invenerat, faciendos locavit*.

[121] *Dig.* 9.2.5.3 mentions both slave and freeborn apprentices.

[122] Nicely demonstrated in Lucian, *Somnium*, though there the narrator ultimately does make a decision contrary to his family's wishes.

[123] Forbes (1955) 328–35; Bradley (1991) 107–12; Liu (forthcoming) shows how they functioned to cement ties between families.

jobs. All these elements suggest that the scale of the apprenticeship system was very large.

If apprenticeships were widespread, and skilled work paid much more than unskilled, the question is how easy was it to cross the line between unskilled and skilled work: could unskilled parents help their children by providing them with a training? In itself the apprenticeship system was not particularly expensive. Yet transaction costs may have been prohibitive.[124] In particular, the loss of labour of family members has to be taken into account. People working in unskilled jobs would have real difficulties in providing a livelihood, and had to mobilize all possible resources to make ends meet. In consequence, there was a limited number of people who could provide children with such an education, and also, given the fact that family ties structured such apprentice-ships, it cannot have been particularly easy to cross the line. Although the acquisition of skill would certainly increase standards of living significantly, it will have been out of reach for many of the unskilled workers, while the semi-skilled workers who were struggling to make ends meet will also not always have been able to pass on their knowledge to the next generation.

It thus seems that the possibilities to acquire a training were relatively large, for both the servile population and the free population. Yet this required an investment that some people were not able to make. The fact that training was available does not imply that everybody obtained it. Many people would end up among the unskilled.

4. FEMALE AND MALE LABOUR

Many discussions of labour implicitly focus on men. However, there is abun-dant evidence that women also worked. Some occupational inscriptions were set up for women, some also by women. Women constituted a significant minority in the sources for workers in Rome.[125] Their position on the labour market is of real interest; the analysis of the labour market must be engendered.

However, it is not particularly easy to progress beyond the simple fact that working women occurred among the labour force. What complicates matters is that within the already biased sources additional gender biases may be at work. There is therefore a real possibility that working women are under-represented in the sources. On the other hand, while the possible biases can hinder the analysis, they might also be in themselves socially significant and indicative of the position of women on the labour market.

---

[124] Hawkins (forthcoming).
[125] For sources, see Kampen (1981) 107–29 with catalogue III; Hasegawa (2005) 32. For some discussion see Kolb (1995) 487–93, and in particular Groen-Vallinga (2013).

A good starting point is the question to what extent the labour market consisted of separate domains for men and women. Given the fact that gendered segregation of labour occurs in many societies, it is unsurprising that some separation existed in Rome. The range of occupations open to women was more limited than for those open to men.[126] It seems likely that certain sectors of the urban economy were closed to women; most notably these were the unskilled jobs that required muscle-power.[127] Few women will have been working in the building or transport industry. On the other hand, there will have been sectors of the economy where women were dominant. Predictably, women are found mostly in jobs associated with the domestic sphere, as child nurses[128] or in textile production.[129] At the same time, the fact that domestic tasks could be formalized into occupations (with the implied possibility of remuneration) is in itself important.[130] Moreover, the 'domestic sphere' turns out to be quite large, extending to midwives and physicians. Textile-working includes the production and sale of luxury items.[131] In addition, women also performed jobs that under any definition fell outside the domestic sphere. Some were of the disreputable type, such as prostitution; others might run the risk of being classified under the same heading, such as innkeeping, dancing, or performing music.[132] But a host of other occupations are also attested, some of them in areas that one would intuitively associate with the male domain.[133] The fact that several reliefs show women at work excludes the possibility that the actual work was delegated to others. It is also clear that some women could acquire substantial incomes from work.[134]

---

[126] Pomeroy (1975) 191; Treggiari (1979*b*).

[127] For a possible exception, Martelli (2013) 101 cites *C.I.L.* 6.25737, mentioning possibly a *saccaria*: *Memoriae saccariae* (or: *Saccariae*) *Zosi[mae]*.

[128] Bradley (1991) 13–36 (and compare 37–75 on the role of men), not all of the nurses are slaves.

[129] Treggiari (1979*b*).

[130] The other possibility is demonstrated by *C.I.L.* 6.11602, where a wife is praised as *lanifica* and *domiseda*; wool-making is here presented as a female *virtue*, not an occupation.

[131] *C.I.L.* 6.9214 = *Terme* 8.13 for a *Sellia Ep(h)yre de sacra via aurivestrix*; *C.I.L.* 6. 9213 for an *aurinetrix*, gold-spinner.

[132] Pomeroy (1975) 201–2. See e.g. *N.S.A.* (1914) 338 = *Terme* 1.19 for a *psaltria*, a female cithara- or lute-player.

[133] Pomeroy (1975) 200, Treggiari (1979*b*); e.g. *C.I.L.* 6.9801 = *Terme* 8.3 (*piscatrix*, though in this case probably a fish-seller rather than a fisherman); *C.I.L.* 6.9855 (*resinaria*, a vendor of resins); *C.I.L.* 6.5184 (*argent(aria)*, silver smith); *C.I.L.* 6.5865 (*tonstr(ix)*, barber), for which see also Mart., *Epig.* 2.17; *C.I.L.* 6.9037 (*sarcinatrix*, tailor); *C.I.L.* 6.37802 (*libraria*, teacher of manuscript writing (?)); *C.I.L.* 6.6939, (*brattia[ria]*, gold-leaf beater).

[134] So, the *piscatrix* of *C.I.L.* 6.9801 = *Terme* 8.3 mentioned above was wealthy enough to finance a substantial grave altar, in which space was also reserved for her patron and a third person (both in the text mentioned in a subordinate position). The *aurivestrix* of *C.I.L.* 6.9214 was wealthy enough to own a series of niches in a *columbarium* at the Vigna Codini at the Via Appia, see *C.I.L.* 6.5287 with *Terme* 8.13.

Conversely, many jobs within the domestic domain were not monopolized by women. Servants in elite households seem to have been predominantly male, not female. The case of male child nurses is the best example,[135] but one might also point to men working in textile production. Given the fact that in many societies the separation between male and female domains of labour was rather strict and formalized, the fact that in Rome the boundaries were ill-defined and permeable is more remarkable than the fact that they existed at all.

It is important to distinguish between the free and the servile population, however. The jobs just mentioned could be held both by freeborn women and by women of the servile population, and there is evidence for both. Nevertheless, it is clear that a disproportionately large number of the attested cases of working women concern the servile population, mostly freedwomen.[136] It is certainly possible that this was again the product of biases in the epigraphy. At the same time, it revives in a somewhat different form the question raised earlier of the extent to which slave and free labour were substitutes for one another.

Conceptualizing the position of female slaves is relatively unproblematic. They were simply put to work by their owners. They also continued with what they were doing after they entered *contubernia* relationships: there are clear cases where women with jobs are mentioned together with husbands.[137] More generally, if slave marriage occurred for slave women as early as for free women, the possibility that women gave up their own jobs after marriage is an academic one: marriage and full labour activity would start more or less simultaneously. At the same time, it is noteworthy that in the *columbaria* a significant proportion of the women, a larger proportion than that of men, did not have a formal occupation. In the *columbaria*, of the people with occupations only 10 per cent are female (against 36 per cent of all persons).[138] Their jobs may simply have been omitted on their epitaphs, perhaps because they performed unskilled work not worth recording, but they might also have been part of the flexible workforce. On the other hand, it should not be forgotten that in a slave system that was at least partly based on slave breeding, many women will have been engaged in just that: producing and caring for new slaves. This might perhaps have limited the emphasis on other types of work they were doing.

What applies to the acquisition of skills mentioned earlier applies to female slaves as well. The evidence from Egypt suggests that female slaves could be and were apprenticed. In Rome much of the education could, in addition, also

---

[135] Bradley (1991) 37–75. [136] Kolb (1995) 488; Mouritsen (2013) 59.

[137] Hasegawa (2005) 70 for examples of couples with different jobs in the *columbaria*; Treggiari (1979*b*) for cases in which freedmen and -women having the same occupation mentioned these separately.

[138] Hasegawa (2005) 32 (slaves and freedmen together).

have taken place within elite households. The evidence from the Egyptian apprenticeship contracts suggests at the same time that the range of skills women acquired is likely to have been more limited, and much more directed at the domestic sphere as described earlier.[139]

Manumission seems to have led to little change with respect to female occupations. Given the fact that manumission normally occurred relatively late, and in any case, almost by definition long after the person had started to work, the possibilities (or need) to change occupation will have been slight. Perhaps some freedwomen were so well off that they could afford to stop working altogether (and would drop out of the epigraphic record), but normally freedwomen continued with their work. There are both cases of freed couples with different occupations, and cases of women with the same occupation as their husband.[140]

The position of free women is more ambiguous and more difficult to evaluate. Elite disdain for working women among the lower classes is well known. They were usually classified as prostitutes and slaves, or something akin to this. If elite ideology had any effect lower down the social scale, this would have resulted in a prejudice against free working women, with detrimental effects both on their possibilities to work and on their identification with it. At the same time, it seems likely that no matter what ideological preferences might have been held, economic necessity will have forced many women to work.

In that respect it may be useful—at least for analytical purposes, as the reality was undoubtedly more complex—to distinguish between unskilled and skilled female labour and bring in the concept of the adaptive family economy.[141] As we saw earlier, skilled labour had the capability not only to generate a substantial income, but in so doing it also offered much more room for manoeuvre for the members of the households. The necessity for women to work in such situations was much less, and there would be more room to adhere to the ideal of a woman as being engaged in domestic tasks.[142] By contrast, the unskilled were more likely to be disadvantaged: if they had families at all, the members of the families would almost certainly be forced to work alongside the principal, simply to survive. At the same time, the chances that they could find work at all were less, as the options for unskilled work were severely limited.

---

[139] Bradley (1991) 107–12.

[140] For shared occupations e.g. *C.I.L.* 6.6939, for different ones e.g. *C.I.L.* 6.5865.

[141] Groen-Vallinga (2013); see also, briefer, Groen-Vallinga and Tacoma (forthcoming). A somewhat similar concept is employed for rural Italy by Erdkamp (forthcoming), see also Bang (2007) 25.

[142] *C.I.L.* 6.11602 for the adjective *domiseda*, 'who stays at home', applied to a wife; note, however, that this is its only attestation.

In this context, the ability of women to receive a training is relevant. Free women are by and large absent from the Egyptian apprenticeship contracts.[143] It is certainly relevant that women married young, around the same time that apprenticeships were concluded. Marriage is likely to have impeded receiving an education outside the new home, and in that sense to have served as a barrier to work. At the same time, this increases the likelihood that newlywed young women received a more informal training within marriage, and that as a consequence this training focused on domestic and/or supporting roles. It seems therefore intrinsically likely that, in the case of skilled workers, many women worked in a subsidiary role next to their husbands. The sources show a number of cases of women who worked alongside their husbands without mentioning an occupation, or who were in a subordinate position, assisting their husbands with whatever was at hand.[144]

The position of working women was thus ambiguous. Female work was sometimes formalized into an occupation, and sometimes their roles were subsumed in those of the husband or simply regarded as part of the household chores. The labour market was dominated by men in more than one way, but women clearly also participated in it. Freeborn women were at a disadvantage, however. In the case of women belonging to families of skilled workers, both ideology and relative economic well-being militated against participation in the labour market. To the extent that unskilled workers would be able to start families, women would be forced to work to make ends meet, but the number of possible occupations will have been severely limited. A positive identification with work was less problematic in the case of female slaves and freedwomen.

5. PERMANENT, TEMPORARY, AND SEASONAL WORK

Lastly, it is of obvious importance to understand how flexible labour arrangements were. Again we might envisage a spectrum running from permanent, lifelong occupations to extremely flexible arrangements of hired day-labourers. Many people will have found themselves somewhere in between these extremes, working for longer spells, but not necessarily for the whole of their life.

---

[143] Bradley (1991) 108.

[144] The occupational reliefs of Zimmer (1982) can be used to demonstrate the range of possibilities. See e.g. no. 2 (showing a seated woman with a polyptych in her hand next to a butcher at work—doing his administration?); no. 13 (strict division between 'female' and 'male' tools of trade); no. 144 (a couple working together). Treggiari (1979*b*) for some exceptions in which men and women having the same occupation mentioned these separately (incidentally concerning freedmen and -women).

We may start with general considerations. In recent years, scholars have started to put more emphasis on the flexible nature of the economy of Rome.[145] The vulnerability of the food supply is, of course, well known,[146] but changes in the availability of cheap or free food will also have had a direct effect on purchasing power, especially at the lower end of the scale where people had to make ends meet. At the higher end of the production scale products were probably often made on a bespoke basis, again causing irregularities. Business will have been very volatile, and craftsmen may have frequently found themselves without work through a lack of orders.[147] Furthermore, seasonal cycles will have produced fluctuations. The regular exodus of aristocrats in the hottest months no doubt caused a lull in demand. Similarly, the presence or absence of the emperor is likely to have affected the demand for luxury goods.[148] Games and spectacles would have created periods of economic frenzy, with large amounts of money being spent, providing work for many.[149] The urban economy of Rome was a breathing organism. It seems natural to suppose that at least some forms of labour responded to these fluctuations in the economy.

At one end of the spectrum, we may expect that some work was done on a permanent basis. In principle, the workshops that dotted Rome would provide such lifelong occupations, perhaps even involving multiple generations. Skilled work offered a relatively high income, which no doubt increased independence and offered higher possibilities of ownership of the premises. It allowed children and slaves to be trained, and thus created possibilities for inter-generational continuity. Independently owned workshops might thus have been passed on, together with the skills, to the next generation: both occupation and place were inherited. At the same time, it is noticeable that we do not find the claims to continuity that in current society forms such an important part of shop advertisement. The partibility of inheritances, the fact that many crafts used moveable equipment, and the fact that the premises of many workshops were located within *insulae* and therefore are more likely to have been rented rather than owned suggests that there were few obstacles to starting or terminating activity. In combination with the vagaries created by a fluctuating demand, permanency will have remained an ideal.

There were other forms of long-term employment. Serving as a soldier offered the clearest example of a long-term and fixed-salary employment of a

---

[145] Erdkamp (2008); Hawkins (forthcoming).
[146] e.g. Tac., *Hist.* 4.38. See Garnsey (1988).   [147] Pleket (1988) 272.
[148] Cf. Suet., *Vesp.* 19.1, in which Vespasian gives dinner parties 'to help the marketmen', *ut macellarios adiuaveret.*
[149] For the effects visible on a small scale, see Suet., *Iul.* 26.2, in which Caesar organizes a gladiatorial combat and feast in memory of his daughter. In order to raise expectations, he orders the food to be prepared by his own household, though he had also led contracts to the markets. Apparently the latter is the normal way, but the former ensures quality.

finite nature. Service was completed at a particular moment in time, and also physically terminated because normally the veteran left the city. Afterwards a new phase of his life would begin, often as small landowner. Sons might, of course, follow in their father's footsteps, but that would simply replicate the pattern.

The employment of slaves by the imperial household, the *domus*, and the small workshops shows some similarities with the situation of soldiers, but only some. In the case of slaves we may also assume that the bulk of their work coincided with the years of their highest physical strength, and provided that the slave was manumitted, the work for their master was also finite. We may, in fact, guess that slaves would often be employed for roughly the same time-span as soldiers (though with more variation). But manumission was never completely certain, and whereas soldiers upon discharge could embark upon a different career, as was stated previously freedmen very often continued with the same type of economic activity and remained with their patrons.

Then there were jobs which would normally be performed for a number of years. This would apply to a job like that of a schoolteacher. In itself the setting up of a school was extremely simple.[150] Perhaps sometimes a space needed to be rented, but normally a free open space could be used. If conditions deteriorated, it was easy to try one's luck elsewhere. However, the acquisition of pupils was very much based on reputation, and schools were to a large extent embodied in the person of the teacher. The creation of a network of pupils required time. We may therefore suppose that it made little economic sense to leave too soon, and that normally teachers would work for a decade or so before moving elsewhere.[151]

The quintessential type of short-term temporary labour would be hired labour. Lucian's *On working in great houses* shows that hired labour was not necessarily unskilled labour, though higher up the social scale somewhat different arrangements could be used for remuneration: architects worked on the basis of *mandata*, contracts in which an honorarium rather than a wage was stipulated.[152] Lower down the scale *mercenarii* were employed, people who hired out their labour—these could be slaves as well. The problem in the study of them is that, by the very nature of their activity, they were less prone to record themselves: *mercenarius* is not a term frequently encountered.[153] Conditions could vary, from informal oral agreements to perform a specific

---

[150] Cf. Plin., *Ep.* 4.13, for an attempt by Pliny to bring in teachers to set up a local school; but the letter suggests normally teachers moved on their own initiative.

[151] Cribiore (2007) for a late antique model in the case of Libanius.

[152] DeLaine (2000) 123.

[153] e.g. Petr., *Sat.* 117.10 for one, in this case fittingly involved in some comical role-reversal between freeborn and slave. Mrozek (1986) 705.

task or work for a day, to written *locatio conductio* contracts.[154] The same applied to types of remuneration.[155] We learn by chance from Suetonius that carriers, *geruli*, received a daily wage,[156] and it seems likely that daily wages were the norm in many unskilled occupations. From Egypt it is known that payment by the day could offer higher wages than payment by the month.[157] Yet conditions could be very hard, especially for the day-labourers. Work not done was work not paid, and often the work was dangerous. Markets for hired labour were, almost by definition, very volatile.[158]

The prime example of truly temporary labour was the building industry. This industry offered work to thousands of people. Given the high speed with which buildings were constructed, there must have been virtual explosions of demand for labour. The contracts were probably divided between several *redemptores*, who each brought in their own small workforces, so it is also possible that actual spells of working for individuals were even shorter than the projects themselves. At the same time, the chances of finding new work must have been large: to the streams of imperial projects we should add repair and maintenance work, and private building projects. It must have been an extremely volatile labour market, with high levels of demand, but also large swings in the numbers employed.[159]

The building industry was also subject to seasonality.[160] It seems likely that economic activity slackened during the winter months. This was the time when imports from the provinces overseas came to a halt. It was the period in which the weather became unpredictable, with the possibilities of storms, heavy rainfall, even snow; it was also the period in which there were high risks of the Tiber flooding the city.[161] The building industry may have come to a halt, or at least have changed its activities and continued at a slower speed.

The other major sector which employed unskilled labour in large numbers, the transport sector, will have been somewhat less subject to seasonality. With respect to the food supply, the seasonal swings in labour demand would probably be more dramatic in Ostia than in Rome itself—transport over land continued, and the warehouses of Ostia were built precisely to

---

[154] Treggiari (1978) 163 with n. 4; (1980) 51; DeLaine (2000) 125 for verbal promises to do a specified type of work in the case of private building.

[155] See Groen-Vallinga and Tacoma (forthcoming) on types of remuneration in Diocletian's *Prices Edict*. Underlying arrangements could vary as well: see Plin., *Ep.* 4.13 for pooling of resources to finance a teacher, whereas normally they would be paid per pupil, by the parents.

[156] Suet., *Cal.* 40.   [157] Cuvigny (1996) 141, 144.

[158] Treggiari (1978); (1980); Holleran (2011) 169–70. See e.g. Apul., *Met.* 9.5–6 for a *faber* leading a precarious existence; it is implied that he gets no pay if the work is cancelled.

[159] Holleran (2011) 171–4; Erdkamp (forthcoming), both with further refs.

[160] Brunt (1980) 93; Erdkamp (forthcoming).   [161] Aldrete (2007) 58–9.

ensure a continuous food supply all year round. Nevertheless, economic activity would probably slacken during the winter months.[162]

It thus seems likely that much of Rome's labour was of a temporary nature, but the conditions and modes in which this occurred varied greatly. Much temporary labour related to longer-term arrangements of at least a number of years. Some of them, like those of the soldiers, were fixed. Others were less clearly defined: slaves might have a reasonable expectation of manumission after age 30, but were never certain of this, and might be expected to continue working for their masters afterwards. The building industry would probably be the most volatile. It seems plausible to locate the truly short-term labour arrangements that were subject to seasonal fluctuations at the unskilled end of labour relations, but the overlap between seasonal and unskilled labour is not complete.

6. LOCATING LABOUR MIGRATION

What remains is the need to locate the migrants within this labour market. The relationship between labour and migration is obviously particularly relevant for voluntary migration. Slaves had little choice in moving to Rome. But the interplay between various forms of labour is important. Slaves may not have had choices, but their owners certainly did when they employed labour. As was argued in Chapter 2, Section 3, in the sending regions the pools of voluntary, forced, and state-organized migrants are likely to have overlapped geographically, at least partially.

The crucial issue is the openness of the labour market. If we look at the four structuring dichotomies that have been discussed, it emerges that in each case we should imagine a spectrum in which large numbers of persons can be found between the extremes. Although the legal status distinction between slave and free was clear-cut, many slaves had much room for manoeuvre, while many free were enmeshed in ties of dependency. Both skilled and unskilled work was available in large quantities. Although women were clearly at a disadvantage on the labour market, the boundary separating male and female occupations was permeable. Rather than performing lifelong jobs, many people were doing work on a temporary basis, though the modes in which they did so varied greatly.

In the case of the elite, the employment of large retinues of slaves was almost mandatory.[163] The aristocracy operated within the ideal of self-sufficiency,

---

[162] Erdkamp (forthcoming). Martelli (2013) 103 emphasizes all-year-round activity of the *saccarii* of Ostia.

[163] Holleran (2011) 167.

and may have lived at least partly from the produce of their own estates.[164] Much activity was directed towards the maintenance of all members of the household. Not just the principal family, but also the staff had to be fed, clothed, and housed. Quite a number of people were engaged in textile production, and we may assume that they primarily catered to the needs of their own staff. The activity was not confined to the physical *domus*, but concerned all economic activities of the owner within the city. Hence the *insularii* we find, and the architects and builders. Activities might even have concerned property outside the city; some of the estate management would take place in the *domus*, and the city will also have been the place where at least a part of the produce of the estates may have ended up.[165] But considerations of scale will have been important. There were significant differences in the size of elite households. Larger households can be assumed to have used particular slaves for highly specialized tasks. They would also be able to replace deceased slaves either by new slaves that had been trained in advance, or by buying replacements on the market. Smaller-sized households would face more dif- ficult options: they would either have to use slaves and freedmen for more than one task, risking the loss of skills, or employ well-trained outsiders on a temporary basis.

The small workshops often contained one or two slaves or freedmen. It has been noted that most Roman 'firms' consisted of such *familiae*.[166] In a situation of fluctuating demand, it made sense to keep workshops relatively small. The concept of the adaptive family economy is helpful to understand the choices that were made: although slaves were integrated into the house- hold, their employment might also be thought of as the most adaptive of all.[167] Additional labour might have been hired for specific tasks if and when the need arose.

Interestingly enough, the one dichotomy that seems not to be relevant in structuring Roman labour is that between migrant and non-migrant labour. There is little evidence for competition between migrant and Rome-born labour. If slaves were employed, no thought was given to their origin, or at least no distinction seems to have been made between the employment of *vernae* and imported slaves. Likewise, in hiring labour ethnicity played no role. There is no evidence for particular groups of migrants taking up specific niches of the urban economy—a phenomenon that is in itself well known in modern societies. Some caution is needed, because it is unusual for people to

---

[164] For the ideal, see e.g. Mart., *Epig.* 7.31, where it is contrasted to buying in the shops of the Subura, and Varro, *De agr.* 1.16.2–6, in the context of a discussion of the location of one's holdings.

[165] Hasegawa (2005) 30–51.   [166] Mouritsen (2011) 218.

[167] Hawkins (forthcoming).

mention both occupation and origin in the same inscription.[168] Nevertheless, it seems that the silence of our sources is real—we might expect that the satirists would immediately have seized the opportunity if it were otherwise. It might also be relevant that the ethnic names that were sometimes given to slaves were not connected to particular occupations: a slave named after Lesbos was not automatically associated with, say, mule-driving.[169]

In some circumstances ethnicity did matter. Some people might have travelled together with the goods that were imported. It is hardly surprising that many foreigners can be found especially among traders or production involving the import of raw goods.[170] Just as goods are said to come from all over the empire, so traders can be found from the same areas. Furthermore, some particular occupations were associated with foreignness: astrologers were supposed to come from the East, the medical professions were supposedly dominated by Greeks.[171] But this type of ethnicity was rather vaguely and broadly defined. Both the Greek world and the East had elastic boundaries, and were mainly used to establish credentials and invoke the source of wisdom that the practitioners were supposedly drawing on.

Being an immigrant was thus in itself not a disadvantage on Rome's labour market—though the absence of fixed avenues and particular economic niches also created few advantages which would help the migrants to find work. In that respect one might regard the labour market of Rome as a level playing-field, with equal chances for immigrants and Rome-born inhabitants alike.

But the problem was that immigrants operated in a crowded market and that most of the labour was enmeshed in some ties of dependency. Some of these were formalized, others left implicit. Many people will have found themselves somewhere between the two outer ends of complete independency and complete dependency, in some form of dependency but with room for

---

[168] For exceptions, see e.g. *C.I.L.* 6.9707, a grave monument for a Thracian money-changer, *nummul(arius) de basilica Iulia natione Bess(us)* and his family; *C.I.L.* 6.9719 for a Thracian slave *olearius*, oil-dealer; *A.E.* (1972) 14 with Noy (2010*a*) 15 for a *medicus ocularius*, eye doctor, from Thebes; *A.E.* (1979) 75 for a *vestiarius*, clothes dealer, from Narbonensis; *C.I.L.* 6.710 for a bilingual text in Latin and Palmyrene which implies that a group of Palmyrenes worked in the *horrea Galbana*. Cf. from Ostia *I.S.I.S.* 21 with Wierschowski (2001) 15 no. 3, where initially *pict(oris)*, painter, rather than *Pict(onis) ex Aquitanica pro(vincia)* was read. In literature, see e.g. Cass. Dio 59.26 for a shoemaker from Gaul.

[169] For a *Lesbius mulio* see *C.E.Iaia* 23 (Ostia); it is clear that the combination is random.

[170] Noy (2000) 114–17 discusses the available epigraphic evidence.

[171] Noy (2000) 110–13 for doctors. It is a *topos* in Roman literature that going to a doctor entailed serious health-risks, and this was coupled with ethnic and servile stereotyping, see e.g. Plin., *N.H.* 29.7.14, claiming *iurarunt inter se barbaros necare omnes medicina*. As McKeown (2007) 60–1 dryly notes, 'the continuing popularity of Greek medicine suggests that Pliny is not necessarily the best representative of upper-class Roman thought'. In addition, Adams (2003) 358–60 points to some bilingual epitaphs in which the switch to Greek seems to be inspired by the profession of the deceased: *C.I.L.* 6.9829 = *I.G.U.R.* 2.460 διδασκάλωι, *C.I.L.* 6.2210 = *I.G.U.R.* 2.707 *paedagogo suo* καὶ καθηγητῇ; *C.I.L.* 6.10122 = *I.G.U.R.* 2.746 for a χοραυλίς. But again it is a vaguely defined Greekness rather than Greek origin that is important.

manoeuvre. In a general sense, one might argue that this dependency would therefore favour the Rome-born population, whether slave or free, for the simple reason that physical proximity to the elite increased the possibility to interact with this group. With regard to freedmen, Mouritsen has argued convincingly that independence would hardly offer the advantages that were so central to previous scholarship, for it cut off the former's slave access to patronage.[172] The arguments might be extended. Free migrants would have to create new networks, or enter an existing one, by gaining access to patronage.[173] Both were certainly possible, but neither was easy.

For immigrating skilled workers, setting up an independent business was in itself certainly possible, and there were no legal or institutional obstacles, such as guild approval, to doing so. The possibilities to find a space to work were certainly there: the rental market was open[174] and there were possibilities to buy premises. Migrants can indeed be found among the craftsmen in Rome and elsewhere.[175] Creating a clientele and investing might have been more difficult. Although credit was available, free craftsmen will not easily have had access to funds needed to start up with.[176] In practice this meant that those who had already had success at home would be the best placed to make the move, but at the same time they were exactly the persons who might have had the least incentive to do so: they would already have settled and might have started a family.

An alternative that would in all probability be much simpler would be to hire oneself out on a temporary basis. The arguments about the lack of stability of the urban economy plead in favour of such shorter-term labour arrangements. This applies both to the skilled and the unskilled parts of the labour market. It would favour temporary over permanent migration.

It follows from the arguments about the family and migration that young migrating men were of the proper age to enter into apprenticeships. Slaves certainly did so. Apprenticeship systems from early modern Europe suggest, on the one hand, that apprenticeship systems could generate substantial

---

[172] Mouritsen (2011) 234; cf. Garnsey (1981).

[173] For one clear expression of a patronage relationship, see *C.I.L.* 6.1625a, but there the couple from Trier seems of relatively high status; see the (somewhat speculative) comments of Wierschowski (2001) no. 69.

[174] Despite the misgivings of Mouritsen (2011) 213; the fact that *insulae* might have been let out to single contractors for longer time-spans does not affect this, as the contractors would have sublet smaller rooms and workspaces to individuals. For traders setting up premises of various types (*tabernulam pergulam horreum armarium officinam*) to sell their wares, see *Dig.* 5.1.19.2.

[175] For a shoemaker from Gaul, see Cass. Dio 59.26. Outside Rome, see the sarcophagus *I.G.* 14.928 with *Terme* 8.26 for an Ephesian in Ostia, very likely a freedman, who is depicted in one of the two reliefs working as a shoemaker together with the male dedicator. For a Carthaginian glass-worker who migrated to Lyon, see *C.I.L.* 13.2000. Further *C.I.L.* 13.5154, cited by Verboven (forthcoming) for a goldsmith from Lydia in Amsoldingen in the builders' guild.

[176] Holleran (2011) 168.

rural–urban migration by prospective apprentices, with sometimes extremely high numbers of apprentices, but on the other hand, that the regions of supply were normally not very far away.[177] Given the networked nature of Roman apprenticeships, we might expect that under normal circumstances only the population of Rome's *suburbium* participated in them, and of course most apprenticeships would simply be held by young persons born in Rome itself. We might locate migrant apprentices from further away, especially at the upper end of the occupational ladder.

The one section of the immigrants that was clearly at a disadvantage was formed by free female migrants. There were simply fewer jobs available for them, much of the work being taken up by servile women. In the *domus* there was very little chance of finding employment—much domestic work was performed by men, and the presence of female slaves provided little reason to hire external female labour. Outside the *domus* there were few unskilled jobs available for women. Even in prostitution—the time-honoured route for impoverished women—they still had to compete with female slaves. Female immigrants had the highest chance of entering Rome alongside their families, yet for skilled workers, resettling on a permanent basis would not be particularly easy.

The structure of the Roman labour market was relatively open, but this does not imply that immigrants could be absorbed indiscriminately. There were simply too many people living in the city to offer a living to all newcomers. Permanent resettlement was certainly possible, but not particularly easy. The possibilities to engage in temporary forms of labour were much greater, which will have worked in favour of temporary migration. The limited number of possibilities for free women to find work will have strongly encouraged the immigration of young males.

---

[177] Moch (2003²) 46 for discussion of early modern Europe.

7

Migration and Acculturation

Though Rome was a 'melting pot', immigrants from the same area would tend to cluster together and preserve their language and culture, at least as long as the links with their country of origin were maintained. This loyalty to their socio-cultural traditions was also furthered by a number of economic and religious associations, in particular in connection with the celebration of funeral rites. The Syrians constituted several groups around the sanctuaries of Jupiter Heliopolitanus on the Janiculum and the Esquiline, as well as around the shrine of Baal—the Dolichenum—on the Aventine, also keeping their language and customs according to Juvenal's testimony.[1]

1. A MULTICULTURAL SOCIETY?

In a study of migration the subject of acculturation is almost unavoidable. For some scholars it is even the *raison d'être* for studying migration. While its importance is certainly great, the attention paid to these subjects can at times seem to be excessive.[2] In the present book I hope to have shown that there is more to the subject of migration—that migration does in fact constitute a subject in its own right. At the same time, the relation between migration and acculturation deserves further study precisely because we now know so much more about the nature of migration to Rome.

When engaging in further study, one of the problems that immediately arises is that of pluriformity. Throughout the book the variety of the patterns of mobility has been emphasized: many people remained for shorter periods in the city, permanent migration forms just the outer edge of the spectrum of mobility, and it does not seem far-fetched to assume that the modes and motives which brought migrants to the city varied significantly from each

---

[1] Polomé (1983) 514, with reference to La Piana (1927) 204 and Juv., *Sat.* 3.62–5.
[2] Cf. a somewhat similar complaint by Sanjek (2003) 317 on modern (mainly US) migration studies: 'the assimilation framework continues to dominate migration studies.'

other.[3] This makes it problematical to generalize about what was no doubt a variety of experiences. At the same time, the variation also alters the nature of the problem. Put simply: variation and fluid movement suggest that migrant communities were more difficult to create and to maintain, though at the same time the need for arrangements to come to terms with the new situation was all the more pressing.

Given the value normally attached to the subject of acculturation, it comes as no surprise that there is a large volume of literature at our disposal.[4] Numerous studies have been devoted to theories of ethnicity and processes of acculturation, and the ancient world has proven to be exceptionally fertile ground to apply them. This is in particular visible in the stream of studies of romanization. While the debates surrounding its usefulness have mostly concerned Italy and the provinces, it is worth exploring some of the ideas and models that have been advanced for Rome itself. In doing so, the term 'acculturation' is used as a neutral umbrella term to cover the outcome of processes of interaction between migrants and the host society. This outcome itself is not predetermined. It can vary significantly and might run along a spectrum from complete absorption to complete rejection.[5]

When Polomé in 1983 used the image of the melting pot, he expressed a series of ideas that have a long pedigree. As Polomé acknowledged in a footnote, similar ideas had been voiced already by La Piana in 1927. The latter wrote:

> It is to-day, and has always been everywhere, the natural tendency of a body of immigrants from the same nationality in a foreign city to live together as much as possible in the same district, where they can reproduce the main characteristics of the social and religious life of the country from which they came. They form sections of their own, separate to a certain extent from the rest of the population, and keep their own language and customs at least as long as the current of immigration remains active. This is a universal phenomenon, of which we have evidence on a large scale in the numerous communities of immigrants from Europe and Asia in the large cities of America. There are reasons for believing that the foreign populations of ancient Rome were no exception to this rule, and that they yielded to this tendency so far as the social and economic conditions of the city allowed them to follow this instinctive need.[6]

Together, the two statements by La Piana and Polomé summarize a type of argument that still pervades the scholarly literature.[7] In fact, it seems to be

---

[3] Morley (2003). Cf. MacMullen (1993) for the idea that many people in Rome stood aloof from society.

[4] Naerebout (2013) for an overview of the related subject of integration.

[5] Naerebout and Versluys (2006).   [6] La Piana (1927) 204.

[7] e.g. in Ricci (2005) 47–51.

reiterated in the concept of diaspora, which envisages migrants as individuals who almost automatically formulate their identity in response to the loss of a homeland to which they feel still connected. Diaspora migrants are conceived of as bridging personally the gap between two cultures.[8] As I will argue, it is not the best way to think about Rome's migrants. Rome was a cosmopolis, and in that sense might also be regarded as a melting pot. There can be little doubt that due to their presence the cultural landscape became more complex and divergent. But the notion that Rome was a multicultural society in which cultural diversity was cherished by immigrants and at least condoned by the Roman state is highly questionable. Community formation by migrants did occur, but it was not the rule, and immigrants to Rome felt no 'instinctive need' to express a migrant identity. Some did, sometimes, but hardly consistently so.

It goes without saying that acculturation is a slippery subject. There is both a risk of over-theorizing and of under-theorizing, and it seems of paramount importance to conduct the discussion on the basis of empirical observations and concrete research questions. The range of possible subjects is also extremely wide. It is plainly impossible to include all subjects and to discuss all sources that are potentially relevant.[9] Instead, the focus here will be on four specific subjects that figure prominently in the debate, and in fact are all mentioned by Polomé cited above: expressions of ethnic identity, language use, religious choices, and the social functions of associations.

The central argument of this chapter is that community ties were relatively weak: there is little sign of the formation of migrant communities in a real sense.[10] Only in some situations can we find elements that point in such directions. We would do better to envisage a spectrum of arrangements: the Jews, who *did* have a strong sense of community, were at one end of this spectrum, slaves, Italian migrants, and senators at the other. Many immigrants should be placed somewhere in between, expressing on occasion something that we can call a migrant identity, but not usually forming ethnically homogeneous migrant groups. At the end of this chapter it is argued that their

[8] See e.g. Eckardt (2010) 7: 'Diasporas communities are characterised by initial dispersal, either forced or voluntary, a distinction from the host society, and a continuous social or spiritual link to the homeland.'

[9] MacMullen (1993) included many in his discussion, arguing that many immigrants remained unintegrated. I have treated one other subject, residential clustering, in Tacoma (2013), where I argue against the existence of migrant quarters. For bioarchaeological analysis of dietary habits in the context of acculturation theory, see Killgrove (2010a) 147–80, concluding at 304: 'On the whole, the dietary data provide evidence that immigrants to Rome were most likely to adopt a local diet, whether by choice or by necessity. There is no conclusive evidence that any individual retained past foodways that were significantly different than the local Roman tradition.'

[10] Contrast, for example, Cracco Ruggini (1980), who described conflicts elsewhere in the Roman world (Alexandria, most notably) as the product of tensions between locals and immigrant groups claiming more civic privileges.

situation can better be analysed in terms of networks than in terms of group formation. Network analysis is more appropriate to investigate situations in which ties were fluid and a strong sense of community was absent.

2. MIGRATION AND ETHNICITY

The first question to address is to what extent migrants formulated their identity in ethnic terms. In what ways and in what contexts did immigrants describe themselves as originating from a specific region? How often were they described as such by others?

Any discussion of ethnic identity must start from the now generally accepted position that ethnicity is subjective.[11] As genetic studies have shown, ethnicity is not an ontological fact deriving from birth: biological races are a construct.[12] The fact that identities are subjective also makes them malleable and responsive to external circumstances. In fact, studies of identity (not just ethnic ones) emphasize that identities are formulated in relation to someone or something else. In consequence, the way an ethnic or other identity is created or reformulated depends on the situation, on the context.[13]

The fact that identities are subject to construction does not mean that ethnic groups cannot have a basis in reality. They can 'exist', in a very real sense, and their boundaries might be demarcated with precision. In fact, in creating groups the drawing of boundaries is of prime importance: membership and exclusion are the main issues.[14] Again, the boundaries of such groups are not fixed. Rather, the formulation of ethnicity is a continuous and dynamic process of negotiation and asserting and reasserting claims about belonging and exclusion.

Ethnic identities can be self-assumed or ascribed by others. If ethnicity is subjective, and formulations of ethnicity concentrate on the boundaries that define membership of a group, then it follows that there are two perspectives:

[11] For the Roman world Boatwright (2012) 11–13; Ivleva (2012) 3–7 for discussion with further bibliography. See also Amory (1997) 14–18, in the context of late antiquity. Gruen (2012) for a critical re-evaluation.

[12] Hirschman (2004); Orlin (2010) 13: 'the genetic differences between accepted members of the same group can be as great as or greater than those between members of distinct groups.' Eckardt et al. (2010) 111–12 and Leach et al. (2010) 135 discuss the implications for craniometry.

[13] Lund (2005) 3: 'Die ethnische Identität eines Individuums ist nun einmal vielschichtig (kumulativ), auch hangt die Selbstidentifikation von der jeweiligen Lage und dem Kontext ab, ist situativ. Vor allem ist sie aber nicht statisch und auch nicht an ein bestimmtes Territorium gebunden, wie in der Forschung früher gewöhnlich angenommen wurde, sondern dynamisch.'

[14] Orlin (2010) 13–14: 'The group is real, but the criteria are decided by the group, and the perception that someone is a member of the group is perhaps the key to defining membership.' See also Orlin (2008) 242.

that of the host society, which may ascribe an ethnic identity to a specific group, and that of the incomers, which operates on the basis of self-identification as a group.[15] Obviously, it is likely that the two perspectives overlap to some extent, but it is certainly possible that the overlap is not complete. There might also be radical differences in appreciation of ethnic labels: outsiders may attach a negative value to what is perceived by insiders as something positive. 'Syrian' may convey different things to different people.

To start with the ethnic identities ascribed by the host society, Romans had strong ideas about foreignness, but the groups of people who comprised the category of 'foreign' changed over time. The progressive inclusion of foreigners exemplified by the ever-widening extension of Roman citizenship is the best expression of how the notion of what was considered 'foreign' shifted.[16] 'Identity in Rome seems to have been constantly renegotiated as the Roman citizen base expanded and citizens and others changed their locations and circumstances.'[17] As can be seen in the case of the Gauls, with the progressive incorporation of this group the geographic location of what was considered barbarian territory shifted northwards,[18] and at least from Caesar onwards Germans took over the dubious honour of being regarded as the typical barbarian.[19]

Those Gauls and Germans were safely located at the margins of the empire, and as the empire expanded the horizon shifted ever further away. But the peoples that could be regarded as foreign were also present in the heart of the empire, in Rome itself. In a situation in which a large part of the population originated from elsewhere, it gave rise to a discourse about the boundaries of Romanness. In such discussions ethnicity normally played a negative role, marking certain groups as non-Roman, intruders, and not belonging properly to the community.[20]

The issue about who was to be included and excluded was acted out in debates on whether to widen the recruitment pool of the senate. On more than one occasion senators debated the admittance of outsiders. The best-documented case is that of Claudius' plea for the admission of senators from Gaul in AD 48.[21] As discussions of Claudius' policies make clear, in political

---

[15] The dichotomy is used for analytical purposes, to obtain a sense of the complexity without over-complicating the discussion. Given the fuzziness of Roman migration, the boundaries between them were in reality not clear. Furthermore, there is at least one other collective perspective that might be relevant: that of other migrant groups. Not all migrant groups positioned themselves in the same way; the Jews once again form a case in point.

[16] Ricci (2005) 4–5.   [17] Boatwright (2012) 18.   [18] Boatwright (2012) 33–64.

[19] Cracco Ruggini (1987) 192–3. For a small vignette in which Batavians function as the completely uncultured Other, see Mart., *Epig.* 6.82.

[20] For a very strong, sexualized image, see Mart., *Epig.* 7.30, in which a *Romana puella* receives indiscriminately foreigners from all parts of the world, but to whom *Romana mentula nihil placet.*

[21] *C.I.L.* 13.1668 (the Lyon tabulae) and Tac., *Ann.* 11.23–5 for Claudius' speech.

discourse the issue could be used to judge imperial behaviour. The way the emperor Claudius was evaluated was very much in the form of accusations that he wished to make everybody a Roman citizen.[22] Such debates on imperial inclusions and exclusions formed a prime vehicle to negotiate the ever-shifting boundaries of the acceptable.[23]

The procedure can best be seen in Roman literature, which also makes clear how complex the ways the imagery was employed could be. Juvenal's third Satire, with the famous image of the Orontes flooding into the Tiber, functions as a key text and has been cited frequently (if not *ad nauseam*), and is often used as the starting point for discussions of ethnic prejudice. In the text the character Umbricius inveighs against the presence of so many foreigners, and leaves Rome. The text has often been read as a straightforward expression of ethnic prejudice: no doubt Juvenal exaggerated to satirical effect, but Umbricius is the spokesman for what some, if not many, Romans must have felt when they were confronted with the influx of foreigners. But the crucial question is how to read Juvenal. Rather than taking it as a literal statement, the text might be understood to have been written without too much commitment by its author to any particular view.[24] As in all of Juvenal's work, irony plays a large role, and at the end the reader is left wondering about the author's intentions. On the one hand it seems that Juvenal plays on the theme of expulsion: instead of those who do not belong to the true Roman community and would need to be expelled, it is honest, hard-working, poor Umbricius who in disgust imposes exile upon himself; 'impoverished Roman citizens should have massed together and marched out long ago'.[25] At the same time, it is clear that Umbricius is ranting, and the fact that he ends with the statement that he is leaving for Baiae can hardly be without significance: the person who flees Rome to escape from the foreigners goes to the very place in Italy

---

[22] Cass. Dio 60.5–8, according to whom Claudius was liberal with awarding citizenship; Messalina and his freedmen actually sold it; cf. Sen., *De Ben.* 6.19.2 for the theoretical possibility of the emperor giving citizenship to all the Gauls. Sherwin-White (1973[2]) 237, 241. The theme recurs in Sen., *Apocol.* 3, where Claudius is accused of wanting to see all Greeks, Gauls, Spaniards, and Britons in togas; 5, where Claudius arriving in heaven is not recognized as Roman; and 6, where the Goddess Febris says Claudius originates from Lyon. See Braund (1980) and Nauta (1987) for the literary tactics employed.

[23] Farney (2007), similar ideas underlie the more general analysis of Boatwright (2012). For the wider resonance of such issues, see Suet., *Iul.* 80.2–3, songs were sung and fake edicts were being posted in jest against the admission of Gauls into the senate; Suet., *Aug.* 40.3, Augustus wanted to keep the citizen body pure and therefore was very reluctant to grant citizenship to foreigners.

[24] Laurence (1997).

[25] Juv., *Sat.* 3.162–3, *agmine facto debuerant olim tenues migrasse Quirites*; this is paired with the possibility that ego visits Aquinum for a break. Umbricius is presented as an average Roman of modest wealth *inter alia* in 3.10, where all his belongings (*tota domus*) are loaded on a single wagon.

that is most associated with Greek decadence.[26] It has also been argued that Umbricius' name is significant: 'Shadowy' can be understood both as a shadow of Romanness, and as jealous failure, Mr Shady.[27] And perhaps self-irony plays a role as well: Juvenal was, after all, himself a foreigner. We are clearly dealing with a discourse about the boundaries of Romanness that does not present a fixed and absolute point of view. The Satire might certainly be read as a response to the presence of migrants. But it is an indirect and rather dim reflection, and Umbricius' rant is implicitly presented as no more than one response in a series of possible reactions.[28]

One element that is perhaps of more importance than the question who Umbricius represents is how Juvenal's invective against foreigners works. The mechanism is one of deliberate lumping together of ethnic and other labels. Slaves, freedmen, parasites, Greeks, Egyptians, Jews, the sexually depraved, they are all part of the same rabble.[29] The lack of differentiation is deliberate and is meant to be both funny and insulting. It also works at the level of individuals, for example, when Juvenal in his first Satire, in the verses leading to the famous *difficile est saturam non scribere*, describes the Egyptian Crispinus as *pars Niliacae plebis, verna Canopi*. In these few words low standing, slave status, ethnic origin, exoticism, and decadence (Canopus) all merge into one.[30] The deliberate conflating of categories can be seen in many other parts of Juvenal's work, as well as elsewhere.[31]

Equally important is what is left out, what is not problematized. In Juvenal's third Satire the focus is on a specific segment of the immigrants: Greeks, Syrians, Egyptians, Asians, Jews, in short, those from the East. Language, slave origins, and origins from the East are all subsumed under one label of Greekness. Much less invective is directed at western immigrants than at eastern ones. There is very little at all on Italians coming from outside Rome. It is tempting to assume that this implies that immigrants who came from western, Latin-using parts of the empire were better accepted by the host society. This may be so, but it also seems likely that the most meaningful way for the satirists to make their point and discuss identity politics was in terms of an opposition between us (Romans) and them (Greeks/Orientals, etc.).

---

[26] Edwards (1996) 125–9, noting at 127 that 'Umbricius' role here is compromised in numerous ways'.

[27] So Braund, in the LCL.   [28] Morley (2003).

[29] Juv., *Sat.* 3.60–80. Cf. Garrido-Hory (1998) 201–4 on the way ethnicity is used by Juvenal with respect to slaves.

[30] Juv., *Sat.* 1.26. Crispinus reappears in *Sat.* 4 (1: *ecce iterum Crispinus*), where he is part of the emperor's *consilium*.

[31] e.g. in Juv., *Sat.* 6.295–300, where in another image of streams flooding into Rome, wealth, crime, and effeminacy are linked to foreign intrusion. Further e.g. Livy 36.17.5, where in a battle speech situated in 191 BC reference is made to Syrians and Asian Greeks, most worthless of peoples and born for slavery.

As for the other aspect of ethnicity, the self-assumed identification of immigrants claiming to belong to a particular ethnic group, it is clear that on some public occasions ethnic identity could serve as a group marker. One example is the funeral of Caesar: 'At the height of the public grief a multitude of foreign peoples went about lamenting each in his own way, in particular the Jews, who even flocked to the pyre for several successive nights.'[32] Foreigners lamented each after the fashion of their country, in what were no doubt highly ritualized displays showing the whole world was united in its grief, but each community in its own way. However, we hear otherwise nothing of the employment of foreign burial rites, and burials of immigrants themselves are characterized by a lack of ethnic markers. What happened at Caesar's funeral was hardly standard procedure. This suggests that such expressions were employed only selectively. The fact that the Jews were singled out also points to the fact that different groups could behave differently. It is not without reason that the Jews were mentioned separately. Not only had they obtained various privileges from Caesar, but they were, of course, famous for their strong communal ties, cemented by the fact that ethnicity and religion coincided.[33]

As far as individual rather than collective expressions of self-assumed ethnic identity are concerned, the first place to look for evidence of these is in the inscriptions. As was discussed in Chapter 1, some inscriptions (the DOC inscriptions) contain explicit references to ethnicity and origins. No matter how brief and factual, such statements are important acts of self-representation. Inscriptions cost money, had little space, and choices were made in what was inscribed. They were erected to demarcate important moments of individuals—mainly their death. With the exception of soldiers,[34] origin was not part of the standard naming pattern in the inscriptions from Rome. The decision to mention origin thus depended on choice (though probably not always a conscious one).

Some individuals made a factual statement about their origin. There is no region that is absent from the list of epigraphically attested origins. As was stated in Chapter 2, Section 3, in contrast to Juvenal and other authors, there is no dominance by people from the East in the inscriptions. Moreover, the use of such indications does not seem to depend on social status. For example, among the civilian Egyptians there occur slaves, possibly a peregrine, some Roman citizens (free or freed), gladiators, an Egyptian priest, a pankratiast, a *naukleros*, and a city councillor.[35] Similar patterns (or lack of patterns) can be

---

[32] Suet., *Iul.* 84.5: *In summo publico luctu exterarum gentium multitodo circulatim suo quaeque more lamentata est praecipueque Iudaei, qui etiam noctibus continuis bustum frequentarunt.*

[33] Noy (2000) 255–67 for an overview.   [34] Noy (2010a) 14.

[35] Slave: *A.E.* (1916) 57 (from a *columbarium*). Freedman(?): *I.G.U.R.* 2.875 (from a *columbarium*). Gladiators: *A.E.* (1988) 24; *C.I.L.* 6.10194 (with *tria nomina*); *C.I.L.* 6.10197. Egyptian priest: *I.G.U.R.* 1.77. Pankratiast: *I.G.U.R.* 1.240. *Naukleros*: *I.G.U.R.* 2.393 (with *tria nomina*). *Peregrinus* (possibly): *I.G.U.R.* 2.610. City councillor: *I.G.U.R.* 2.1060.

observed in other provincial samples. The absence of a correlation with status suggests that such statements about origins were regarded as unproblematic, if not positive.

However, there are clear biases in the types of geographical units that were used. In the sample of the Egyptians just mentioned a relatively high number of Alexandrians occurs, while very few inscriptions mention other place names within Egypt.[36] One could perhaps think that this would reflect the special position of Alexandria *ad Aegyptam* or could be explained by the prominence of Alexandrian traders in grain and other wares, but the pattern is similar in other samples of provincial migrants. A large number of the immigrants state that they originated from the larger centres; while the rest simply state that they came from the region, without providing further geographical detail. For example, among the forty civilian Syrians that have been identified,[37] we find that many express their identity in broad terms referring to Syria, without being more specific. The same patterns emerge from the military inscriptions.[38] The choice suggests that in such cases a common larger territorial homeland overrode more precise identifications. Where we do find more precise identifications, they often referred to Antioch, or one of the other important cities—places with a resonance to a wider audience, places which gave some additional lustre to those who could claim to originate from there. Whether the predominance of larger cities reflects a pattern of stepwise migration is unclear, but in any case it also points to selectivity in what was mentioned.

Other inscriptions have a much more muted suggestion of foreignness, using foreign-sounding names,[39] local phrases, and regional calendars. Some such indications are difficult to assign to a particular homeland, and, as was stated in Chapter 1, epigraphers have been rightly cautious in using them as certain indications of immigration. The elements that were employed were not natural attributes that needed to be inserted in the text.

The ethnic references were meant to be seen by others. The inscriptions were set up in places where others came or could see them. As was stated in Chapter 1, there were no immigrant graveyards in Rome in the Principate, and in consequence the inscriptions were not put up for internal consumption.

---

[36] Noy (2000) 247 gives the following figures (which include the late antique inscriptions): province 13, Alexandria 21, other cities 3, villages 4. In the case of the Alexandrians, it is not always clear whether it is Alexandrian origin or Alexandrian citizenship that is meant—the two obviously overlapped, but the overlap was not complete.

[37] Noy (2000) 319–20 for the list, 234–40 for discussion.

[38] Tacoma and Tybout (forthcoming *b*) on soldiers from the Near East stationed in Rome. Something similar may even be observed in the cases where ethnic origins of slaves are specified, see *A.E.* (1972) 14 of 47/46 BC for a small *familia* of freedmen and freedwomen.

[39] e.g. *C.I.L.* 6.10781 and *C.I.L.* 6.19716, in which the names point to Egyptian origin; the Cappadocian name Iazemus in *C.I.L.* 6.6476 and 6.37415, or the rare female cognomen Athena in *C.I.L.* 1(2). 2997a = *Terme* 4.16.

Given the fact that Roman commemorative practice was to a large extent directed at outsiders, it is not far-fetched to assume that the ethnic labels were intended to be seen by the outside world. Moreover, many of the references that were used only acquired meaning outside the place of birth. In fact, normally the ethnic labels that are employed in Rome are not encountered in the home region. Partly this was no doubt for practical reasons: it would be strange indeed to describe yourself as 'Egyptian' in an epitaph in, say, Oxyrhynchus—or it would in fact convey something different (hostility to Greek culture, say). Following from that, it seems highly likely that the wider regional identities were assumed only when people were abroad. By moving to Rome, immigrants *became* Syrian, Egyptian, and so on, or at least presented themselves on occasion as such.

What the patterns in the inscriptions demonstrate is that the ethnicity of immigrants was a constructed one, that it was malleable, and that its employment depended on choice. What determined this choice in individual cases is impossible to reconstruct—also because the cases in which it was omitted are invisible for us. How much selectivity was involved can be intimated from the crude statistics: there are approximately 1,000 inscriptions in which migrants make explicit reference to their provincial origins out of an estimated total of *c.*60,000 inscriptions from the city of Rome (1.6 per cent).[40] Surely more than 1 in 60 persons living in Rome was born in the provinces.[41]

Selectivity is not the same as repression. There can be little doubt that in itself the mention of origin was unproblematic. There is no hint that negative connotations were attached to the cases where ethnic origin was mentioned. It is particularly important that the mentions of origin were also used by persons of relatively high status. There was no conscious masking of migrant origins. Foreignness was clearly cherished at certain moments, in certain contexts, and

---

[40] The total number of inscriptions from Rome is admittedly a guess, and the figure is dependent on the criteria used. The Clauss-Slaby database as of April 2015 lists slightly over 40,000 inscriptions for *C.I.L.* 6, but almost 120,000 inscriptions found in Rome. The former figure obviously excludes inscriptions published post-*C.I.L.*, while the latter figure includes *instrumentum domesticum*, and Republican and late antique material. The actual number must thus be somewhere in between. Subtracting from the *c.*120,000 the *c.*20,000 texts of the *instrumentum* published in *C.I.L.* 15 and the *c.*40,000 texts of *I.C.U.R.* (late antique catacombs, mainly) results in 60,000 inscriptions. For lower estimates for figures of Roman epitaphs based on *C.I.L.* 6 see Huttunen (1974) 16 (26,000), Eck (1998) 32 (35,000), and Rawson (2013) 99 (at least 30,000).

[41] In late antiquity, the proportions decrease further, see Nieddu (2003) for *c.*200 migrant inscriptions on a total of *c.*40,000 Christian inscriptions (0.5%). On a smaller scale the same is visible in the Isola Sacra necropolis at Ostia. Among the persons buried in over 100 tombs, there is only one person who is explicitly called an immigrant: Tomb 1, *I.S.I.S.* 21, a tomb for *C(ai) Annaei Attici Pict(onis) ex Aquitanica pro(vincia)*. The isotopic research of Prowse et al. (2007) based on the skeletons from the same graveyard suggests a percentage in the order of 30% immigrants (20 out of 61 cases, though see Chapter 4, Section 3 for the difficulties in interpretation). See for more discussion Tacoma (forthcoming *c*).

this could be done both by private persons (in epitaphs) and collectively (in public rituals like Caesar's funeral). But origin was just one of a series of possible identity markers, and the important thing is that it seems not to have figured particularly highly on the list.[42]

The finding about the selective employment of ethnic markers finds support in current thinking about more recent forms of migration, where what has been dubbed the 'ethnicity forever' approach is increasingly criticized.[43] Hoerder, for example, argues that in the case of the Germans of the seventeenth century and beyond, belonging to polities was only partly defined by ethnicity, and that language, religion, and occupation were more important markers of identity.[44]

Selectivity was at work in both the internal and external perspective on the ethnic identity of immigrants, but each was selective in a different way. From the viewpoint of the host community, the presence of foreigners in the heart of the empire generated a discourse about the boundaries of Romanness. In Juvenal we see how such a discourse could be employed: ethnic categories were pejorative, and were deliberately imprecise. When ethnic labels were used by the migrants themselves, they could also be used imprecisely to create wider labels, such as 'Syrian', but such labels were used in a neutral, if not positive way. It seems likely that the ethnic identity that was thus expressed made use of categories that were relevant in Rome rather than at home, and were employed only in certain circumstances.

3. LANGUAGE USE

From ethnicity we need to move to language, for it might be expected that language choice acted as a major marker of identity for migrants.[45] Did language help in fostering or creating a migrant group identity? Language use may also have acted as a means of integration into the host society. At a

---

[42] A somewhat similar argument is developed in Gruen (2012), who applies it to the ancient world at large.

[43] Lesger, Lucassen, and Schrover (2002) 45.   [44] Hoerder (2008) 18.

[45] Haarmann (1999) 64: 'Language is a major marker of ethnicity for many local groups around the world, and there have been historical periods when language was assigned an ideological role as the marker par excellence of ethnic identity'; Ricci (2005) 52: 'Una delle spie più eloquenti dell'acculturazione di un immigrato o di un gruppo di immigrati era certamente la lingua impiegata.' Adams (2003), in his study of Roman bilingualism, emphasizes the role of language choice in identity formation rather than its putative practical aims, e.g. 32: 'it should not be assumed that the aim of a bilingual inscription was always simply to reach the maximum readership', and 32–4 for the idea that language choice depends on geographical and historical context.

more practical level, to what extent did language facilitate entrance into society, or, conversely, might lack of knowledge have formed an obstacle?

In the strict sense of the word, there were no migrant languages in Rome: we do not hear of Egyptians using Egyptian in Rome, of Syrians using Syriac, of North Africans using Punic, and so on. When Juvenal has Umbricius complaining about the Syrians whose language was carried by the Orontes into the Tiber, in all probability he had in mind Greek, not Syriac.[46] It is, in fact, legitimate to ask to what extent vernacular languages were used at all in Rome.[47] As we will see, language choice was essentially confined to two languages, Greek and Latin. The very restricted availability implies almost automatically that although some connection between language and expressions of ethnicity certainly might have existed, the overlap between ethnicity and language was far from complete. At most, language choice is to be regarded as an expression of ethnic allegiance rather than directly of immigrant status itself.

The question what it meant or implied when a migrant from Syria used Greek when he was in Rome has no easy answer. Some basic ideas formulated in sociolinguistics may offer help in avoiding thinking too schematically of language use as either expressing one's own group identity or expressing integration in the host society. Sociolinguistics studies how language varieties differ between social groups, and how language is employed to demarcate such groups. It is based on the assumption that people make, consciously or unconsciously, choices in the way they employ language, and that such changes are socially significant. Sociolinguistics originally focused on distinctions between groups of different status, who formed what was called a speech community or *Sprechbund*: a homogenous group with well-demarcated boundaries that adopted a particular type of speech. Nowadays the focus has shifted from the way language marks off community boundaries to the multiplicity of interactions and to code switching.[48] Language use, it has been recognized, is situational and selective. The question then is in what contexts migrant groups made particular language choices, and what types of connotations such choices may have had.

Obviously, there are only a limited number of contexts available where we can evaluate language choice. We are, after all, dependent on written sources,

---

[46] Juv., *Sat.* 3.63: *iam pridem Syrus in Tiberim defluxit Orontes, et linguam et mores et cum tibicine chordas obliquas nec non gentilia tympana secum vexit et ad circum iussas prostare puellas.* Solin (1983) 720 with n. 288, cf. Polomé (1983) 514, quoted at the beginning.

[47] I use the term 'vernacular' languages as a convenient shorthand term to cover all languages that were used in the Roman Empire other than Latin and Greek. These languages were only 'vernacular' from the perspective of Rome, and differed significantly from each other in importance and geographical spread; in addition, some of them had writing systems, while others did not.

[48] Adams (2003), esp. 18–29 and 297–346.

in particular on inscriptions. Especially in terms of informal, oral contexts, the possibilities of obtaining meaningful information are severely limited.[49] Yet the fact that most of what we can see refers to public contexts is not in itself a hindrance: we are, after all, studying the way migrants might have used language to create or maintain a collective identity or express allegiance in the public sphere.

The general linguistic situation in the regions of origin of the immigrants has been analysed *in extenso*. It is likely that many immigrants will have known some Latin before arriving in Rome. Immigrants from Italy can, of course, be supposed to have known Latin well; for many of them it was their first language. Outside Rome, Latin had spread in the third and second centuries BC, and by the first century BC it was dominant. We can safely assume that during the Principate Latin was the first language for most people in Italy.[50] In the case of people living in the western provinces, knowledge of Latin will have been widespread, not least because in many areas vernacular languages simply did not survive the presence of the Romans.[51] Soldiers will either have known Latin or acquired knowledge of it during their service.[52] In the eastern provinces people will have been much less likely to do so.[53] There, the use of Latin was reserved for situations where larger numbers of Italians were present, most notably in the Roman colonies, and in the army.

As regards Greek, this played a marginal role in the western parts of the empire—though formerly it had been dominant in the areas where Greek colonies had been located.[54] Greek was widely used in the eastern part of the empire, where it was the administrative language. The Greek used in Roman times was itself still diversified. It comprised not only *koine*, but the main dialects were also used.[55]

However, many people in the provinces will have had another first language than Latin or Greek. Even among the local elites, the knowledge of languages other than Latin and Greek might have been common.[56] The position of these languages is much more difficult to evaluate, as many of them lacked a writing

[49] Kaimio (1979) 321: 'we have not found sufficient material to determine the dominant language use in various spheres and at different times; this applies especially to most private functions.' Adams (2003), in his study of code-switching, emphasizes the differences between oral and written utterances.
[50] Balsdon (1979) 116; Harris (1989) 178–9; Adams (2003) 111–84 on the evidence for Oscan, Umbrian, Venetic, and Messapic in contact with Latin, see also 184–99 on Celtic in Cisalpine Gaul. The position of Greek in Magna Graecia (and, outside Italy, in Sicily) is more complex.
[51] Adams (2003) 289–91 on the factors contributing to language death.
[52] Adams (2003) 20, 760–1 adds some nuance to the thought that the army made *exclusively* use of Latin, but it can hardly be doubted that it was dominant.
[53] See the detailed study of Rochette (1997).   [54] Polomé (1983) 511.
[55] Kaimio (1979) 9; cf. Adams (2003) 13.
[56] *Epit. de Caes.* 20.8 (Sept. Severus knowing Latin, Greek, and Punic), SHA, *Sept. Sev.* 15.7 (Septimius Severus' sister as *vix Latine loquens*).

system and thus have left little trace.[57] '[T]he epigraphic remains severely under-record the linguistic heterogeneity of the Roman Empire.'[58] Tantalizing hints are given by the question discussed by the jurists whether pronouncements in other languages than Latin or Greek (Punic, Gallic, and Assyrian are mentioned) had legal validity.[59] What is most difficult to ascertain is not so much the occurrence of such languages, but rather the extent to which there were people in the empire with no Latin or Greek at all. For Harris, 'many of the inhabitants of the Roman Empire spoke neither Greek nor Latin', and he plays down the extent of bilingualism.[60] Others have emphasized the prevalence of bilingualism: 'We must assume that most language communities of the Roman Empire were diglot or even polyglot.'[61] The difference of opinions may perhaps be alleviated if we assume that in the former view the countryside is factored in, and that the latter view describes urban communities. What seems relatively certain is that the use of first languages other than Greek or Latin was confined to restricted areas of life, and outside urban contexts: we should locate such language use primarily at home and in the countryside.[62] In Egypt, where we can follow the linguistic interaction between Greek and Egyptian in some detail, under the Principate Demotic texts were only produced in a very limited number of contexts, and their numbers declined significantly over time.

In the city of Rome itself the situation with respect to written language is relatively clear, at least from what the epigraphy suggests. Latin was dominant in Rome at all levels. All state communication in Rome was in Latin; in cases of treaties with Greek communities translations were made, but these were for use in the home community, not for Rome itself.[63] No such effort at translation is recorded for any other language than Greek.[64] As regards the private use of written language, it is surely significant that the great majority of inscriptions were written in Latin. As for spoken language, there can again be little doubt about the dominance of Latin, though Latin itself was spoken

[57] Balsdon (1979) 117–18; Harris (1989) 175–90 for a survey; see also Adams (2003) 108–296 with further refs. As Adams observes, 'the Romans behaved as if vernacular languages did not exist' (xix, on the Roman East); this attitude, while socially significant, did not help their documentation.
[58] Harris (1989) 177.
[59] *Dig.* 32.11pr. (*fideicommissa* in Punic or Gallic or any other language); *Dig.* 45.1.1.6 (*stipulationes* in Punic, Assyrian, or other languages).
[60] Harris (1989) 175, see also 185 ('we see the indigenous tongues persisting even many centuries after the establishment of Roman power').
[61] Kaimio (1979) 14; likewise MacMullen (1966; 1990) 32. See esp. Adams (2003), who on the one hand emphasizes that in the Roman world 'bilingualism cannot be quantified' (1), yet on the other states that in world history it is more common than monolingualism. Note, however, that his definition of bilingualism is deliberately inclusive; it need not (and normally does not) imply perfect knowledge of both languages (3–8).
[62] Balsdon (1979) 118.   [63] Kaimio (1979) 61–3.
[64] Kaimio (1979) 109. For the symbolic importance of translation, see Moatti (2006) 111–17.

with many accents, which at the upper end of the social scale gave rise to snobbery.[65]

The use of Greek came second. However, in epigraphy it was used significantly less than Latin. With regard to official texts, some Greek inscriptions were put up by cities from the East.[66] *Stationes* and some *collegia* also put up inscriptions in Greek.[67] As might be expected, epitaphs form the bulk of the Greek texts. But the number of gravestones in Greek dwindles in comparison to the Latin ones: they formed only 3 per cent of all epitaphs from Rome.[68] Although the evidence is hardly unequivocal, the Greek inscriptions from Rome seem to contain a relatively high percentage of immigrants.[69] There are also a number of cases where Greek in inscriptions is retained by second-generation migrants who were born in Rome, though it seems that it normally gave rapidly way to Latin.[70] But Greek was certainly not a migrant language in the stricter sense of the term. The relations are not straightforward: many migrants also employed Latin,[71] and the use of Greek was not the exclusive domain of migrants (no matter how defined). The relatively high proportion of epigrams among the Greek inscriptions points to the fact that sometimes the choice in favour of Greek may have had a cultural rather than a practical basis. In fact, Latin prose often preceded such Greek epigrams; as epigrams could, of course, just as well be composed in Latin, the switch must have been deliberate.[72] In a significant number of cases the Greek is also found as part of bilingual texts. As is the norm in such texts, the contents are similar but not exactly the same; in consequence, inscriptions where both languages figure on an equal footing are rare.[73] As Adams, in his study of Roman bilingualism, remarks, 'bilingual inscriptions are often intended to confer a mixed cultural/linguistic identity on the referent(s), and to that end one of the versions may

---

[65] Balsdon (1979) 128–31; Adams (2003) 16–17, 237; e.g. Lucian., *De merc.* 24 (Greek philosophers speaking Latin with difficulty); SHA, *Hadr.* 3.1 (Hadrian speaking initially with a rustic accent); SHA, *Sept. Sev.* 19.9 (the emperor retained his African accent even in old age).

[66] Kaimio (1979) 64–6: dedications to Dea Roma and Jupiter Capitolinus; honorific inscriptions for the imperial house or local governors.

[67] Kaimio (1979) 64–7.

[68] Kaimio (1979) 172, based on an estimate of 1,200 pagan Greek epitaphs; a similar percentage of 2.8% is obtained by comparing the *c.*1,700 Greek inscriptions of *I.G.U.R.* to the *c.*60,000 Latin inscriptions from Rome. At a smaller scale, the graveyard from Isola Sacra, Ostia, produces the same picture: the *I.S.I.S.* publication contains 13 Greek texts against 372 Latin ones (3.5%). Note that this is supposedly a graveyard with many migrants, see Prowse et al. (2007) and Tacoma (forthcoming *c*).

[69] Kajanto (1963) 2–4 (84 contain direct statements about origin, the great majority of these concern places in the East); Kaimio (1979) 23, 174–5.

[70] Kajanto (1963) 4; Noy (2000) 172, 176.

[71] As Noy (2010*a*) 13–14 observed in his discussion of *A.E.* (1972) 13–14, in households in which slaves hailed from different linguistic backgrounds Latin would be the logical choice.

[72] Boyancé (1956) 124.

[73] Adams (2003) 30; cf. Kaimio (1979) 176; e.g. *I.G.U.R.* 2.291 (with Adams (2003) 35–6) is a Greek epitaph of which only the protection clause is bilingual.

have symbolic rather than communicative value'.[74] A similar interpretative framework can be used for inscriptions using a Greek script for a Latin text or vice versa, or texts in one language and script in which phrases from the other creep in.[75]

As is well known, the status of Greek was ambiguous: it was both regarded as the language of culture and associated with slavery.[76] Already at the end of the Republic the absence of knowledge of Greek among the elite was considered something of an anomaly, though its actual use was also politically charged.[77] Emperors, like other members of the elite, normally knew Greek well, though individual emperors differed in their attitudes.[78] It seems almost certain that elite children in Rome were taught Greek.[79]

When it comes to spoken language, Latin was clearly dominant, but Greek might have been used more than the proportions of Latin and Greek inscriptions suggest.[80] It also seems likely that many people in Rome had at least some knowledge of Greek.[81] It has further been argued that the type of bilingualism on display in the Latin–Greek epitaphs of Rome reflects more general usage.[82]

Despite the presence of so many migrants, other languages hardly occur at all in written form in Rome. Nor is there much evidence for the intrusion of foreign words. There is only a handful of inscriptions in other languages than Greek or Latin. Palmyrene was used in some bilingual inscriptions, mainly from the shrine of Bel near Porta Portuense discussed below. A line of Nabataean is used in two bilingual inscriptions (in which Latin is the first language), one by a person from Petra, the other for someone from

---

[74] Adams (2003) 40.

[75] Numerous examples in many variations in Adams (2003); e.g. in *I.G.U.R.* 2.615 Δις Μαν(ιβους). Γ(άιος) Ἰούλους Τιλέσφορος φηκετ ετ σιβι ετ σουεις λειβ<ε>ρτεις λειβερταβουσκε εωρυμ· Τερεντία Ἄκτη φηκετ Τερεντίῳ Ἀνεικήτῳ ετ λ<ει>βερτω ετ κονιουγει βενεμερεντει ετ σιβι ετ σουεις λειβερτεις λειβερταβουσκε εωρουμ· οκ μονομεντου ηδεφικατου ες κομουνε αβ Ιουνιω Τελεσφορω <ε>τ Τερεντια Ακτη (with commentary of Adams (2003) 47–52, arguing that the scribe displays good knowledge of Latin and that the choice for Greek script must therefore have been made by the dedicator). Further *I.G.U.R.* 2.728 with Adams (2003) 71, where Greek creeps into the Latin text, or *I.G.U.R.* 2.570 with Adams (2003) 348–9, written in Greek script, but in a mixture of Latin and Greek.

[76] Kaimio (1979) 322–3. For the general ambiguity with which the Romans regarded the Greeks, see Woolf (1994).

[77] Dubuisson (1992) 188–91; Adams (2003) 9–14; Boatwright (2012) 72.

[78] Kaimio (1979) 130–43. Cass. Dio 60.17.4 has Claudius stripping a Lycian of his Roman citizenship when it appeared that he could not speak Latin, see Eck (2009*a*) 15–16.

[79] Quint., *Inst. Or.* 1.1.12–13 for Greek taking in fact precedence; Tac., *Dial.* 29 for a hostile account. Kaimio (1979) 317; Dubuisson (1992) 195–200.

[80] Noy (2000) 171: 'The fact that Latin inscriptions (principally epitaphs) outnumber Greek ones in Rome by about 50:1 does not necessarily reflect the proportion of people whose first language was Latin. There are numerous epitaphs in Latin for immigrants whose home areas suggest that they almost certainly spoke Greek.'

[81] See again Quint., *Inst. Or.* 1.1.12–13. Kaimio (1979) 317–18.   [82] Polomé (1983) 515.

Palmyra.[83] Jews normally used Greek and to a lesser extent Latin in their epitaphs; while stock phrases or tags in Hebrew and Aramaic sometimes appeared at the end of such texts.[84] When two ambassadors from the Nabataean king came to Rome, they commemorated their visit on a bilingual inscription in Latin and Greek, not in Aramaic.[85]

Vernacular languages may have been spoken more than that they were used in writing, but there is a noticeable lack of references to their use. In a tantalizing half-sentence that occurs in the biographies of Caesar and Augustus, Suetonius states that both had actors 'of all languages' performing plays in the neighbourhoods, but it is unclear what is referred to: plays in other languages than Latin and Greek are otherwise unknown, and further references to vernacular languages (let alone to their clustering by quarter) are almost entirely lacking. If not just Latin and Greek were meant, Oscan is the most likely candidate.[86] Suetonius relates how a staged supplication by the Armenian king Tiridates before Nero was translated by an ex-praetor; the king's words might have been in Armenian, but Greek is also a possibility.[87] Beside the possibility that the ex-praetor knew Armenian well enough to act as interpreter, there is no substantial evidence for interpreters of foreign languages other than Greek in Rome in the first two centuries AD.[88] Whatever use was made of languages other than Latin or Greek is thus almost completely obscured from our view. It may be that such languages were used at home—it is certainly relevant that at least some of the attested migrant marriages were between people originating from the same region. That its use was extensive outside

[83] *C.I.L.* 6.19134 (Palmyra) and 34196 (Petra) with Noy (2000) 178 and Terpstra (2015); Noy (2010*a*) 15–17 and (2010*b*) for some general remarks.

[84] The classic analysis is from Leon (1995²) 75–92; see also Noy (2000) 177–8; Cappelletti (2006) 179–80 for an convenient overview of language use in the Jewish inscriptions from Rome based on revised figures (75% in Greek, 20% Latin, but with significant differences between sites); Adams (2003) 21–2 for the symbolism of tags and 271–2 for the absence of knowledge of Hebrew in Rome.

[85] *I.G.U.R.* 1.16.

[86] Suet., *Iul.* 39.1: *edidit spectacula varii generis: munus gladiatorum, ludos etiam regionatim urbe tota et quidem per omnium linguarum histriones, item circenses athletas naumachiam.* Suet., *Aug.* 43.1–2: *fecitque nonnumquam etiam vicatim ac pluribus scaenis per omnium linguarum histriones.* See among others Polomé (1983) 517; Noy (2000) 177 n. 107; Adams (2003) 117–18. For the survival of Oscan and its use on stage see Strabo 5.3.6; for the performance of Greek and Oscan *ludi* see Cic., *ad fam.* 7.1.3, though it is not certain whether Cicero refers to the language that is used.

[87] Suet., *Nero* 13 with Kaimio (1979) 108 (Greek); Rochette (1996) no. 21 (Armenian); Noy (2000) 177 (presumably Armenian); Ricci (2005) 55 (Armenian). Considering the theatrical setting, not much can be inferred from the scene anyway.

[88] Rochette (1996) for a useful appendix of attested interpreters; though Rochette seems to suggest otherwise, most of them operate far from Rome, or translate from Greek to Latin. Interpreters of other languages are usually situated at or outside the borders of the empire: see e.g. Plin., *N.H.* 6.5.15 on 130 interpreters employed by Roman traders to do business with tribes around the Black Sea.

private contexts seems extremely unlikely, however. The satirists would almost certainly have seized the opportunity to mention it if this were the case.[89]

In explaining how immigrants made their linguistic choices, several factors can be adduced. In the regions of origin the provincial languages were already leading a shadowy existence: they were used in certain areas of life, but their use was restricted. For all public purposes Latin or Greek would be used. In many (though not all) cases, the provincial languages lacked a writing system—both a practical obstacle for their use, and an expression of their marginalized position. It would have been remarkable indeed—though not completely impossible—if upon arrival in Rome immigrants had suddenly started to use such languages in the public domain.

It remains possible that many immigrants to Rome had another language than Greek or Latin as their first language, and some might not have known Greek or Latin at all. However, the almost complete absence of references to the employment of other languages than Greek and Latin in Rome also suggests that migration was itself selective. As modern studies show, prior knowledge of the language of the intended destination serves as a selective device in the decision of prospective migrants. Those who do know the language are more prone to move, those who do not are more likely to stay put.[90] Thus it seems reasonable to expect that a relatively high proportion of people who had at least a rudimentary knowledge of Latin or Greek immigrated to Rome. For soldiers serving in Rome, prior knowledge of Latin might have been one factor in the decision to recruit them (and some of those serving in Rome were only recruited in stages (most notably the *equites singulares*), which automatically meant that they would have already acquired Latin in the army). In the case of slaves, selection may have been made not upon enslavement itself, but rather at the moment when it was decided which slaves were fit to serve in the households, that is, when they were bought at the slave market. For urban slavery, a least some knowledge of Latin or Greek is likely to have been a vital requirement.[91] We do not know enough about the situation in the regions of origin to know exactly how selective such processes were, but it seems likely that linguistic selection played at least some role in governing migration streams.

In Rome, Latin was the default option in many contexts. It is clear that in more formal, official and public contacts Latin was to be used by migrants and locals alike, and that its use was in principle unmarked. Immigrants from the

---

[89] Though cf. Juv., *Sat.* 3.63 for the language of the Syrians, discussed above.

[90] Noy (2000) 169.

[91] In *Dig.* 21.1.65.2 the possibility is envisaged that a slave is 'experienced' without knowing Latin (*nec ad rem pertinere, Latine sciat nec ne*); the context suggests skilled household slavery. I assume such slaves would normally at least know some Greek. Also relevant is Artemid. 1.53, on a free Greek who dreams to learn Latin and in the real world is sentenced to slavery; in this case slavery is paired with knowing Latin. For use of Greek, see Adams (2003) 761–2.

West can be supposed to have used it as a common and self-evident means of communication, including in their daily interactions, even if their own first language had been different. By contrast, its use by migrants from the East may be taken to be a conscious choice. In inscriptions this is particularly clear in those cases where Latin is used in combination with an ethnic identifier stating that someone originated from the East.

For immigrants from the East, Greek may at a practical level have acted as a migrant language, as a common language that all immigrants knew. The use of Greek in writing was much more marked than that of Latin: the relative paucity of Greek inscriptions suggests it was used sporadically and only in some contexts. Even migrants who came from areas where Greek was the main language did not use it in a systematic fashion, and often employed Latin as well. Moreover, Greek was more than just a marker of foreign origin. It served both as a slave language and as the language of high culture. The multiplicity of connotations is important.[92]

Given the paucity of vernacular languages in Rome and the dominance of Latin, it is tempting to see the language choices of immigrants as a straightforward expression of integration, of a wish to be or become part of the host society. As we saw, however, choices were not always self-evident, and although the choice was normally confined to Latin or Greek only, still the connotations would depend on the context and the user. The use of Greek in particular may have meant many different things in many different contexts. At the same time, it would be difficult to deny the integrative roles of Latin and Greek. At a practical level, their use will have created an easy means of communication and strongly facilitated their entrance into the host society. At a symbolic level, its use is likely to have fostered a sense of belonging to one community.

A series of twenty-five inscriptions from a shrine dedicated to Bel and some other eastern gods near Porta Portuensis shows the complexity of the linguistic choices.[93] The sanctuary served a clientele with a marked Syrian flavour. In the inscriptions, Latin, Greek, and Palmyrene were used, and in five of them two languages were used next to each other: nineteen used Latin (of which sixteen solely Latin), eight Greek (four solely Greek), and three Palmyrene (all three of them in combination with Latin or Greek). In one of the texts that employ two languages, a dedication to Sol, Latin and Palmyrene seem to have an equal status, and each is used for one side of the altar. Interestingly enough,

---

[92] Cf. Adams (2003) 365, who in his otherwise stimulating and nuanced treatment of bilingualism understands the use of Greek script and Greek language in monolingual inscriptions from Rome as 'indicating non-integration'.

[93] Chausson (1995) for an impressive and painstaking reconstruction of the full dossier, with further references; as Chausson stresses, not all inscriptions are equally certain to belong to the same sanctuary, but the general picture cannot be in doubt. For the bilingual texts see also Noy (2000) 243 and Adams (2003) 248–53.

the phrasing of the two texts differs significantly from each other, and only in the Palmyrene text is reference made to the origin of some of the dedicants as Palmyrene.[94] A second one used Palmyrene and Greek, just below each other, without, it seems, much difference between the two: the languages seem to have had equal status, though it may be significant that Palmyrene came first.[95] In a third one, Greek and Palmyrene were used by someone who identified himself in the Greek part as Palmyrene; this element was lacking in the Palmyrene text, but there his use of a Palmyrene naming system clearly marked him as such.[96] In a fourth and fifth inscription Latin and Greek were used by two persons, of whom only one described himself as Palmyrene.[97] If we assume—no doubt somewhat over-schematically—that in all the five bilingual texts one language was assigned the role of language of the host society and the other the role of the immigrants' language, it follows that both Latin and Greek could figure as host language, when they were paired with Palmyrene. In the Latin–Greek bilingual texts, however, the role of Greek was reversed, and it could also be used as the immigrant's language. If this interpretation is correct, Greek played more than one role. Furthermore, the fact that even in a sanctuary like this no dedications are attested using solely Palmyrene is striking: at most Palmyrene was used on an equal footing, but not as the main language. Even here Latin was dominant.

4. MIGRANT CULTS?

The shrine of Bel near Porta Portuense also raises questions about the existence of migrant cults. Immigrants can, after all, be expected to have brought their own gods and to have continued venerating them. It is well known that many foreign cults could be found in harbour cities: Piraeus in the Hellenistic period was full of foreign cults, and so were Puteoli and Ostia in Roman Italy. Likewise, the religious history of the city of Rome has often been described in terms of a continuous process of introducing new gods. For our purposes it is not so much the introduction of foreign gods itself that

---

[94] *C.I.L.* 6.30817 with Chausson (1995) no. N, also for the copious further bibliography.

[95] *I.G.U.R.* 1.120 with Chausson (1995) no. F and Adams (2003) 252–3 (though note that the text survives only partially, and the phrasing of the Greek is restored with the help of the Palmyrene and vice versa).

[96] *I.G.U.R.* 1.119 with Chausson (1995) no. O and Noy (2000) 182, 243 and Adams (2003) 251–2 for the onomastics.

[97] *C.I.L.* 6.50 = *I.G.U.R.* 1.117; *C.I.L.* 6.51 = *I.G.U.R.* 1.118 with Chausson (1995) nos. D and E and Adams (2003) 248. The two inscriptions are very similar, but not exactly the same; the fact that in the latter a consular date has been read of AD 116 excludes the possibility that Heliodorus is the same as the one in *I.G.U.R.* 1.119 of AD 236, as Noy (2000) 243 cautiously ventured.

matters,[98] but the way their cults functioned. Can we expect them to have functioned as institutions that catered for the needs of the migrants? Did they serve as a gateway into society, offering a place where migrants met and shared information? Did they help to express or reaffirm a collective identity for migrants? Can we find 'migrant cults': cults of foreign gods serving a migrant clientele, in which the origin of god and members overlapped and the identity of the one reinforced that of the other?

A degree of caution seems warranted. The idea of the prominent presence of migrant cults is based on a modern model of the way ethnically strongly segregated churches function in some present-day societies, often forming the main institutional gateway into the host society.[99] However, such a function is not a natural feature of all societies, and the risk of introducing anachronisms is large indeed. The repeated warnings not to approach Roman polytheism with Christian preconceptions are also highly relevant to the present subject— obviously temples did not play the same social roles as churches.

The notion that something that we might call migrant cults existed once was very strong, especially with regard to cults coming from the East. The argument was that 'Oriental' cults, often mystery cults, had entered Rome that were fundamentally different from the rest of Roman religion. They would eventually pave the way for the rise of Christianity. They were attractive to outsiders, who, after all, had been responsible for their importation.[100] Such a binary model, in which 'Oriental' cults are placed in opposition to traditional Roman religion, is no longer adhered to. The supposedly Oriental cults are so diverse that a single label obscures rather than helps in understanding. There was no strict division between these cults and official Roman religion, and they were attractive to more than one group. The supposed eastern origin was often notional: the form such cults took in Rome or in the Roman Empire bore only a vague resemblance to their original cult.[101]

Yet at the same time the idea of migrant cults is not wholly implausible, and there is some value in maintaining a dichotomy at least for analytical

---

[98] And even for the introduction of foreign cults, the assumption that they were brought by migrants is not the only plausible option. See Squarciapino (1962), arguing that the chronology suggests that in Ostia at least some of the cults were taken over from the capital rather than being introduced by traders. Despite the fact that the black stone had been brought from Pessinus to Rome via Ostia in 204 BC, the large temple complex of Magna Mater dates only from imperial times, though cult practice started earlier. For the building history of the temple at the Palatine in Rome, see Richardson (1992), s.v. 'Magna Mater, aedes' and Steinby (ed.) (1993–2000), s.v. 'Magna Mater, aedes'.

[99] Putnam (2007) 161: 'Historically, Americans worshipped in such complete racial segregation that it was proverbial among sociologists of religion that "11:00 am Sunday is the most segregated hour in the week".'

[100] e.g. LaPiana (1927).

[101] Beard, North, and Price (1998) 246–7 for a summary of a complicated subject.

purposes.[102] Religion is known to be very important in the formulation and creation of ethnic identities.[103] In both ancient perceptions of Roman religion and modern thinking about foreignness, religion forms a central issue. Religion is regarded as the area par excellence where debates about Roman identity were played out.[104]

The city of Rome under the high empire contained a variety of cults that was extremely wide, even by Roman standards, including Magna Mater, Isis, Sarapis, Mithras, Jahweh, and Jupiter Dolichenus. Some cults had been incorporated into the official religious landscape long before or gradually became part of it in the first two centuries AD, while others led an existence more in the background, or were physically located outside the *pomerium*. Sanctuaries of various sorts and sizes were strewn over the city. In many cases, multiple sanctuaries are found for particular cults: there are at least three sanctuaries for Jupiter Dolichenus, for Isis at least fourteen different sacred places have been identified, and forty Mithras caves have been located.[105] The variety of the cults and their wide dispersion over the city can be taken as an expression of the 'continuum of religious institutions and practices'.[106]

In many such cults foreignness played a central role. Gods were said to originate from outside Italy, sometimes from very specific places, as in the case of Jupiter Dolichenus. Priests could be foreigners. Sanctuaries could have an architecture that marked them off as different from that of Italian (or Greek) temples, as in the case of Isaeum Campense and the Syrian sanctuary on the Janiculum.[107] The iconography of the cult could be different from the trad-itional religious repertoire, and ritual procedures could be distinctly foreign. All these aspects marked them off from traditional Roman religion, no matter how diverse and inclusive this traditional religion itself was.[108]

Some of these cults were also highly visible, although this did not, of course, apply to all of them. Some cultic places were no more than adapted rooms in

[102] Cf. Price (2012) for a different analytical distinction, between ethnic and elective cults.
[103] Orlin (2010) 15.
[104] Beard, North, and Price (1998) 167: 'Roman religion continued under the empire to be a key set of practices which permitted reflections and debates on Roman identity.'
[105] Beard, North, and Price (1998) 266; for Jupiter Dolichenus, see later in this section; for Mithras, see also Richardson (1992), s.v. 'Mithraeum' and Steinby (ed.) (1993–2000), s.v. 'Mithra'.
[106] Beard, North, and Price (1998) 247; for the variety in cultic practice in the Roman world in general see MacMullen (1981).
[107] For the Isaeum Campense, see Richardson (1992), s.v. 'Isis Aedes' (noting that 'the complex was architecturally very exotic') and Steinby (ed.) (1993–2000), s.v. 'Iseum et Serapeum in Campo Martio; Isis Campensis' (F. Coarelli). For the Syrian sanctuary, see Richardson (1992), s.v. 'Iuppiter Heliopolitanus'; Steinby (ed.) (1993–2000), s.v. 'Iuppiter Heliopolitanus (Reg. XIV)' (J. Calzini Gysens), though admittedly it is only the third phase of the temple, dated to the second half of the fourth century AD and characterized by religious eclecticism, that is noted for its peculiar ground-plan.
[108] Beard, North, and Price (1998) 278–9.

houses, and in a case like that of Mithras the seclusion must have been deliberate. But others had large temples in prominent places. Their members could appear in processions, their priests and initiates distinguished by dress and attributes.

At the same time, the foreignness of these cults was subject to construction, both in the eyes of the participants and in the eyes of outsiders. What for Romans exactly constituted foreign religion was again left unclear—it depended on context and could change, as, for example, the fluctuating treatment of the Isis cult in the first century showed.[109] The Romans themselves never defined fully or coherently the foreignness of foreign cults.[110] Boundaries were also permeable: many connections existed between seemingly foreign and seemingly official Roman religions. One clear expression of this was the fact that many sanctuaries (including the Aventine Dolichenum and the Syrian sanctuary on the Janiculum) were home to an assemblage of gods, of whom only a proportion were foreign. Another was that some of the supposedly foreign cults had a clear connection with the imperial house or tied themselves to the imperial family.[111]

Many of the foreign cults fostered a strong sense of allegiance and were henotheistic: the existence of other gods was not denied, but their own god clearly took precedence above the rest. Some were mystery cults with secret initiation rituals that marked the complete transformation of the individual, and many can be considered to be 'elective': they were entered through personal choice and had what we would call members—the fact that some of these cults inscribed lists of participants on stone is in itself indicative of this notion of membership.[112] The elective cults seem to have employed various strategies to regulate membership: some included slaves, while others allowed women to participate.[113]

Thus, some of the cults can be regarded as clearly demarcated institutions in which notions of foreignness played an important role. The question is to what extent their membership was dominated by migrants.

We should begin with a negative observation. Conventional expressions like *Dis Manibus* apart, in Noy's list of provincial migrant inscriptions religious allegiances are not often mentioned. Ethnic origin and cultic preference did not form an automatic or standard part of a migrant's self-definition, at least

---

[109] Beard, North, and Price (1998) 250; cf. Chapter 3, Section 5 on expulsions.

[110] Orlin (2010) 11–12. For an example, see SHA, *Hadr.* 22.10: Hadrian 'observed Roman cults, but despised foreign ones', *sacra Romana diligentissime curavit, peregrina contempsit*, in which neither Roman nor foreign is defined any further.

[111] For a relatively simple example, see *A.E.* (1926) 116 with *Terme* 5.8 and Steinby (ed.) (1993–2000), s.v. 'Mithra, Anthrum (Horti Sallustiani, Reg. VI)', in which two imperial freedmen finance a cave (*antrum*) with a Mithras statue for the wellbeing and return and the victory of the Severan imperial family.

[112] Beard, North, and Price (1998) 245.   [113] North (2013) on female participation.

not simultaneously. This does not, of course, exclude any form of religious allegiance. It is certainly legitimate to wonder whether and in what form such expressions should be expected to occur in epitaphs. In some cases the physical context—now often unknown—would have made the connection plain; for example, when a dedication was erected at a sanctuary, no words would be necessary to establish the connection.

The best example of strong ties between cults and immigrants does not come from Rome but from Puteoli, Rome's prime harbour before it was eclipsed by Ostia. A famous dossier contains a letter by the *statio* of the Tyreans who resided in Puteoli to the council of their home-town Tyrus, and a partly preserved record of the session of the city council of Tyrus discussing its request for financial help.[114] In the letter, the Tyreans in Puteoli claimed that, due to their dwindling numbers, their *statio* was in difficulties. The debate by the council of Tyrus is unfortunately only partly preserved, but it is clear that the relationship of the *statio* of Puteoli with a parallel *statio* of the Tyreans in Rome had become strained. The precise nature of the relations between the city of Tyrus, its *statio* in Rome, and its *statio* in Puteoli need not occupy us here. What is important is that in the documents the religious activities of the *statio* in Puteoli are described in some detail. They financed 'sacrifices and rites of our paternal gods that are established here in temples', while in addition, the *statio* was charged for 'the bull sacrifice at the games of Puteoli', and they were 'fitting out the *statio* for the sacred days of the emperor as they occur'.[115] The three religious activities nicely encapsulate the three spheres in which the *statio* operated: they stressed the ties with their homeland through their ancestral cults; they showed their integration in the civic community of Puteoli by the bull sacrifice during the city's games (though the phrasing in the document suggests this may not have entirely to their own liking); and they displayed their loyalty towards the emperor on imperial birthdays. It is further noteworthy that in the document the Tyreans resident in Puteoli are presented as distinct from the Tyrean traders and businessmen who came to Puteoli, which suggests that the former had immigrated on a more or less permanent basis to Puteoli, though the fact that they organized themselves as a *statio* does make it likely that they remained involved in its trade.[116] The dossier is the best example of a straightforward connection between a foreign cult, a well-demarcated community of immigrants, and a

---

[114] *I.G.* 14.830 with Sosin (1999). Other examples are mentioned in Price (2012) 3–7.

[115] *I.G.* 14.830, lines 9–10, cf. 23–4, τε θυσίας καὶ θρησκείας τῶν πατρίων ἡμῶν θεῶν ἐνθά δε ἀφωσιωμένων ἐν ναοῖς; 11–12, cf. 26–7 τὰ ἀναλώματα εἰς τὸν ἀγῶνα τὸν ἐν Ποτιόλοις τῆς βουθουσίας ἡμεῖν προσετέθη; 14–15, cf. 26–7 εἰς τὰς ἱερὰς ἡμέρας τοῦ κυρίου Αὐτοκράτορος συνπεσούσης.

[116] *I.G.* 14.830, lines 3–4, 7–8 οἱ ἐν Ποτιόλοις κατοικοῦντες, 16–17 οὔτε παρὰ ναυκλήρων οὔτε παρὰ ἐμπόρων. In addition, the name of the ambassador of the *statio* that presented the letter to the council, Laches, son of Preimogenia and Agathopous, may imply that Laches' father had

home-town. Although the evidence for such ties is less strong in other cases, it may be assumed that other *stationes* of other cities and regions operated along similar lines,[117] and that such organizational forms also occurred in Rome. The dossier itself explicitly refers to the *statio* of the Tyreans in Rome, and it seems likely that this implies that it was operating in a similar way as the one in Puteoli (though its financial arrangements differed somewhat).

Such well-demarcated communities of immigrants that identified themselves through their cultic activities with their homelands made particular sense in the case of long-distance trade networks. As Terpstra explains with respect to another community of traders living in Puteoli, the Nabateans:

> Because geographical provenance and religious identity formed the defining element of this group, it was effectively a closed network with fixed membership. Non-Nabataeans would not have been able to join, nor would Nabateans, if expelled, have been able to join another network (at least not easily). The members making up the network as a collective therefore had a large amount of coercive power over individual members; they possessed the definitive power to include and exclude, and they thus controlled access to Nabataean business in Puteoli. As members of a foreign trade network, centered on geographical provenance, they will have had more occasion for monitoring and punishment than their native business partners. They could, for example, ostracize members from the collective, or spread negative reports about them, thereby ensuring that misbehaving members could no longer get any business. The result of all this will have been that trust was established between Nabataeans and Puteolans, and that both sides could feel secure that trade conflicts could be resolved through the proper legal channels, even in the absence of government enforcement.[118]

Rome, however, contained many more migrants than Puteoli, and more groups than traders alone. Even if there was a *statio* that took care of a cult of the ancestral gods, it is unlikely that there would be an obligation to participate in it. Terpstra's argument that in Puteoli traders were effectively forced to join the exclusive network is convincing, but it seems likely that in Rome such exclusivism would be applicable only to a limited number of its immigrants. In fact, it is telling that even in the dossier of the Tyreans, membership turns out to be one of the main issues in the question who should finance the cultic activities: in the letter from the *statio* it was implied that the dwindling numbers of resident Tyreans were causing the financial difficulties, suggesting a system of membership and contributions. However, it emerges

---

married a Roman woman from Puteoli (note that she was mentioned first, suggesting higher status), and that Laches was a second-generation immigrant.

[117] Verboven (forthcoming) argues that such arrangements may be lurking behind inscriptions referring to 'worshippers of god X from place Y residing in place Z', e.g. *C.I.L.* 10.1634 'Worshippers of Jupiter Heliopolitanus from Beirut residing in Puteoli', *cultores Iovis Heliopolitani Berytenses qui Puteolis consistunt.*

[118] Terpstra (2015) 88–9. Cf. Price (2012) for more possibilities.

from the ensuing debate in Tyrus that in reality the *statio* of Rome had paid Puteoli's costs, and that membership was not the real issue.[119] The *statio* could make its claim precisely because effectively the resident Tyrians had no choice but to join (just as Terpstra maintains), but there was no formal obligation to do so.

It is rather unlikely that in Rome every foreign cult would have a *statio* behind it to finance it, and that the 'members' of such a *statio* were the main or sole participants in such cults. No doubt financial arrangements were diverse, and equally doubtless the worshippers could be organized along different principles. A hint of more open arrangements is provided by the Bel sanctuary near Porta Portuense that has already been discussed. From the twenty-five inscriptions it emerges that in fact a whole array of gods was associated with it, not just one ancestral god. And while it is clear that at least some of the worshippers were Palmyreans or other Syrians, it is also clear that some were not.[120] It is surely possible that behind some of the Greek and Roman names that occur in its inscriptions there lurk people with a Syrian background, but even if this was the case, it remains significant that they chose not to identify themselves as such. Although the sanctuary had unmistakable Syrian and Palmyrean overtones, ties between cult and immigrant worshippers were less strong than in the case of the *statio* of Puteoli.

One of the best examples of how diverse membership could come from another sanctuary, that of Jupiter Dolichenus on the Aventine. Its god Dolichenus originated from the otherwise relatively obscure city of Doliche in Commagene (mod. Dülük, Turkey), where he was worshipped in a temple overlooking the city.[121] The iconography of the god (his pose on a bull, thunderbolt, and double axe) seems to refer to his Hittite predecessor. The intervening history of the god and the cult in the Achaemenid and Hellenistic period is very obscure, until the Dolichenus cult spread rather suddenly over the Roman Empire in the second century. Worship flourished especially in the later second and early third centuries AD; it is thought that the capture of Doliche by Shapur in AD 253 dealt a significant blow to the cult. Some seventeen sanctuaries have been identified in the Roman Empire, and over 600 inscriptions referring to the cult have been published.[122] Many of the finds originate from the frontier zones in Britain, along the Rhine and the Danube, and it is therefore not surprising that a significant number of the participants in

---

[119] See Sosin (1999), showing that the implicit claims made in the *statio*'s letter are contradicted by the statements during the debate.

[120] Among the inscriptions cited by Chausson (1995), some mention worshippers of whom only a part are described as Syrian or Palmerene, implying that the others were not. In a number of other cases no ethnic identifiers are used at all. Note that the sanctuary is seen by Price (2012) 4 as a prime example of an ethnic cult.

[121] *New Pauly*, s.v. 'Doliche' (J. Wagner).

[122] *C.C.I.D.* (1987) numbers 642 inscriptions, but this includes some vacant numbers.

the cult belonged to the army. Although one of the (if not *the*) main characteristics of the god was that he originated from a specific place, there was no obvious connection between these sanctuaries and the temple in Doliche.

In the city of Rome there were at least three sanctuaries of Jupiter Dolichenus.[123] Interestingly enough, they had markedly different profiles and served rather different clienteles. One sanctuary was part of a series of temples at or near the camp of the *equites singulares* near the Lateran palace, located next to others for Sol Invictus, Apollo, and Diana. Both its location and the attested dedicants show it belonged to and was used by the *equites*.[124] A second Dolichenum was on the Esquiline (at the north side of the current Piazza Vittorio Emmanuelle). This one also had a military or paramilitary clientele, but not exclusively so, as some other worshippers are attested as well.[125]

It is the third sanctuary that is particularly relevant for the present discussion, as it is often presented as one of the quintessential migrant cults. The sanctuary on the Aventine is by far the best-known Dolichenus sanctuary in the Roman world, not least because it is from this sanctuary that membership lists survive.[126] Judging by the names, its exclusively male membership shows a variety of backgrounds. One of the larger and more important inscriptions lists thirty-four names, that are suggestive of Celtic, Egyptian, Greek, and Roman backgrounds and different social and legal statuses, probably including slaves, and with some people related to each other. Remarkably enough, though, among all the names preserved there is only one that may perhaps point in the direction of Syria, and even that one is extremely uncertain.[127] This makes it rather difficult to maintain that the cult served as a magnet for Syrians living in Rome.[128]

Similar situations can be found for other cults, though our evidence is usually not as complete as for the Aventine Dolichenum. Both in the case of the Aventine Dolichenum and similarly composed cult groups, it is possible

---

[123] Though some of the find spots remain unknown, the strong dispersal over the rest of the city of inscriptions that cannot be connected to any of the three known sanctuaries suggests that at one time more cult places existed; see *C.C.I.D.* 422–34. Richardson (1992), s.v. 'Iupiter Dolichenus (3)' and Steinby (ed.) (1993–2000), s.v. 'Iuppiter Dolichenus, aedes' (L. Chioffi) refer to a shrine in Transtiberim.

[124] *C.C.I.D.* 417 for a description, 418–21 for the inscriptions.

[125] *C.C.I.D.* 407 (description) 408–16 (inscriptions); Richardson (1992), s.v. 'Iupiter Dolichenus (2)'; Steinby (ed.) (1993–2000) s.v. 'Iuppiter Dolichenus, sacrarium' (L. Chioffi).

[126] *C.C.I.D.* 355 (description), 356–439 (inscriptions); Richardson (1992), s.v. 'Iupiter Dolichenus, Templum (1)'.

[127] *C.C.I.D.* 373; many of the names also occur in other inscriptions. As the editors rightly observe, 'Zumindest nach der Namen der hier genannten Gemeindemitglieder setzte sich die Aventiner Kultgemeinschaft insgesamt aus verschiedenen ethnischen Gruppen zusammen'. A possibly Semitic name occurs in col. 5, line 13, Suetrius Bacradis, but this requires the name to be read as Bar-cadis.

[128] Cf. Polomé (1983) 514, quoted at the beginning of this chapter.

that the membership of the Aventine shrine simply comprised a more or less random cross-section of Rome's general population, which was, after all, rather heterogeneous. In that case, it would be a sobering corrective to the standard interpretation of the Aventine Dolichenus temple as a migrant cult. However, it might perhaps also be hypothesized that in such cases the cult did in fact function as a migrant cult, but in a much looser sense: it may have attracted people who felt themselves to be foreigners and identified with a foreign god, no matter where they came from and independent of the question where the god had his home-town. Which of these two options is correct is difficult to say, but the possibility that some foreign cults reaffirmed in such a vague way a much more broadly defined immigrant identity should be taken seriously, especially if one wants to salvage the notion of migrant religions.

> So are any generalizations possible at all about the social composition of these cults and the social range of their members? It is easy enough to imagine how a rootless immigrant, lost in a great city, might have found attraction in the community of worshippers of Isis. But there is no reason to suppose that such people made up the majority of the cult's adherents or explain its success.[129]

> Of course, many foreigners who moved to Rome did continue to worship their ancestral gods, according to the customs of their original countries; but did not necessarily seek new cult members from the population at large. People flocked to Rome from both the eastern and western parts of the empire. No doubt almost all of them kept to some of the religious traditions of their homeland.[130]

This is what Beard, North, and Price have to say, and there is little to disagree with. Yet migrant cults in the stricter sense can only be detected with difficulty. There were certainly some cults in which the overlap between the foreignness of the cult and the origin of its members was more or less complete. In many more, however, migrant identity played a vaguer role, or hardly any role at all. In the religious landscape of Rome its role was not a prominent one, and it was certainly not consistently the same.

A small vignette from Apuleius' *Golden Ass* shows the complexities. When Apuleius' Lucius arrived in Rome, he went straight to the Isaeum Campense, describing himself in a beautiful image as 'a stranger to her shrine, but a native to her religion'.[131] Perhaps the Isaeum did function for him as a gateway into Roman society, and it certainly functioned in the narrative as a trap for the priests to help recently arrived believers spend more money on her cult. Yet Lucius was a recent convert to Isis, and the fact that he immediately turned to the temple was not caused by the fact that he was—or regarded himself as—an Egyptian in any sense. In fact, and ironically, the Isaeum Campense was a

---

[129] Beard, North, and Price (1998) 300.   [130] Beard, North, and Price (1998) 271–2.
[131] Apul., *Met.* 11.26: *fani quidem advena, religionis autem indigena.*

temple, the *raison d'être* of which was precisely that it had established itself in the heart of city, integrated in the Roman religious landscape, and built by the emperor.[132]

5. MIGRANT ASSOCIATIONS?

The last area that remains to look at is that of the associations.[133] Given the fact that in recent research the approach has shifted from a study of the way they provided internal sociability to wider societal and symbolic roles,[134] it is certainly important to take them into account. The associations may have offered a platform to organize migrants, functioned as a gateway into urban society, and offered a surrogate family. At a symbolic level, they might have formed a place of interaction with local society, provided their members with symbolic capital, and have helped to establish network ties with patrons.[135] The associations claimed their place in the urban landscape: they were very visible, had their own buildings in prominent places, their own festivals, and their own designated places in theatres.

As is well known, associations were organized along various principles, and it seems they used whatever was available as an immediate point of identification.[136] They could provide burial for their members, they could contain the *familia* of an aristocratic *domus* and be responsible for the burials in its *columbarium*, they could be professional associations of people with the same occupation, they could be *stationes* of traders from a particular area, a particular product, or both. The boundaries between the various forms of associations were vague—so vague that it might be argued that the elective cults described above simply formed part of the same spectrum. Associations normally had a patron god to whom regular sacrifices were made, so the cultic element was never completely absent.

From a functional perspective, the immediate and concrete roles of associations were limited. Some provided a savings mechanism for payment of burial costs, but from their surviving rules it is clear that communal feasts

---

[132] See Richardson (1992), s.v. 'Isis Aedes' and Steinby (ed.) (1993–2000), s.v. 'Iseum et Serapeum in Campo Martio; Isis Campensis' (F. Coarelli). The building history is for the earlier period somewhat obscure, but it is certain that Domitian rebuilt the temple after the fire of AD 80.

[133] See Ricci (2005) 55–64 for an overview.

[134] Perry (2011); Liu (forthcoming), placing the shift in the context of social capital theory and new institutional economics.

[135] Perry (2011) 507; Verboven (2011).

[136] Rives (2001) 132: 'Any attempt to catalogue them appears to be overly schematic.' Verboven (forthcoming) also points to the fact that in inscriptions only part of the full title of *collegia* could be employed, so that what appears to be a cultic association might in fact (also) be a professional one.

formed a very important ingredient of their activities.[137] Professional associations are best known for what they did not do: they did not interfere in the urban economy, at least not before late antiquity. No price-setting occurred, they had no intermediary role in assigning apprenticeships, they offered no control of the quality of products, they did not monopolize labour. Mostly their activities were social, centring again especially on the organization of communal meals for their members.[138] But they are likely to have played more indirect economic roles, such as sharing expertise, strengthening internal trust and solidarity, and offering protection against outsiders.[139] They did, after all, bring together people who might work on the same projects, or might compete for the same orders. In the case of the professional associations in a situation of variable demand, with production organized in small workshops, co-operation would be advantageous.[140] It is in this context that the often observed engagement with the elite might be seen: they recruited patrons from the elite, set up dedications to high-placed persons, and sometimes received direct financial help, while their own magistrates could enter higher circles.[141]

It is clear that membership of such associations offered many advantages. If the state offered privileges and immunities, they were normally given to the associations. For some occupations, especially those that concerned the exploitation of natural resources, a government licence was required, though true monopolization by the professional associations of such exploitation seems only a later (though logical) development.[142] However, membership was not particularly cheap, and also brought obligations with it.[143]

Surprisingly little is known about actual procedures for admission, except that the associations themselves decided who was admitted, not the local authorities.[144] Membership lists suggest that membership was both controlled and restricted. In general, one might say that associations favoured membership of free adult males to the detriment of all other persons. However, practices varied significantly, and freedmen were often included. There were also some associations with a mixed slave and free membership.[145] One dedication in Rome was set up by a *collegium mulierum*, function unknown.[146] Women also acquired roles as patronesses and 'mothers'.[147] In the case of the

---

[137] Perry (2011) 507. The overlap in functions is readily visible in *C.I.L.* 14.2112, concerning the association of the *cultores Dianae et Antinoi* at Lanuvium. See Ebel (2004) 12–75.

[138] For sociability as a key element, see Perry (2011).

[139] Cf. Liu (forthcoming), who discusses the context of such arguments, and cautions against seeing the associations as efficient institutional solutions to societal problems.

[140] DeLaine (2000) 132; Verboven (forthcoming).

[141] Perry (2011) 508–11. See (again) *C.I.L.* 14.2112, documenting in some detail the relation between the patron and the *cultores Dianae et Antinoi* at Lanuvium.

[142] Verboven (forthcoming).   [143] Liu (forthcoming).   [144] Perry (2011) 512.

[145] Kampen (1981) 27 n. 25.   [146] *C.I.L.* 6.10423: *Ti(berio) B() M() colleg(ium) mulierum.*

[147] Hemelrijk (2008).

occupational associations, it is also clear that there were also members who were not active themselves: there were minors (some probably apprentices), elderly people who presumably had previously worked in the profession, and those owned the production facilities (and/or the slaves) rather than working there themselves, and then there was the occasional honorary member.[148] Although it is clear that many poorer members of the population were buried through the services of a *collegium*, obviously for many others burial was arranged independently. As for the professional associations, membership was not a formal requirement for working in a particular occupation.[149]

There were numerous *collegia* in Rome: some 500 different ones are attested from the first four centuries, in some 700 inscriptions.[150] Some *collegia* could be rather large, with hundreds of members, but most were relatively small, with a couple of tens of members. Nevertheless, although exact figures are unavailable, it seems likely that only part of the population was a member of any association. For the professional associations, previous estimates suggested that about one-third of the adult male population was a member, but even this may be too high. If the 500 *collegia* that are known from Rome each had an average membership of 100, only 5 per cent of the population would be a member, or some 10 per cent of the males of 14 and over. The figures might in reality be higher, because not all *collegia* are attested, but even if they would be doubled, the associations will have comprised only a part of the working population.[151] Something similar can be observed in the case of a particular association. The *collegium* of *fabri tignariorum* ('builders') is known to have had at one point a membership of about 1,300; it was organized in sixty *decuriae* of around twenty-two members each. This was an extremely large *collegium*, and its activities are attested from the first to the fourth century AD. Yet by any estimate far more people will have been engaged in the building industry; and slaves, who were surely employed in large numbers, are not known to have been admitted to this *collegium* (freedmen were).

Notwithstanding their integrative roles, *collegia* were thus to some extent exclusivist.[152] The question, then, is to what extent migrants were active in such organizations. La Piana wrote that, 'it is evident that the foreign population had a large share in the membership of the various associations': 'foreigners invaded the old Roman guilds and formed many new ones in the case of crafts, trades, and professions brought into Rome from outside'.[153]

---

[148] Verboven (forthcoming).   [149] Verboven (forthcoming).

[150] Liu (forthcoming).

[151] Calculation of Liu (forthcoming), who also cites previous estimates. Liu argues that the actual figures might be lower, because not all 500 associations will have existed simultaneously. In addition, it is possible that some people were members of more than one association, see *Terme* 8.12 on *C.I.L.* 14.4234.

[152] Liu (forthcoming).   [153] La Piana (1927) 245, 246.

Neither 'evident' nor 'invaded' seem appropriate, though that some foreigners will have been included seems more than likely. The question is in what form.

Outside Rome, it is known that sometimes parallel associations were set up by immigrants next to local ones. Obviously, members of such non-local organization were set apart and had to find a balance between finding their way into local society and protecting their own interests.[154] Such parallel organizations are not attested for Rome. La Piana remarks that normally there were no *collegia* of foreigners—they joined existing ones.[155]

One organizational form quite obviously catered for the need of some immigrants: the trading stations. Their religious activities have already been discussed above, in the case of the *statio* of the Tyreans at Puteoli. The *stationes* clearly served as bridgeheads, and formed part of a network of similar *stationes* elsewhere. The evidence shows that *stationes* were normally organized by city (in a few cases by larger entities, such as provinces). Traders could also be organized around the products they imported.[156] This will no doubt also have given their organizations an immigrant membership, but less exclusively so, for they could also comprise Rome-born traders in the same product. They could be formed basically by any community that saw the need to protect its interests. It seems that their actual premises were small (there was no storage space of any substance),[157] that they were clustered (in Ostia to the extent that they formed a separate square),[158] and that their offices were rented from the city.[159] The Puteoli inscription shows that there was some link between the *statio* and the governing bodies of the home-town (at least at a financial level) and between *stationes* of the same home-town, that some *stationes* received contributions of one sort or another from their traders, and, as was discussed above, that *stationes* were involved in the upkeep of home cults in their place of destination.[160] The extent to which *stationes* were

---

[154] Liu (forthcoming) for parallel organizations of *consistentes*. One of their strategies seems to have been to engage locals as patrons. Cf. Noy (2010*a*) on the attestations of *collegia peregrinorum* in Britain and Germania and Verboven (2011) on *collegia* of merchants and other foreigners in general.

[155] La Piana (1927) 265. See also Bruun (forthcoming) on *Tribu* p.165 from Ostia, probably a membership list of an association of *fabri navales*. The list comprises *c*.90 names, almost all are Roman citizens, but seven belong to *peregrini*. Although not all need to be first-generation migrants, the association clearly admitted outsiders.

[156] Meiggs (1973²) 283–9; Ricci (2005) 60, mentioning *inter alia C.I.L.* 6.1935 (a dedication set up by *mercatori olei Hispani ex provincia Baetica*) and *C.I.L.* 6.1620 (a dedication by *mercatores frumentari(i)/et oleari(i) Afrari*). See also Terpstra (2013).

[157] Sixty-one small rooms at Ostia. Suet., *Nero* 37.1 speaks of *tabernae* at Rome. In the case of Puteoli, there has been much debate about the height of the *misthos*, and this has implications for our understanding of the size of the *statio* of the Tyrians. If Sosin (1999) is right that the sum was no more than 250 *denarii*, we should imagine likewise a small office; if otherwise, there might have been substantial differences between the sizes of *stationes*.

[158] For Rome, cf. Plin., *N.H.* 16.86.236, for *stationes municipiorum* at the Forum of Caesar.

[159] Not so in Suet., *Nero* 37.1, but with rather unhappy consequences for the lessor.

[160] *I.G.* 14.830 with Sosin (1999).

subject to state control (either by their home-towns or the Roman state—some were involved in transporting grain) is debated, but current discussions tend to see them as relatively autonomous organizations.

The fundamental question is to what extent the *stationes* can be regarded as associations.[161] If they are regarded as similar, the implication is that many of the attested associations operated in the same way. Verboven, in a thorough discussion of trans-local merchants, seems to think they were equivalent.[162] Yet some caution is needed. Although in their public cultic activities they behaved very much like local associations and—we may suppose—modelled their behaviour upon them, in other important respects they may not have been identical. There is much less evidence for the commensality that is so characteristic of associations, and the size of their buildings militates against regular communal gatherings. Furthermore, the evidence for funerary activities is flimsy.[163] *Stationes* may perhaps have sometimes provided for burials of its 'members', but it is most unlikely that they did so on a significant scale, since this would produce a funerary landscape with clusters of burials of particular migrant groups (for example, in *columbaria*) that is completely at odds with what we actually find in Rome and Ostia. It seems clear that they primarily served the needs of traders and businessmen. For those immigrants that were not directly involved with them, we might imagine that the *stationes* formed not so much the point of entrance but rather the bridge with the home community: in practical terms, they helped to find out news, or book a passage on a ship, in symbolic terms giving the participating immigrants a place in society. This would be a place within the community that kept marking them as outsiders and would emphasize their immigrant status explicitly. It seems no coincidence that most epigraphical attestations of the eastern *stationes* were put up in Greek.

Another model might lurk behind the *collegium Aesculapii et Hygeae*.[164] Though this is not explicitly stated, this might have been in fact a *collegium* of people working in the medical professions. As was stated before, the medical profession was one of the few that did have an ethnic colouring: doctors were supposed to have a Greek background—a background which was in itself flexible and subject to construction. Although we lack precise knowledge about the membership of this *collegium*, it seems likely that it contained a membership that was dominated by migrants—though itself of rather diverse origins. The situation will have been similar in the case of various types of stage artists (like actors, mime artists, dancers), whose associations are known

---

[161] Noy (2000) 163.   [162] Verboven (2011).
[163] By contrast, *C.I.L.* 6.9677 shows the opposite. It is a grave monument of a *q(uin)q(uennalis) corporis negotiantium Malacitanorum*, for himself, his wife, his children, and their freedmen and descendants. Clearly he was buried separately.
[164] *C.I.L.* 6.10234.

relatively well and whose professions were also sometimes dominated by 'Greeks'.[165] However, there were few such professions, and this makes it unlikely that this type of covert migrant association was widespread.

In the case of many other associations, we may suppose that immigrants would simply join the ranks of the local *collegium*, or would not join any association at all. Once more, the variety is striking. Purely and openly visible migrant clubs were certainly present in the form of the *stationes*, but it seems likely that they predominantly played a role for businessmen and traders. In other areas of urban society, professional identity took precedence. Slaves were mostly excluded from such organizations, which, given the fact that many of them were highly skilled and worked beside free persons, is remarkable. After manumission they were able to obtain entrance. In the case of the aristocratic *domus*, they were made members of the *domus collegium*; it seems unlikely they had much choice, though it is known that some slaves could also be members of an external association that catered for their burial, and that conflicts between owners of slaves and such associations could arise.[166]

6. MIGRANT NETWORKS

Knowledge about migration patterns is a vital requisite before acculturation can be addressed, since it affects the nature of the problem. A sense of scale helps: it does matter if roughly a quarter of Rome's population consisted of people born elsewhere. Geographically, the origins of migrants were extremely diverse, and the large degree of heterogeneity will have affected the possibilities for community formation. At the same time, migrants came predominantly from within the empire rather than outside it, and although that empire was culturally certainly not homogeneous, the power and allure of things Roman were felt everywhere. Engagement with Roman culture can hardly be assumed to have started only upon arrival in Rome. Socially, migrants covered the full spectrum of statuses, running from the elite to slaves, and given the importance attached to status, ethnic bonding is unlikely to have transcended such class differences. Some migrant groups will have entered Roman society seamlessly. In consequence, migrants such as the Italians have become almost invisible for us. Others had every reason to participate actively in Roman elite culture, like senators. Slaves will have had every incentive to

---

[165] Ricci (2005) 60–1.

[166] See *C.I.L.* 14.2112, containing the rules of the *cultores Dianae et Antinoi* at Lanuvium, with detailed provisions for burial. The association was open to slaves; see esp. col. 2, line 4 for a *funus imaginarium* in a case where a master refuses to hand over the body of his slave. See Ebel (2004) 39–41.

show adaptive behaviour, no matter how traumatic the experience of being enslaved might have been. Other migrants, faced with a new environment, sometimes emphasized their origins.

In the previous sections, scepticism was expressed about the extent to which immigrants in Rome could profitably be described in terms of migrant communities. It seems rather unlikely that Polomé's quote cited at the beginning of the chapter accurately captures the nature of a migrant's experiences. As a rule, they did not cluster together, they did not preserve their own language, they did not use economic and religious associations to foster loyalty to their socio-cultural traditions, and they did not have their own exclusive sanctuaries.[167] The notion is based on the incorrect assumption that closed migrant communities are natural phenomena. In most—though not all—cases, the sources rather suggest a weak sense of community among migrants living in Rome. Although we saw that the drawing of boundaries was in some respects important for immigrants, the boundaries themselves were permeable and negotiable. However, this may easily be reduced to the negative argument that, with a few exceptions, well-defined immigrant communities cannot be distinguished. It is hardly satisfactory to leave the argument there, as migrant studies have time and again emphasized that migrants often use formal or informal institutions to help them come to terms with their new surroundings.[168]

Rather than looking for communities that lead a shadowy existence anyway, network theory might help to probe deeper. Network theory seems better suited because it focuses on the structure of the network and the nature of the ties rather than ill-defined group boundaries. It is especially Granovetter's distinction between weak and strong ties that seems useful.[169] Its attraction for our purposes is that it works with simple binary opposites that are good to think with and that obviate the need for sophisticated data that we do not have.

Granovetter introduced in 1973 a principle that did not so much concern the structure of networks but rather the nature of the ties between members. The starting point formed a distinction between strong and weak ties, expressed in degrees of social relation: a crucial distinction between friends (strong ties) and acquaintances (weak ties) was made. The higher the prevalence of strong ties, the more overlap in the network: participants tend to befriend each other's friends. Put differently, network density is much higher. The weaker the ties, the less dense the network becomes. Networks consisting of close friends show much overlap, and therefore are more closed, whereas

---

[167] Cf. Polomé (1983) 514.

[168] Manning (2013²) 193: 'While some individuals may migrate as wanderers, moving unassisted, most migration takes place with the support of institutions and networks.'

[169] Granovetter (1972–3), formulated in the context of his strength of weak ties (SWT) model. Cf. Boyd (1989) 654–5, noting its potential for the study of migration, and Manning (2013²).

networks consisting of people who know each other vaguely are bound to be more open.

Granovetter's argument was that, paradoxically, a network having weak ties performs in some respects better than a well-integrated network of strong ties. A network with many weak ties is better at diffusing knowledge and adapting itself.

> Granovetter's insight is that ties that are weak in the relational sense—that the relations are less salient or frequent—are often strong in the structural sense— that they provide shortcuts across the social topology. Although casual friend-ships are relationally weak, they are more likely to be formed between socially distant actors with few network 'neighbors' in common. These 'long ties' between otherwise distant nodes provide access to new information and greatly increase the rate at which information propagates, despite the relational weakness of the tie as a conduit.[170]

Granovetter's model has been highly influential, not only in modelling net-works but also in understanding social relations. In particular, there is a strong connection between Granovetter's model and the concept of social capital, and hence even with the general notion that establishing and using connec-tions is central to the way societies are structured.[171] It therefore hardly comes as a surprise that the model has had resonance in migration studies, where community formation is one of the central issues. At the same time, migration historians (and others) have added a number of refinements that can be profitably employed here as well.

Granovetter himself already observed that the distinction between networks with weak ties and strong ties might be class-specific: lower-class networks have a higher propensity to rely on strong ties, and the insulated nature of such groups helps to explain why it is difficult to escape from them.[172] This distinction has also been applied to understand variations between different migrant groups in contemporary society.[173] Better-skilled and higher-educated migrants have less propensity to rely on fellow countrymen. A crucial factor is, of course, language acquisition: better-educated migrants are inherently more likely to speak the language of their host country. One may add that higher up the social hierarchy status tends to override ethnicity. Sometimes there is even a deliberate choice to stay aloof from co-patriots.[174] The class distinction also coincides with a different use of institutions. Higher-status migrants tend to make more use of formal institutions, including those of the host country. Lower-status migrants tend to pool resources informally.

---

[170] Centola and Macy (2007) 704.   [171] Borgatti et al. (2009) 893.
[172] Granovetter (1983) 210, 213–14, though the class-specificity does not always apply. The difficulty with the distinction is that some elite groups may also be characterized by strong ties.
[173] Gill and Bialsi (2011) 243, though again the distinction does not always hold.
[174] Gill and Bialsi (2011) 245–6.

Crucial information like job openings is usually passed informally rather than through official institutions.[175]

A second addition to Granovetter's model is the notion that networks are highly dynamic. Particularly in the case of migrants, networks are created very quickly: 'the necessity to build up one's support network for a lower socio-economic status migrant is imperative in functioning and adapting in the host community. Because of this necessity, networks must be created very quickly.'[176] Networks are easily formed, but also easily dissolved.[177] They are 'are often highly localised, and formed and disbanded relatively quickly', as Gill and Bialsi emphasize:

> Recent work in migration and transnational studies emphasises the ways in which migrants' networks change upon arrival in their destination countries... A range of empirical work has demonstrated that migrant networks are by no means static, and that ties both to origin countries and to fellow migrants change once larger migrant communities are established and migrants themselves begin to settle in their destination countries.[178]

In the Roman world, there were some cases where ethnicity did form a significant marker for the persons involved. The best example is surely that of trade networks. As was discussed in the previous section, traders could organize themselves around the products they sold, but they could also identify themselves around their place of origin. In such an organizational form trust played a large role, and ethnicity could be used to cement ties between otherwise unrelated persons.[179] In such situations we may assume that ties between immigrants were relatively strong.

In other cases it seems that immigrant ties were rather weak. The absence of significant forms of community formation suggests that ties were created along different lines, with people of the same profession, the same legal or social status, or in patronage relations. Especially when class-specificity and the dynamic nature of networks are factored in, the 'weak ties' model seems a good way to conceptualize how many immigrants found their way to Rome. We may envisage their networks as being quickly formed, but also quickly dissolved. Upon arrival, migrants suddenly found themselves originating from the same nation, and this may temporarily override distinctions of status. But ties to compatriots quickly give way to ties to others. The model helps us understand the weak sense of community among the immigrants, which can then be described as a group characterized with a low network density and a significant number of bridges to others living in Rome.

---

[175] See also Boyd (1989) 652: in contemporary illegal immigration, informal networks are vital.
[176] Gill and Bialsi (2011) 246.   [177] Gill and Bialsi (2011) 242.
[178] Gill and Bialsi (2011) 241.   [179] Terpstra (2015).

8

Conclusion: Rome's Migration System

Our understanding of history alters dramatically with the realization that
its actors were not sedentary.[1]

1. DRAMATIC CHANGES?

There can be little doubt that the claim of Moch in her book on migration in
Europe since 1650 is correct: the understanding of European history has
changed dramatically since migration has been taken seriously as an object
for historical study. The character of the economy, labour relations, marriage
patterns, and urban demography: all have been reconsidered.[2] The world we
thought we had lost turns out to have never existed in the first place.[3] There
certainly were, as Zelinsky so forcefully phrased it, communities with 'an array
of cells firmly fixed in space with rather strong, if invisible, membranes
surrounding each unit',[4] but more often than not, on closer inspection the
membranes turn out to have been permeable.

But does our understanding also change dramatically in the Roman case,
now that it is clear that there, too, people were not sedentary? 'It is one thing
to accept that Romans moved around a lot; it is another to appreciate what it
really meant.'[5] The question is worth addressing explicitly. If connectivity
was the hallmark of the ancient Mediterranean world, the argument that in
the first two centuries AD levels of mobility were substantial is not in itself
particularly spectacular. Moreover, migration in the first two centuries AD was

---

[1] Moch (2003[2]) 1.
[2] e.g. Moch (2003[2]) 2 'Our view of the building and growth of the cities of Europe and of the
rise of the modern state takes on a new cast when we realize that country folk and people from
small towns built the expanding cities of the eighteenth and nineteenth centuries. Some went
home when their job was completed, but others returned annually for more work in the
construction trades, and still others took up long-term residence in the city.'
[3] Lucassen and Lucassen (1997) on Laslett's *World we have lost*: Laslett (1983[3]).
[4] Zelinsky (1971) 234.   [5] Scheidel (2004) 24.

arguably a relatively smooth process: there were few intervening obstacles or institutional barriers. It is thus the particular modes of migration in the Principate that invite scrutiny of its implications, not the fact that it occurred at all.

The question about the implications of Roman migration is a rather open one. It is surely not the intention to reconsider the whole history of the Roman Empire in this concluding chapter.[6] Instead, it seems advisable to proceed step by step, and move from the known to the unknown. This chapter will therefore start with a summary of the argumentation by picking up some strands and tying them together. First, the family resemblances between the various forms of migration will be discussed. In a following section urban migration theory will be revisited. In the Introduction it was claimed that one good reason to analyse Roman migration is that it allows us to study the relationship between urbanization, labour, and migration without interference from the modernization debate. Although much of the book has been devoted to precisely these issues, it is worth broadening the scope and discussing its application to the Roman world at large. As will be clear, quantification remains a crucial but almost insoluble issue. In a following section the problem of numbers will be addressed once again. A subsequent section endeavours to approach the question of scale by studying one crucial variable in a qualitative way: transport. Finally, some of the wider implications of the findings for the understanding of Roman society are discussed.

2. FAMILY RESEMBLANCES

As always, much is dependent on definition. In the case of pre-industrial Europe, a large part of the migration streams came into view by relaxing the definition of migration to include semi-permanent forms of migration that need not necessarily imply lifelong resettlement. With this change, the focus shifted away from trans-national to trans-local migration. The altered perspective is visible in a subtle change of words: instead of focusing on immigration and emigration, it is now migration *tout court* that is studied. The change might be demonstrated with Zelinsky's quote that was cited at the beginning of the book. According to Zelinsky, before the mobility transition that was postulated by him, societies were fundamentally sedentary: 'Some circulation might occur, but normally within a well-trodden social space—for example, the daily journey to field, pasture, fishery, or quarry, trips to fairs,

---

[6] For wider-ranging attempts to formulate the importance of Roman mobility, see Scheidel (2004); Moatti (2006); Woolf (forthcoming *a*). For a comparative perspective, see Woolf (forthcoming *b*).

shrines, and courts, or the rather more extended sojourns of apprentices and students.'[7] Part of the response to Zelinsky's model was the idea that forms of mobility that he thought were uninteresting, consisting of mere 'circulation' 'within a well-trodden social space', actually merited inclusion in studies of mobility and migration. Not only could they be massive in volume and structure the rhythms of daily life, but they also were socially significant.

In the case of Roman migration, definition is equally important. In this book, migration is defined as a permanent or semi-permanent transfer between settlements, along the lines of the definition used for early modern European studies. Both what is included in the definition and what is left out is important. Legal status is not part of the definition, and in consequence forced and state-organized migration are taken into account alongside voluntary migration. This is not merely an attempt to broaden the perspective by including more types of movers. It is of real importance, because in the Roman world forced, state-organized, and voluntary migration show many similarities, and it is their interaction that forms one of the most interesting aspects of Roman migration.

Moreover, just as in the case of early modern European migration, it is the inclusion of 'semi-permanent' forms of migration that is important for the discussion of Roman migration. Permanent immigration certainly occurred in Rome. In the case of slaves, permanent resettlement on a large scale is virtually certain. Many other migrants will of their own accord have resettled on a permanent basis. But much migration was semi-permanent: many immigrants stayed for shorter or longer terms in Rome and then returned, while others came on a seasonal basis to Rome. Almost all soldiers stationed in Rome left at the end of their term of service. An exclusive focus on permanent migration alone runs the risk of missing a significant part of the migration streams.

The inclusion in the definition of semi-permanent migration has one beneficial effect that is very important from a practical perspective. It allows us to bypass prolonged discussions of identifying 'true' permanent immigrants in the sources. In fact, such real immigrants can only be discerned with great difficulty.[8] The sources consist mainly of epitaphs that record foreigners who died in the city; similarly, isotopic studies identify non-locals in samples of skeletons. These are static records that are used to document a dynamic process.[9] As has been recognized by many scholars, it was not necessarily the intention of the foreigners who died in the city to stay there: some may in fact simply have been passers-by who were unfortunate enough to die en

---

[7] Zelinsky (1971) 234.

[8] e.g. Foubert (2013) 395, noting with respect to the epigraphical attestions of female travellers that '[t]here is . . . a thin line between travel and migration'.

[9] Woolf (2013) 357: 'measuring mobility from gravestones is a little like trying to measure coin circulation from the evidence of hoards.'

route. In fact, in the sources it is neither easy to find people who made a conscious decision to stay—barring those few immigrants who made *inter vivos* grave monuments in their new home-town and thus signalled their intention to transfer permanently—nor to find evidence for return migration.[10] To complicate matters, it seems likely that people themselves were not aware of their own intentions: many permanent resettlements might have begun as temporary stays.[11] For these reasons, limiting the sources to attestations of 'pure' forms of permanent migration seems to lead into a blind alley.

Including semi-permanent forms of migration thus solves a problem with our sources. But the relaxation of the definition of migration at the same time creates new practical problems, for the spectrum of mobility is wide indeed. What exactly is constituted by 'semi-permanent' remains difficult to define. It seems futile to impose too strict limits on what types of temporary mobility are to be in- and excluded. What about, say, ambassadors who stayed for prolonged periods in Rome? Rather than imposing a strict time-limit in which people have to stay in order to be considered semi-permanent migrants, it seems best to create some order on the basis of a typology.

Several such typologies and categorizations may be devised. Obviously, some work better than others in the Roman case, but ultimately their usefulness depends on the type of problem being addressed.[12] The complex composition of Rome's population is sufficient to suggest that no single typology or organizing criterion will in itself be able to capture migration fully in all its aspects. Three classifications have been discussed in this book.

Agency is the most obvious organizing principle, and on its basis three major forms of forced, state-organized, and voluntary migration can be distinguished. It is a very useful distinction for analytical purposes, and an important part of the arguments in this book has been structured around it. It is, at the same time, somewhat ironic that part of the argument has been that agency matters less than is normally thought. Throughout the book there is a recurring theme that the three forms share a number of characteristics—though without being identical.

A different categorization was used in Chapter 2, where ten types of migration were presented. These ten types work well to capture the rather complex reality of Roman migration. Interestingly enough, most of these types show that various types of mobility occurred simultaneously. The categorization

---

[10] Woolf (2013) 352: 'when we find evidence of individuals who have moved significant distances it is not always easy to tell whether they had intended to return home or had aimed to migrate in search of a new life, whether their journeys were regular ones or once-in-a-lifetime displacements, even whether they were voluntary or compelled, and if involuntary by need or by force majeure.'

[11] For Augustine's stepwise migration, see Tacoma (forthcoming *c*).

[12] De Ligt and Tacoma (forthcoming); Zerbini (forthcoming *a*).

also helps in making guestimates for the number of migrants, or, as was done in Chapter 3, guestimates for proportions of Roman citizens among them. But for other purposes a tenfold distinction is rather unwieldy to use. Moreover, it invites continuous further sub-categorization: the moment one starts to study one type in more detail, it turns out that various sub-types can be distinguished within it, which might also be considered independently.

It is also possible to categorize migrants by ethnic group on the basis of origin. The categorization is mainly relevant to provincial immigrants. It is certainly an extremely useful way to categorize the sources: it allows us to compile lists of Gauls, Egyptians, and so on. It is not without reason that this is the normal way to group sources and structure discussions of migration. Despite appearances, such *Listenwissenschaft* is not value-free, however. Ethnic identity should not be confused with ontological fact: it was not very important, or rather, it was important at certain moments, for certain groups, but not in a consistent manner. In that sense, such lists easily mislead, because they might suggest the formation of solid ethnic communities living in Rome. It is certainly important to use the lists, because it is not a given that community formation worked for each group in the same way, but otherwise such categorization is not particularly helpful.

The benefit of employing multiple perspectives is that it increases awareness of the lacunae in our knowledge. We know much more about state-organized mobility of the soldiers stationed in Rome than we do about the forced mobility of imported slaves. We know quite a lot about elite mobility, but very little about temporary labour migration. We know much about provincial migration, but less about migration within Italy. It is extremely important to be aware of this, especially because an almost inverse relation seems to exist between coverage by the sources and numerical importance.

Obviously then, migration to Rome was a complex phenomenon. Migrants can be found in all groups of the population of Rome, across the social spectrum: they cross all our familiar social taxonomies. They were not only stakeholders in society. They were not only *peregrini*, but could also be Roman citizens; they were not only members of the plebs, but also members of the elite; not only freeborn, but also slaves and freedmen. Migrants were often equated in the literary sources with slaves and ex-slaves, but this does not mean that all migrants were slaves. The reverse was not true either: many slaves were home-bred and will not have left their *familia*. Among the *peregrini* will have been persons who had lived for generations in Rome. The result was a very diffuse population.

It is easy to argue that migration was complex and stop there. Fragmentation is easily demonstrated (migration *was* indeed unruly), but intellectually not very satisfactory. What is more interesting is that, despite the wide variety of forms, these forms share common traits. The metaphor of family resemblances captures the phenomenon best, for the forms did not merely share superficial resemblances, they were also related. They really did form a family.

Voluntary, forced, and state-organized migration shared, at least in principle, the same geography. This is best visible in the discussion of slave origins: one would intuitively expect that imported slaves would come from over the borders of the Roman world. But the evidence suggests otherwise: a high proportion of the slaves that we find in Rome originated from within the empire. Soldiers and free civilians might come from the same territories. This implies that most migrants were recruited from the same population pool. Obviously, the instant we start looking in more detail, differences emerge: different groups came from different territories; for some types of migration, such as seasonal labour migration, geographical proximity to Rome was an important determinant. But the fundamental fact of shared geographical origins remains. It is telling that the mere knowledge of the origin of a migrant does not in itself help to determine the type or form of migration. Someone hailing from Syria could be senator, slave, soldier, astrologer, and so on.

The strong similarities are reinforced by the demographic profiles of voluntary migrants, slaves, and soldiers. Young adult males dominated migration streams in all three cases. Again, it is also clear that differences existed between the various groups at a more detailed level. In particular, there was some variation in the amount of female and sub-adult migration. For obvious reasons, the demographic profile of soldiers was the most coherent, while more variation occurs among slaves and voluntary migrants.

Paradoxical though it may sound, despite the shared characteristics of all forms of migration in terms of demographical profile or geographical background, there was no collective immigrant identity shared by all migrants. Senators originating from the provinces would be horrified to find themselves lumped together with slaves. Soldiers saw themselves primarily as soldiers, slaves as slaves. Only in some contexts was a migrant identity explicitly demarcated. The clearest case is that of trade networks, where there was a functional component to it: shared membership of an ethnic group enabled the creation of trust networks.[13] In many other contexts ethnic identity was overridden by other identities. There was no automatic migrant community formation along ethnic lines.

What the typologies show is that Rome functioned as a centre around which a series of streams of migration revolved. Soldiers lived in the city for years, and then left again (not always for home). Members of the elite set up a household in Rome, but were often on the move. Seasonal labourers moved within Italy. And so on, in an endless choreography of smaller and larger movements.

---

[13] Terpstra (2015).

3. URBANIZATION—LABOUR—MIGRATION

The relation between urbanization, labour, and migration was essentially discussed in Chapter 5 (urbanization) and Chapter 6 (labour), but what was presented in the other chapters impinges on it. For this book, only the top of the urban pyramid was considered, the city of Rome, and not the urban system as a whole. It is useful to address the question of wider application here.

Soldiers, slaves, and voluntary migrants all moved to Rome. In the Roman world at large, however, most soldiers were normally sent to frontiers, slaves often ended up at rural estates, and voluntary migration could also not be directed at cities. In consequence, studying urban migration captures only a part of all Roman migration. However, given the centrality of cities to Roman society, there can be no doubt that urban migration was an important part of all migration streams.

In discussions of the relation between urbanization, labour, and migration, urban migration theory plays a prominent role. Its starting point is the assumption of urban excess mortality: more people die in the city than are born there. There are two explanations for the deficit. A model of urban natural decrease predicts that urban populations are unable to reproduce themselves and need an external supply of immigrants. An alternative explanation suggests that, rather than urban natural decrease, diminished fertility among urban immigrants caused urban birth deficits. It was argued in Chapter 5 that both models apply in the case of Rome: excess mortality and reduced immigrant fertility occurred simultaneously.

The arguments need not be repeated here. What matters is that if urban migration theory is applied to the Roman world at large, it requires some modifications. This does not just concern the application of the two varieties of the theory simultaneously; rather, the model must be modified in all three respects that are relevant for the present discussion: urban systems, labour, and migration.

Seen from a distance, the urban system of the Roman world is in itself straightforward. The Roman world was a world of cities, with an extremely hierarchical urban system. This hierarchy is in itself sufficient reason to merit the application of urban migration theory and allow the creation of a single urban migration model based on rank-size distribution. However, although some of the arguments made for Rome can be easily transposed to other cities, others cannot. An important part of the model works on the assumption that mortality is dependent on diseases, whose transmission is thought to be dependent on population densities, which we assume to be a function of city size, which we pretend to know—not exactly the surest of foundations. In fact, the transmission of diseases differs from disease to disease. In a number of cases urban density matters directly or indirectly for the spread of diseases, but in others it does not. In consequence, urban rank-size distributions can only function as a very rough approximation of the actual position in the hierarchy of sending and receiving settlements.

It is also clear that location, access, and connectivity of cities were important factors. Harbour cities housed many immigrants, but many other cities might still have conformed to Finley's consumer city model, forming a closed unit with its surrounding countryside, in which a sedentary urban population lived essentially from the proceeds of the countryside.[14] The onomastic profile of the large commercial centres of Ostia and Aquileia suggest that they received large streams of immigrants, whereas a smaller inland city like Asisium seems to have had a much more stable local onomastic repertoire, suggesting a much more limited presence of outsiders.[15] Somewhat similarly, Strabo claimed that in Gaul the city of Narbo (mod. Narbonne) housed more foreigners than Nemausus (mod. Nîmes).[16]

It is also noteworthy that applications of the theory have done little to confront them with what we know of Roman urban population dynamics. Survey archaeology has made it possible to obtain a much improved idea of settlement hierarchies. One of the major problems in translating the model to historical reality is that little remains known about the Roman peasant and the smaller settlements peasant families supposedly lived in.[17] Archaeological surveys have done much to fill the gaps in our knowledge, but have produced no uniform results and only added to the complexity.[18] In the case of Roman Italy, it has been argued that in the first two centuries AD in many areas (though not all) the landscape emptied out, and that rural sites were on the decline.[19] Although it is possible to combine a scenario of population decline with emigration—the villages may have simply sent more than their surplus population to higher-order settlements and thus have contracted—even such a relatively simple explanation already adds an important element to the model.

The largest challenge in the application of the theory is to conceptualize the population dynamics of the small cities that dotted the Roman Empire. Although they have been regarded as suffering from urban natural decrease,[20] it is more attractive to assume that they were major suppliers of migrants to Rome. The rather difficult question whether migrants came straight from the

---

[14] Patterson (2006) 41.   [15] Salomies (2002), esp. 137–8.

[16] Strabo 4.1.12 Νέμαυσος, κατὰ μὲν τὸν ἀλλότριον ὄχλον καὶ τὸν ἐμπορικὸν πολὺ Νάρβωνος λειπομένη.

[17] MacMullen (1974); Garnsey (1979).

[18] see Van Tol et al. (2014) with further literature for discussion of minor centres in Roman Italy.

[19] Patterson (2006) 5–9, though emphasizing that there were also areas with continuity and even growth of rural settlements. A similar increase in settlement clustering has been observed on the basis of survey data from Roman Greece, see Alcock (1993).

[20] As Scheidel (2004) 16 noted, 'it is not at all obvious that a small and generously laid-out town of 1,000 or 2,000 ought to have experienced any natural decrease at all'. Yet he nevertheless assumes that such towns did.

countryside or moved stepwise through the settlement hierarchy loses much of its force if we assume that they often came from such small-sized cities. It would also help to understand why, at least to some extent, migration was a selective process: as was argued in Chapters 3 and 7, people with citizenship and people with knowledge of Latin or Greek might have been more prone to move to Rome than others. This will have worked in favour of better-educated or more urbanized parts of the population, which in its turn makes migration straight from the countryside to Rome less likely.

According to urban migration theory, the populations of minor cities were so small that they must have been suppliers of migrants rather than receivers. Yet their city status is also relevant. Given the prevalence of urban slavery in general, it is likely that small cities were not just supplying larger settlements with migrants, but also received them, in the form of imported slaves. This was certainly the case in Herculaneum. This city had a small population, in the order of 4,000–5,000 persons. On the basis of its small size, we might expect that it produced a surplus of people who moved off to settlements of higher order. Yet the presence of very large numbers of freedmen in the community suggests that slaves were imported in high numbers.[21] This does not preclude that substantial emigration also took place to higher-order settlements, but Herculaneum is clearly much more than a simple sending settlement. Whether the Herculanean situation was exceptional or not is difficult to determine, but the fact remains that a very large number of similar-sized towns dotted the Italian landscape.[22]

It is becoming increasingly clear that in the Roman world regional urban networks had different shapes.[23] The function of Rome as a hub becomes clear when provincial patterns of migration are taken into account. As was discussed in Chapter 2, Section 3, within the Roman Empire we find mostly regional zones of movement, from which a single extension ran to Rome. Such a pattern warns against taking Rome as the model for all migration: other cities were not small-scale Romes. Much movement within specific areas of the Roman world will have remained regional—though even there the distances that were traversed could be substantial. Rome formed in that sense a real node, connecting urban networks that remained otherwise distinct.[24] This in turn might be one of the explanations why, despite the overall centrality of the

---

[21] Wallace-Hadrill (2011) 123–45, 303–4; Mouritsen (2011) 129–30, and in particular De Ligt and Garnsey (2012) and De Ligt and Garnsey (forthcoming) for in-depth analysis of the album of Herculaneum, in which, in addition, some (though not many) *incolae* are also attested. They also refer to theories that many of the persons in the nearly contemporaneous wax tablets were outsiders as well.

[22] Morley (1996) 182 estimated 400 minor cities in Roman Italy with populations between 1,000 and 5,000 inhabitants. Further Scheidel (2004) 14; Patterson (2006) 38–9.

[23] De Ligt (2008) for a pilot study of regional urban networks.

[24] Tacoma and Tybout (forthcoming *a*).

city in the Roman world and the marked hierarchy in settlements, regional urban networks could retain various shapes.

As for labour, the second element, the original model of the urban migration theory simply assumed that people moved to the city attracted by the possibilities for finding work. The motives for coming to the city were not even discussed. Implicitly finding work was taken to be unproblematic (at least for the application of urban migration theory). The possibility that there was friction in the labour market was not taken into account.

At first sight this assumed absence of friction might seem justified in the case of Rome. As appeared in Chapter 3, there were no serious institutional obstacles to immigrate voluntarily or bring people as slaves or soldiers to Rome. There was only a limited amount of state intervention. To the extent that mobility was controlled, it concerned the movement of the aristocracy, for political reasons. Administrative procedures of census-taking created cumbersome situations in which people were supposed to return home. But all in all, the number of intervening obstacles was not very large. Neither were there major institutional impediments for immigrants to enter the labour market. Outsiders were not demarcated collectively as such, nor was there any legal status by which immigrants were marked from the rest of the population. *Peregrini* might, in some respects, have been at a disadvantage compared to Roman citizens, but not all (perhaps not even many) immigrants were peregrines, nor were all peregrines first-generation immigrants in the definition used here. Although entering professional associations might not in itself have been particularly easy (one needed to get accepted and had to pay fees), the problem would be the same for outsiders and locals alike. There was hardly any monopolization of particular jobs, either by the local population or by immigrants.

The fact that young males dominated migration streams fits with the fact that the opportunities for female labour were more modest. The preponderance of males almost automatically impinges on urban fertility levels, and merits the application of the depressed fertility model of Sharlin beside that of Wrigley's model based on urban natural decrease.

From the perspective of labour, the mixed nature of the migration streams is also not a problem. Slaves participated in what was to a significant extent a unified economic space. Soldiers may have remained aloof from the civilian labour force, but in the regions where they came from people might have had some choice between joining the army and entering a civilian occupation. Agency—the question whether migrants moved voluntarily or were forced to do so—is from the perspective of labour migration less important than it may seem.

In Rome the labour market was thus relatively open, but the real problem was the overcrowding and instability within the city. There was insufficient work to provide stable incomes for all its inhabitants, and more importantly, irregularities in supply and demand created uncertainties. For a part of the population the grain dole cushioned people from these effects. But the dole also distorted the functioning of the market, for the simple reason that some had access to it and others did not. Immigrants were not excluded on principle (as long as they met the criteria for eligibility), but we might assume that new arrivals were at a disadvantage in gaining access, if only because they would have to wait to be enrolled. The lack of sufficient opportunities to find an income will have served as a check on further population growth, and might have encouraged return migration.

A major issue for the wider applicability of urban migration theory is whether the urban labour market elsewhere in the Roman world was comparable to that of Rome. In some respects the urban economy of other cities will certainly have looked similar, though obviously on a smaller scale. It seems highly likely that the occupational structure was more pronounced in Rome than it was anywhere else in the ancient world, and it may also be assumed that specialization was a function of population size. To be sure, not all cities will have had the need for large numbers of unskilled workers, and smaller urban economies might perhaps also have been less subject to short-term fluctuations. Yet even in small cities the social emulation of aristocratic behaviour by local elites helped to create a vibrant local building industry, providing work for both skilled and unskilled workers. If the cities were of sufficiently large size, a large sector might also have come into existence involved in the importation and processing of foodstuffs. However, labour opportunities might not just be a question of size. The composition of migrant populations might have been rather different, and voluntary migrants might have been more visible, marked as *incolae*. It seems that at least some cities possessed associations of non-locals that were exclusively reserved for them.[25] Exactly what the more marked demarcation of immigrants in these cities implies is not entirely clear, but the fact that they were institutionally set apart may indicate that other Roman cities were less open to outsiders than Rome was. This might be reconciled with the larger model if openness and city size correlated to some extent: precisely because Rome needed so many immigrants and immigration was so varied, there might have been fewer institutional barriers to immigration than in the other, much smaller, cities.

As for the third and last element, it is somewhat ironic that urban migration theory says very little about migration. It does not make predictions about the nature of it. All that is needed is that humans move into the city; it does not matter who they are or where they come from. The theory does not make predictions about the legal status of the immigrants. It does make predictions about the required level of net immigration, but not about crude migration

---

[25] Liu (forthcoming).

levels. Nor does it predict the demographic profile of the immigrants, though it helps in understanding the implications of the gender and age structure once they are known.

What is relevant to the application of urban migration theory to the larger Roman world is that the composition of immigrants was mixed: migrant streams will have normally consisted of a mixture of voluntary immigrants and imported slaves, with soldiers sometimes being added. The balance between these migrant groups will have varied from settlement to settlement.

One important element that affects the application of urban migration models is the question of the extent to which migration was permanent. In the case of Rome, it appears that the degree of permanency differed between the three forms of migration. In the case of slaves, it is reasonable to assume that almost all slaves (or ex-slaves) remained circling around their masters (or patrons). In the case of soldiers, it seems certain that most veterans left Rome, though it is also likely that their patterns of return were more varied than the term 'return-migration' may suggest. In the case of voluntary migrants, it seems likely that a large proportion left Rome again, but clearly patterns were varied. Neither a model based solely on permanent resettlement nor a model based on permanent movement between Rome and the homelands is entirely apt to describe the situation in Rome. As in other cities the balance between voluntary, forced, and state-organized migrants is likely to have been different,[26] this will also have affected the degree of return migration. Urban migration theory needs to take such variation into account.

All in all, urban migration theory remains the best starting point to study the relation between urbanization, labour, and migration, but it should be used as a point of departure, not as an aim in itself. Ultimately, it works better to describe migration to Rome than it does to describe what happened in the rest of the settlement hierarchy. Given the advances made in our understanding of urbanization, labour, and migration, amendments should be made to the model if it is applied to the wider Roman world. Because population densities were high, the urban–rural divide remained important: villages had a higher likelihood of producing a surplus population. But the landscape of supply and demand was not just based on population densities. Some regions experienced much worse mortality conditions than other areas, independent of the question whether they housed cities or villages. The patterns were also complex because many of the immigrants that came to Rome were brought there as slaves, and because Rome attracted a relatively high number of provincial migrants that did not necessarily come from the countryside. It is difficult to maintain a simple distinction between settlements that were receiving a stream of immigrants and settlements that were producing a surplus population.

---

[26] De Ligt and Garnsey (forthcoming).

It might in a sense be regarded as a natural process that refinements occur in urban migration theory; increases in our knowledge almost automatically lead to greater awareness of the intricacies and complexities of the relation between urbanization, labour, and migration. The aim is to find an appropriate level of generalization that at the same time does justice to the complexities of historical reality. Any model is by definition a mere approximation of reality, but it is certainly legitimate to require that such an approximation is reasonably close.

4. QUANTIFYING MIGRATION

In a book like this, it is difficult to avoid the impression that migration was significant not only in qualitative terms but also in quantitative terms. In the stable conditions of the Principate, levels of mobility can be assumed to have been high. But were they really? Woolf has warned against naive optimism: many, if not most, people are likely to have been stayers rather than movers.[27]

Quantification represents a challenge—if not an almost insurmountable problem. It is not without reason that in Roman demography migration is usually simply ignored. Whereas mortality levels can be modelled on the basis of biological and ecological constraints, human mobility has no such natural limits. Especially in those cases where voluntary migration becomes a significant factor, even abstract modelling becomes very difficult.[28]

We are obviously dependent on which yardstick we use, how we measure, and what we compare it with. For example, in the year 2000 an estimated 130 million people lived outside their birth nation.[29] The figure is stunning, but it also shows immediately the difficulties of drawing comparisons, for transnational migration is by and large irrelevant to Roman migration. More to the point is that the claim that the more than 10 million slaves who were transported to the New World represented 'the human migration largest in number and longest in duration in world history' cannot be maintained

[27] Woolf (forthcoming *a*). Somewhat similarly, though much more briefly, Shaw (2001) 432 pointed out in response to the arguments of Horden and Purcell (2000) that the Mediterranean Sea not only connected regions and people, but also could isolate them from each other, implying that connectivity can be overestimated.

[28] Cf. Scheidel (2004) 14: 'Unlike relevant information on colonization programmes, quantifiable evidence for private population transfers is almost completely unavailable.' Note that Scheidel in modelling migration under the Republic and the early part of the reign of Augustus equates voluntary migration with net urban migration. No doubt his argument is correct that state-organized migration in the form of colonization and serving in the legions was dominant in the period under consideration, but it is possible that voluntary migration was significantly higher than net urban migration.

[29] Sanjek (2003) 315.

in view of what is known about Roman slavery.[30] Some migration historians have used an annual rate of people who move per 100 persons.[31] But there are so many guesses involved in producing such a figure for the Roman Principate, in which voluntary migration was significant, that it seems futile to try to calculate it.

In the case of this book, the easiest way to approach the problem is to try to quantify the proportion of people who lived in Rome but were born elsewhere. Such an approach, crude though it is, fits with the definition employed in this book, and allows one to use the evidence from the isotopic studies, which produces figures for non-locals in sample populations. It also enables us to use the extensive literature about urban population size. In Chapter 2, findings from isotopic studies were placed against guestimates for the ten migrant groups. The former were in themselves relatively precise but concerned very small samples, while the latter were crude approximations enveloped in uncertainties. They can be used to balance each other: the fact that the imprecise and rather speculative figures for migrant groups suggest lower totals than the figures from the isotopic samples serves as a brake on inflating the figures. Together, they suggest a percentage of migrants in the order of 20–30 per cent of the total population.

One of the indirect virtues of the calculation is that it creates an awareness that in situations in which the population remains stable (that is, mortality and fertility do not change) net migration must remain the same. If something changes in the volume of one part of the migration streams, compensation must occur in one of the other parts. In the case of expansion or contraction of the urban population size, similar mechanisms operate, though in a more complex way.

How this might have worked can be demonstrated in the case of slaves. Given the large size of the slave population in Rome, small changes in the balance between *vernae* and imported slaves would have immediately affected the balance between forced and voluntary immigration even if total numbers of slaves remained the same. Scheidel has advocated a model in which the majority of slaves in the Principate were produced by slave breeding.[32] His major argument was that the extremely high number of slaves in Italy would have put a demographically insupportable pressure on the population to produce such slaves. Especially since a large part of the slaves originated from within the empire, it was inconceivable that so many Roman families produced slaves. It seems relatively certain that in the Republic the major (or main) supply of slaves came from warfare, that is, from external sources.

---

[30] Sanjek (2003) 322.
[31] Tilly (1978) 52; Scheidel (2004) on a Net Rate of Migration, the average annual incidence of relocations.
[32] See Chapter 2, Section 4 on Scheidel (1997).

Although the change to slave breeding is in principle also connected to the slowing down of urban growth in Rome at the end of the Republic and the end of sustained warfare, it seems plausible that we are dealing with a slow process in which the balance tipped gradually in favour of home-bred slavery rather than a radical switch from one system to another.[33] If we see the shift as a process rather than a one-time event, and assume for the sake of argument a stable population, the gradual diminishment of imported slaves created vacancies in the urban population. The vacuum will have been filled partly by an increase in the number of soldiers (whose increase in numbers over time is certain), but mostly by voluntary migrants. In this book the structural similarity of the various forms of migration was argued. Somewhat ironically, the families that Scheidel thought were incapable of producing slaves were certainly capable to produce soldiers and voluntary migrants.

However, the easiest approach is admittedly not necessarily the best for all purposes. The major disadvantage of a calculation of proportions of immigrants among the urban population is that it is only able to very limited extent to capture the dynamism inherent in migration. The urban population is unlikely to have remained stable over the course of the Principate. It is very likely that, in reality, compensatory mechanisms of the type described in the case of Scheidel's model were much more complex. There will have been short-term oscillations in population size, in parallel with longer-term trends; possible scenarios include further modest growth after the time of Augustus, and a decline as a consequence of the impact of the Antonine plague. Political decisions also impinged on the urban economy, and these will have affected the possibility to earn a stable income and hence have impacted on migration decisions. The gradually increasing absence of the emperor is likely to have had serious repercussions on the urban economy of Rome. Precisely because of its high level, migration created flexibility in the population. More perhaps than fertility or mortality, migration would have been a highly responsive property of the urban demographic regime.

In principle, the estimated ratio of 20–30 per cent for migrants living in Rome creates a benchmark against which we can try to compare other cities and settlements. That Rome formed the apex of the Roman migration system cannot be in doubt. Patterns of zoning strongly suggest that Rome was the centre of migration streams. How this works out quantitatively is more difficult to determine, however, and it goes without saying that the written sources are woefully inadequate to judge this matter. Isotopic evidence suggests roughly similar or higher percentages of migrants in various samples

---

[33] See Harris (1999; 2011) 107, 'something like Scheidel's model...must in the end have imposed itself. When?' See also his 2011 addendum, at 108: 'If I were to address this problem again, I would argue for an upwards curve in the proportion of Roman slaves who were born to slave mothers.'

from widely different places.[34] There are certainly issues of comparability, but the isotopic studies, in any case, do not point to a straightforward relation between percentages of migrants and settlement size.[35] In fact, it is certainly possible that some cities contained proportionally more migrants than Rome did. But given its enormous size and the fact that Rome was by far the largest city in the empire, in absolute terms Rome is likely to have contained the largest number of migrants.

How the figures changed over longer time-spans is also difficult to envisage, at least in a detailed manner. What seems probable is that the balance between the various forms of migration changed over time from the Republic to late antiquity. Colonizations under the Republic involved massive transfers of people.[36] Together with the movement of soldiers and the high levels of importation of slaves, state-organized and forced migration will have been high. It is therefore likely that the proportion of voluntary migration was significantly lower before the Principate. At the other end of our period, in late antiquity, the massive movements of armies, the invasions of various tribes, the population displacements that were caused by the invasions, the widespread use of exile as a weapon in theological struggles,[37] imperial attempts to tie people to their territory or occupation, and the probable increasing reliance on convict labour[38] make it likely that again the proportion of voluntary movement decreased. But as these two cases also immediately make clear, it is very hard to move beyond such generalities. They are also based on rather conventional understandings of the two periods, which in both cases are contested. In fact, for both periods arguments have been presented in favour of relatively high levels of voluntary mobility.[39] Rome itself, to be sure,

---

[34] For a summary of the analysis of four sites in Roman Britain, see Eckardt et al. (2010) 122, table 7.2, suggesting percentages of non-locals running from 41% to 59%, though note that Leach et al. (2010) 132 give a lower percentage of up to 20% for samples from Roman Britain. For oxygen isotopic analysis of a sample from the imperial estate at Vagnari, S. Italy, 1st–3rd centuries AD, producing six out of twenty-three immigrants, or 26%, see Prowse et al. (2010). For Ostia, see Prowse et al. (2007) with Chapter 4, Section 3. However, at the late antique mine of Phaeno in modern Jordan, strontium and oxygen isotopes identified only one out of thirty-one individuals as a foreigner (3%). See Perry et al. (2009), with comments and further refs. in Groen-Vallinga and Tacoma (2015).

[35] And cf. the no doubt highly rhetorical Sen., *ad Helv.* 6.4: 'Then leave this city [i.e. Rome], which in a sense may be said to belong to all, and travel from one city to another; everyone will have a large proportion of foreign population', *Deinde ab hac civitate discede, quae veluti communis potest dici, omnes urbes circumi; nulla non magnam partem peregrinae multitudines habet.*

[36] Scheidel (2004). Cf. also for the Hellenistic East, Loman (2004) on the importance of Greek colonization in mobility streams.

[37] Todd (2001); Allen and Neil (2013) 37–52. Note, however, that aristocratic banishment was also a standard weapon in earlier elite struggles.

[38] Millar (1984); Groen-Vallinga and Tacoma (2015). Cf. Woolf (forthcoming *b*).

[39] For the Republic, see e.g. Erdkamp (2008); cf. already Knapp (1907) on freedom of travel in the plays of Menander, Plautus, and Terence. See for late antiquity Leyerle (2009) 113, claiming

continued to attract voluntary immigrants in large numbers even in late antiquity, when its automatic role as *caput mundi* was far less self-evident.[40]

It is certainly possible to produce wider quantitative models, but the uncertainties are rather large. There is an inherent difficulty that the wish for precision calls for quantification, but that calculations only add further imprecision. Quantification should not be abandoned, but should be approached with lowered expectations.

5. A TRANSPORT TRANSITION?

A qualitative rather than quantitative approach may also be used to assess the importance of migration in the Principate. For obvious reasons, good possibilities for travel are a vital prerequisite for migration. Transport costs energy, time, and money. Transport is also scarce in an economic sense. It might not be available to everyone in equal measure; instead, its accessibility might depend on such factors as status, age, and gender. Moreover, transportation systems might change over time: the cost of travel might decline, or its accessibility might improve. The mile (Roman or otherwise) might in that sense have shrunk or increased in size.[41] Such changes could be very important. Ideas about the emergence of tmodern western society place great emphasis on improvements in communications and transport. Underlying Zelinsky's idea of a mobility transition was a transport revolution.[42]

One dominant line of thought in the Roman case is that under the high empire mobility reached unprecedented levels because the possibilities for travel were virtually unrestricted. 'Roman citizens, freedmen, slaves and allies swarmed across the Mediterranean: traders, soldiers and captives criss-crossed the sea.' 'Single rule over *mare nostrum* ensured freedom of movement and resulted in cultural mixing in the Mediterranean on a scale never seen before or since.' These statements, taken from a recent general history of the Mediterranean Sea, are unremarkable in themselves.[43] The notion that under the *pax romana* of the first two centuries AD people could travel far and wide,

---

that it was 'an astonishingly mobile society'; cf. already MacMullen (1964) on the wide gap between social reality and imperial attempts to tie people to land, occupation, and social position; see further Handley (2011) for a detailed study of the late antique West.

[40] For attestations of foreigners in late antique Rome, see e.g. Avraméa (1995); the lists of Christian and Jewish inscriptions in the appendix of Noy (2000) and Nieddu (2003).

[41] See Hoerder, Lucassen, and Lucassen (2007) 38 for changes in nineteenth-century transportation affecting the distances covered in migration.

[42] Zelinsky (1971); this idea is even reinforced by the important revisions of Lucassen and Lucassen (2009).

[43] Abulafia (2011) 199 and 211 respectively.

that levels of mobility were high, and that there were hardly any impediments to such movement, is widespread and can be found in various forms.[44] There is nothing inherently implausible with this picture, and at a general level there can be little doubt that it is correct. The volume of internal trade, the Roman penchant for infrastructure, and the internal peace and stability offered by the *pax romana* were all surely conducive to the rise of a *culture voyageuse*.[45]

The idea of unrestricted movement under peaceful conditions seems to be echoed in the ancient sources. For example, Velleius Paterculus, in a eulogy on Augustus, writes that: 'the *pax augusta*, which has spread to the regions of the east and of the west and to the bounds of the north and of the south, preserves every corner of the world safe from the fear of brigandage.'[46] But at the same time it is precisely such corroboration by the ancient sources that makes the notion also problematical. In fact, the modern statements just quoted turn out to barely extend beyond the continuation of a Roman idea: it is we who echo them. That Roman idea itself formed part of a wider discourse of empire in which the benefits of imperial rule, *pax romana* (or, as in Velleius Paterculus' case, *pax Augusta*), and free travel were all inextricably mixed.[47] It comes as no surprise that the statement by Velleius Paterculus is placed in the context of a much wider list of the beneficial effects of Augustus' rule.[48] That does in itself not imply that the set of ideas is wrong. After all, discourses do not operate outside of reality, but rather inform thought and structure behaviour. But the similarities between ancient and modern arguments give us reason to pause.

In the pre-industrial context of a Roman society that invested only very little in technical innovation, it cannot reasonably be expected that a fundamental transport revolution occurred. But the question whether, at a more modest level, a *transition* in transport took place is nevertheless worth posing. The question has been answered in the affirmative by Laurence, who, in his work on mobility in Roman Italy, stressed how connections between places had a unificatory effect: individual cities became part of networks, and through increased ease of communication 'a fundamental alteration of the space economy' took place.[49]

Yet there is also room for doubt. The traditional scepticism from the primitivist school still holds some force.[50] There were no substantial innovations in

---

[44] e.g. in a standard work on travel in the ancient world, Casson (1974) 122: 'The first two centuries of the Christian Era were halcyon days for a traveller.' Or in the comparative overview of pre-modern travel of Gosch and Stearns (2008) 36: 'Political unity and a vibrant economy put Romans on the roads and sea lanes in unprecedented numbers.'

[45] André and Baslez (1993) 7.

[46] Vell. Pat. 2.126.3 (trans. F. W. Shipley, LCL 1951): *Diffusa in orientis occidentisque tractus et quidquid meridiano aut septentrione finitur, pax augusta omnis terrarum orbis angulos a latrocinium metu servat immunes.* Grünewald (1999) 26 n. 25 for similar statements.

[47] Adams (2001) 2 for a short description.   [48] Vell. Pat. 2.126.

[49] Laurence (1999), quote at 80. See also Greene (1986) 40–3; Horden and Purcell (2000) 128.

[50] In particular Yeo (1946). For further bibliography Laurence (1999) 1.

the technology of transport. Travel remained irregular, in more than one sense. Sea travel was seasonal and dangerous, and normally followed indirect coastal routes.[51] Transport over land was slow and costly, and roads primarily catered for state needs: the movement of the army and state officials. Given these limitations, is it legitimate to speak of a transport transition through which levels and the nature of mobility were altered in a fundamental way? Did the Roman mile indeed shrink in size? More concretely, an analysis needs to be made of how the network of Roman roads, the available means of transport, the perceived dangers of travel, and social biases in travel affected Roman mobility levels.

One—if not *the*—argument in favour of a transition is the high quality of Roman infrastructure. It is not so much technological change that is central, but the creation, maintenance, and continuous improvement of the infrastructure. This required enormous investments, which were largely made by the state, sometimes in combination with private financiers.[52] The Roman network of paved roads in long, straight stretches constituted the glory of the Roman world.[53] A finely tuned network of public highways, local roads, private roads, bridges, dams, and sometimes even tunnels had come into existence, with approximately 80,000 km of main roads.[54] Alongside these roads arose a fully developed network of lodging houses. Although the main emphasis was clearly on road building, the Romans also improved waterways: some major canalization projects were undertaken, and huge investments were made in harbour installations, of which the major example is Ostia/Portus.

In the Roman world, road building and conquest had gone hand in hand, right from the construction of the first paved road, the famous Via Appia, in 312 BC Initially, roads were not intended for private travel or to facilitate trade but for the army and administrators. However, the volume of traffic by administrators and soldiers may have been relatively low, meaning that the actual use by state officials would have been limited.[55] A similar line of reasoning may apply to the *cursus publicus*, the state message and transport

---

[51] e.g. Syn., *Ep.* 4. See Gambash (forthcoming); Horden and Purcell (2000) 365: '[t]he short hops and unpredictable experiences of *cabotage* are . . . the basic modality for all movements of goods and peoples in the Mediterranean before the age of steam.'

[52] e.g. SHA, *Pertinax* 9.2 for road maintenance as a major item in the state budget. For the stunning sums involved, see *C.I.L.* 9.6075 on Hadrian improving the Via Appia over a distance of 15,75 miles, adding HS 1,147,000 to the HS 569,100 contributed by the landowners. Cf. also the *Tabula Heracleensis* for the interplay between state and private finance in maintaining streets in the city of Rome under the late Republic.

[53] Horden and Purcell (2000) 126–8 for brief but perceptive remarks on the symbolism involved. Among many others Strabo 5.3.8 regarded roads (and aqueducts and sewers) as hallmarks of Roman civilization, and contrasted them with Greek achievements. Cf. Plut., *G.Gracch.* 7. See Laurence (1999) 47, 65 on Statius' eulogy on the Via Domitiana in *Silvae* 4.4.

[54] Greene (1986) 35–6 for basic introduction; Van Tilburg (2007) 6 for discussion of figures.

[55] Van Tilburg (2007) *passim*.

system that was established by Augustus and reformed by Trajan and Hadrian, that grew into a very efficient communications system.[56] Use of the *cursus* was strictly controlled and was therefore a privilege; *diplomata* were bestowed on individuals by the emperor or by provincial governors on his behalf.[57] The restrictive policy with regard to the bestowal of these *diplomata*, plus the admittedly vague figures we have for the use of the *cursus*, again suggest relatively low levels of official traffic.[58] Although use by non-officials was of secondary concern to the state, Roman infrastructure was free for use by anyone, and was used for transport of goods and people.[59] In fact, it has been argued that the roads in the vicinity of Rome will have been very crowded, not with state officials, but with carts used to transport food and building materials to Rome.[60]

The roads will by no means have been crowded only with carts, but also with people. Yet the lack of a sustained development of passenger transport gives reason to pause. Whatever development there was in this direction was haphazard.[61] No doubt most people travelled on foot, certainly in the case of ordinary people travelling short distances.[62] But for longer distances, usually more than one type of transport was involved.[63] It is noteworthy that many of these forms did not cater specifically for human needs. At sea, people normally travelled on merchant ships;[64] even high-ranking persons used them.[65] At the same time, the number of passengers that could be carried on such ships seems not insignificant—even if we allow for numerical inflation in the sources.[66] Slaves were also transported on merchant ships, alongside other

---

[56] Suet., *Aug.* 49.3–50; SHA, *Hadr.* 7.5; SHA, *Ant. Pius* 12.3; SHA, *Sept. Sev.* 14.2. Kolb (2000).

[57] Bender (1978) 13–14. Plin., *Ep.* 10.120, where Pliny gives his wife a *diploma*; Sen., *De Clem.* 1.10.3, where Augustus' clemency is shown by the fact that he provided banished aristocrats with *diplomata* to travel safely; Tac., *Hist.* 2.54, where *diplomata* for the *cursus publicus* are bestowed by Otho but quickly lose their validity at his fall; idem 2.65, for the importance of the imperial name; SHA, *Pertinax* 1.6, where Pertinax, before he became emperor, used the *cursus* without *diploma* and was subsequently forced by the governor to travel on foot. For an important discussion on requisitioned transport, Mitchell (1976), with Kolb (2000) 96–7. For the wider use of the term *diploma*, see Moatti (2000) 941–4, who also offers a more detailed discussion of the changes in the authorities issuing them.

[58] Kolb (2000) 98–102; van Tilburg (2007) 61–2.

[59] Or, as Adams (2001) 4 states: 'It is fair to say that the road network of the empire served the needs of the state, both administrative and military, before those of the private individuals, but the latter could certainly benefit.'

[60] De Laine (1995) 558.   [61] Woolf (forthcoming *a*).

[62] For a relief from Stobi of people travelling on foot (two men, one child, one woman), see Bender (1978) fig. 18.

[63] Salway (2001) 34.

[64] For a depiction of a cargo ship with passengers on board (a couple), see Casson (1994) 112–1,3 fig. 84 (Portus, *c.* AD 200).

[65] e.g. Philo, *In Flacc.* 26, for King Agrippa travelling from Puteoli to Alexandria.

[66] The figures we have come from shipwreck narratives, and are suspiciously large: Wierschowski (1995) 22. Jos., *Vita* 3 (600, but note that Josephus' figures are often inflated); Acts 27: 37 (276); Syn., *Ep.* 4 with Casson (1974) 159–62 (over 50 passengers on a crew of 13).

wares.[67] Although the numbers of transported slaves were high, and the capacity of the Romans to design very large ships is impressive, there is no evidence that slaves were transported on ships specifically designed for the purpose. On the roads there was certainly a distinction between carts for goods and carriages for persons, though people could have their belongings loaded on a wagon which they accompanied.[68] But again we do not find carriages for larger numbers of persons, and the speed of travel of most carriages remained relatively slow. At the same time, it is certainly relevant that carriages could also be hired, implying wider availability and a high enough demand for wheeled transport by third parties.[69]

Then there is the point of travel risks. In any society the perceived dangers of travel can in themselves constitute an inhibiting factor in the decision to undertake a journey.[70] For example, seasonal labourers travelling back with their pay would have formed an easy prey for brigands.[71] In the Roman world, travel remained conceptualized as a major decision, subject to religious taboos. Oracles were consulted, vows were made, dedications were set up to ensure or give thanks for safe journeys.

It was not entirely without reason that people gave serious consideration to embarking on a journey. Roaming bands or individual brigands could pose serious dangers.[72] We hear of the disappearance of travellers, even members of the elite.[73] Medical authors have pointed out that wounded or dead travellers offered a good opportunity for anatomical study—suggesting the frequent occurrence of attacks.[74] Suetonius famously relates how in the last days of the Republic travellers in Italy, free and slave alike, had often disappeared without a trace in the *ergastula*,

---

[67] Petr., *Sat.* 76; cf. Syn., *Ep.* 4 for a female slave from Pontus among the passengers. For mixed cargoes, see Horden and Purcell (2000) 369.

[68] As in the case of Juvenal's Umbricius, see Juv., *Sat.* 3.10, where the *raeda* is hired at the Porta Capena, cf. 317 for the waiting *mulio*.

[69] Bender (1978) 26.   [70] See Hoerder, Lucassen, and Lucassen (2007) 34.

[71] Moch (2003²) 1, for a vignette from eighteenth-century rural France.

[72] See, for a brief empire-wide survey, MacMullen (1966) 255–68; for a full study, Grünewald (1999), who emphasizes that the imagery used in the sources is closely akin to that employed in the novels. Latin *latro* and Greek *leistes* were increasingly used in political invective and should primarily be regarded as subjective labels rather than statements of fact.

[73] Plin., *Ep.* 6.25 describes two cases, one a knight, the other a centurion, from Pliny's home-town. Cf. SHA, *Comm.* 5.12 for a senator being killed by Commodus, ostensibly by bandits. A similar ploy is found in SHA, *Carac.* 3.8. For dogs trained to guard large estates and to bite passing travellers, see Apul., *Met.* 8.17; 9.36. The inscriptions occasionally refer to death by robbers, see e.g. *C.I.L.* 6.20307a; *C.I.L.* 13.259 (commemoration in Aquitania of two persons *a latronibus interfecti*, one of them from Carthagina Nova in Spain); with some more sources in Fuhrmann (2012) 113. Jesus' parable of the Samaritan in *N.T. Luke* 30–7 shows a traveller from Jerusalem to Jericho attacked by robbers and left half-dead along the road. For the possibility that slaves were killed en route, see *Dig.* 12.4.5.4.

[74] Cels., *de Med.* pr. 43.

workhouses-cum-prisons.[75] Soldiers did not always offer protection, but might also requisition transport animals.[76] Some people travelled armed,[77] or were protected by dogs,[78] or attached themselves to more important persons.[79] Only the poor were safe: 'even along an infested road, the poor may travel in peace.'[80] Even within Italy some areas remained difficult to control. Those areas in the south that combined few roads with large-scale transhumance were well known for their problems,[81] but brigands also operated nearer to Rome, for example, at the Pontine marshes.[82] At the beginning of the third century, a band of 600 robbers was able to move throughout Italy for two years before its leader, Bulla Felix, was finally caught.[83] Near to Italy, Sardinia was difficult to control.[84] Brigands of various sorts remained 'konstante Erscheinungen des alltäglichen Lebens in der römischen Gesellschaft'.[85]

With the establishment of the Principate, the state took on a more active role in ensuring safety.[86] It was considered a prime duty of provincial governors to suppress brigands.[87] Soldiers were stationed along roads, workhouses inspected, and guilds disbanded.[88] These were not just practical measures; there was a clear link with the ideology of empire: the empire was symbolically created by sweeping the sea clean of pirates and by suppressing brigands. Whether these measures were entirely successful can be doubted,[89] but the

---

[75] Suet., *Aug.* 32.1, *Tib.* 8.2 adds that they also contained people wishing to escape enlistment in the army. SHA, *Hadr.* 18.9 has Hadrian forbidding *ergastula servorum et liberorum*. Cf. *Dig.* 4.6.9 for imprisonment by bandits or the powerful.

[76] For soldiers as a major risk rather than as protectors, see Apul., *Met.* 9.39.

[77] For members of the elite travelling within Italy with bands of armed slaves in the late Republic, see Laurence (1999) 178–9. Apul., *Met.* 8.17 for armed travellers running the risk of being regarded as brigands; cf. Fronto, *Ep.* 2.12 (LCL vol. 1, p.150) for shepherds fearing that horsemen were brigands. Dion. Hal., *Ant.Rom.* 4.48.1 and *Dig.* 48.6.1 for illegal possession of more weapons than necessary for a journey.

[78] Plin., *N.H.* 8.61.144 for two cases of people protected by their dogs.

[79] Epict., *Diss.* 4.1.91.

[80] Sen., *Ep.* 14.9, *etiam in obsessa via paupera pax est*; in a similar vein Juv., *Sat.* 10.22.

[81] Laurence (1999) 185.

[82] Juv., *Sat.* 3.306–8: bringing them under control would simply drive the robbers to Rome.

[83] Cass. Dio 77.10.1–7; MacMullen (1966) 267; Fuhrmann (2012) 134–5.

[84] Cass. Dio 55.28.1, for pirates occupying Sardinia for some time in AD 6. Cf. Tac., *Ann.* 2.85, for the expulsion of Jews in AD 19, part of whom were conscripted to combat bandits there. Marasco (1991) 655–7 for the background.

[85] Grünewald (1999) 27.

[86] Nippel (1995) 101; in general Fuhrmann (2012). For the subsequent period, see e.g. SHA, *Sept. Sev.* 18.6: *latronum ubique hostis*.

[87] Fronto, *Ant. Pius* 8 (LCL p.236–7). MacMullen (1966) 265–6; André and Baslez (1993) 127; Laurence (1999) 185.

[88] Suet., *Aug.* 32.1–2; *Tib.* 37.1; Tert., *Apol.* 2.8, stating that tracking down bandits was assigned to the army. Cf. *C.I.L.* 6.234. Moatti (2000) 936. As Ramin and Veyne (1981) 487, with respect to *ergastula* point out, this behaviour is more characteristic of the beginning of each new reign than with imperial policy per se.

[89] Kelly (2007) 158 on differences between imperial ideology and reality.

point remains that they may have helped to mitigate the negative perceptions of the dangers of travel.

Then there is the factor of the temporality of travel. Unsurprisingly, most travel took place during the day.[90] On land, people stayed for the night in lodging houses. On sea, many—though certainly not all—ships took indirect routes and went into a harbour at night. What is more important is that much travel remained confined to certain parts of the year. It is clear that sea travel remained seasonal, with the sailing season being limited from roughly May to October.[91] Outside this period, storms and heavy clouds hindered navigation.[92] Arguably, the *raison d'être* of Ostia/Portus was to ensure year-round food supply in a situation in which imports occurred only for part of the year. In contrast, the major benefit of travelling by road was that it was much less subject to seasonality than travelling by sea. Due to heavy snows, the crossing of the Alps remained rather dangerous during winter, but for the rest the roads could be used all year round, though there can be little doubt that travelling in winter would be slower and less comfortable. However, roads were clearly built to be used at all times of the year; great attention was paid to drainage and to ensuring the durability of the pavement.[93]

On balance, it seems likely that the Roman mile shrunk in size, but not in an unequivocal or dramatic way. Only minor developments in the direction of passenger transport can be discerned. Although the speed of state communication could be high, under normal circumstances the duration of voyages did not improve significantly. Travel speed was hardly any faster than the pace of travel by foot. In Horace's famous description of a journey from Rome to Brundisium, the itinerary took ten days, covering 360 miles on the Via Appia, averaging a mere 36 miles (53.2 km) a day.[94] It does seem unlikely that elite travel was slower than normal travel—if anything, rather the reverse. It is telling that summations to the court by the praetor used a rather low average distance of 20 miles per day (almost 30 km) to calculate the period within which someone had to appear in Rome.[95]

---

[90] For travel after dark, see Plin., *N.H.* 8.61.144, where a person returning from his suburban residence near Rome is attacked by a robber.

[91] Abulafia (2011) 202: a stop on sailing from mid-November to early March, and sailing was regarded as dangerous from mid-September to early November and from March to the end of May. In consequence, the sailing season was effectively limited to 3–4 months. Horden and Purcell (2000) 142 observe that, throughout the centuries, 'the contrast between open and close seasons remained quite pronounced' (though there are some qualifications to be made). Cf. Suet., *Claud.* 18.2–19: Claudius reputedly tried with extensive privileges to tempt owners of grain ships to bring grain to Rome even during the winter, but such privileges will have done little to mitigate the risks themselves.

[92] Casson (1974) 150.   [93] Casson (1974) 166.

[94] Hor., *Sat.* 1.5, with Laurence (1999) 92–3. Admittedly, Horace advocated slow travel on the Via Appia, see 1.5.6: *minus est gravis Appia tardis.* For the duration of travel recorded in other literary works, see Greene (1986) 28.

[95] *Inter alia, Dig.* 38.15.2.3; 50.16.3 pr. Laurence (1999) 62–73, 82; Salway (2001) 32.

The speed of travel improved only little, but at the same time there are numerous (and rather varied) indications that the *volume* of traffic increased. There are increasing mentions of frequent voyages by individuals.[96] Trade on particular sea routes intensified.[97] The average and maximum size of ships increased, both with respect to their length and their tonnage; it would only be superseded from the fifteenth century onwards.[98] Another indicator is the increase in shipwrecks: in the Mediterranean it is clear that the number of wrecks from the Roman period is larger than in any other historical period before 1500,[99] and within the Roman period the peak falls within the Principate.[100] Though the ships themselves were freighters, they did carry passengers. There can be little doubt that the volume of human mobility rose.

Travel, then, remained clearly subject to limitations. But given the pre-modern nature of society, Roman possibilities for travel were relatively good. It should not be naively supposed that the high quality of Roman roads implies that travelling posed no obstacle at all, but Adams remarked 'how far the discussion of mobility has come from the seemingly entrenched theories of Finley—a static population hemmed into local communities by the high cost of land transport'.[101] One can only agree.

6. SOME IMPLICATIONS

But does migration really matter? The *raison d'être* of this book is the claim that migration can and should be studied as a subject in its own right. Its patterns and modes can be analysed profitably by having recourse to theories and models developed for other periods. Migration historians of these other periods have at the same time advocated an integral approach: migration should be studied in its societal context. In the Roman case this is in fact imperative. It is otherwise hardly possible to advance the study of Roman

---

[96] For the famous voyage of Paul, see Bender (1978) 28–9 (with fig), Gosch and Stearns (2008) 38–9, and Abulafia (2011) 202–3.

[97] See Henning (2001) on the route around Cape Malea; most *euploia* inscriptions and most shipwrecks in the area date to the Principate, while the harbour infrastructure was expanded in the same period.

[98] Casson (1974) 158–9; Greene (1986) 24–6; Abulafia (2011) 201. Variation in ship size is also visible in *P.Bingen* 77, a register of cargo ships in Alexandria. For some comparative data of ships in the seventeenth century, see Cressy (1987) 145–6.

[99] Greene (1986) 18.

[100] MacMullen (1988) 8–11 for discussion with further refs, focusing on the date of the peak. Horden and Purcell (2000) 371–2 with their table 5, showing the stunning height of the Roman peak; though they caution that it may be partly produced by the fact that the use of amphorae makes wrecks from the Roman period better visible archaeologically than those from periods.

[101] Adams (2001) 5. Cf. Woolf (forthcoming *a*) for a less optimistic assessment of the possibilities for long-distance travel.

migration. For example, one does not get very far studying labour migration by confining the research to those few migrants who were helpful enough to mention both origin and occupation in the same inscription. Indirect means—in this case studying labour relations—are more profitable. The result is somewhat paradoxical: the case for the independence of the subject is made by studying it indirectly. However, the interdependence between migration and other subjects can be turned into an advantage, since as a last step the causality can be turned around, and one can ask to what extent knowledge of migration affects our understanding of these other subjects.

As for the role of the state, there can be little doubt that under the Principate coercion was no longer the main determinant in migration. In the Republic the state had taken an active role in colonization programmes, movements of the army, and conducting wars that led to massive imports of slaves.[102] The creation of an army consisting of professionals not only changed recruitment patterns but also altered the relation between the state and the citizens and *peregrini* that chose to enlist. At the same time, the monopolization of power by the emperor at the expense of aristocratic competition changed the nature of Roman expansionism. The connection between warfare and enslavement was not completely severed, but wars fought on behalf of the Roman state were not anymore the main mechanism by which slaves were produced. Under the Principate the state did not actively stimulate or facilitate voluntary migration, though it certainly condoned it. Its role thus seems to have become smaller.

Migration might also be seen as a social process. The state (and the emperor as its embodiment) presented itself as the guardian of society and of the moral and social order. Though there can be no doubt that Roman societal organ-ization was strongly hierarchical, there is an increasing awareness among scholars that society was not static.[103] Roman society is now seen as a field of negotiation, in which positions continuously needed to be reaffirmed and claims needed to be accepted by others in order to be effective. In that sense, Roman society was more open than it may otherwise seem. This idea of openness is reinforced if we assume that there was a slow trickle of outsiders who tried to join the community: if the array of competitors was constantly changing, fragile equilibria were continuously being disturbed and needed to be re-established time and again. Additional complexity arose when people moved to and fro between communities: claims made in the new environment might give rise to changes in standing at home. It is not entirely surprising that the main response of the state to geographical mobility was not so much to try to curb it, but rather to focus on controlling status claims and prevent illegal status absorption. Ideologically, everybody was supposed to know his place.

[102] The classic discussion is Hopkins (1978). See further Scheidel (2004).
[103] Tacoma (2006); (forthcoming *b*), both with further refs.

In discussions of the Roman family, the fact that some family members could be geographically mobile is not often taken into account, at least not as a structural element. It is certainly relevant for our understanding of decision-taking by parents and others: such decisions are likely not to have been only about careers and marriage, but also about moving out. At the same time, family forms are more and more approached as dynamic structures: the question whether the Roman family was nuclear has lost some of its force, as all families almost by definition will have gone through cycles of contraction and expansion. Adding geographical mobility obviously reinforces the picture of dynamism. The dominance of young men in migration streams is closely connected to the late male age at marriage, and is certainly relevant for understanding the age gap between spouses. Likewise, the functioning of the marriage market gains a new aspect if we assume that young men could reside elsewhere before marriage, and that women could move over substantial distances to marry.

In the study of demography, there is an increasing awareness of the existence of regional differences in demographic regimes, though there are severe difficulties in analysing these in any detail. If people were moving to and fro, there is a possibility that differences between demographic regimes were evened out, both through transport of cultural norms about marriage and through transmission of diseases. No matter how we interpret its meaning exactly, the prevalence of the nuclear family in epitaphs found in regions that are wide apart remains stunning. In other aspects demographic variation might have been reinforced. This concerns in particular the dichotomy between city and countryside. The dominance of men in migration streams will have created gender imbalances in urban populations which will in turn have affected fertility and marriage patterns in the city.

With respect to labour, the mixed form of labour has been taken as the central characteristic of Roman labour relations. In addition, there is an increasing awareness that different types of labour might have been at least in part structurally equivalent. It is clear that the composition of workforces differed from region to region and from setting to setting. Why choices were made for specific types of labour in particular circumstances is beyond recovery, but it is possible to arrive at a general understanding by analysing the openness of the labour market, that is, by studying labour mobility. Geographical mobility of people who are looking for work and labour mobility in an abstract sense are not exactly the same thing, but they come reasonably close, and the former certainly helps to understand the latter.

Migration surely led to a cumulation of affiliations.[104] In formulating new models of cultural interaction, a new consensus has arisen in the approach to

---

[104] Moatti (forthcoming).

cultural interaction in the Roman provinces. It is taken to be a series of adaptive responses to uniforming tendencies by the selective borrowing of the culture and ideas of the Roman cultural repertoire and reassigning meaning to them. It offered strategies to negotiate one's place in the world and to participate in an empire-wide society while simultaneously retaining a local identity. The process resulted in cultural homogeneity and heterogeneity at the same time.[105] Such forms of cultural interaction may not be the direct result of migration; in fact, arguably in the Roman world people, goods, and ideas did not travel together, at least not always.[106] But the diversity in migration patterns suggests that a single overriding model of cultural behaviour might not be particularly helpful to capture the wide variety of possible responses. The current models of cultural interaction seem to allow enough room to cover this variety, but the case of the migrants in Rome, who for a large part reaffirmed their ethnic identity only selectively and haphazardly, might serve as a useful reminder that not everybody sought continuously to express his local identity.

Much more can be said about these topics, but such discussions fall outside the scope of this book. It is, of course, not particularly surprising that migration adds dynamism to our understanding of Roman society. The fact that migration has been placed higher on the ancient historical agenda is surely due to the fact that we *wish* to emphasize the dynamic aspects of society. But there is a paradox: by adding dynamic complexity, we very soon reach the limits of our knowledge.

---

[105] Naerebout (2013). These brief sentences can hardly do justice to two decades of scholarship. Key works include Woolf (1994 and 1998), the essays in Goldhill (ed.) (2001), and Whitmarsh (ed.) (2010). For all its briefness, the trenchant remarks of Scheidel (2004) 22–4 are very important, though his own plea to reinstate a model of romanization is more apt to describe interaction as a result of colonization where the agency is relatively clear than cultural interaction in general.

[106] Though cf. Schörner (forthcoming), for a clear case where they did, and Price (2012) for a nuanced model of the transfer of religious ideas throughout the empire.

Bibliography

Abulafia (2011): D. Abulafia, *The great sea: a human history of the Mediterranean* (London).

Adams (2001): C. Adams, 'Introduction', in C. Adams and R. Laurence (eds.), *Travel and geography in the Roman Empire* (London), 1–6.

Adams (forthcoming): C. Adams, 'Migration in Roman Egypt: problems and possibilities', in L. de Ligt and L. E. Tacoma (eds.), *Migration and mobility in the early Roman Empire* (Leiden), 264–84.

Adams (2008): G. W. Adams, *Rome and the social role of élite villas in the suburbs* (British Archaeological Reports Int. Ser. 1760) (Oxford).

Adams (2003): J. N. Adams, *Bilingualism and the Latin language* (Cambridge).

van Aerde (2015): M. E. J. J. van Aerde, 'Egypt and the Augustan cultural revolution: an interpretative archaeological overview' (diss. Leiden).

Alcock (1993): S. E. Alcock, *Graecia Capta: the landscapes of Roman Greece* (Cambridge).

Aldrete (2004): G. S. Aldrete, *Daily life in the Roman city: Rome, Pompeii, and Ostia* (Westport and London).

Aldrete (2007): G. S. Aldrete, *Floods of the Tiber in ancient Rome* (Baltimore).

Aldrete and Mattingly (1999): G. S. Aldrete and D. J. Mattingly, 'Feeding the city: the organization, operation and scale of the supply system for Rome', in D. S. Potter and D. J. Mattingly (eds.), *Life, death and entertainment in the Roman Empire* (Ann Arbor, Mich.), 171–204.

Allen and Neil (2013): P. Allen and B. Neil, *Crisis management in late antiquity (410–590 CE): a survey of the evidence from episcopal letters* (Leiden).

Ameling (1983): W. Ameling, *Herodes Atticus* (Hildesheim, Zürich, and New York), 2 vols.

Amory (1997): P. Amory, *People and identity in Ostrogothic Italy, 489–554* (Cambridge 1997).

André and Baslez (1993): J. M. André and M. F. Baslez, *Voyager dans l'antiquité* (Paris).

Aubert (1994): J.-J. Aubert, *Business managers in Ancient Rome: a social and economic study of institores, 200 BC–AD 250* (Leiden).

Augenti (2008): D. Augenti, *Il lavoro schiavile a Roma* (Rome).

Avraméa (1995): A. Avraméa, 'Mort loin de la patrie. L'apport des inscriptions paléochrétiennes', in G. Cavallo and C. Mango (eds.), *Epigrafia medievale Greca e Latina. Ideologia e funzione* (Atti del Seminario di Erice, 12–18 settembre 1991) (Spoleto), 1–65.

Bade et al. (eds.) (2007): K. J. Bade, P. C. Emmer, L. Lucassen, and J. Oltmer (eds.), *Enzyklopädie Migration in Europa. Vom 17. Jahrhundert bis zur Gegenwart* (Munich).

Bagnall and Frier (1994): R. S. Bagnall and B. W. Frier, *The demography of Roman Egypt* (Cambridge, etc.).

Balsdon (1979): J. P. V. D. Balsdon, *Romans and aliens* (London).

Bang (1910): M. Bang, 'Die Herkunft der römischen Sklaven', *Mitteilungen des kaiserlich deutschen archaeologischen Instituts, römische Abteilung*, 25: 223–51.

Bang (2007): P. F. Bang, 'Trade and empire: in search of organizing concepts for the Roman economy', *Past and Present*, 195: 3–53.

Barry (2008): W. D. Barry, 'Exposure, mutilation, and riot: violence at the "Scalae Gemoniae" in early imperial Rome', *Greece & Rome*, 55: 222–46.

Beard, North, and Price (1998): M. Beard, J. North, and S. Price, *Religions of Rome I: a history* (Cambridge).

Bender (1978): H. Bender, *Römischer Reiseverkehr: Cursus publicus und Privatreisen* (Stuttgart).

Bernard (forthcoming *a*): S. Bernard, 'Workers in the Roman imperial building industry', in C. Laes and K. Verboven (eds.), *Work, labor and professions in the Roman world*.

Bernard (forthcoming *b*): S. Bernard, 'Food distributions and immigration in imperial Rome', in L. de Ligt and L. E. Tacoma (eds.), *Migration and mobility in the early Roman Empire* (Leiden), 50–71.

Bertinelli and Donati (eds.) (2005): M. G. A. Bertinelli and A. Donati (eds.), *Il cittadino, lo straniero, il barbaro, fra integrazione ed emarginazione nell'antichità* (Atti del I incontro internazionale di Storia Antica, Genova 2003) (Rome).

Bertinelli and Donati (eds.) (2006): M. G. A. Bertinelli and A. Donati (eds.), *Le vie della storia. Migrazioni di popoli, viaggi di individui, circolazione di idee nel Mediterraneo antico* (Atti del II incontro internazionale di Storia Antica, Genova 2004) (Rome).

Bertolino (1997): A. Bertolino, '"*Pannonia terra creat, tumulat Italia tellus*". Presenze Pannoniche nell'area di S. Sebastiano', *Rivista di archeologia Christiana*, 73: 115–27.

Boatwright (2012): M. T. Boatwright, *Peoples of the Roman world* (Cambridge).

Bodel (2000): J. Bodel, 'Dealing with the dead: undertakers, executioners and potter's fields in ancient Rome', in V. M. Hope and E. Marshall (eds.), *Death and disease in the ancient city* (London and New York), 128–51.

Bonner (1977): S. F. Bonner, *Education in ancient Rome: from the elder Cato to the younger Pliny* (Berkeley and Los Angeles).

Borbonus (2014): D. Borbonus, *Columbarium tombs and collective identity in Augustan Rome* (Cambridge).

Borgatti et al. (2009): S. P. Borgatti, A. Mehra, D. J. Brass, and G. Labianca, 'Network analysis in the social sciences', *Science*, 323: 892–5.

Bowersock (1965): G. W. Bowersock, *Augustus and the Greek world* (Oxford).

Boyancé (1956): P. Boyancé, 'La Connaissance du grec à Rome', *Revue des Études Latines*, 34: 111–31.

Boyd (1989): M. Boyd, 'Family and personal networks in international migration: recent developments and new agendas', *International Migration Review*, 23.3: 638–70.

Bradley (1987): K. Bradley, 'On the Roman slave supply and slave breeding', in M. I. Finley (ed.), *Classical slavery* (*Slavery & Abolition* 8) (London), 42–64.

Bradley (1991): K. R. Bradley, *Discovering the Roman family: studies in Roman social history* (New York).

Bradley (1994): K. Bradley, *Slavery and society at Rome* (Cambridge).

Braund (1980): D. C. Braund, 'The Aedui, Troy and Apocolocyntosis', *Classical Quarterly*, NS 30: 420–5.

Braunert (1964): H. Braunert, *Die Binnenwanderung. Studien zur Sozialgeschichte Ägyptens in der Ptolemäer- und Kaiserzeit* (Bonn).

Broadhead (2004): W. Broadhead, 'Rome and the mobility of the Latins: problems of control', in C. Moatti (ed.), *La Mobilité des personnes en méditerranée de l'antiquité à l'époque moderne: procédures de contrôle et documents d'identification* (Rome), 315–35.

Brunt (1980): P. A. Brunt, 'Free labour and public works at Rome', *Journal of Roman Studies*, 70: 81–100.

Bruun (1992): C. Bruun, 'The spurious "Expeditio Ivdaeae" under Trajan', *Zeitschrift für Papyrologie und Epigrafik*, 93: 99–106.

Bruun (2010): C. Bruun, 'Water, oxygen isotopes, and immigration to Ostia-Portus', *Journal of Roman Archaeology*, 23: 109–32.

Bruun (forthcoming): C. Bruun, 'Tracing familial mobility: female and child migrants in the Roman West', in L. de Ligt and L. E. Tacoma (eds.), *Migration and mobility in the early Roman Empire* (Leiden). 176–204.

Buchi (2005): E. Buchi, 'La Venetia fra immigrazione e integrazione', in M. G. A. Bertinelli and A. Donati (eds.), *Il cittadino, lo straniero, il barbaro, fra integrazione ed emarginazione nell'antichità* (Atti del I incontro internazionale di Storia Antica, Genova 2003) (Rome), 213–44.

Budd et al. (2004): P. Budd, A. Millard, C. Chenery, S. Lucy, and C. Roberts, 'Investigating population movement by stable isotope analysis: a report from Britain', *Antiquity*, 78: 127–41.

Candilio and Bertinetti (2011): D. Candilio and M. Bertinetti, *I marmi antichi del Palazzo Rondinini* (Rome).

Cappelletti (2006): S. Cappelletti, *The Jewish community of Rome: from the second century* BC *to the third century C.E.* (Leiden and Boston).

Capponi and Mengozzi (1993): S. Capponi and B. Mengozzi, *I vigiles dei Cesari: l'organizzazione antincendio nell'antica Roma* (Rome).

Carcopino (1939): J. Carcopino, *La Vie quotiedienne a Rome à l'apogée de l'empire* (Paris).

Carroll (2006): M. Carroll, *Spirits of the dead. Roman funerary commemoration in western Europe* (Oxford).

Casson (1974): L. Casson, *Travel in the ancient world* (London).

Casson (1978): L. Casson, 'Unemployment, the building trade and Suetonius, *Vesp.* 18', *Bulletin of the American Society of Papyrologists*, 15: 43–51.

Casson (1994): L. Casson, *Ships and seafaring in ancient times* (London).

Catalano et al. (2013): P. Catalano, G. Fornaiari, V. Gazzaniga, A. Piccioli, and O. Rickards, *Scritto nelle ossa. Vivere, ammalarsi e curarsi a Roma in età imperiale* (Rome).

Centola and Macy (2007): D. Centola and M. Macy, 'Complex contagions and the weakness of long ties', *American Journal of Sociology*, 113: 702–34.

Chausson (1995): F. Chausson, 'Vel Iovi vel Soli: quatre études autour de la Vigna Barberini (191–354)', *Mélanges de l'Ecole française de Rome. Antiquité*, 107: 661–765.

Cherry (1990): D. Cherry, 'The Minician law: marriage and the Roman citizenship', *Phoenix*, 44: 244–66.

Ciuffarella (1998): L. Ciuffarella, 'Palynological analyses of resinous materials from the Roman mummy of Grottarossa, second century AD: a new hypothesis about the site of mummification', *Review of Palaeobotany and Palynology*, 103: 201–8.

Claridge (2010^2): A. Claridge, *Rome: an Oxford archaeological guide* (Oxford; 1st edn. 1998).

Coarelli (2007): F. Coarelli, *Rome and environments: an archaeological guide* (Berkeley, Los Angeles, and London).

Coleman (1990): K. M. Coleman, 'Fatal charades: Roman executions staged as mythological enactments', *Journal of Roman Studies*, 80: 44–73.

Coleman (2000): K. Coleman, 'Entertaining Rome', in J. Coulston and H. Dodge (eds.), *Ancient Rome: the archaeology of the eternal city* (Oxford) 210–58.

Cool (2010): H. E. M. Cool, 'Finding the foreigners', in H. Eckardt (ed.), *Roman diasporas: archaeological approaches to mobility and diversity in the Roman empire* (Journal of Roman Archaeology Suppl. 78) (Portsmouth), 27–44.

Corbier (2001): M. Corbier, 'Child exposure and abandonment', in S. Dixon (ed.), *Childhood, class and kin in the Roman world* (London and New York), 52–73.

Cornell (1995): T. J. Cornell, *The beginnings of Rome: Italy and Rome from the Bronze Age to the Punic Wars (c. 1000–264 BC)* (London and New York).

Coulston (2000): J. Coulston, '"Armed and belted men": the soldiery in imperial Rome', in J. Coulston and H. Dodge (eds.), *Ancient Rome: the archaeology of the eternal city* (Oxford), 76–118.

Cracco Ruggini (1980): L. Cracco Ruggini, 'Nuclei immigrati e forze indigene in tre grandi centri commerciali dell' impero', in J. D'Arms and E. C. Kopff (eds.), *The seaborne commerce of ancient Rome* (Rome), 55–76.

Cracco Ruggini (1987): L. Cracco Ruggini, 'Intolerance: equal and less equal in the Roman world', *Classical Philology*, 82: 187–205.

Cramer (1951): F. H. Cramer, 'Expulsion of astrologers from ancient Rome', *Classica et Mediaevalia*, 12: 9–50.

Crawford (1996): M. H. Crawford, *Roman statutes* (BICS Suppl 64) (London), 2 vols.

Cressy (1987): D. Cressy, *Coming over: migration and communication between England and New England in the seventeenth century* (Cambridge).

Cribiore (2007): R. Cribiore, *The school of Libanius in late antique Antioch* (Princeton and Oxford).

Crook (1967): J. A. Crook, *Law and life of Rome* (London and Southampton).

Cuvigny (1996): Cuvigny, H., 'The amount of wages paid to the quarry-workers at Mons Claudianus', *Journal of Roman Studies*, 86: 139–45.

D'Arms (1970): J. H. D'Arms, *Romans on the Bay of Naples: a social and cultural study of the villas and their owners from 150 BC to AD 400s* (Cambridge).

Daube (1951): D. Daube, 'The peregrine praetor', *Journal of Roman Studies*, 41: 66–70.

DeLaine (1995): J. DeLaine, The supply of building materials to the city of Rome', in N. Christie (ed.), *Settlement and economy in Italy 1500 BC–AD 1500: papers of the fifth conference of Italian archaeology* (Oxford), 555–62.

DeLaine (2000): J. DeLaine, 'Building the eternal city: the construction industry of imperial Rome', in J. Coulston and H. Dodge (eds.), *Ancient Rome: the archaeology of the eternal city* (Oxford), 119–41.

DeLaine (2005): J. DeLaine, 'The commercial landscape at Ostia', in A. MacMahon and J. Price (eds.), *Roman working lives and urban living* (Oxford), 29–47.

Dietz and Weber (1982): K. Dietz and G. Weber, 'Fremde in Rätien', *Chiron*, 12: 409–33.

Dixon (1992): S. Dixon, *The Roman family* (Baltimore and London).

Dobson and Mann (1973): B. Dobson and J. C. Mann, 'The Roman army in Britain and Britons in the Roman army', *Britannia*, 4: 191–205.

von Domaszewski (1967^2): A. v. Domaszewski, *Die Rangordnung des römischen Heer* (1st edn. 1908), repr. with same pagination and commentary by B. Dobson in *Beihefte der Bonner Jahrbücher*, 14 (Bonn).

Dresken-Weiland (2003): J. Dresken-Weiland, 'Fremde in der Bevölkerung des kaiserzeitlichen Rom', *Römische Quartalschrift für christliche Altertumskunde und Kirchengeschichte*, 98: 18–34.

Drogula (2011): F. K. Drogula, 'Controlling travel: deportation, islands and the regulation of senatorial mobility in the Augustan Principate', *The Classical Quarterly*, 61: 2011.

Dubuisson (1992): M. Dubuisson, 'Le Grec à Rome à l'époque de Cicéron: extension et qualité du bilinguisme', *Annales ESC*, 47: 187–97.

Dupras and Schwarcz (2001): T. Dupras and H. P. Schwarcz 'Strangers in a strange land: stable isotope evidence for human migration in the Dakhleh Oasis, Egypt', *Journal of Archaeological Science*, 28: 1199–208.

Durry (1938): M. Durry, *Les Cohortes prétoriennes* (Paris).

Ebel (2004): E. Ebel, *Die Attraktivität früher christlicher Gemeinden: die Gemeinde von Korinth im Spiegel griechisch-römischer Vereine* (Tübingen).

Eck (1998): W. Eck, 'Grabmonumente und sozialer Status in Rom und Umgebung', in P. Fasold, T Fischer, H. von Hesberg, and M. Witteyer (eds.), *Bestattungssitte und kulturelle Identität* (Xanthener Berichte 7) (Cologne), 29–40.

Eck (2009*a*): W. Eck, 'The presence, role and significance of Latin in the epigraphy and culture of the Roman Near East', in H. M. Cotton, R. G. Hoyland, J. J. Price, and D. J. Wasserstein (eds.), *From Hellenism to Islam: cultural and linguistic change in the Roman Near East* (Cambridge), 15–42.

Eck (2009*b*): W. Eck, 'There are no cursus honorum Inscriptions: the function of the cursus honorum in epigraphic communication', *Scripta Classica Israelica*, 28: 79–92.

Eck (forthcoming): W. Eck, 'Ordo senatorius und Mobilität: Auswirkungen und Konsequenzen im Imperium Romanum', in E. Lo Cascio and L. E. Tacoma, with M. J. Groen-Vallinga (eds.), *The impact of mobility and migration in the Roman Empire* (Impact of Empire 12) (Leiden).

Eckardt (2010): H. Eckardt, 'Introduction: diasporas in the Roman world', in H. Eckardt (ed.), *Roman diasporas: archaeological approaches to mobility and diversity in the Roman Empire* (Journal of Roman Archaeology Suppl. 78) (Portsmouth), 7–11.

Eckardt (ed.) (2010): H. Eckardt (ed.), *Roman diasporas: archaeological approaches to mobility and diversity in the Roman empire* (Journal of Roman Archaeology Suppl. 78) (Portsmouth).

Eckardt et al. (2010): H. Eckardt, with C. Chenery, S. Leach, M. Lewis, G. Müldner, and E. Nimmo, 'A long way from home: diaspora communities in Roman Britain', in H. Eckardt (ed.), *Roman diasporas: archaeological approaches to mobility and diversity in the Roman Empire* (Journal of Roman Archaeology Suppl. 78) (Portsmouth) 99–130.

Edwards (1996): C. Edwards, *Writing Rome: textual approaches to the city* (Cambridge).

Eltis (ed.) (2002): D. Eltis (ed.), *Coerced and free migration: global perspectives* (Stanford).

Elsner (1992): J. Elsner, 'Pausanias: a Greek pilgrim in the Roman world', *Past and Present*, 135: 3–29.

Erdkamp (2008): P. Erdkamp, 'Mobility and migration in Italy in the second century BC', in L. de Ligt and S. Northwood (eds.), *People, land, and politics: demographic developments and the transformation of Roman Italy 300 BC–AD 14* (Leiden), 417–50.

Erdkamp (forthcoming): P. Erdkamp, 'Seasonal labour and rural–urban mobility in Roman Italy', in L. de Ligt and L. E. Tacoma (eds.), *Migration and mobility in the early Roman Empire* (Leiden), 33–49.

Farney (2007): G. D. Farney, *Ethnic identity and aristocratic competition in Republican Rome* (Cambridge).

Fassbender (2005): A. Fassbender, *Untersuchungen zur Topographie von Grabstätten in Rom von der späten Republik bis in die Spätantike* (Berlin).

Ferrandini Troisi (1996): F. Ferrandini Troisi, 'Professionisti "di giro" nel Mediterraneo antico. Testimonianze epigrafiche', in M. G. A. Bertinelli and A. Donati (eds.), *Le vie della storia. Migrazioni di popoli, viaggi di individui, circolazione di idee nel Mediterraneo antico* (Atti del II incontro internazionale di Storia Antica, Genova 2004) (Rome), 145–54.

Finlay (1981a): R. A. P. Finlay, *Population and metropolis: the demography of London, 1580–1650* (Cambridge).

Finlay (1981b): R. Finlay, 'Natural decrease in early modern cities', *Past and Present*, 92: 169–74.

Finley (1977): M. I. Finley, 'The ancient city from Fustel de Coulanges to Max Weber and beyond', *Comparative Studies in Society and History*, 19: 305–27.

Finley (1980): M. I. Finley, *Ancient slavery and modern ideology* (London).

Flory (1978): M. B. Flory, 'Family in *familia*: kinship and community in slavery', *American Journal of Ancient History*, 3: 78–95.

Forbes (1955): C. A. Forbes, 'The education and training of slaves in antiquity', *Transactions of the American Philological Association*, 86: 321–60.

Foubert (2013): L. Foubert, 'Female travellers in Roman Britain: Vibia Pacata and Julia Lucilla', in E. Hemelrijk and G. Woolf (eds.), *Women and the Roman city in the Latin West* (Leiden and Boston), 391–404.

Foubert (forthcoming): L. Foubert, 'Migrant women in P.Oxy. and the port cities of Roman Egypt: tracing women's travel behaviour in papyrological sources', in L. de Ligt and L. E. Tacoma (eds.), *Migration and mobility in the early Roman Empire* (Leiden), 285–304.

Frank (1916): T. Frank, 'Race mixture in the Roman Empire', *American Historical Review*, 21: 689–708.

Frank (1927²): T. Frank, *An economic history of Rome* (New York; 1st edn. 1920).

Frank (1934): T. Frank, 'The people of Ostia', *Classical Journal*, 29: 481–93.

Freeman (1997): P. W. M. Freeman, 'Mommsen through to Haverfield: the origins of romanization studies', in D. J. Mattingly (ed.), *Dialogues in Roman imperialism: power, discourse, and discrepant experience in the Roman Empire* (Journal of Roman Archaeology Suppl. 23) (Portsmouth), 27–50.

Freis (1967): H. Freis, *Die Cohortes Urbanae* (Cologne and Graz).

Frézouls (1987): E. Frézouls, 'Rome ville ouverte. Réflexions sur les problèmes de l'expansion urbaine d'Auguste à Aurélien', in: *L'Urbs. Espace urbain et histoire (1er siècle av. J.C.–IIIe siècle ap. J.C.)* (Rome), 373–92.

Frézouls (1989): E. Frézouls, 'Déplacements à l'interieur des provinces occidentales sous le Haut-Empire: quelques exemples', *Ktèma*, 14: 123–38.

Fuhrmann (2012): C. J. Fuhrmann, *Policing the Roman Empire: soldiers, administration, and public order* (Oxford).

Galley (1995): C. Galley, 'A model of early modern urban demography', *Economic History Review*, 48: 448–69.

Galli and Pisani Sartorio (eds.) (2009): M. Galli and G. Pisani Sartorio (eds.), *Machina. Tecnologia dell'antica Roma* (Rome).

Gallivan and Wilkins (1997): P. Gallivan and P. Wilkins, 'Familial structures in Roman Italy: a regional approach', in B. Rawson and P. Weaver (eds.), *The Roman family in Italy: status, sentiment, space* (Canberra and Oxford), 239–79.

Gambash (forthcoming): G. Gambash, 'Between mobility and connectivity in the Roman Mediterranean', in E. Lo Cascio and L. E. Tacoma, with M. J. Groen-Vallinga (eds.), *The impact of mobility and migration in the Roman Empire* (Impact of Empire 12) (Leiden).

Gardner (1993): J. F. Gardner, *Being a Roman citizen* (London).

Garnsey (1979): P. D. A. Garnsey, 'Where did Italian peasants live?', *Proceedings of the Cambridge Philological Society*, 25: 1–25.

Garnsey (1981): P. Garnsey, 'Independent freedmen and the economy of Roman Italy under the Principate', *Klio*, 63: 359–71.

Garnsey (1988): P. Garnsey, *Famine and food supply in the Graeco-Roman world: responses to risk and crisis* (Cambridge).

Garnsey (1991): P. Garnsey, 'Mass diet and nutrition in the city of Rome', in A. Giovannini (ed.), *Nourrir la plèbe. Actes du Colloque en honneur de D. Van Berchem, Genève 1989* (Geneva), 67–101.

Garnsey and Saller (1987): P. Garnsey and R. P. Saller, *The Roman Empire: economy, society, and culture* (London).

Garrido-Hory (1998): M. Garrido-Hory, *Juvénal. Esclaves et affranchis à Rome* (Paris).

Gill and Bialsi (2011): N. Gill and P. Bialski, 'New friends in new places: network formation during the migration process among Poles in the UK', *Geoforum*, 42: 241–9.

Goldhill (ed.) (2001): S. Goldhill (ed.), *Being Greek under Rome: cultural identity, the second sophistic and the development of empire* (Cambridge).

Gordon (1924): M. L. Gordon, 'The nationality of slaves under the early Roman Empire', *Journal of Roman Studies*, 14: 93–111.

Gosch and Stearns (2008): S. S. Gosch and P. N. Stearns, *Premodern travel in world history* (New York and London).

Gowland and Garnsey (2010): R. L. Gowland and P. Garnsey, 'Skeletal evidence for health, nutritional status and malaria in Rome and the empire', in H. Eckardt (ed.), *Roman diasporas: archaeological approaches to mobility and diversity in the Roman Empire* (Journal of Roman Archaeology Suppl. 78) (Portsmouth), 131–56.

Graham (2011): E.-J. Graham, 'From fragments to ancestors: re-defining the role of os resectum in rituals of purification and commemoration in Republican Rome', in M. Carroll and J. Rempel (eds.), *Living through the dead: burial and commemoration in the classical world* (Oxford and Oakville), 91–109.

Granovetter (1972–3): M. Granovetter, 'The strength of weak ties', *American Journal of Sociology*, 78: 1360–80.

Granovetter (1983): M. Granovetter, 'The strength of weak ties: a network theory revisited', *Sociological Theory*, 1: 201–33.

Gray (2011): C. L. Gray, 'Foreigners in the burial ground: the case of the Milesians in Athens', in M. Carroll and J. Rempel (eds.), *Living through the dead: burial and commemoration in the classical world* (Oxford and Oakville) 47–64.

Gregori (2012a): G. L. Gregori, 'Recinti d'incerta identificazione', in D. Rossi (ed.), *Sulla Via Flaminia. Il mausoleo di Marco Nonio Macrino* (Rome) 162–4.

Gregori (2012b): G. L. Gregori, 'Le sei nuove stele di militari', in D. Rossi (ed.), *Sulla Via Flaminia. Il mausoleo di Marco Nonio Macrino* (Rome), 165–70.

Greene (1986): K. Greene, *The archaeology of the Roman economy* (Berkeley and Los Angelos).

Griffin (1991): M. Griffin, 'Urbs Roma, plebs and princeps', in L. Alexander (ed.), *Images of empire* (Journal for the study of the Old Testament Suppl. 122) (Sheffield), 19–46.

Groen-Vallinga (2013): M. J. Groen-Vallinga, 'Desperate housewives? The adaptive family economy and female participation in the Roman urban labour market', in E. Hemelrijk and G. Woolf (eds.), *Women and the Roman city in the Latin West* (Leiden and Boston), 295–321.

Groen-Vallinga and Tacoma (2015): M. Groen-Vallinga and L. E. Tacoma, 'Contextualising condemnation to hard labour in the Roman empire', in C. de Vito and A. Lichtenstein (eds.), *Global convict labour* (Leiden), 49–78.

Groen-Vallinga and Tacoma (forthcoming): M. J. Groen-Vallinga and L. E. Tacoma, 'The value of labour: Diocletian's Price Edict', in: C. Laes and K. Verboven (eds.), *Work, labor and professions in the Roman world*.

Gruen (2012): E. Gruen, 'Did ancient identity depend on ethnicity? A preliminary probe', *Phoenix*, 67: 1–22.

Grünewald (1999): T. Grünewald, *Raüber, Rebellen, Rivalen, Rächer. Studien zu 'latrones' im römischen Reich* (Stuttgart).

Haarmann (1999): H. Haarmann, 'History', in J. A. Fishman (ed.), *Handbook of language and ethnic identity* (New York and Oxford), 60–76.

Habicht (2001): C. Habicht, 'Tod auf der Gesandtschaftsreise', in B. Virgilio (ed.), *Studi Ellenistici*, 13 (Pisa), 9–17.

Hajnal (1965): J. Hajnal, 'European marriage patterns in perspective', in D. V. Glass and D. E. C. Eversley (eds.), *Population in history* (London), 101–43.

Hajnal (1982): J. Hajnal, 'Two kinds of preindustrial household formation system', *Population and Development Review*, 8: 449–94.

Hajnal (1983): 'Two kinds of pre-industrial household formation system', in R. Wall, J. Robin, and P. Laslett (eds.), *Family forms in historic Europe* (Cambridge), 65–104 [reprint with minor alterations of Hajnal (1982)].

Haley (1991): E. W. Haley, *Migration and economy in Roman Imperial Spain* (Barcelona).

Hamdoune (2006): C. Hamdoune, 'Mouvements de population dans les carmina funéraires africaines', in A. Akerraz, P. Ruggeri, A. Siraj, and C. Vismara (eds.), *L'Africa Romana. Mobilità delle persone e dei populi, dinamiche migratorie, emigrazioni ed immigrazioni nelle province occidentali dell'Impero Romano* (Atti del XVI Convegno di Studio, Rabat, 15–19 dicembre 2004) (Rome), 1001–20.

Hammond (1957): M. Hammond, 'Composition of the senate, AD 68–235', *Journal of Roman Studies*, 47: 74–81.

Handley (2011): M. Handley, *Dying on foreign shores: travel and mobility in the late-antique West* (Portsmouth).

Harkness (1896): A. G. Harkness, 'Age at marriage and at death in the Roman Empire', *Transactions of the American Philological Association*, 37: 35–72.

Harris (1980, 2011): W. V. Harris, 'Towards a study of the slave trade', *Journal of Roman Studies*, 70 (1980), 126–45, revised and reprinted in: id. (ed.), *Rome's imperial economy: twelve essays* (Oxford 2011), 57–87.

Harris (1989): W. V. Harris, *Ancient literacy* (Cambridge and London).

Harris (1994): W. V. Harris, 'Child-exposure in the Roman empire', *Journal of Roman Studies*, 84: 1–22.

Harris (1999; 2011): W. V. Harris, 'Demography and the sources of Roman slaves', *Journal of Roman Studies*, 89 (1999), 62–75, revised and reprinted in id. (ed.), *Rome's imperial economy: twelve essays* (Oxford 2011), 88–109.

Harris (2005): W. V. Harris, 'The Mediterranean and ancient history', in id. (ed.), *Rethinking the Mediterranean* (Oxford and New York), 1–42.

Harris (2011): W. V. Harris, 'Poverty and destitution in the Roman Empire', in id. (ed.), *Rome's imperial economy: twelve essays* (Oxford), 27–54.

Hasegawa (2005): K. Hasegawa, *The familia urbana during the early empire: a study of columbaria inscriptions* (British Archaeological Reports Int. Ser. 1440) (Oxford).

Hawkins (forthcoming): C. Hawkins, 'Contracts, coercion, and the boundaries of Roman manufacturing firms', in C. Laes and K. Verboven (eds.), *Work, labor and professions in the Roman world*.

Hemelrijk (2008): E. A. Hemelrijk, 'Patronesses and "mothers" of Roman collegia', *Classical Antiquity*, 27: 115–62.

Henning (2001): D. Henning, 'Die antiken Seehandelsroute um Kap Malea', *Münstersche Beiträge zur antiken Handelsgeschichte*, 20.1: 23–37.

Hermansen (1978): G. Hermansen, 'The population of imperial Rome: the regionaries', *Historia*, 27 (1978), 129–68.

Hin (2013): S. Hin, *The demography of Roman Italy: population dynamics in an ancient conquest society, 201 BCE–14 CE* (Cambridge).

Hin (forthcoming): S. Hin, 'Revisiting urban graveyard theory: migrant flows in post-classical Athens', in L. de Ligt and L. E. Tacoma (eds.), *Migration and mobility in the early Roman Empire* (Leiden), 234–63.

Hingley (1996): R. Hingley, 'The "legacy" of Rome: the rise, decline, and fall of the theory of romanization', in J. Webster and N. Cooper (eds.), *Roman imperialism: post-colonial perspectives* (Leicester Archaeology Monographs 3) (Leicester), 35–48.

Hingley (2005): R. Hingley, *Globalizing Roman culture: unity, diversity and empire* (London).

Hirschman (2004): C. Hirschman, 'The origins and demise of the concept of race', *Population and Development Review*, 30: 385–415.

Hochstadt (1983): S. Hochstadt, 'Migration in preindustrial Germany', *Central European History*, 16: 195–224.

Hoerder (2002): D. Hoerder, *Cultures in contact: world migrations in the second millennium* (Durham, NC and London).

Hoerder (2008): D. Hoerder, 'Migration and cultural interaction across the centuries: German history in a European perspective', *German Politics and Society*, 26: 1–23.

Hoerder, Lucassen, and Lucassen (2007): D. Hoerder, J. Lucassen, and L. Lucassen, 'Terminologien und Konzepte in der Migrationsforschung', in K. J. Bade, P. C. Emmer, L. Lucassen, and J. Oltmer (eds.), *Enzyklopädie Migration in Europa. Vom 17. Jahrhundert bis zur Gegenwart* (Munich), 28–53.

Hoffmann (1986): J. Hoffmann, *Die soziale Ausgliederung als Strafe. Eine sozialhistorische Untersuchung* (Saarbrücken).

Holleran (2011): C. Holleran, 'Migration and the urban economy of Rome', in C. Holleran and A. Pudsey (eds.), *Demography and the Graeco-Roman world* (Cambridge), 155–80.

Holleran (2012): C. Holleran, *Shopping in ancient Rome: the retail trade in the late Republic and the Principate* (Oxford).

Holleran (forthcoming *a*): C. Holleran, 'Getting a job: finding work in the city of Rome', in C. Laes and K. Verboven (eds.), *Work, labor and professions in the Roman world*.

Holleran (forthcoming *b*): C. Holleran, 'Labour mobility in the Roman world: a case study of mines in Iberia', in L. de Ligt and L. E. Tacoma (eds.), *Migration and mobility in the early Roman Empire* (Leiden), 95–137.

Hope (2000): V. Hope, 'The city of Rome: capital and symbol', in J. Huskinson (ed.), *Experiencing Rome: culture, identity and power in the Roman Empire* (London), 63–93.

Hope (2009): V. M. Hope, *Roman death: the dying and the dead in ancient Rome* (London and New York).

Hopkins (1964/5): M. K. Hopkins, 'The age of Roman girls at marriage', *Population Studies*, 18: 309–27.

Hopkins (1978): K. Hopkins, *Conquerors and slaves: sociological studies in Roman history 1* (Cambridge).

Hopkins (1983): K. Hopkins, *Death and renewal: sociological studies in Roman history 2* (Cambridge).

Hopkins and Burton (1983): K. Hopkins and G. Burton, 'Ambition and withdrawal: the senatorial aristocracy under the emperors', in K. Hopkins, *Death and renewal: sociological studies in Roman history 2* (Cambridge), 120–200.

Horden and Purcell (2000): P. Horden and N. Purcell, *The corrupting sea: a study of Mediterranean history* (Oxford).

Horden and Purcell (2005): P. Horden and N. Purcell, 'Four years of corruption: a response to critics', in W. V. Harris (ed.), *Rethinking the Mediterranean* (Oxford and New York), 348–75.

Huttunen (1974): P. Huttunen, *The social strata in the imperial city of Rome: a quantitative study of the social representation in the epitaphs published in the Corpus Inscriptionum Latinarum volumen VI* (Oulu).

Isaac (2004): B. Isaac, *The invention of racism in classical antiquity* (Princeton).

Isayev (2013): E. Isayev, 'Mediterranean ancient migrations, 2000–1 BCE', in I. Ness (ed.), *Encyclopedia of global human migration* (Oxford), 4: 2126–9.

Ivleva (2012): T. Ivleva, 'Britons abroad: the mobility of Britons and the circulation of British-made objects in the Roman Empire' (diss. Leiden).

Ivleva (forthcoming): T. Ivleva, 'Peasants into soldiers: recruitment and military mobility in the early Roman empire', in L. de Ligt and L. E. Tacoma (eds.), *Migration and mobility in the early Roman Empire* (Leiden), 158–75.

Jackson and Moch (1989; 1996): J. Jackson jr. and L. Moch, 'Migration and the social history of Europe', *Historical Methods*, 22 (1989), 27–36; repr. in D. Hoerder and L. Moch (eds.), *European migrants: global and local perspectives* (Boston 1996), 52–69.

Jansen (2011): G. C. M. Jansen, 'Toilets and health', in G. C. M. Jansen, A. O. Koloski-Ostrow, and E. Moormann (eds.), *Roman toilets: their archaeology and cultural history* (Leuven), 157–62.

Jongman (1990): W. M. Jongman, 'Het Romeins imperialisme en de verstedelijking van Italië', *Leidschrift*, 7: 43–58.

Jongman (2003): W. M. Jongman, 'Slavery and the growth of Rome: the transformation of Italy in the second and first centuries BCE', in C. Edwards and G. Woolf (eds.), *Rome the cosmopolis* (Cambridge), 100–22.

Joshel (1992): S. R. Joshel, *Work, identity and legal status at Rome: a study of the occupational inscriptions* (Norman, Okla., and London).

Joshel (2010): S. R. Joshel, *Slavery in the Roman world* (Cambridge).

Kaimio (1979): J. Kaimio, *The Romans and the Greek language* (Commentationes Humanarum Litterarum 64) (Helsinki).

Kajanto (1963): I. Kajanto, *A study of the Greek epitaphs of Rome* (Acta Instituti Romani Finlandiae 2.3) (Helsinki).

Kakoschke (2002): A. Kakoschke, *Ortsfremde in den römischen Provinzen Germania inferior und Germania superior. Eine Untersuchung zur Mobilität in den germanischen Provinzen anhand der Inschriften des 1. bis 3. Jahrhunderts n. Chr.* (Osnabrücker Forschungen zu Altertum und Antike-Rezeption 5) (Möhnesee).

Kampen (1981): N. Kampen, *Image and status: Roman working women in Ostia* (Berlin).

Kaster (1988): R. A. Kaster, *Guardians of language: the grammarian and society in late antiquity* (Berkeley, Los Angeles, and London).

Kelly (2007): B. Kelly, 'Riot control and imperial ideology in the Roman Empire', *Phoenix*, 61: 150–76.

Keppie (1983): L. Keppie, *Colonisation and veteran settlement in Italy, 47–14 BC* (London).

Killgrove (2010a): K. Killgrove, 'Migration and mobility in imperial Rome' (diss. Chapel Hill, NC).

Killgrove (2010*b*): K. Killgrove, 'Response to C. Bruun, "Water, oxygen and immigration to Ostia-Portus"', *Journal of Roman Archaeology*, 23: 133–6.

Killgrove (2010*c*): K. Killgrove, 'Identifying immigrants to imperial Rome using strontium isotope analysis', in H. Eckardt (ed.), *Roman diasporas: archaeological approaches to mobility and diversity in the Roman Empire* (Journal of Roman Archaeology Suppl. 78) (Portsmouth), 157–74.

Knapp (1907): C. Knapp, 'Travel in ancient times as seen in Plautus and Terence', *Classical Philology*, 2: 1–24 and 281–304.

Kolb (1995): F. Kolb, *Rom. Die Geschichte der Stadt in der Antike* (Munich).

Kolb (2000): A. Kolb, *Transport und Nachrichtentransfer im römischen Reich* (Berlin).

Komlos and Baten (2004): J. Komlos and J. Baten, 'Looking backward and looking forward: anthropometric research and the development of social science history', *Social Science History*, 28: 191–210.

Kron (2012): G. Kron, 'Nutrition, hygiene and mortality: setting parameters for Roman health and life expectancy consistent with our comparative evidence', in E. Lo Cascio (ed.), *L'impatto della 'peste antonina'* (Bari), 193–252.

Kudlien (1991): F. Kudlien, *Sklaven-Mentalität im Spiegel antiker Wahrsagerei* (Stuttgart).

La Piana (1927): G. La Piana, 'Foreign groups in Rome during the first centuries of the empire', *Harvard Theological Review*, 20: 183–403.

Laes and Verboven (forthcoming): C. Laes and K. Verboven (eds.), *Work, labor and professions in the Roman World*.

Lampe (2003): P. Lampe, *From Paul to Valentinus: Christians at Rome in the first two centuries* (Minneapolis).

Laslett (1983[3]): P. Laslett, *The world we have lost: further explored* (London; 1st edn. 1965).

Lassère (1977): J.-M. Lassère, *Ubique populus. Peuplement et mouvements de population dans l'Afrique romaine de la chute de Carthage à la fin de la dynastie des Sévères (146 a.C.–235 p.C.)* (Paris).

Laurence (1997): R. Laurence, 'Writing the Roman metropolis', in H. M. Parkins (ed.), *Roman urbanism: beyond the consumer city* (London and New York), 1–20.

Laurence (1999): R. Laurence, *The roads of Roman Italy: mobility and cultural change* (London).

Laurence (2001): R. Laurence, 'The writing of archaeological discourse—a view from Britain?', *Archaeological Dialogues*, 8: 90–122.

Le Roux (2004): P. Le Roux, 'La Romanisation en question', *Annales (HSS)*, 59: 287–311.

Leach et al. (2009): S. Leach, M. Lewis, C. Chenery, G. Müldner, and H. Eckardt, 'Migration and diversity in Roman Britain: a multidisciplinary approach to the identification of immigrants in Roman York, England', *American Journal of Physical Anthropology*, 140: 546–61.

Leach et al. (2010): S. Leach, H. Eckardt, C. Chenery, G. Müldner, and M. Lewis, 'A lady of York: migration, ethnicity and identity in Roman Britain', *Antiquity*, 84: 131–45.

Lee (1966): E. S. Lee, 'A theory of migration', *Demography*, 3: 47–57.

Lelis, Percy, and Verstraete (2003): A. Lelis, W. A. Percy, and B. C. Verstraete, *The age of marriage in ancient Rome* (Lewinston, Queenston, and Lampeter).

Leon (1995²): H. J. Leon, *The Jews of ancient Rome* (Peabody; 1st edn. 1960).

Lesger, Lucassen, and Schrover (2002): C. Lesger, L. Lucassen, and M. Schrover, 'Is there life outside the migrant network? German immigrants in XIXth century Netherlands and the need for a more balanced migration typology', *Annales de démographie historique*, 2: 29–50.

Lewis (1991): N. Lewis, 'Hadriani sententiae', *Greek, Roman and Byzantine Studies*, 32: 267–80.

Leyerle (2009): B. Leyerle, 'Mobility and the traces of empire', in P. Rousseau with J. Raithel (eds.), *A companion to late antiquity* (Oxford), 110–24.

Lieb (1986): H. Lieb, 'Die constitutiones für die stadrömischen Truppen', in W. Eck and H. Wolff (eds.), *Heer und Integrationspolitik. Die römische Militärdiplome als historische Quelle* (Cologne and Vienna), 322–46.

Liebs (1976): D. Liebs, 'Rechtsschulen und Rechtsunterricht im Prinzipat', in H. Temporini (ed.), *Aufstieg und Niedergang der römischen Welt. Geschichte und Kultur Roms im Spiegel der neueren Forschung* (Berlin and New York), vol. 2.15: 288–362.

de Ligt (2008): L. de Ligt, 'The population of Cisalpine Gaul in the time of Augustus', in L. de Ligt and S. Northwood (eds.), *People, land, and politics: demographic developments and the transformation of Roman Italy 300 BC–AD 14* (Leiden and Boston), 139–83.

de Ligt and Garnsey (2012): L. de Ligt and P. Garnsey, 'The album of Herculaneum and a model of the town's demography', *Journal of Roman Archaeology*, 25: 69–94.

de Ligt and Garnsey (forthcoming): L. de Ligt and P. Garnsey, 'Migration in early-imperial Italy: Herculaneum and Rome compared', in L. de Ligt and L. E. Tacoma (eds.), *Migration and mobility in the early Roman Empire* (Leiden), 72–95.

de Ligt and Northwood (eds.) (2008): L. de Ligt and S. Northwood (eds.), *People, land, and politics: demographic developments and the transformation of Roman Italy 300 BC–AD 14* (Leiden and Boston).

de Ligt and Tacoma (forthcoming): L. de Ligt and L. E. Tacoma, 'Approaching migration in the early Roman empire', in L. de Ligt and L. E. Tacoma (eds.), *Migration and mobility in the early Roman Empire* (Leiden), 1–22.

Lis and Soly (forthcoming): C. Lis and H. Soly, 'Work, identity and self-representation in the Roman Empire and the West-European Middle Ages: different interplays between the social and the cultural', in C. Laes and K. Verboven (eds.), *Work, labor and professions in the Roman world*.

Liu (forthcoming): L. Liu, 'Work, occupation, and group membership', in C. Laes and K. Verboven (eds.), *Work, labour, and professions in the Roman world*.

Lo Cascio (2000): E. Lo Cascio, 'La popolazione', in E. Lo Cascio (ed.), *Roma imperiale: una metropolis antica* (Rome), 17–69.

Lo Cascio (2012): E. Lo Cascio, 'Il mondo di lavoro e la vita economica nella città', in R. Friggeri, M. G. Granino Cecere, and G. L. Gregori (eds.), *Terme di Diocleziano. La collezione epigrafica* (Rome), 470–5.

Lo Cascio (forthcoming): E. Lo Cascio, 'The impact of migration on the demographic profile of the city of Rome: a reassessment', in L. de Ligt and L. E. Tacoma (eds.), *Migration and mobility in the early Roman Empire* (Leiden), 23–32.

Loman (2004): P. Loman, 'Mobility of Hellenistic women' (diss. Nottingham).

Lucassen and Lucassen (1997): J. Lucassen and L. Lucassen, 'Migration, migration history, history: old paradigms and new perspectives', in id. (eds.), *Migration, migration history, history: old paradigms and new perspectives* (Bern) 9–38.

Lucassen and Lucassen (2009): J. Lucassen and L. Lucassen, 'The mobility transition revisited, 1500–1900: what the case of Europe can offer to global history', *Journal of Global History*, 4: 347–77.

Lucassen and Lucassen (2010): J. Lucassen and L. Lucassen, 'The mobility transition revisited, 1500–1900: sources and methods' (ISSH-Research Paper 46), www.issg.nl.

Lucassen, Lucassen, and Manning (eds.) (2010): J. Lucassen, L. Lucassen, and P. Manning (eds.), *Migration history in world history: multidisciplinary approaches* (Leiden and Boston).

Lund (2005): A. A. Lund, 'Hellenentum und Hellenizität: Zur Ethnogenese und zur Ethnizität der antiken Hellenen', *Historia*, 54: 1–17.

MacMullen (1964): R. MacMullen, 'Social mobility and the Theodosian code', *Journal of Roman Studies*, 54: 49–53.

MacMullen (1966): R. MacMullen, *Enemies of the Roman order* (Cambridge).

MacMullen (1966; 1990): R. MacMullen, 'Provincial languages in the Roman empire', *American Journal of Philology*, 87: 1–17; repr. in id., *Changes in the Roman Empire: essays in the ordinary* (Princeton), 32–40.

MacMullen (1974): R. MacMullen, 'Peasants, during the principate', in H. Temporini (ed.), *Aufstieg und Niedergang der römischen Welt. Geschichte und Kultur Roms im Spiegel der neueren Forschung* (Berlin and New York), vol. 2.1.1: 253–61.

MacMullen (1981): R. MacMullen, *Paganism in the Roman Empire* (New Haven and London).

MacMullen (1988): R. MacMullen, *Corruption and the decline of Rome* (New Haven and London).

MacMullen (1993): R. MacMullen, 'The unromanized in Rome', in S. J. D. Cohen and E. S. Frerichs (eds.), *Diasporas in Antiquity* (Atlanta, Ga.), 47–64.

Maier (1953–4): F. G. Maier, 'Römische Bevökerungsgeschichte und Inschriftenstatistik', *Historia*, 2: 318–51.

Malkin, Constantakopoulou, and Panagopoulou (eds.) (2009): I. Malkin, C. Constantakopoulou, and K. Panagopoulou (eds.), *Greek and Roman networks in the Mediterranean* (London).

Manning (2013^2): P. Manning, *Migration in world history* (New York, etc.; 1st edn. 2005).

Marasco (1991): G. Marasco, 'Tiberio e l'esilio degli Ebrei in Sardegna nel 19 d.C.', in A. Mastino (ed.), *L'Africa Romana* (Atti del VIII Convegno di studio, Cagliari, 14–16 XII 1990) (Sassari), 649–60.

Marshall (1966): A. J. Marshall, 'Governors on the move', *Phoenix*, 20: 231–46.

Martelli (2013): E. Martelli, *Sulle spalle dei saccarii. Le rappresentazioni di facchini e il trasporto di derrate nel porto di Ostia in epoca imperiale* (BAR Int. Ser. 2467) (Oxford).

Martin (1996): D. B. Martin, 'The construction of the ancient family: methodical considerations', *Journal of Roman Studies*, 86: 39–60.

Martin (2001): S. D. Martin, 'Imperitia: the responsibility of skilled workers in classical Roman law', *American Journal of Philology*, 122: 107–29.

Mattingly (1997): D. J. Mattingly, 'Introduction: dialogues of power and experience in the Roman Empire', in id. (ed.), *Dialogues in Roman imperialism: power, discourse, and discrepant experience in the Roman Empire* (Journal of Roman archaeology Suppl. 23) (Portsmouth), 7–24.

Maxey (1938): M. Maxey, *Occupations of the lower classes in Roman society* (Chicago); repr. with same pagination in M. E. Park and M. Maxey, *Two studies on the Roman lower classes* (New York, 1975).

McGinn (2004): T. A. J. McGinn, *The economy of prostitution in the Roman world: a study of social history and the brothel* (Ann Arbor, Mich.).

McKeown (2007): N. McKeown, *The invention of ancient slavery?* (London).

Meiggs (1973²): R. Meiggs, *Roman Ostia* (Oxford; 1st edn. 1960).

Millar (1981): F. Millar, 'The world of the Golden Ass', *Journal of Roman Studies*, 71: 63–75.

Millar (1984): F. Millar, 'Condemnation to hard labour in the Roman Empire, from the Julio-Claudians to Constantine', *Papers of the British School at Rome*, 52: 124–47.

Mitchell (1976): S. Mitchell, 'Requisitioned transport in the Roman empire: a new inscription from Pisidia', *Journal of Roman Studies*, 66: 106–31.

Moatti (2000): C. Moatti, 'Le contrôle de la mobilité des personnes dans l'Empire romain', *Mélanges de l'École française de Rome. Antiquité*, 112 (2): 925–58.

Moatti (2004): C. Moatti, 'Introduction', in id. (ed.), *La Mobilité des personnes en méditerranée de l'antiquité à l'époque moderne: procédures de contrôle et documents d'identification* (Rome), 1–24.

Moatti (ed.) (2004): C. Moatti (ed.), *La Mobilité des personnes en méditerranée de l'antiquité à l'époque moderne: procédures de contrôle et documents d'identification* (Rome).

Moatti (2006): C. Moatti, 'Translation, migration, and communication in the Roman Empire: three aspects of movement in history', *Classical Antiquity*, 25(1): 109–40.

Moatti (2007): C. Moatti, 'Le Contrôle des gens de passage à Rome aux trois premiers siècles de notre ère', in C. Moatti and W. Kaiser (eds.), *Gens de passage en Méditerranée de l'Antiquité à l'époque moderne: procédures de contrôle et d'identification* (Paris), 79–116.

Moatti (forthcoming): C. Moatti, 'Migration et droit dans l'empire romain: catégories, contrôles et intégration', in: E. Lo Cascio and L. E. Tacoma, with M. J. Groen-Vallinga (eds.), *The impact of mobility and migration in the Roman Empire* (Impact of Empire 12) (Leiden).

Moatti and Kaiser (2007): C. Moatti and W. Kaiser, 'Introduction', in id. (eds.), *Gens de passage en Méditerranée de l'Antiquité à l'époque moderne: procédures de contrôle et d'identification* (Paris).

Moatti and Kaiser (eds.) (2007): C. Moatti and W. Kaiser (eds.), *Gens de passage en Méditerranée de l'Antiquité à l'époque moderne: procédures de contrôle et d'identification* (Paris).

Moch (1996): L. Moch, 'Introduction', in D. Hoerder and L. Moch (eds.), *European migrants: global and local perspectives* (Boston), 1–18.

Moch (2003²): L. Moch, *Moving Europeans: migration in western Europe since 1650* (Bloomington and Indianapolis; 1st edn. 1992).

Moch (2007): L. Moch, 'Connecting migration and world history: demographic patterns, family systems and gender', *International Review of Social History*, 52: 97–104.

Modéran (2004): Y. Modéran, 'L'Établissement de barbares sur le territoire romain à l'époque impériale', in C. Moatti (ed.), *La Mobilité des personnes en méditerranée de l'antiquité à l'époque moderne: procédures de contrôle et documents d'identification* (Rome), 337–97.

Moretti (1958): L. Moretti, 'Sulle "stationes municipiorum" del Foro Romano', *Athenaeum*, 36: 106–16.

Morley (1996): N. Morley, *Metropolis and hinterland: the city of Rome and the Italian economy 200 BC–AD 200* (Cambridge).

Morley (2003): N. Morley, 'Migration and the metropolis', in C. Edwards and G. Woolf (eds.), *Rome the cosmopolis* (Cambridge), 147–57.

Morley (2005): N. Morley, 'The salubriousness of the Roman city', in H. King (ed.), *Health in antiquity* (London and New York), 192–204.

Morley (2006): N. Morley, 'The poor in the city of Rome', in M. Atkins and R. Osborne (eds.), *Poverty in the Roman world* (Cambridge), 21–39.

Mouritsen (1998): H. Mouritsen, *Italian unification: a study in ancient and modern historiography* (London).

Mouritsen (2011): H. Mouritsen, *The freedman in the Roman world* (Cambridge and New York).

Mouritsen (2013): H. Mouritsen, 'Slavery and manumission in the Roman elite', in M. George (ed.), *Roman slavery and material culture* (Toronto), 43–68.

Mrozek (1986): S. Mrozek, 'Zur Verbreitung der freien Lohnarbeit in der römischen Kaiserzeit', in H. Kalcyk, B. Gullath, and A. Graeber (eds.), *Studien zur alten Geschichte: Siegfried Lauffer zum 70. Geburtstag am 4. August 1981 dargebracht von Freunden, Kollegen und Schülern* (Rome), vol. 2: 705–16.

Müller and Hasenohr (eds.) (2002): C. Müller and C. Hasenohr (eds.), *Les Italiens dan le monde grec, IIe siècle av. J.-C.—Ier siècle ap. J.-C.: circulation, activités, intégration. Actes de la Table Ronde, École Normale Supérieure, Paris, 14–16 mai 1998* (Bulletin de Correspondance Hellenique Suppl. 41) (Athens).

Musco et al. (2008): S. Musco, P. Catalano, A. Caspio, W. Pantano, and K. Killgrove, 'Le Complexe archéologique de Casal Bertone', *Les Dossiers d'archéologie*, 330: 32–9.

Naerebout (2013): F. G. Naerebout, 'Convergence and divergence: one empire, many cultures', in G. de Kleijn and S. Benoist (eds.), *Integration in the Roman world* (Impact of Empire 10) (Leiden), 263–82.

Naerebout and Versluys (2006): F. Naerebout and M. J. Versluys, '"L'acculturation n'est qu'un mot". Cultuurcontact en acculturatieprocessen in de oudheid: een inleiding', *Leidschrift*, 21.3: 7–23.

Nauta (1987): R. R. Nauta, 'Seneca's "Apocolocyntosis" as Saturnalian literature', *Mnemosyne*, 40: 69–96.

Nieddu (2003): A. M. Nieddu, 'Fremde in der Nekropole von S. Paolo fuori le mura', *Römische Quartalschrift für christliche Altertumskunde und Kirchengeschichte*, 98: 112–20.

Nippel (1995): W. Nippel, *Public order in Rome* (Cambridge).

Nock (1932): A. D. Nock, 'Cremation and burial in the Roman empire', *Harvard Theological Review*, 25: 321–59.

North (2013): J. North, 'Gender and cult in the Roman West: Mithras, Isis, Attis', in E. Hemelrijk and G. Woolf (eds.), *Women and the Roman city in the Latin West* (Leiden and Boston), 109–28.

Noy (1998): D. Noy, 'Where were the Jews of the diaspora buried?', in M. Goodman (ed.), *Jews in a Graeco-Roman world* (Oxford), 75–89.

Noy (2000): D. Noy, *Foreigners at Rome: citizens and strangers* (London).

Noy (2010a): D. Noy, 'Epigraphic evidence for immigrants at Rome and in Roman Britain', in H. Eckardt (ed.), *Roman diasporas: archaeological approaches to mobility and diversity in the Roman empire* (Journal of Roman Archaeology Suppl. 78) (Portsmouth), 13–26.

Noy (2010b): D. Noy, 'Immigrant and Jewish families at Rome in the 2nd–5th centuries', in E. Rebillard and C. Sotinel (eds.), *Les Frontières du profane dans l'antiquité tardive* (Collection de l'École française de Rome 428) (Rome), 199–211.

Oerlemans and Tacoma (2014): A. P. A. Oerlemans and L. E. Tacoma, 'Three great killers: infectious diseases and patterns of mortality in imperial Rome', *Ancient Society*, 44: 213–41.

Orlin (2008): E. M. Orlin, 'Octavian and Egyptian cults: redrawing the boundaries of romanness', *American Journal of Philology*, 129: 231–53.

Orlin (2010): E. M. Orlin, *Foreign cults in Rome: creating a Roman Empire* (Oxford).

Osborne (1991): R. Osborne, 'The potential mobility of human populations', *Oxford Journal of Archaeology*, 10: 231–52.

Osborne (2006): R. Osborne, 'Introduction: Roman poverty in context', in M. Atkins and R. Osborne (eds.), *Poverty in the Roman world* (Cambridge), 1–20.

Panciera (1993): S. Panciera, 'Soldati e civili a Roma nei primi tre secoli dell'impero', in W. Eck (ed.), *Prosopographie und Sozialgeschichte* (Cologne), 261–76.

Parker (2008): G. Parker, 'The gender of travel: Cynthia and others', *Materiali e Discussioni per l'analisi dei testi classici*, 61: 85–99.

Patterson (1992): J. R. Patterson, 'Patronage, collegia and burial in imperial Rome', in S. Bassett (ed.), *Death in towns: urban responses to the dying and the dead, 100–1600* (Leicester), 15–27.

Patterson (2000a): J. R. Patterson, 'On the margins of the city of Rome', in V. M. Hope and E. Marshall (eds.), *Death and disease in the ancient city* (London and New York), 85–103.

Patterson (2000b): J. R. Patterson, 'Living and dying in the city of Rome: houses and tombs', in J. Coulston and H. Dodge, *Ancient Rome: the archaeology of the eternal city* (Oxford), 259–89.

Patterson (2006): J. R. Patterson, *Landscapes and cities: rural settlement and civic transformation in early imperial Italy* (Oxford).

Patterson (2010): J. R. Patterson, 'The city of Rome revisited: from mid-Republic to mid-Empire', *Journal of Roman Studies*, 100: 210–32.

Pearce (2010): J. Pearce, 'Burial, identity and migration in the Roman world', in H. Eckardt (ed.), *Roman diasporas: archaeological approaches to mobility and diversity in the Roman empire* (Journal of Roman Archaeology Suppl. 78) (Portsmouth), 79–98.

Perry (2011): J. S. Perry, 'Organized societies: collegia', in M. Peachin (ed.), *The Oxford handbook of social relations in the Roman world* (Oxford), 499–516.

Perry et al. (2009): M. A. Perry, D. S. Coleman, D. L. Dettman, and A.-H. Al-Shiyab, 'An isotopic perspective on the transport of Byzantine mining camp laborers into Southwestern Jordan', *American Journal of Physical Anthropology*, 140: 429–41.

Petersen (1958): W. Petersen, 'A general typology of migration', *American Sociological Review*, 23: 256–66.

Phang (2001): S. E. Phang, *The marriage of Roman soldiers (13 BC–AD 235): law and family in the imperial army* (Leiden, etc.).

Pleket (1988): H. W. Pleket, 'Labor and unemployment in the Roman empire: some preliminary remarks', in I. Weiler (ed.), *Soziale Randgruppen und Aussenseiter im Altertum. Referate vom Symposium 'Soziale Randgruppen und antike Sozialpolitik', in Graz (21. bis 23. September)* (Graz), 267–76.

Pleket (1993): H. W. Pleket, *Kapitalisme en oudheid. Was Rome een kwaadaardige metropool?* (Leiden).

Pollard (2012): A. M. Pollard, 'Science, archaeology and the Romans, or "What has scientific archaeology ever done for the Romans?"', in I. Schrüfer-Kolb (ed.), *More than just numbers? The role of science in Roman archaeology* (Journal of Roman Archaeology Suppl. 91) (Portsmouth), 177–88.

Polomé (1983): E. Polomé, 'The linguistic situation in the western provinces of the Roman empire', in W. Haase (ed.), *Aufstieg und Niedergang der römischen Welt* (Berlin and New York) vol. 2.29.2: 509–53.

Pomeroy (1975): S. B. Pomeroy, *Goddesses, whores, wives, and slaves: women in classical antiquity* (New York).

Pooley and Turnbull (1998): C. G. Pooley and J. Turnbull, *Migration and mobility in Britain since the eighteenth century* (London).

Price (2012): S. Price, 'Religious mobility in the Roman Empire', *Journal of Roman Studies*, 102: 1–19.

Prowse (forthcoming): T. L. Prowse, 'Isotopes and mobility in the ancient Roman world', in L. de Ligt and L. E. Tacoma (eds.), *Migration and mobility in the early Roman Empire* (Leiden), 205–33.

Prowse et al. (2007): T. L. Prowse, H. P. Schwarcz, P. Garnsey, M. Knyf, R. Macchiarelli, and L. Bondioli, 'Isotopic evidence for age-related immigration to imperial Rome', *American Journal of Physical Anthropology*, 132: 510–19.

Prowse et al. (2010): T. L. Prowse, J. L. Barta, T. E. von Hunnius, and A. M. Small, 'Stable isotope and mitochondrial DNA evidence for geographic origins on a Roman estate at Vagnari (Italy)', in H. Eckardt (ed.), *Roman diasporas: archaeological approaches to mobility and diversity in the Roman Empire* (Journal of Roman Archaeology Suppl. 78) (Portsmouth), 175–98.

Putnam (2007): R. W. Putnam, '*E pluribus unum*: diversity and community in the twenty-first century', *Scandinavian Political Studies*, 30 (2): 137–74.

Rajak (1984): T. Rajak, 'Was there a Roman charter for the Jews?', *Journal of Roman Studies*, 74: 107–23.

Ramage (1983): E. S. Ramage, 'Urban problems in ancient Rome', in R. T. Marchese (ed.), *Aspects of Greek and Roman urbanism: essays on the classical city* (British Archaeological Reports Int. Ser. 188) (Oxford), 61–92.

Ramin and Veyne (1981): J. Ramin and P. Veyne, 'Droit romain et société: les hommes libres qui passent pour esclavages et l'esclavage volontaire', *Historia*, 30: 472–97.

Ravenstein (1885): E. G. Ravenstein, 'The laws of migration', *Journal of the Royal Statistical Society*, 46: 167–235.

Ravenstein (1889): E. G. Ravenstein, 'The laws of migration: second paper', *Journal of the Royal Statistical Society*, 52: 241–305.

Rawson (ed.) (1986): B. Rawson (ed.), *The family in ancient Rome: new perspectives* (Ithaca, NY).

Rawson (2013): B. Rawson, 'Marriages, families, households', in P. Erdkamp (ed.), *The Cambridge companion to ancient Rome* (Cambridge), 93–109.

Rebuffat (2004): R. Rebuffat, 'Mobilité des personnes dans l'Afrique romaine', in C. Moatti (ed.), *La mobilité des personnes en méditerranée de l'antiquité à l'époque moderne: procédures de contrôle et documents d'identification* (Rome), 155–203.

Reinhold (1971): M. Reinhold, 'Usurpation of status and status symbols in the Roman Empire', *Historia*, 20: 275–302.

Ricci (1993): C. Ricci, 'Egiziani a Roma', *Aegyptus*, 73: 71–91.

Ricci (1994): C. Ricci, *Soldati delle milizie urbane fuori di Roma. La documentazione epigrafica* (Opuscula Epigrafica 5) (Rome).

Ricci (1996): C. Ricci, 'Principes et reges externi (e loro schiavi e liberti) a Roma e in Italia: testimonianze epigrafiche di età imperiale', *Rendiconti della Classe di Scienze morali, storiche e filologiche dell'Academia dei Lincei*, 7: 561–92.

Ricci (2005): C. Ricci, *Orbis in urbe. Fenomeni migratori nella Roma imperiale* (Rome).

Richardson (1992): L. Richardson, *A new topographical dictionary of ancient Rome* (Baltimore and London).

Rickman (1980): G. Rickman, *The corn supply of ancient Rome* (Oxford).

Rives (2001): J. Rives, 'Civic and religious life', in J. Bodel (ed.), *Epigraphic evidence: ancient history from inscriptions* (London and New York), 118–36.

Rochette (1996): B. Rochette, '*Fidi interpretes*. La traduction orale à Rome', *Ancient Society*, 27: 75–89.

Rochette (1997): B. Rochette, *Le Latin dans le monde grec. Recherches sur la diffusion de la langue et des lettres latines dans les provinces hellénophones de l'Empire romain* (Brussels).

Rood (2011): T. C. B. Rood, 'Black Sea variations: Arrian's *Periplus*', *Cambridge Classical Journal*, 57: 137–63.

Roselaar (forthcoming): S. Roselaar, 'State-organized mobility in the Roman Empire: legionaries and auxiliaries', in L. de Ligt and L. E. Tacoma (eds.), *Migration and mobility in the early Roman Empire* (Leiden), 138–57.

Ross Taylor (1961): L. Ross Taylor, 'Freedmen and freeborn in the epitaphs of imperial Rome', *American Journal of Philology*, 82: 113–32.

Rostovtzeff (1926): M. Rostovtzeff, *The social and economic history of the Roman Empire* (Oxford).

Rutgers (1994; 1998): L. V. Rutgers, 'Roman policy towards the Jews: expulsions from the city of Rome during the first century C.E.', *Classical Antiquity*, 13 (1994) 56–74; repr. in K. P. Donfried and P. Richardson (eds.), *Judaism and Christianity in first-century Rome* (Grand Rapids, Mich. 1998), 93–116.

Rutgers (1998): L. Rutgers, *The hidden heritage of diaspora Judaism* (Leuven).

Saller (1987): R. P. Saller, 'Men's age at marriage and its consequences in the Roman family, *Classical Philology*, 82: 21–34.

Saller and Shaw (1984): R. P. Saller and B. D. Shaw, 'Tombstones and Roman family relations in the Principate: civilians, soldiers, and slaves', *Journal of Roman Studies*, 74: 124–56.

Sallares (2002): R. Sallares, *Malaria and Rome: a history of malaria in ancient Italy* (Oxford, etc.).

Salomies (2002): O. Salomies, 'People in Ostia: some onomastic observations and comparisons with Rome', in C. Bruun and A. G. Zevi (eds.), *Ostia e Portus nelle loro relazioni con Roma* (Rome), 135–60.

Salway (2001): B. Salway, 'Travel, *itineraria* and *tabellaria*', in C. Adams and R. Laurence (eds.), *Travel and geography in the Roman Empire* (London), 22–66.

Sanjek (2003): R. Sanjek, 'Rethinking migration, ancient to future', *Global Networks*, 3: 315–36.

Scheidel (1994): W. Scheidel, 'Libitina's bitter gains: seasonal mortality and endemic disease in the ancient city of Rome', *Ancient Society*, 25: 151–75.

Scheidel (1997): W. Scheidel, 'Quantifying the sources of slaves in the early Roman Empire', *Journal of Roman Studies*, 87: 156–69.

Scheidel (2001): W. Scheidel, *Death on the Nile: disease and the demography of Roman Egypt* (Mnemosyne Suppl. 228) (Leiden, etc.).

Scheidel (2003): W. Scheidel, 'Germs for Rome', in C. Edwards and G. Woolf (eds.), *Rome the cosmopolis* (Cambridge), 158–76.

Scheidel (2004): W. Scheidel, 'Human mobility in Roman Italy I: the free population', *Journal of Roman Studies*, 104: 1–26.

Scheidel (2005): W. Scheidel, 'Human mobility in Roman Italy, II: the slave population', *Journal of Roman Studies*, 95: 64–79.

Scheidel (2011): W. Scheidel, 'The Roman slave supply', in K. Bradley and P. Cartledge (eds.), *The Cambridge world history of slavery* (Cambridge), 287–310.

Scheidel (2013): W. Scheidel, 'Disease and death', in P. Erdkamp (ed.), *The Cambridge companion to ancient Rome* (Cambridge), 45–59.

Schörner (forthcoming): G. Schörner, 'Mobile Handwerker—wandernde Werkstätten: Techniktransfer im Imperium Romanum', paper presented at the twelfth workshop of Impact of Empire, Rome, June 17–19, 2015, 'Mobility and migration in the Roman world'.

Schultz (1942-3): F. Schultz, 'Roman registers of birth and birth certificates', *Journal of Roman Studies*, 32: 78–91; 33: 55–64.

Scobie (1986): A. Scobie, 'Slums, sanitation and mortality in the Roman world', *Klio*, 68: 399–433.

Sharlin (1978): A. Sharlin, 'Natural decrease in early modern cities: a reconsideration', *Past and Present*, 79: 126–38.

Sharlin (1981): A. Sharlin, 'A rejoinder to an article by R. Finlay', *Past and Present*, 92: 175–80.

Shaw (1987): B. D. Shaw, 'The age of Roman girls at marriage: some reconsiderations', *Journal of Roman Studies*, 77: 30–46.

Shaw (1996): B. D. Shaw, 'Seasons of death: aspects of mortality in imperial Rome', *Journal of Roman Studies*, 86: 100–38.

Shaw (2001): B. D. Shaw, 'Challenging Braudel: a new vision of the Mediterranean', *Journal of Roman Archaeology*, 14: 419–53.

Shaw (2006): B. D. Shaw, 'Seasonal mortality in imperial Rome and the Mediterranean: three problem cases', in G. R. Storey (ed.), *Urbanism in the pre-industrial world: cross-cultural approaches* (Tuscaloosa, Fla.), 86–109.

Sherwin-White (1973²): A. N. Sherwin-White, *The Roman citizenship* (Oxford; 1st edn. 1939).

Sidebotham (1986): S. E. Sidebotham, *Roman economic policy in the Erythra Thalassa: 30 BC–AD 217* (Leiden).

Silver (2011): M. Silver, 'Contractual slavery in the Roman economy', *Ancient History Bulletin*, 25: 73–132.

Simelon (1992): P. Simelon, 'Les Mouvements migratoires en Lucanie romaine (Iᵉʳ–IIᵉ siècles)', *Mélanges de l'École française de Rome. Antiquité*, 104: 691–708.

Solin (1983): H. Solin, 'Juden und Syrer im westlichen Teil der römischen Welt. Eine ethnisch-demographische Studie mit besonderer Berücksichtigung der sprachlichen Zustände', in H. Tempori and W. Haase (eds.), *Aufstieg under Niedergang der römischen Welt* (Berlin and New York), vol. 2.29.2: 587–789.

Solin (1996): H. Solin, *Die stadtrömischen Sklavennamen: ein Namenbuch* (Stuttgart).

Solin (2003²): H. Solin, *Die griechischen Personennamen in Rom* (Berlin and New York; 1st edn. 1982), 3 vols.

Solin (2007): H. Solin, 'Mobilità socio-geografica nell'impero romano. Orientali in occidente. Considerazione isagogiche', in M. Mayer i Olivé, G. Baratta, and A. Guzmán Almagro (eds.), *XII Congressus Internationalis Epigraphiae Graecae et Latinae* (Barcelona), 1363–80.

Sordi (ed.) (1994): M. Sordi (ed.), *Emigrazione e immigrazione nel mondo antico* (Milan).

Sordi (ed.) (1995): M. Sordi (ed.), *Coercizione e mobilità umana nel mondo antico* (Milan).

Sosin (1999): J. D. Sosin, 'Tyrian stationarii at Puteoli', *Tyche*, 14 (1999), 275–84.

Speidel (1994a): M. P. Speidel, *Riding for Caesar: the Roman emperors' horse guards* (Cambridge).

Speidel (1994b): M. P. Speidel, *Die Denkmäler der Kaiserreiter* Equites Singulares Augusti (Cologne).

Sperduti, Bondioli, and Garnsey (2012): A. Sperduti, L. Bondioli, and P. Garnsey, 'Skeletal evidence for occupational structure at the coastal towns of Portus and Velia (1st–3rd c. AD)', in I. Schrüfer-Kolb (ed.), *More than just numbers? The role of science in Roman archaeology* (Journal of Roman Archaeology Suppl. 91) (Portsmouth), 53–70.

Squarciapino (1962): M. F. Squarciapino, *I culti orientali ad Ostia* (Leiden).

Stambaugh (1988): J. E. Stambaugh, *The ancient Roman city* (Baltimore and London).

Stanley (1990): F. H. Stanley, 'Geographical mobility in Roman Lusitania: an epigraphical perspective', *Zeitschrift für Papyrologie und Epigrafik*, 82: 249–69.

Steidl (2009): A. Steidl, 'Introduction', in J. Ehmer, A. Steidl, and S. Nadel (eds.), *European mobility: internal, international, and transatlantic moves in the 19th and early 20th centuries* (Göttingen), 7–16.

Steinby (ed.) (1993–2000): E. M. Steinby, *Lexicon topographicum urbis Romae* (Rome), 6 vols. with suppl.

Stevens (forthcoming): S. Stevens, *City boundaries and urban development in Roman Italy: 4th century BC–AD 271* (Leuven).

Tacoma (2006): L. E. Tacoma, *Fragile hierarchies: the urban elites of third-century Roman Egypt* (Mnemosyne suppl. 271) (Leiden).

Tacoma (2012): L. E. Tacoma, 'Settlement and population', in C. Riggs (ed.), *The Oxford Companion to Roman Egypt* (Oxford), 122–35.

Tacoma (2013): L. E. Tacoma, 'Migrant quarters at Rome?', in G. de Kleijn and S. Benoist (eds.), *Integration in the Roman world* (Impact of Empire 10) (Leiden), 127–46.

Tacoma (forthcoming *a*): L. E. Tacoma, 'The labour market', in A. Claridge and C. Holleran (eds.), *A companion to the city of Rome* (Oxford).

Tacoma (forthcoming *b*): L. E. Tacoma, 'Roman elite mobility under the Principate', in H. van Wees and N. Fisher (eds.), *'Aristocracy' in antiquity. Redefining Greek and Roman elites* (Swansea), 125–145.

Tacoma (forthcoming *c*): L. E. Tacoma, 'Bones, stones, and Monica. Isola sacra revisited', in: E. Lo Cascio and L. E. Tacoma, with M.J. Groen-Vallinga (eds.), *The impact of mobility and migration in the Roman Empire* (Impact of Empire 12) (Leiden).

Tacoma and Tybout (forthcoming *a*): L. E. Tacoma and R. A. Tybout, 'Moving epigrams: migration and mobility in the Greek East in the Hellenistic and Roman period', in L. de Ligt and L. E. Tacoma (eds.), *Migration and mobility in the early Roman Empire* (Leiden), 345–89.

Tacoma and Tybout (forthcoming *b*): L. E. Tacoma and R. A. Tybout, 'Inscribing Syrian mobility in the Hellenistic and Roman period', in A. J. Yoo and A. Zerbini (eds.), *A home away from home: new paths to the study of migration and migrant identities in the eastern Mediterranean from the Roman period to the Crusades* (Farnham).

Taylor (2011): C. Taylor, 'Migration and the demes of Attica', in C. Holleran and A. Pudsey (eds.), *Demography and the Graeco-Roman world: new insights and approaches* (Cambridge), 117–34.

Temin (2003/4): P. Temin, 'The labour market of the early Roman Empire', *Journal of Interdisciplinary History*, 34: 513–38.

Terpstra (2013): T. Terpstra, *Trading communities in the Roman World: a microeconomic and institutional perspective* (Leiden and Boston).

Terpstra (2015): T. Terpstra, 'Roman trade with the Far East: evidence for Nabataean middlemen in Puteoli', in F. de Romanis and M. Maiuro (eds.), *Across the ocean: nine essays on Indo-Mediterranean trade* (Leiden), 73–94.

Thüry (2001): G.E. Thüry, *Müll und Marmorsäulen. Siedlungshygiene in der römischen Antike* (Mainz am Rhein).

Van Tilburg (2007): C. van Tilburg, *Traffic and congestion in the Roman Empire* (London).

Tilly (1978): C. Tilly, 'Migration in modern European history', in W. H. McNeill and R. S. Adams (eds.), *Human migration: patterns and policies* (Bloomington and London), 48–72.

Todd (2001): M. Todd, *Migrants and invaders: the movement of peoples in the ancient world* (Stroud).

Tol et al. (2014): G. Tol, T. de Haas, K. Armstrong, and P. Attema, 'Minor centres in the Pontine Plain: the cases of Forum Appii and Ad Medias', *Papers of the British School at Rome*, 82: 109–34.

Tomlin (2003): R. S. O. Tomlin, '"The girl in question": a new text from Roman London', *Britannia*, 34: 41–51.

Toynbee (1971): J. M. C. Toynbee, *Death and burial in the Roman World* (London and Southampton).

Tozzi (2014): G. Tozzi, 'Un nuovo epigramma Greco da Roma', *Rivista di filologia e di istruzione classica*, 142: 408–26,

Treggiari (1973): S. Treggiari, 'Domestic staff at Rome in the Julio-Claudian period, 27 BC to AD 68', *Histoire sociale—Social History*, 6: 241–55.

Treggiari (1978): Treggiari, S., 'Rome: urban labour', *Seventh International Economic History Congress* (Edinburgh) Theme B3, 162–5.

Treggiari (1979a): S. Treggiari, 'Questions on women domestics in the Roman west', in *Schiavitù, manomissione e classi dipendenti nel mondo antico* (Rome), 185–201.

Treggiari (1979b): S. Treggiari, 'Lower class women in the Roman economy', *Florilegium*, 1: 65–79.

Treggiari (1980): S. Treggiari, 'Urban labour in Rome: *mercennarii* and *tabernarii*', in P. Garnsey (ed.), *Non-slave labour in Graeco-Roman antiquity* (Proceedings of the Cambridge Philological Society 6) (Cambridge), 48–64.

Tschiedel (2003): H. J. Tschiedel, 'Das Fremde als Signum römischer Identität', *Römische Quartalschrift für christliche Altertumskunde und Kirchengeschichte*, 98 (2003), 5–17.

Tybout (forthcoming): R. A. Tybout, 'Dead men walking: the repatriation of mortal remains', in L. de Ligt and L. E. Tacoma (eds.), *Migration and mobility in the early Roman Empire* (Leiden), 390–437.

Verboven (2011): K. Verboven, 'Resident aliens and translocal merchant collegia in the Roman world', in O. Hekster and T. Kaizer (eds.), *Frontiers in the Roman World* (Impact of Empire 9) (Leiden and Boston), 335–48.

Verboven (forthcoming): K. Verboven, 'Guilds and organizing urban populations in the Roman world during the Principate', in C. Laes and K. Verboven (eds.), *Work, labor and professions in the Roman world.*

Virlouvet (1991): C. Virlouvet, 'La Plèbe frumentaire à l'époque d'Auguste. Une tentative de définition', in A. Giovannini (ed.), *Nourrir la plèbe. Actes du Colloque en honneur de D. Van Berchem, Genève 1989* (Geneva), 43–65.

Virlouvet (1997): C. Virlouvet, 'Existait-il des registres de décès à Rome au 1er siècle ap. J.C.?', *La Rome impériale: démographie et logistique* (Actes de la table ronde, Rome, 25 mars 1994) (Rome), 77–88.

De Visscher (1958): F. de Visscher, 'La Condition des peregrins à Rome jusqu'a la constitution Antonine de l'an 212', *L'étranger. Recueils de la société J. Bodin*, 9: 195–208.

De Vries (1984): J. de Vries, *European urbanization, 1500–1800* (London).

Vout (2003): C. Vout, 'Embracing Egypt', in C. Edwards and G. Woolf (eds.), *Rome the cosmopolis* (Cambridge), 177–202.

Wallace-Hadrill (2011): A. Wallace-Hadrill, *Herculaneum: past and future* (London).

Walters (1997): J. Walters, 'Invading the Roman body: manliness and impenetrability in Roman thought', in J. P. Hallett and M. B. Skinner (eds.), *Roman sexualities* (Princeton).

Weaver (2004): P. Weaver, 'P.Oxy. 3312 and joining the household of Caesar', *Zeitschrift für Papyrologie und Epigrafik*, 149: 196–204.

Webster (2001): J. Webster, 'Creolizing the Roman provinces', *American Journal of Archaeology*, 105: 209–25.

Webster (2010): J. Webster, 'Routes to slavery in the Roman world: a comparative perspective on the archaeology of forced migration', in H. Eckardt (ed.), *Roman diasporas: archaeological approaches to mobility and diversity in the Roman empire* (Journal of Roman Archaeology Suppl. 78) (Portsmouth), 45–65.

Wells (ed.) (2013): P. S. Wells (ed.), *Rome beyond its frontiers: imports, attitudes and practices* (Portsmouth).

Wesch-Klein (2007): G. Wesch-Klein, 'Recruits and veterans', in P. Erdkamp (ed.), *A companion to the Roman army* (Oxford), 435–50.

Whitmarsh (2001): T. Whitmarsh, ' "Greece is the world": exile and identity in the second sophistic', in S. Goldhill (ed.), *Being Greek under Rome: cultural identity, the second sophistic and the development of empire* (Cambridge, etc.), 269–305.

Whitmarsh (ed.) (2010): T. Whitmarsh, *Local knowledge and microidentities in the imperial Greek world* (Cambridge).

Whittaker (1993): C. R. Whittaker, 'The poor in the city of Rome', in id. (ed.), *Land, city and trade in the Roman Empire* (Aldershot), 1–25.

Whittaker (1994): C. R. Whittaker, *Frontiers of the Roman Empire: a social and economic study* (Baltimore).

Whittaker (2004): C. R. Whittaker, 'The use and abuse of immigrants in the later Roman Empire' in C. Moatti (ed.), *La Mobilité des personnes en méditerranée de l'antiquité à l'époque moderne: procédures de contrôle et documents d'identification* (Rome, 2004), 127–53; repr. in: C. R. Whittaker (ed.), *Rome and its frontiers: the dynamics of empire* (London and New York, 2004), 199–218.

Wiedemann (1985): T. Wiedemann, 'The regularity of manumission at Rome', *Classical Quarterly*, 35: 162–75.

Wierschowski (1995): L. Wierschowski, *Die regionale Mobilität in Gallien nach den Inschriften des 1. bis 3. Jahrhunderts n. Chr. Quantitative Studien zur sozial- und wirtschaftsgeschichte der westlichen Provinzen des römischen Reiches* (Historia Einzelschriften 91) (Stuttgart).

Wierschowski (2001): L. Wierschowski, *Fremde in Gallien—'Gallier' in der Fremde. Die epigraphisch bezeugte Mobilität in, von und nach Gallien vom 1. bis 3. Jh. n.Chr. (Texte—Übersetzungen—Kommentare)* (Historia Einzelschriften 159) (Stuttgart).

Wilson (1966): A. J. N. Wilson, *Emigration from Italy in the Republican age of Rome* (Manchester and New York).

Woods (1989): R. Woods, 'What would one need to know to solve the "natural decrease in early modern cities" problem?', in R. Lawton (ed.), *The rise and fall of great cities* (London) 80–95.

Woods (2003): R. Woods, 'Urban–rural mortality differentials: an unresolved debate', *Population and Development Review*, 29: 29–46.

Woods (2007): R. Woods, 'Ancient and early modern mortality: experience and understanding', *Economic History Review*, 60: 373–99.

Woolf (1994): G. Woolf, 'Becoming Roman, staying Greek: culture, identity and the civilizing process in the Roman East', *Proceedings of the Cambridge Philological Society*, 10: 116–43.

Woolf (1998): G. Woolf, *Becoming Roman: the origins of provincial civilization in Gaul* (Cambridge and New York).

Woolf (2006): G. Woolf, 'Writing poverty in Rome', in M. Atkins and R. Osborne (eds.), *Poverty in the Roman world* (Cambridge), 83–99.

Woolf (2013): G. Woolf, 'Female mobility in the Roman West', in E. Hemelrijk and G. Woolf (eds.), *Women and the Roman city in the Latin West* (Leiden and Boston), 351–68.

Woolf (forthcoming *a*): G. Woolf, 'Movers and stayers: the limits of mobility', in L. de Ligt and L. E. Tacoma (eds.), *Migration and mobility in the early Roman Empire* (Leiden), 438–62.

Woolf (forthcoming *b*): G. Woolf, 'Moving peoples in early empires', in E. Lo Cascio and L. E. Tacoma, with M.J. Groen-Vallinga (eds.), *The impact of mobility and migration in the Roman Empire* (Impact of Empire 12) (Leiden).

Van der Woude (1982): A. M. van der Woude, 'Population developments in the northern Netherlands (1500–1800) and the validity of the "urban graveyard" effect', *Annales de démographie historique*: 55–75.

Wrigley (1967): E. A. Wrigley, 'A simple model of London's importance in changing English society and economy', *Past and Present*, 37: 47–70.

Wrigley (1969): E. A. Wrigley, *Population and history* (London).

Yeo (1946): C. Yeo, 'Land and sea transport in imperial Italy', *Transactions of the American Philological Association*, 77: 221–5.

Zelinsky (1971): W. Zelinsky, 'The hypothesis of the mobility transition', *Geographical Review*, 61: 219–49.

Zerbini (forthcoming *a*): A. Zerbini, 'Human mobility in the Roman Near East: patterns and motives', in L. de Ligt and L. E. Tacoma (eds.), *Migration and mobility in the early Roman Empire* (Leiden), 305–44.

Zerbini (forthcoming *b*): A. Zerbini, 'Forced displacement in Rome and Byzantium: patterns and responses', paper presented at the twelfth workshop of Impact of Empire, Rome, June 17–19, 2015, 'Mobility and migration in the Roman world'.

Zimmer (1982): G. Zimmer, *Römische Berufsdarstellungen* (Berlin).

Index of Sources

Literary

Index of Subjects